Oracle8™ Server Reference

Release 8.0

June, 1997

Part No. A54645-01

In memory of Bob Miner and Bob Kooi--

As you will see in this and other Oracle8 manuals, a number of new and exciting concepts and capabilities for information management are available in Oracle8. The members of Oracle's Server Technologies Division would like to dedicate Oracle8 to the memory of Bob Miner and Bob Kooi, whose contributions to prior versions made Oracle8 possible. We wish we could still thank them in person.

ORACLE®

Enabling the Information Age™

Oracle8 Server Reference

Part No. A54645-01

Release 8.0

© Copyright 1997 Oracle Corporation. All Rights Reserved.

Primary Author: Paul Lane

Contributors: John Bellemore, Roger Bodamer, William Bridge, Allen Brumm, Sumanta Chatterjee, Greg Doherty, Alan Downing, Masane Hayashi, Alex Ho, Amit Jasuja, Robert Jenkins, Boris Klotts, Anjo Kolk, Susan Kotsovolos, Andre Kruglikov, Michael Kung, Nina Lewis, Juan Loaiza, William Maimone, Moham-mad Monajjemi, Gary Ngai, Anil Nori, Alok Pareek, Kant Patel, Thomas Pfaeffle, Tuomas Pystynen, Mark Ramacher, Sriram Samu, Richard Sarwal, Ekrem Soylemez, Anand Srinivasan, James Stamos, Alvin To, Alex Tsukerman, Radek Vingralek, William Waddington, Joyo Wijaya, Graham Wood, Gail Yamanaka, Sofia Yeung,

Contents

Chapter 2   **Static Data Dictionary Views** 2-1

Preface

This manual provides reference information about the Oracle8 Server, running on all operating systems. This information includes:

- Initialization Parameters
- Static Data Dictionary Views
- Dynamic Performance (V$) Views
- National Language Support
- Database Limits
- SQL Scripts
- Oracle Wait Events
- Enqueue and Lock Names
- Statistics Descriptions

Audience

This manual is written for database administrators, system administrators, and database application developers.

Knowledge Assumed of the Reader

It is assumed that readers of this manual are familiar with relational database concepts, basic Oracle Server concepts, and with the operating system environment under which they are running Oracle.

Installation and Migration Information

This manual is not an installation or migration guide. If your primary interest is installation, refer to your operating system-specific Oracle documentation. If your primary interest is database and application migration, refer to *Oracle8 Server Migration*.

Information Database Administration

While this manual describes the architecture, processes, structures, and other concepts of the Oracle Server, it does not explain how to administer the Oracle Server. For that information, see the *Oracle8 Server Administrator's Guide*.

Application Design Information

In addition to administrators, experienced users of Oracle and advanced database application designers will find information in this manual useful. However, database application developers should also refer to the *Oracle8 Server Application Developer's Guide* and to the documentation for the tool or language product they are using to develop Oracle database applications.

How Oracle8 Server Reference Is Organized

This manual is organized as follows:

Chapter 1, "Initialization Parameters"

This chapter contains detailed descriptions of the database initialization parameters in the parameter file that are required to start an instance.

Chapter 2, "Static Data Dictionary Views"

This chapter contains descriptions of the Oracle data dictionary tables and views.

Chapter 3, "Dynamic Performance (V$) Views"

This chapter contains descriptions of the dynamic performance views, also known as the V$ views.

Chapter 4, "National Language Support"

This chapter describes features that enable Oracle8 applications to operate with multiple languages using conventions specified by the application user.

Chapter 5, "Database Limits"

This chapter lists the limits of values associated with database functions and objects.

Chapter 6, "SQL Scripts"

This chapter describes the SQL scripts that are required for optimal operation of the Oracle8 Server.

Appendix A, "Oracle Wait Events"

This appendix describes the event name, wait time and parameters for wait events displayed by the V$SESSION_WAIT and V$SYSTEM_EVENT views.

Appendix B, "Enqueue and Lock Names"

This appendix describes the enqueues and locks used by the Oracle Server.

Appendix C, "Statistics Descriptions"

This appendix describes the statistics stored in the V$SESSION_WAIT and V$SYSSTAT dynamic performance table.

Conventions Used in This Manual

The following sections describe the conventions used in this manual.

Text of the Manual

The following textual conventions are used:

UPPERCASE WORDS	Uppercase text is used to call attention to command keywords, object names, parameters, filenames, and so on. For example:

"If you create a private rollback segment, the name of the rollback segment must be included in the ROLLBACK_SEGMENTS parameter of the parameter file."

Italicized Words	Italicized words within text indicate the definition of a term. For example:

"A database is a collection of data to be treated as a unit. The general purpose of a database is to store and retrieve related information, as needed."

Italics also call out specific book titles and emphasized words.

Examples of Commands and Statements

SQL, Server Manager line mode, and SQL*Plus commands and statements appear separated from the text of paragraphs in a monospaced font. For example:

```
INSERT INTO emp (empno, ename) VALUES (1000, 'SMITH');

ALTER TABLESPACE users ADD DATAFILE 'users2.ora' SIZE 50K;
```

Punctuation , ' "	Example statements can include punctuation such as commas or quotation marks. All punctuation given in example statements is required. All example statements are terminated with a semicolon. Note that depending on the application being used, a semicolon or other terminator might or might not be required to end a statement.
Uppercase Words: INSERT, SIZE	Uppercase words in example statements are used to indicate the keywords within Oracle SQL. However, note that when issuing statements, keywords are not case sensitive.
Lowercase Words: emp, users2.ora	Lowercase words in example statements are used to indicate words supplied only for the context of the example. For example, lowercase words can indicate the name of a table, column, or file.

Your Comments Are Welcome

We value and appreciate your Comments as an Oracle user and reader of the manuals. As we write, revise, and evaluate our documentation, your opinions are the most important input we receive. At the back of this manual is a Reader's Comment Form which we encourage you to use to tell us what you like and dislike about this manual or other Oracle manuals.

If the form is not available, please use the following address.

Server Technologies Documentation Manager
Oracle Corporation
500 Oracle Parkway
Redwood Shores, CA 94065   U.S.A.

1

Initialization Parameters

This chapter contains detailed descriptions of the database initialization parameters.

The following topics are included in this chapter:

- Initialization Parameter File
- Specifying Values in the Parameter File
- Reading the Parameter Descriptions
- Parameter Descriptions

Initialization Parameter File

The initialization parameter file is a text file that contains a list of parameters and a value for each parameter. The file should be written in the client's default character set. Specify values in the parameter file which reflect your installation.

The following are sample entries in a parameter file:

```
PROCESSES = 100
OPEN_LINKS = 12
GLOBAL_NAMES = TRUE
```

The name of the parameter file varies depending on the operating system. For example, it can be in mixed case or lowercase, or it can have a logical name or a variation on the name INIT.ORA. As the database administrator, you can choose a different filename for your parameter file. There is also an INITDW.ORA file which contains suggested parameter settings for data-warehouses and data-marts.

See your Oracle operating system-specific documentation for the default locations and filenames for these parameter files. The INIT.ORA file is what the Oracle Server reads for its parameter information upon startup.

Sample parameter files are provided on the Oracle Server distribution medium for each operating system. A distributed sample file is sufficient for initial use, but you will want to make changes in the file to tune the database system for best performance. Any changes will take effect the next time you completely shut down the instance and then restart it.

Database administrators can use initialization parameters to do the following:

- optimize performance by adjusting memory structures, for example, the number of database buffers in memory

- set some database-wide defaults, for example, how much space is initially allocated for a context area when it is created

- set database limits, for example, the maximum number of database users

- specify names of files

Many initialization parameters can be fine-tuned to improve database performance. Other parameters should never be altered or only be altered under the supervision of Oracle Corporation Worldwide Support staff.

Note: If you are using Trusted Oracle, see the *Trusted Oracle Server Administrator's Guide* for information about additional initialization parameters.

Specifying Values in the Parameter File

This section describes several aspects of setting parameter values in the parameter file. The following topics are included:

- Rules

- Changing Parameter Values

- Displaying Current Parameter Values
- Uses of Parameters
- Types of Parameters
- Parameters You Should Not Specify in the Parameter File
- When Parameters Are Set Incorrectly

Rules

The following rules govern the specification of parameters in the parameter file:

- All parameters are optional.
- Only parameters and comments should appear in the parameter file.
- A pound sign (#) starts a comment; the rest of the line is ignored.
- The server has a default value for each parameter. This value may be operating system dependent, depending on the parameter.
- Parameters can be specified in any order.
- Case (upper or lower) in filenames is only significant if case is significant on the host operating system.
- To enter several parameters on one line, use spaces between parameter names and values, as in the following:

```
PROCESSES = 100 SAVEPOINTS = 5 OPEN_CURSORS = 10
```

- Some parameters, such as ROLLBACK_SEGMENTS, accept multiple value entries. You can enter multiple values enclosed in parentheses and separated by commas. For example:

```
ROLLBACK_SEGMENTS = (SEG1, SEG2, SEG3, SEG4, SEG5)
```

  Or, you can enter multiple values without parentheses and commas. For example:

```
ROLLBACK_SEGMENTS = SEG1 SEG2 SEG3 SEG4 SEG5
```

  Either syntax is valid.

- A backslash or *escape character* (\) indicates continuation of the parameter specification. If a backslash continues a line, the continued line must have no preceding spaces. For example:

```
ROLLBACK_SEGMENTS = (SEG1, SEG2, \
SEG3, SEG4, SEG5)
```

- The keyword IFILE can be used to call another parameter file, which must be in the same format as the original parameter file.

- Enclose parameter values which contain whitespace in double quotes. For example:

```
NLS_TERRITORY = "CZECH REPUBLIC"
```

Suggestion: It is advisable to list parameters in alphabetical order in the parameter file. That makes it easier to find them and helps ensure that each parameter is specified only once. If a parameter is specified consecutively "n" number of times, it is associated with a list of "n" values. If a parameter is specified "n" number of times, but not all consecutively, then the last consecutive list of values is used.

See your operating system-specific Oracle documentation for more information on parameter files.

Using Special Characters in Parameter Values

If a parameter value contains a special character, then either the special character must be preceded by an escape character or the entire parameter value must be contained in double quotes. For example:

```
DB_DOMAIN = "JAPAN.ACME#.COM"
```

or

```
DB_DOMAIN = JAPAN.ACME\#.COM
```

Table 1-1 lists the special characters.

Table 1-1: Special Characters in the Initialization Parameter File

Character	Description
#	Comment
(	Start list of values
)	End list of values
"	Start or end of quoted string
'	Start of end of quoted string
=	Separator of keyword and value(s)
,	Separator of elements
–	Precedes UNIX-style keywords
\	Escape character

Wherever a special character must be treated literally in the initialization parameter file, it must be either prefaced by the escape character or the entire string that contains the special character must be surrounded by single or double quotes.

Using the Escape Character

As described in "Rules" on page 1-3, the escape character (\) can also signify a line continuation. If the escape character is followed by an alphanumeric character, then the escape character is treated as a normal character in the input. If it is not followed by an alphanumeric, then the escape character is treated either as an escape character or as a continuation character.

Using Quotes

Quotes can be nested in any of three ways. One method is to double the quotes in the nested string. For example:

```
NLS_DATE_FORMAT = """Today is"" MM/DD/YYYY"
```

Another method is to alternate single and double quotes. For example:

```
NLS_DATE_FORMAT = '"Today is" MM/DD/YYYY'
```

The third method is to escape the inner quotes. For example:

```
NLS_DATE_FORMAT = "\"Today is\" MM/DD/YYYY"
```

Changing Parameter Values

To change a parameter's value, edit the parameter file. The next time the instance starts, it uses the new parameter values in the updated parameter file. Note that the change does not take effect until the instance is shut down and restarted.

Dynamic Parameters

Some initialization parameters are *dynamic*, that is, they can be modified using the ALTER SESSION, ALTER SYSTEM, or ALTER SYSTEM DEFERRED commands while an instance is running.

Use this syntax for dynamically altering the initialization parameters:

```
ALTER SESSION SET parameter_name = value
ALTER SYSTEM SET parameter_name = value
ALTER SYSTEM  SET parameter_name = value DEFERRED
```

Whenever a dynamic parameter is modified using the ALTER SYSTEM, or ALTER SYSTEM DEFERRED command, then the command that modifies the parameter is also recorded in the alert log.

The ALTER SESSION command changes the value of the parameter specific to the session that invokes this command. The value of this parameter does not change for other sessions in the instance. The value of the initialization parameters listed in Table 1-2 can be changed with ALTER SESSION.

Table 1-2: Initialization Parameters Alterable with ALTER SESSION

ALLOW_PARTIAL_SN_RESULTS	B_TREE_BITMAP_PLANS
DB_FILE_MULTIBLOCK_READ_COUNT	GLOBAL_NAMES
HASH_AREA_SIZE	HASH_MULTIBLOCK_IO_COUNT
MAX_DUMP_FILE_SIZE	NLS_CURRENCY
NLS_DATE_FORMAT	NLS_DATE_LANGUAGE
NLS_ISO_CURRENCY	NLS_LANGUAGE
NLS_NUMERIC_CHARACTERS	NLS_SORT
NLS_TERRITORY	OBJECT_CACHE_MAX_SIZE_PERCENT
OBJECT_CACHE_OPTIMAL_SIZE	OPS_ADMIN_GROUP
OPTIMIZER_MODE	OPTIMIZER_PERCENT_PARALLEL
OPTIMIZER_SEARCH_LIMIT	PARALLEL_INSTANCE_GROUP
PARALLEL_MIN_PERCENT	PARTITION_VIEW_ENABLED
PLSQLV2_COMPATIBILITY	REMOTE_DEPENDENCIES_MODE
SORT_AREA_RETAINED_SIZE	SORT_AREA_SIZE
SORT_DIRECT_WRITES	SORT_READ_FAC
SORT_WRITE_BUFFER_SIZE	SORT_WRITE_BUFFERS
SPIN_COUNT	STAR_TRANSFORMATION_ENABLED
TEXT_ENABLE	TIMED_STATISTICS

The ALTER SYSTEM command modifies the global value of the parameter until the database is shut down. The ALTER SYSTEM command does not always change the parameter value for the current session. Use the ALTER SESSION command to change the parameter value for the current session. The value of the initialization parameters listed in Table 1-3 can be changed with ALTER SYSTEM.

Table 1-3: Initialization Parameters Alterable with ALTER SYSTEM

AQ_TM_PROCESSES	CONTROL_FILE_RECORD_KEEP_TIME
DB_BLOCK_CHECKPOINT _BATCH	DB_BLOCK_CHECKSUM
DB_BLOCK_MAX_DIRTY _TARGET	DB_FILE_MULTIBLOCK_READ_COUNT
FIXED_DATE	FREEZE_DB_FOR_FAST_INSTANCE_RECOVERY
GLOBAL_NAMES	HASH_MULTIBLOCK_IO_COUNT
LICENSE_MAX_SESSIONS	LICENSE_MAX_USERS
LICENSE_SESSIONS_WARNING	LOG_ARCHIVE_DUPLEX_DEST
LOG_ARCHIVE_MIN_SUCCEED _DEST	LOG_CHECKPOINT_INTERVAL
LOG_CHECKPOINT_TIMEOUT	LOG_SMALL_ENTRY_MAX_SIZE
MAX_DUMP_FILE_SIZE	MTS_DISPATCHERS
MTS_SERVERS	OPS_ADMIN_GROUP
PARALLEL_INSTANCE_GROUP	PARALLEL_TRANSACTION_ RESOURCE_TIMEOUT
PLSQL_V2_COMPATIBILITY	REMOTE_DEPENDENCIES_MODE
RESOURCE_LIMIT	SPIN_COUNT
TEXT_ENABLE	TIMED_OS_STATISTICS
TIMED_STATISTICS	USER_DUMP_DEST

The ALTER SYSTEM DEFERRED command does not modify the global value of the parameter for existing sessions, but the value will be modified for future sessions that connect to the database. The value of the initialization parameters listed in Table 1-4 can be changed with ALTER SYSTEM DEFERRED.

Table 1-4: Initialization Parameters Alterable with ALTER SYSTEM DEFERRED

ALLOW_PARTIAL_SN_RESULTS	BACKUP_DISK_IO_SLAVES
BACKUP_TAPE_IO_SLAVES	DB_FILE_DIRECT_IO_COUNT
OBJECT_CACHE_MAX_SIZE _PERCENT	OBJECT_CACHE_OPTIMAL_SIZE
SORT_AREA_RETAINED_SIZE	SORT_AREA_SIZE
SORT_DIRECT_WRITES	SORT_READ_FAC
SORT_WRITE_BUFFER_SIZE	SORT_WRITE_BUFFERS
TRANSACTION_AUDITING	

Displaying Current Parameter Values

To see the current settings for initialization parameters, use the following server manager command:

```
SVRMGR> SHOW PARAMETERS
```

This displays all parameters in alphabetical order, with their current values.

Enter the following text string to see a display for all parameters having BLOCK in their name.:

```
SVRMGR> SHOW PARAMETERS BLOCK
```

If you display all the parameters, you might want to use the SPOOL command to write the output to a file.

Uses of Parameters

Initialization parameters can be grouped by function in several different ways. For example, there are parameters that perform the following functions:

- set database-wide limits
- set user or process limits
- name files or directories required by a database system
- set limits on database resources

- affect performance (these are called *variable parameters*)

The set of variable parameters are of particular interest to database administrators because these parameters are used primarily for improving database performance.

Types of Parameters

The Oracle Server has the following types of initialization parameters:

- Derived Parameters
- Global Cache Parameters with Prefix GC
- Operating System-Dependent Parameters
- Variable Parameters (these can be dynamic parameters or any of the above)
- Heterogeneous Services Parameters

Derived Parameters

Some initialization parameters are noted as *derived*. This means that their values are calculated from the values of other parameters. Normally, you should not alter values for derived parameters, but if you do, the value you specify overrides the calculated value.

Global Cache Parameters with Prefix GC

Initialization parameters with the prefix GC, such as GC_DB_LOCKS, apply to systems using the Oracle Parallel Server. The prefix GC stands for Global Cache. The settings of these parameters determine how the Oracle Parallel Server coordinates multiple instances. The settings you choose have an effect on the use of certain operating system resources.

Additional Information: For more information about the Parallel Server, see *Oracle8 Parallel Server Concepts & Administration*.

See your system release bulletins or other operating system-specific Oracle documentation for platform-specific information on Parallel Server parameters.

Operating System-Dependent Parameters

For some initialization parameters, the valid values or ranges depend upon the host operating system. This is denoted in the default, or range column as operating system-dependent. For example, the parameter DB_BLOCK_BUFFERS indicates the *number* of data buffers in main memory, and its maximum value depends on the operating system. The *size* of those buffers, set by DB_BLOCK_SIZE, has a system-dependent default value.

See your operating system-specific Oracle documentation for more information on operating system dependent Oracle parameters and operating system parameters.

Variable Parameters

The variable initialization parameters offer the most potential for improving system performance. Some variable parameters set capacity limits but do not affect performance. For example, when the value of OPEN_CURSORS is 10, a user process attempting to open its 11th cursor receives an error. Other variable parameters affect performance but do not impose absolute limits. For example, reducing the value of DB_BLOCK_BUFFERS does not prevent work even though it may slow down performance.

Increasing the values of variable parameters may improve your system's performance, but increasing most parameters also increases the System Global Area (SGA) size. A larger SGA can improve database performance up to a point. In virtual memory operating systems, an SGA that is too large can degrade performance if it is swapped in and out of memory. Operating system parameters that control virtual memory working areas should be set with the SGA size in mind. The operating system configuration can also limit the maximum size of the SGA.

Heterogeneous Services Parameters

There are a number of initialization parameters specific to Heterogeneous Services which must be set using a package called DBMS_HS.

For information about specifying these parameters, see *Oracle8 Server Distributed Database Systems*.

Parameters You Should Not Specify in the Parameter File

The following types of parameters might never have to be specified in the parameter file:

- parameters that you never alter except when instructed to do so by Oracle Corporation to resolve a problem

- derived parameters that normally do not need altering because their values are automatically calculated by the Oracle Server

When Parameters Are Set Incorrectly

Some parameters have a minimum setting below which an Oracle instance will not start. For other parameters, setting the value too low or too high may cause Oracle to perform badly, but it still runs.

You may see messages indicating that a parameter value is too low or too high, or that you have reached the maximum for some resource. Frequently, you can wait a short while and retry the operation when the system is not as busy. If a message occurs repeatedly, you should shut down the instance, adjust the relevant parameter, and restart the instance.

Reading the Parameter Descriptions

The parameter descriptions in this chapter follow the format shown below.

PARAMETER_NAME

Parameter type:	Whether the type is integer, boolean, string, and so on.
Parameter class:	Whether the parameter is dynamic or static. If dynamic, then it also describes whether it can be changed by an ALTER SYSTEM or ALTER SESSION statement.
Default value:	The value this parameter assumes if not explicitly specified.
Range of values:	The valid range of values that this parameter can assume, shown as a minimum and maximum value. Not applicable to all parameters.
Multiple instances:	How the values for this parameter must be specified for multiple instances in an Oracle Parallel Server. Not applicable to all parameters.
OK to change:	Notes on changing the parameter value; not specified for all releases.

The remaining paragraphs provide a textual description of the parameter and the effects of different settings.

For more information, see references to chapters or books that contain more detailed information on this subject.

Parameter Descriptions

Descriptions of the individual initialization parameters follow in alphabetical order.

Most initialization parameter values are global (on a database-wide basis), not per user, unless otherwise specified.

For more information, see your system release bulletins or other operating system-specific Oracle documentation.

O7_DICTIONARY_ACCESSIBILITY

Parameter type:	boolean
Parameter class:	static
Default value:	TRUE
Range of values:	TRUE, FALSE

O7_DICTIONARY_ACCESSIBILITY is intended to be used for migration from Oracle7 to Oracle8. O7_DICTIONARY_ACCESSIBILITY controls restrictions on SYSTEM privileges. If the parameter is set to TRUE, access to objects in SYS schema is allowed (Oracle7 behavior). If this parameter is set to FALSE, SYSTEM privileges that allow access to objects in other schema do not allow access to objects in dictionary schema.

For example, if O7_DICTIONARY_ACCESSIBILITY=FALSE, then the SELECT ANY TABLE statement will allow access to views or tables in any schema except SYS schema (for example, dictionaries could not be accessed). The system privilege, EXECUTE ANY PROCEDURE will ALLOW ACCESS on the procedures in any other schema except in SYS schema.

If you need to access objects in the SYS schema, then you must be granted explicit object privilege. Also, the following roles, which can be granted to the database administrator, also allow access to dictionary objects: SELECT_CATALOG_ROLE, EXECUTE_CATALOG_ROLE, and DELETE_CATALOG_ROLE.

For more information on this parameter and the roles mentioned above, see the *Oracle8 Server Administrator's Guide*.

ALLOW_PARTIAL_SN_RESULTS

Parameter type:	boolean
Parameter class:	dynamic, scope = ALTER SESSION, ALTER SYSTEM DEFERRED
Default value:	FALSE
Range of values:	TRUE, FALSE
Multiple instances:	should have the same value

ALLOW_PARTIAL_SN_RESULTS is a Parallel Server parameter. This parameter allows for partial results to be returned on queries to global performance tables (GV$) even if a slave could not be allocated on the instance.

If the value of MAX_PARALLEL_SERVERS equals 0, then a query on the global dynamic performance table (GV$) will revert to a sequential query on the local instance. If the value of MAX_PARALLEL_SERVERS is greater than 0 and a slave cannot be allocated on an instance in a GV$ query, then the value of ALLOW_PARTIAL_SN_RESULTS determines whether the query returns partial results or returns a failure.

If ALLOW_PARTIAL_SN_RESULTS is TRUE, then the query succeeds and returns results from all of the instances which were able to allocate a slave for the query. If ALLOW_PARTIAL_SN_RESULTS is FALSE, then the query fails and returns an error message.

ALWAYS_ANTI_JOIN

Parameter type:	string
Parameter class:	static
Default value:	NESTED_LOOPS
Range of values:	NESTED_LOOPS/MERGE/HASH

ALWAYS_ANTI_JOIN sets the type of antijoin that the Oracle Server uses. The system checks to verify that it is legal to perform an antijoin, and if it is, processes the subquery depending on the value of this parameter. When set to the value NESTED_LOOPS, the Oracle Server uses a nested loop antijoin algorithm. When set to the value MERGE, the Oracle Server uses the sort merge antijoin algorithm. When set to the value HASH, the Oracle Server uses the hash antijoin algorithm to evaluate the subquery.

AQ_TM_PROCESSES

Parameter type:	integer
Parameter class:	dynamic, scope=ALTER SYSTEM
Default value:	0
Range of values:	either 0 or 1

AQ_TM_PROCESSES specifies whether a time manager is created. If AQ_TM_PROCESSES is set to 1, then one time manager process is created to monitor the messages. If AQ_TM_PROCESSES is not specified or is set to 0, then the time manager is not created. Setting the parameter to a value greater than 1 results in an error, and no time manager is created.

For more information about this parameter and Advanced Queuing, see the *Oracle8 Server Application Developer's Guide*.

ARCH_IO_SLAVES

Parameter type:	integer
Parameter class:	static
Default value:	0
Range of values:	0 - 15

ARCH_IO_SLAVES specifies the number of I/O slaves used by the ARCH process to archive redo logfiles. The ARCH process and its slaves always write to disk. By default the value is 0 and I/O slaves are not used.

This parameter is normally adjusted when an I/O bottleneck has been detected in the ARCH process. Typically, I/O bottlenecks in this process will occur on platforms that do not support asynchronous I/O or implement it inefficiently.

AUDIT_FILE_DEST

Parameter type:	string
Parameter class:	static
Default value:	$ORACLE_HOME/RDBMS/AUDIT

AUDIT_FILE_DEST specifies the directory where auditing files are stored.

AUDIT_TRAIL

Parameter type:	string
Parameter class:	static
Default value:	NONE
Range of values:	NONE (FALSE), DB (TRUE), OS

AUDIT_TRAIL enables or disables the writing of rows to the audit trail. Audited records are not written if the value is NONE or if the parameter is not present. The OS option enables system-wide auditing and causes audited records to be written to the operating system's audit trail. The DB option enables system-wide auditing and causes audited records to be written to the database audit trail (the SYS.AUD$ table).

The values TRUE and FALSE are also supported for backward compatibility. TRUE is equivalent to DB, and FALSE is equivalent to NONE.

The SQL AUDIT statements can set auditing options regardless of the setting of this parameter.

For more information, see the *Oracle8 Server Administrator's Guide*.

B_TREE_BITMAP_PLANS

Parameter type:	boolean
Parameter class:	dynamic, scope = ALTER SESSION
Default value:	FALSE
Range of values:	TRUE/FALSE

B_TREE_BITMAP_PLANS makes the optimizer consider a bitmap access path even when a table only has regular B-tree indexes. Do not change the value of this parameter unless instructed by Oracle Technical Support.

BACKGROUND_CORE_DUMP

Parameter type:	string
Parameter class:	static
Default value:	FULL
Range of values:	FULL/PARTIAL

BACKGROUND_CORE_DUMP specifies whether the SGA is dumped as part of the generated core file. When BACKGROUND_CORE_DUMP=FULL, the SGA is dumped as part of the generated core file. If BACKGROUND_CORE_DUMP=PARTIAL, then the SGA is not dumped as part of the generated core file.

BACKGROUND_DUMP_DEST

Parameter type:	string
Parameter class:	static
Default value:	operating system-dependent
Range of values:	valid local pathname, directory, or disk

BACKGROUND_DUMP_DEST specifies the pathname for a directory where debugging trace files for the background processes (LGWR, DBWR, and so on) are written during Oracle operations.

An ALERT file in the directory specified by BACKGROUND_DUMP_DEST logs significant database events and messages. Anything that affects the database instance-wide or globally is recorded here. This file records all instance start ups and shut downs, messages to the operator console, and errors that cause trace files to be written. It also records every CREATE, ALTER, or DROP operation on a database, tablespace, or rollback segment.

The ALERT file is a normal text file. Its filename is operating system-dependent. For platforms that support multiple instances, it takes the form ALERT_*sid*.LOG. This file grows slowly, but without limit, so the database administrator might want to delete it periodically. The file can be deleted even when the database is running.

For more information, see the *Oracle8 Server Administrator's Guide*. See your operating system-specific Oracle documentation for the default value.

BACKUP_DISK_IO_SLAVES

Parameter type:	integer
Parameter class:	dynamic, scope = ALTER SYSTEM DEFERRED
Default value:	0
Range of values:	0 - 15 although a value under 7 is recommended

BACKUP_DISK_IO_SLAVES specifies the number of I/O slaves used by the Recovery Manager to backup, copy, or restore. Note that every Recovery Manager channel can get the specified number of I/O slave processes. By default, the value is 0 and I/O slaves are not used.

Typically I/O slaves are used to "simulate" asynchronous I/O on platforms that either do not support asynchronous I/O or implement it inefficiently. However, I/O slaves can be used even when asynchronous I/O is being used. In that case the I/O slaves will use asynchronous I/O.

BACKUP_TAPE_IO_SLAVES

Parameter type:	boolean
Parameter class:	dynamic, scope = ALTER SYSTEM DEFERRED
Default value:	FALSE
Range of values:	TRUE/FALSE

BACKUP_TAPE_IO_SLAVES specifies whether I/O slaves are used by the Recovery Manager to backup, copy, or restore data to tape. When BACKUP_TAPE_IO_SLAVES = TRUE, an I/O slave process is used to write to or read from a tape device. If this parameter is FALSE (the default), then I/O slaves are not used for backups; instead, the shadow process engaged in the backup will access the tape device.

Note, as a tape device can only be accessed by one process at any given time, this parameter is a boolean, that allows or disallows deployment of an I/O slave process to access a tape device.

Typically I/O slaves are used to "simulate" asynchronous I/O on platforms that either do not support asynchronous I/O or implement it inefficiently. However, I/O slaves can be used even when asynchronous I/O is being used. In that case the I/O slaves will use asynchronous I/O.

BITMAP_MERGE_AREA_SIZE

Parameter type:	integer
Parameter class:	static
Default value:	1 Mb
Range of values:	system-dependent value

BITMAP_MERGE_AREA_SIZE parameter specifies the amount of memory used to merge bitmaps retrieved from a range scan of the index. The default value is 1 Mb. A larger value should improve performance because the bitmap segments must be sorted before being merged into a single bitmap. This parameter is not dynamically alterable at the session level.

BLANK_TRIMMING

Parameter type:	boolean
Parameter class:	static
Default value:	FALSE
Range of values:	TRUE/FALSE

BLANK_TRIMMING specifies the data assignment semantics of character datatypes. A value of TRUE allows the data assignment of a source character string/variable to a destination character column/variable even though the source length is longer than the destination length. In this case, however, the additional length over the destination length is all blanks. This is in compliance with SQL92 Transitional Level and above semantics. A value of FALSE disallows the data assignment if the source length is longer than the destination length and reverts to SQL92 Entry Level semantics.

CACHE_SIZE_THRESHOLD

Parameter type:	integer
Parameter class:	static
Default value:	0.1*DB_BLOCK_BUFFERS
OK to change:	yes
Multiple instances:	should have the same value

CACHE_SIZE_THRESHOLD specifies the maximum size of a cached partition of a table split among the caches of multiple instances. If the partition is larger than the value of this parameter, the table is not split among the instances' caches. The default value of this parameter is 1/10 the number of database blocks in the buffer cache. This parameter can also specify the maximum cached partition size for a single instance.

As of Release 8.0.3, the CACHE_SIZE_THRESHOLD parameter is being denigrated.

For more information, see *Oracle8 Parallel Server Concepts & Administration.*

CLEANUP_ROLLBACK_ENTRIES

Parameter type:	integer
Parameter class:	static
Default value:	20

CLEANUP_ROLLBACK_ENTRIES specifies the number of undo records processed at one time when rolling back a transaction. Prevents long transactions from freezing out shorter transactions that also need to be rolled back. Normally this parameter will not need modification.

For more information, see the *Oracle8 Server Administrator's Guide.*

CLOSE_CACHED_OPEN_CURSORS

Parameter type:	boolean
Parameter class:	static
Default value:	FALSE
Range of values:	TRUE/FALSE

CLOSE_CACHED_OPEN_CURSORS specifies whether cursors opened and cached in memory by PL/SQL are automatically closed at each COMMIT. A value of FALSE signifies that cursors opened by PL/SQL are held open so that subsequent executions need not open a new cursor. If PL/SQL cursors are reused frequently, setting the parameter to FALSE can cause subsequent executions to be faster.

A value of TRUE causes open cursors to be closed at each COMMIT or ROLLBACK. The cursor can then be reopened as needed. If cursors are rarely reused, setting the parameter to TRUE frees memory used by the cursor when the cursor is no longer in use.

COMMIT_POINT_STRENGTH

Parameter type:	integer
Parameter class:	static
Default value:	operating system-dependent
Range of values:	0 - 255

COMMIT_POINT_STRENGTH specifies a value that determines the commit point site in a distributed transaction. The node in the transaction with the highest value for COMMIT_POINT_STRENGTH will be the commit point site. A database's commit point strength should be set relative to the amount of critical shared data in the database. For example, a database on a mainframe computer typically shares more data among users than one on a personal computer. Therefore, COMMIT_POINT_STRENGTH should be set to a higher value for the mainframe computer.

The commit point site stores information about the status of transactions. Other computers in a distributed transaction require this information, so it is desirable to have machines that are always available as commit point sites. Therefore, set COMMIT_POINT_STRENGTH to a higher value on your more available machines.

For more information about two-phase commit, see *Oracle8 Server Concepts* and *Oracle8 Server Distributed Database Systems.* See also your operating system-specific Oracle documentation for the default value.

COMPATIBLE

Parameter type:	string
Parameter class:	static
Default value:	8.0.0
Range of values:	default release to current release
Multiple instances:	must have the same value

COMPATIBLE allows you to use a new release, while at the same time guaranteeing backward compatibility with an earlier release. This is in case it becomes necessary to revert to the earlier release. This parameter specifies the release with which the Oracle Server must maintain compatibility. Some features of the current release may be restricted.

When using the standby database and feature, this parameter must have the same value on the primary and standby databases, and the value must be 7.3.0.0.0 or higher.

This parameter allows you to immediately take advantage of the maintenance improvements of a new release in your production systems without testing the new functionality in your environment.

The default value is the earliest release with which compatibility can be guaranteed.

For more information, see *Oracle8 Server Migration.* See also your operating system-specific Oracle documentation for the default value.

COMPATIBLE_NO_RECOVERY

Parameter type:	string
Parameter class:	static
Default value:	release dependent
Range of values:	default version to current version
Multiple instances:	must have the same value

COMPATIBLE_NO_RECOVERY functions like the COMPATIBLE parameter, except that the earlier version may not be usable on the current database if recovery is needed.

The default value is the earliest version with which compatibility can be guaranteed. In some cases, this version may be earlier than the version which can be specified with the COMPATIBLE parameter.

For more information, see *Oracle8 Server Migration.* See also your operating system-specific Oracle documentation for the default value.

CONTROL_FILE_RECORD_KEEP_TIME

Parameter type:	integer
Parameter class:	dynamic, scope = ALTER SYSTEM
Default value:	7 (days)
Range of values:	0 - 365 (days)

Records in some sections in the control file are circularly reusable while records in other sections are never reused.
CONTROL_FILE_RECORD_KEEP_TIME applies to reusable sections. It specifies the minimum age in days that a record must have before it can be reused. In the event a new record needs to be added to a reusable section and the oldest record has not aged enough, the record section expands. If CONTROL_FILE_RECORD_KEEP_TIME is set to 0, then reusable sections never expand and records are reused as needed.

Table 1-5 lists the names of reusable sections.

Table 1-5: Names of Reusable Sections

ARCHIVED LOG	BACKUP CORRUPTION
BACKUP DATAFILE	BACKUP PIECE
BACKUP REDO LOG	BACKUP SET
COPY CORRUPTION	DATAFILE COPY
DELETED OBJECT	LOGHISTORY
OFFLINE RANGE	------------------

CONTROL_FILES

Parameter type:	string
Parameter class:	static
Default value:	operating system-dependent
Range of values:	1 - 8 filenames

CONTROL_FILES specifies one or more names of control files, separated by commas. Oracle Corporation recommends using multiple files on different devices or mirroring the file at the OS level.

For more information, see the *Oracle8 Server Administrator's Guide*.

CORE_DUMP_DEST

Parameter type:	string
Parameter class:	static
Default value:	$ORACLE_HOME/DBS/

CORE_DUMP_DEST specifies the directory where core files are dumped.

CPU_COUNT

Parameter type:	integer
Parameter class:	static
Default value:	automatically set by Oracle
Range of values:	0 - unlimited
OK to change:	no

CPU_COUNT specifies the number of CPUs available to Oracle. Oracle uses it to set the default value of the LOG_SIMULTANEOUS_COPIES parameter. On single-CPU computers, the value of CPU_COUNT is 0.

Warning: On most platforms Oracle automatically sets the value of CPU_COUNT to the number of CPUs available to your Oracle instance. Do not change the value of CPU_COUNT.

If there is heavy contention for latches, change the value of LOG_SIMULTANEOUS_COPIES to twice the number of CPUs you have. Do not change the value of CPU_COUNT.

For more information, see the *Oracle8 Server Administrator's Guide*. See also your operating system-specific Oracle documentation for information about this parameter.

CREATE_BITMAP_AREA_SIZE

Parameter type:	integer
Parameter class:	static
Default value:	8 Mb
Range of values:	operating system-dependent

CREATE_BITMAP_AREA_SIZE specifies the amount of memory allocated for bitmap creation. The default value is 8 Mb. A larger value might lead to faster index creation. If cardinality is very small, you can set a small value for this parameter. For example, if cardinality is only 2 then the value can be on the order of kilobytes rather than megabytes. As a general rule, the higher the cardinality, the more memory is needed for optimal performance. This parameter is not dynamically alterable at the session level.

CURSOR_SPACE_FOR_TIME

Parameter type:	boolean
Parameter class:	static
Default value:	FALSE
Range of values:	TRUE/FALSE

If CURSOR_SPACE_FOR_TIME is set to TRUE, the database uses more space for cursors to save time. It affects both the shared SQL area and the client's private SQL area.

Shared SQL areas are kept pinned in the shared pool when this parameter's value is TRUE. As a result, shared SQL areas are not aged out of the pool as long as there is an open cursor that references them. Because each active cursor's SQL area is present in memory, execution is faster. Because the shared SQL areas never leave memory while they are in use, however, you should set this parameter to TRUE only when the shared pool is large enough to hold all open cursors simultaneously.

Setting this parameter to TRUE also retains the private SQL area allocated for each cursor between executes instead of discarding it after cursor execution. This saves cursor allocation and initialization time.

For more information, see *Oracle8 Server Concepts*.

DB_BLOCK_BUFFERS

Parameter type:	integer
Parameter class:	static
Default value:	50 buffers
Range of values:	4 - operating system-specific
OK to change:	yes
Multiple instances:	can have different values

DB_BLOCK_BUFFERS specifies the number of database buffers available in the buffer cache. It is one of the primary parameters which contribute to the total memory requirements of the SGA on the instance. The DB_BLOCK_BUFFERS parameter, together with the DB_BLOCK_SIZE parameter, determines the total size of the buffer cache. Effective use of the buffer cache can greatly reduce the I/O load on the database. Since

DB_BLOCK_SIZE can be specified only when the database is first created, use DB_BLOCK_BUFFERS to control the size of the buffer cache.

This parameter affects the probability that a data block will be pinged when Parallel Server is enabled: the more buffers, the more chance of pings.

For more information, see *Oracle8 Server Concepts*. See also your operating system-specific Oracle documentation for the default value.

DB_BLOCK_CHECKPOINT_BATCH

Parameter type:	integer
Parameter class:	dynamic, scope = ALTER SYSTEM IMMEDIATE
Default value:	8
Range of values:	0 - derived

DB_BLOCK_CHECKPOINT_BATCH specifies the number of buffers that will be added to each batch of buffers that DBWR writes in order to advance checkpoint processing.

Reducing DB_BLOCK_CHECKPOINT_BATCH prevents the I/O system from being flooded with checkpoint writes and allows other modified blocks to be written to disk. Setting it to a higher value allows checkpoints to complete more quickly.

In general, DB_BLOCK_CHECKPOINT_BATCH should be set to a value that allows the checkpoint to complete before the next log switch takes place. If a log switch takes place every 20 minutes, then this parameter should be set to a value that allows check pointing to complete within 20 minutes.

Setting DB_BLOCK_CHECKPOINT_BATCH to zero causes the default value to be used. If an overly large value is specified for this parameter, Oracle (silently) limits it to the number of blocks that can be written in a database writer write batch.

For more information, see *Oracle8 Server Concepts*.

DB_BLOCK_CHECKSUM

Parameter type:	boolean
Parameter class:	dynamic, scope = ALTER SYSTEM
Default value:	FALSE
Range of values:	TRUE/FALSE

If DB_BLOCK_CHECKSUM is set to TRUE, DBWR and the direct loader will calculate a checksum and store it in the cache header of every data block when writing it to disk.

Warning: Setting DB_BLOCK_CHECKSUM to TRUE can cause performance overhead. Set this parameter to TRUE only under the advice of Oracle Support personnel to diagnose data corruption problems.

For more information, see the *Oracle8 Server Administrator's Guide*.

DB_BLOCK_LRU_EXTENDED_STATISTICS

Parameter type:	integer
Parameter class:	static
Default value:	0
Range of values:	0 - dependent on system memory capacity

DB_BLOCK_LRU_EXTENDED_STATISTICS disables or enables compilation of statistics which measures the effects of increasing the number of buffers in the buffer cache in the SGA. When this facility is enabled, it keeps track of the number of disk accesses that would be saved if additional buffers were allocated. A value greater than zero specifies the additional number of buffers (over DB_BLOCK_BUFFERS) for which statistics are kept. This tuning tool should be turned off during normal operation.

When compiling statistics, set this parameter to the maximum size you want to use to evaluate the buffer cache. It should be set to zero otherwise. (Although you can set this value very high, it is not practical to set it to a size beyond your system's memory capacity.)

Setting this parameter can cause a large performance loss, so it should only be set when the system is lightly loaded.

For more information, see the *Oracle8 Server Administrator's Guide*.

DB_BLOCK_LRU_LATCHES

Parameter type:	integer
Parameter class:	static
Default value:	CPU_COUNT/2
Range of values:	1 - the number of CPUs

DB_BLOCK_LRU_LATCHES specifies the upper bound of the number of LRU latch sets. Set this parameter to a value equal to the desired number of LRU latch sets. Oracle decides whether to use this value or reduce it based on a number of internal checks. If the parameter is not set, Oracle calculates a value for the number of sets. The value calculated by Oracle is usually adequate. Increase this only if misses are higher than 3% in V$LATCH.

DB_BLOCK_LRU_STATISTICS

Parameter type:	boolean
Parameter class:	static
Default value:	FALSE
Range of values:	TRUE/FALSE

DB_BLOCK_LRU_STATISTICS disables or enables compilation of statistics in the X$KCBCBH table, which measures the effect of fewer buffers in the SGA buffer cache.

Set this parameter to TRUE when you want to compile statistics for the X$KCBCBH table; otherwise, leave it set to FALSE. This parameter is a tuning tool and should be set to FALSE during normal operation.

Setting this parameter can cause a large performance loss, so it should only be set when the system is lightly loaded.

For more information, see *Oracle8 Server Administrator's Guide* and *Oracle8 Server Tuning*.

DB_BLOCK_MAX_DIRTY_TARGET

Parameter type:	integer
Parameter class:	dynamic, scope = ALTER SYSTEM set at runtime
Default value:	all the buffers in the cache
Range of values:	100 to all buffers in the cache, setting to 0 disables incremental checkpoint buffer writes
OK to change:	yes, at run-time
Multiple instances:	can have different values

DB_BLOCK_MAX_DIRTY_TARGET specifies the number of buffers that can be dirty (modified and different from what is on disk). If the number of dirty buffers in a buffer cache exceeds this value, DBWR will write out buffers in order to try and keep the number of dirty buffers below the specified value.

Note that this parameter does not impose a hard limit on the number of dirty buffers; in other words, DBWR attempts to keep the number of dirty buffers below this value, but will NOT stop (or slow) database activity if the number of dirty buffers exceeds this value occasionally.

This parameter can be used to influence the amount of time it takes to perform instance recovery since recovery is related to the number of buffers that were dirty at the time of the crash. The smaller the value of this parameter, the faster the instance recovery. Note that this improvement in recovery time is achieved at the expense of writing more buffers during normal processing. Hence, setting this parameter to a very small value might adversely affect performance if the workload modifies large numbers of buffers.

Setting this value to 0 disables writing of buffers for incremental checkpointing purposes; all other write activity continues as before (that is, it is unaffected by setting this parameter to 0).

DB_BLOCK_SIZE

Parameter type:	integer
Parameter class:	static
Default value:	operating system-dependent
Range of values:	operating system-dependent (2048 - 32768)
OK to change:	Only at database creation
Multiple instances:	must have the same value

DB_BLOCK_SIZE specifies the size in bytes of Oracle database blocks. Typical values are 2048 and 4096. The value for DB_BLOCK_SIZE in effect at CREATE DATABASE time determines the size of the blocks; at all other times the value must be set to the original value.

This parameter affects the maximum value of the FREELISTS storage parameter for tables and indexes. DSS (data warehouse) database environments tend to benefit from larger block size values.

For more information about block size, see *Oracle8 Server Concepts.* See also your operating system-specific Oracle documentation for the default value.

DB_DOMAIN

Parameter type:	string
Parameter class:	static
Default value:	WORLD
Range of values:	any legal string of name components, separated by periods and up to 128 characters long, including periods (see valid characters below) —this value cannot be NULL
Multiple instances:	must have the same value

DB_DOMAIN specifies the extension components of a global database name, consisting of valid identifiers, separated by periods. Specifying DB_DOMAIN as a unique string for every database is highly recommended.

For example, this parameter allows one department to create a database without worrying that it might have the same name as a database created by another department. If one sales department's DB_DOMAIN = "JAPAN.ACME.COM", then their "SALES" database (SALES.JAPAN.ACME.COM) is uniquely distinguished from another database with DB_NAME = "SALES" but with DB_DOMAIN = "US.ACME.COM".

The following characters are valid in a database domain name:

- alphabetic characters
- numbers
- underscore (_)
- pound (#)

For more information, see the *Oracle8 Server Administrator's Guide*.

DB_FILES

Parameter type:	integer
Parameter class:	static
Default value:	operating system-dependent
Range of values:	minimum value: either the value that was specified in the MAXDATAFILES clause the last time CREATE DATABASE or CREATE CONTROLFILE was executed, or the current actual number of datafiles in the data
	maximum value: operating system-dependent
Multiple instances:	must have the same value

DB_FILES specifies the maximum number of database files that can be opened for this database. The maximum valid value for DB_FILES is the maximum number of files, subject to operating system constraint, that will ever be specified for the database, including files to be added by ADD DATAFILE statement.

If you increase the value of DB_FILES, you must shut down and restart all instances accessing the database before the new value can take effect.

For more information, see the *Oracle8 Server Administrator's Guide*. See also your operating system-specific Oracle documentation for the default value.

DB_FILE_DIRECT_IO_COUNT

Parameter type:	integer
Parameter class:	dynamic, scope= ALTER SYSTEM
Default value:	64
Range of values:	operating system-dependent

DB_FILE_DIRECT_IO_COUNT is used to specify the number of blocks to be used for IO operations done by backup, restore or direct path read and write functions. The IO buffer size is a product of DB_FILE_DIRECT_IO_COUNT and DB_BLOCK_SIZE. The IO buffer size cannot exceed max_IO_size for your platform.

Assigning a high value to this parameter results in greater use of PGA or SGA memory.

DB_FILE_MULTIBLOCK_READ_COUNT

Parameter type:	integer
Parameter class:	dynamic, scope = ALTER SYSTEM, ALTER SESSION
Default value:	8
Range of values:	operating system-dependent

DB_FILE_MULTIBLOCK_READ_COUNT is used for multi-block I/O and specifies the maximum number of blocks read in one I/O operation during a sequential scan. The total number of I/Os needed to perform a full table scan depends on factors such as these:

- the size of the table
- the multi-block read count
- whether parallel query is being utilized for the operation

The default is 8. OLTP and batch environments typically have values for this parameter in the range of 4 to 16. DSS (data warehouse) database environments tend to get the most benefit from maximizing the value for this parameter.

The actual maximums vary by operating system; they are always less than the operating system's maximum I/O size expressed as Oracle blocks (*max_IO_size*/DB_BLOCK_SIZE). Attempts to set this parameter to a value greater than the maximum will cause the maximum to be used.

For information on the optimizer, see *Oracle8 Server Tuning*. See also your operating system-specific Oracle documentation for the default value.

DB_FILE_NAME_CONVERT

Parameter type:	string
Parameter class:	static
Default value:	none
Range of values:	character string

Use DB_FILE_NAME_CONVERT to convert the filename of a new data file on the primary database to a filename on the standby database. Adding a datafile to the primary database necessitates adding a corresponding file to the standby database. When the standby database is updated, this parameter is used to convert the datafile name on the primary database to the a datafile name on the standby database. The file must exist and be writable on the standby database or the recovery process will halt with an error.

Set the value of this parameter to two strings: the first string is the pattern found in the datafile names on the primary database; the second string is the pattern found in the datafile names on the standby database.

DB_FILE_SIMULTANEOUS_WRITES

Parameter type:	integer
Parameter class:	static
Default value:	4
Range of values:	minimum: 1
	maximum:
	• when striping used: 4 times the number of disks in the file that is striped the most.
	• when striping not used: 4

DB_FILE_SIMULTANEOUS_WRITES specifies the maximum number of simultaneous writes that can be made to a given database file. Oracle also uses the value of this parameter in computing various internal parameters that affect read and write operations to database files.

If you specify an excessively large value for this parameter, significant delays in performing read and write operations to a given database file might occur. This is because I/O requests get queued in the disk. If you set a value which is too small, the number of I/Os that can be issued to a given database file will be limited.

In environments where the database files reside on RAM devices or which use disk striping at the operating system level, it is beneficial to increase the value of this parameter. If striped files are used, Oracle recommends that you set the value of this parameter to 4 times the maximum number of disks in the file that is striped the most.

This parameter is also used to determine the number of reads-per-file in the redo read-ahead when reading redo during recovery.

For more information, see *Oracle8 Server Tuning*. See also your operating system-specific Oracle documentation for the default value.

DB_NAME

Parameter type:	string
Parameter class:	static
Default value:	NULL
Range of values:	any valid database name
Multiple instances:	must have the same value, or else the same value must be specified in STARTUP OPEN *db_name* or ALTER DATABASE *db_name* MOUNT

DB_NAME can specify a database identifier of up to eight characters. If specified, it must correspond to the name specified in the CREATE DATABASE statement. Although the use of DB_NAME is optional, it should generally be set before invoking CREATE DATABASE and then referenced in that statement.

If not specified, a database name must appear on either the STARTUP or the ALTER DATABASE MOUNT command line for each instance of the parallel server.

The following are valid characters in a database name:

- alphabetic characters
- numbers
- underscore (_)
- pound (#)
- dollar symbol ($)

No other characters are valid. Double quotation marks are removed before processing the database name. They cannot be used to embed other characters in the name.

Lowercase characters are not treated with special significance. They are considered the same as their uppercase counterparts.

For more information, see the *Oracle8 Server Administrator's Guide*.

DBLINK_ENCRYPT_LOGIN

Parameter type:	boolean
Parameter class:	static
Default value:	FALSE
Range of values:	TRUE/FALSE

DBLINK_ENCRYPT_LOGIN specifies whether attempts to connect to other Oracle Servers through database links should use encrypted passwords. When you attempt to connect to a database using a password, Oracle encrypts the password before sending it to the database. If the DBLINK_ENCRYPT_LOGIN parameter is TRUE, and the connection fails, Oracle does not re-attempt the connection. If this parameter is FALSE, Oracle re-attempts the connections using an unencrypted version of the password.

For more information, see the *Oracle8 Server Administrator's Guide*.

DBWR_IO_SLAVES

Parameter type:	.integer
Parameter class:	static
Default value:	0
Range of values:	0 to system-dependent value

DBWR_IO_SLAVES specifies the number of I/O slaves used by the DBWR process. The DBWR process and its slaves always write to disk. By default, the value is 0 and I/O slaves are not used.

Typically I/O slaves are used to "simulate" asynchronous I/O on platforms that do not support asynchronous I/O or implement it inefficiently. However, I/O slaves can be used even when asynchronous I/O is being used. In that case the I/O slaves will use asynchronous I/O.

I/O slaves are also useful in database environments with very large I/O throughput, even if asynchronous I/O is enabled.

DELAYED_LOGGING_BLOCK_CLEANOUTS

Parameter type:	boolean
Parameter class:	static
Default value:	TRUE
Range of values:	TRUE/FALSE
OK to change:	yes
Multiple instances:	need not be identical

DELAYED_LOGGING_BLOCK_CLEANOUTS turns the delayed block cleanout feature on or off. This reduces pinging in an Oracle Parallel Server. Keeping this feature set to TRUE sets a fast path, no logging block cleanout at commit time. Logging the block cleanout occurs at the time of a subsequent change to the block. This generally improves Oracle Parallel Server performance, particularly if block pings are a problem.

When Oracle commits a transaction, each block that the transaction changed is not immediately marked with the commit time. This is done later, on demand, when the block is read or updated. This is called *block cleanout*.

When block cleanout is performed during an update to a current block, the cleanout changes and the redo records are appended with those of the update. In previous releases, when block cleanout was needed during a read to a current block, extra cleanout redo records were generated and the block was dirtied. This has been changed.

When a transaction commits, all blocks changed by the transaction are cleaned out immediately. This cleanout performed at commit time is a "fast version" which does not generate redo log records (*delayed logging*) and does not reping the block. Most blocks will be cleaned out in this way, with the exception of blocks changed by long running transactions.

During queries, therefore, the data block's transaction information is normally up-to-date and the frequency of needing block cleanout is greatly reduced. Regular block cleanouts are still needed when querying a block where the transactions are still truly active, or when querying a block which was not cleaned out during commit.

Note: In long-running transactions, block cleanouts will not be performed during the transaction. If the transaction is not long running, block cleanout will be performed and the block cleanout is logged at the change of block.

During changes (INSERT, DELETE, UPDATE), the cleanout redo log records are generated and appended with the redo of the changes.

DISCRETE_TRANSACTIONS_ENABLED

Parameter type:	boolean
Parameter class:	static
Default value:	FALSE
Range of values:	TRUE/FALSE

Set DISCRETE_TRANSACTIONS_ENABLED to TRUE to implement a simpler, faster rollback mechanism that improves performance for certain kinds of transactions. There are strict limits on the kinds of transactions that can occur in discrete mode, but greater efficiency can be obtained for these transactions.

For more information about supplied packages, see the *Oracle8 Server Tuning*.

DISK_ASYNCH_IO

Parameter type:	boolean
Parameter class:	static
Default value:	TRUE
Range of values:	TRUE, FALSE

DISK_ASYNCH_IO can be used to control whether I/O to datafiles, controlfiles and logfiles are asynchronous. If a platform supports asynchronous I/O to disk, it is recommended that this parameter is left to its default. However, if the asynchronous I/O implementation is not stable, this parameter can be set to FALSE to disable asynchronous I/O. If a platform does not support asynchronous I/O to disk, this parameter has no effect.

If DISK_ASYNCH_IO is set to FALSE, then DBWR_IO_SLAVES should also be set.

DISTRIBUTED_LOCK_TIMEOUT

Parameter type:	integer
Parameter class:	static
Default value:	60 seconds
Range of values:	1 - unlimited

DISTRIBUTED_LOCK_TIMEOUT specifies the amount of time in seconds for distributed transactions to wait for locked resources.

For more information on data concurrency, see *Oracle8 Server Concepts* and *Oracle8 Server Distributed Database Systems*.

DISTRIBUTED_RECOVERY_CONNECTION_HOLD_TIME

Parameter type:	integer
Parameter class:	static
Default value:	200 seconds
Range of values:	0 - 1800 seconds

DISTRIBUTED_RECOVERY_CONNECTION_HOLD_TIME specifies the length of time to hold a remote connection open after a distributed transaction fails, in hope that communication will be restored without having to reestablish the connection. Larger values minimize reconnection time, but they also consume local resources for a longer time period. Values larger than 1800 seconds can be specified. Because the reconnection and recovery background process runs every 30 minutes (1800 seconds) (whether or not a failure occurs), a value of 1800 or larger means that the connection never closes.

For more information, see the *Oracle8 Server Administrator's Guide* and *Oracle8 Server Distributed Database Systems*.

DISTRIBUTED_TRANSACTIONS

Parameter type:	integer
Parameter class:	static
Default value:	operating system-dependent
Range of values:	0 - TRANSACTIONS

DISTRIBUTED_TRANSACTIONS specifies the maximum number of distributed transactions in which this database can concurrently participate. The value of this parameter cannot exceed the value of the parameter TRANSACTIONS.

If network failures are occurring at an abnormally high rate, causing many in-doubt transactions, you may want to decrease this parameter's value temporarily. This limits the number of concurrent distributed transactions, which then reduces the number of in-doubt transactions. Thus, the amount of blocked data and possible heuristic decision making (because of in-doubt transactions) is reduced.

If DISTRIBUTED_TRANSACTIONS is set to 0, no distributed transactions are allowed for the database. The recovery (RECO) process also does not start when the instance starts up.

For more information, see the *Oracle8 Server Administrator's Guide* and *Oracle8 Server Distributed Database Systems*. See also your operating system-specific Oracle documentation for the default value.

DML_LOCKS

Parameter type:	integer
Parameter class:	static
Default value:	derived (4 * TRANSACTIONS)
Range of values:	20 - unlimited, 0
Multiple instances:	must all have positive values or must all be 0

DML_LOCKS specifies the maximum number of DML locks—one for each table modified in a transaction. The value should equal the grand total of locks on tables currently referenced by all users. For example, if 3 users are modifying data in one table, then 3 entries would be required. If 3 users are modifying data in 2 tables, then 6 entries would be required.

The default value assumes an average of 4 tables referenced per transaction. For some systems, this value may not be enough.

If the value is set to 0, enqueues are disabled and performance is slightly increased. However, you cannot use DROP TABLE, CREATE INDEX, or explicit lock statements such as LOCK TABLE IN EXCLUSIVE MODE. If the value is set to 0 on one instance, it must be set to 0 on all instances of an Oracle Parallel Server.

For more information on data concurrency, see *Oracle8 Parallel Server Concepts & Administration*, *Oracle8 Server Concepts*, and *Oracle8 Server Distributed Database Systems*.

PDML Restrictions

DML_LOCKS has the following PDML restrictions regarding locks acquired by a parallel UPDATE/DELETE/INSERT statement.

- The coordinator acquires one Table lock SX where there is one Partition lock X per partition.

- For parallel UPDATE/DELETE, unless the UPDATE/DELETE's WHERE clause specifies the partitions involved, the coordinator will acquire partition locks for all partitions.

- For parallel INSERT, the coordinator will acquire partition locks for all partitions.

- Each slave acquires one Table lock SX where there is one Partition lock NULL per partition, and where there is one Partition-Wait lock X per partition.

- A slave can work on one or more partitions but a partition can only be worked on by one slave. So for a table with 600 partitions, running with parallel degree 100, assuming all partitions are involved in the parallel UPDATE/DELETE statement. There are the following requirements:

    - The coordinator acquires one Table lock SX and 600 Partition locks X

    - Total slaves acquire 100 Table locks SX, 600 Partition locks NULL, and 600 Partition-Wait locks X

ENQUEUE_RESOURCES

Parameter type:	integer
Parameter class:	static
Default value:	derived
Range of values:	10 - 65535

An enqueue is a sophisticated locking mechanism which permits several concurrent processes to share known resources to varying degrees. Any object which can be used concurrently can be protected with enqueues. For example, Oracle allows varying levels of sharing on tables: two processes can lock a table in share mode or in share update mode.

One difference between enqueues and latches is that in latches there is no ordered queue of waiting processes as there are in enqueues. Processes waiting for latches can either use timers to wake up and retry or spin (only in multiprocessors).

ENQUEUE_RESOURCES sets the number of resources that can be concurrently locked by the lock manager. The default value of ENQUEUE_RESOURCES is derived from the SESSIONS parameter and should be adequate, as long as DML_LOCKS + 20 is less than ENQUEUE_RESOURCES. For three or fewer sessions, the default value is 20. For 4 to 10 sessions, the default value is ((SESSIONS - 3) * 5) + 20; and for more than 10 sessions, it is ((SESSIONS - 10) * 2) + 55.

If you explicitly set ENQUEUE_RESOURCES to a value higher than DML_LOCKS + 20, then the value you provide is used.

If there are many tables, the value may be increased. Allow one per resource (regardless of the number of sessions or cursors using that resource), not one per lock Only increase this parameter if Oracle returns an error specifying that enqueues are exhausted.

For more information on data concurrency, see *Oracle8 Parallel Server Concepts & Administration*, *Oracle8 Server Concepts* and *Oracle8 Server Distributed Database Systems*.

EVENT

Parameter type:	string
Parameter class:	static
Default value:	NULL

EVENT is used to debug the system. This parameter should not usually be altered except at the direction of Oracle technical support personnel.

FIXED_DATE

Parameter type:	string
Parameter class:	dynamic, scope = ALTER SYSTEM
Default value:	NULL

FIXED_DATE lets you set a constant date that SYSDATE will always return instead of the current date. The format of the date is:

`YYYY-MM-DD-HH24:MI:SS`.

It also accepts the default Oracle date format, without a time. Specify the value with double quotes (but not single quotes) or without quotes. For example,

`FIXED_DATE = "30-nov-95"`

or

`FIXED_DATE = 30-nov-95`

This parameter is useful primarily for testing.

FREEZE_DB_FOR_FAST_INSTANCE_RECOVERY

Parameter type:	boolean
Parameter class:	dynamic, scope = ALTER SYSTEM
Default value:	see below
Range of values:	TRUE, FALSE
OK to change:	yes
Multiple instances:	must have identical values

FREEZE_DB_FOR_FAST_INSTANCE_RECOVERY is a Parallel Server parameter. The value of this parameter lets the database administrator control whether Oracle freezes the entire database during instance recovery. When this parameter is set to TRUE, Oracle freezes the entire database during instance recovery. The advantage of freezing the whole database is that it stops all other disk activities except those for instance recovery. This lets instance recovery complete faster. The drawback of freezing the whole database is that the entire database becomes unavailable during instance recovery.

When this parameter is set to FALSE, Oracle does not freeze the entire database, unless Oracle is responsible for *resilvering* some of the mirrored data files. Resilvering means ensuring data consistency of mirrored data files after a node crash. When Oracle does not freeze the entire database, part of the unaffected database will be accessible during instance recovery.

If all online datafiles use hash locks, the default value of this parameter is FALSE. If any data files use fine-grain locks, the default is TRUE.

For more information, see *Oracle8 Parallel Server Concepts & Administration*.

GC_DEFER_TIME

Parameter type:	integer
Parameter class:	dynamic, scope = ALTER SYSTEM
Default value:	0
Range of values:	any positive integer
Multiple instances:	can have different values
OK to change:	no

GC_DEFER_TIME specifies the time (in 100ths of a second) that the server waits, or *defers,* before responding to forced-write requests for hot blocks from other instances. Specifying the GC_DEFER_TIME parameter makes it more likely that buffers will be properly cleaned out before being written, thus making them more useful when they are read by other instances. It also improves the chance of hot blocks being used multiple times within an instance between forced writes.

The default value, 0, means that the feature is disabled: no deferring occurs.

GC_FILES_TO_LOCK

Parameter type:	string
Parameter class:	static
Default value:	NULL
Multiple instances:	must have identical values
OK to change:	yes

GC_FILES_TO_LOCKS is a Parallel Server parameter. This parameter controls the mapping of PCM locks to datafiles. The value of the parameter should be set to cover as many files as possible. Thus, to avoid performance problems, you should always change GC_FILES_TO_LOCKS when the size of datafiles change or when new datafiles are added. This requires you to shutdown and restart your parallel server.

GC_FILES_TO_LOCKS has the following syntax:

```
GC_FILES_TO_LOCKS = "{file_list=lock_count[!blocks][EACH]}[:]..."
```

where *file_list* is one or more datafiles listed by their file numbers, or ranges of file numbers, with comma separators:

```
filenumber[-filenumber][,filenumber[-filenumber]]...
```

and *lock_count* is the number of PCM locks assigned to *file_list*. If *lock_count* is set to 0, then fine-grain locking is used for these files.

A colon (:) separates each clause that assigns a number of PCM locks to *file_list*. The optional parameter *blocks*, specified with the "!" separator, indicates the number of contiguous blocks covered by one lock. The default is non-contiguous blocks. EACH specifies that each datafile in *file_list* is assigned a separate set of *lock_count* PCM locks. Spaces are not allowed within the quotation marks.

If the number of PCM locks allocated to a datafile is less than or equal to the number of blocks in a datafile, each of these locks will cover a number of contiguous blocks within the datafile equal to *!blocks*. If the number of PCM locks assigned to the datafile is larger than its number of blocks, resources will be wasted since there will be locks which are not covering any blocks.

The datafiles not specified in GC_FILES_TO_LOCKS are covered, by default, by releasable locks. Releasable locks are controlled by a different parameter, GC_RELEASABLE_LOCKS. See "GC_RELEASABLE_LOCKS" on page 1-46.

To find the correspondence between filenames and file numbers, query the data dictionary view DBA_DATA_FILES. See "DBA_DATA_FILES" on page 2-55.

GC_FILES_TO_LOCKS has no effect on an instance running in exclusive mode.

For more information on GC_FILES_TO_LOCKS, see *Oracle8 Parallel Server Concepts & Administration*.

GC_LCK_PROCS

Parameter type:	integer
Parameter class:	static
Default value:	1 (ignored when the database is mounted in exclusive mode)
Range of values:	1 - 10, or 0 for a single instance running in exclusive mode
OK to change:	yes (1 is usually sufficient)
Multiple instances:	must have identical values

GC_LCK_PROCS is a Parallel Server parameter. This parameter sets the number of background lock processes (LCK0 through LCK9) for an instance in a parallel server. The default of 1 is normally sufficient, but you can increase the value if the distributed lock request rate saturates the lock process. The lock process is saturated if it becomes CPU bound.

Increase the value of the PROCESSES parameter by one for each LCKn process, and increase the values of other parameters whose default values are derived from PROCESSES if you do not use their defaults.

For more information, see *Oracle8 Parallel Server Concepts & Administration*.

GC_RELEASABLE_LOCKS

Parameter type:	integer
Parameter class:	static
Default value:	Defaults to the number of buffers (DB_BLOCK_BUFFERS)
Range of values:	0 - DB_BLOCK_BUFFERS or higher
Multiple instances:	can have different values
OK to change:	yes

Lock elements can be fixed or non-fixed. Fixed lock elements are used by hashed PCM locks, in which the lock element name is preassigned. Non-fixed lock elements are used with fine-grain locking.

If the GC_RELEASABLE_LOCKS parameter is set, its value is used to allocate space for fine-grain locking. There is no maximum value, except as imposed by memory restrictions.

This parameter is specific to the Oracle Parallel Server in shared mode.

For more information, see *Oracle8 Parallel Server Concepts & Administration*.

GC_ROLLBACK_LOCKS

Parameter type:	string
Parameter class:	static
Default value:	20
Multiple instances:	must have identical values
OK to change:	yes

GC_ROLLBACK_LOCKS is a Parallel Server parameter. This parameter specifies, for each rollback segment, the number of distributed locks available for simultaneously modified rollback segment blocks. The default is adequate for most applications.

These instance locks are acquired in exclusive mode by the instance that acquires the rollback segment. They are used to force the instance to write rollback segment blocks to disk when another instance needs a read-consistent version of a block.

For more information, see *Oracle8 Parallel Server Concepts & Administration*.

GLOBAL_NAMES

Parameter type:	boolean
Parameter class:	dynamic, scope = ALTER SESSION, ALTER SYSTEM
Default value:	FALSE
Range of values:	TRUE/FALSE

GLOBAL_NAMES specifies whether a database link is required to have the same name as the database to which it connects. If the value of GLOBAL_NAMES is FALSE, then no check is performed. Oracle recommends setting this parameter to TRUE to ensure the use of consistent naming conventions for databases and links.

If you use distributed processing, set GLOBAL_NAMES to TRUE to ensure a unique identifying name for your database in a networked environment.

For more information, see the *Oracle8 Server Administrator's Guide*.

HASH_AREA_SIZE

Parameter type:	integer
Parameter class:	dynamic, scope= ALTER SESSION
Default value:	2 * SORT_AREA_SIZE
Range of values:	0 - system-dependent value

HASH_AREA_SIZE specifies the maximum amount of memory, in bytes, to be used for hash joins. If this parameter is not set, its value defaults to twice the value of the SORT_AREA_SIZE parameter.

HASH_MULTIBLOCK_IO_COUNT

Parameter type:	integer
Parameter class:	dynamic, scope= ALTER SESSION, ALTER SYSTEM
Default value:	1
Range of values:	operating system dependent

HASH_MULTIBLOCK_IO_COUNT specifies how many sequential blocks a hash join reads and writes in one IO. When operating in multi-threaded server mode, however, this parameter is ignored (a value of 1 is used even if you set the parameter to another value).

The maximum value for HASH_MULTIBLOCK_IO_COUNT varies by operating system. It is always less than the operating system's maximum I/O size expressed as Oracle blocks (max_IO_size/DB_BLOCK_SIZE).

This parameter strongly affects performance because it controls the number of partitions into which the input is divided. If you change the parameter value, try to make sure that the following formula remains true:

$$R / M <= Po2(M/C)$$

where:

R = sizeof(*left input to the join*)
M = HASH_AREA_SIZE * 0.9
$Po2(n)$ = largest power of 2 that is smaller than n
C = HASH_MULTIBLOCK_IO_COUNT * DB_BLOCK_SIZE

IFILE

Parameter type:	string
Parameter class:	static
Default value:	NULL
Range of values:	valid parameter filenames
Multiple instances:	can have different values

Use IFILE to embed another parameter file within the current parameter file. For example:

```
IFILE = COMMON.ORA
```

You can have up to three levels of nesting. In this example, the file COMMON.ORA could contain a second IFILE parameter for the file COMMON2.ORA, which could contain a third IFILE parameter for the file GCPARMS.ORA. You can also include multiple parameter files in one parameter file by listing IFILE several times with different values:

```
IFILE = DBPARMS.ORA
IFILE = GCPARMS.ORA
IFILE = LOGPARMS.ORA
```

For more information, see the *Oracle8 Server Administrator's Guide*.

INSTANCE_GROUPS

Parameter type:	string LIST
Parameter class:	static
Allowable values:	a string of group names, separated by commas.

INSTANCE_GROUPS is a Parallel Server parameter. It can be specified in parallel mode only. This parameter assigns the current instance to the specified groups. The value of INSTANCE_GROUPS must be a comma-separated list of instance groups. Instance groups are used when allocating query slaves for a parallel operation.

See also "PARALLEL_INSTANCE_GROUP" on page 1-89.

For more information, see *Oracle8 Parallel Server Concepts & Administration*.

INSTANCE_NUMBER

Parameter type:	integer
Parameter class:	static
Default value:	lowest available number (depends on instance start up order and on the INSTANCE_NUMBER values assigned to other instances)
Range of values:	1 - maximum number of instances specified in CREATE DATABASE statement
Multiple instances:	if specified, instances must have different values
OK to change:	yes (can be specified in both parallel and exclusive modes)

INSTANCE_NUMBER is a Parallel Server parameter. This parameter can be specified in parallel mode or exclusive mode. It specifies a unique number that maps the instance to one group of free space lists for each table created with storage option FREELIST GROUPS.

The INSTANCE option of the ALTER TABLE ALLOCATE EXTENT statement assigns an extent to a particular group of free lists. If you set INSTANCE_NUMBER to the value specified for the INSTANCE option, the instance uses that extent for inserts, and updates that expand rows.

The practical maximum value of this parameter is the maximum number of instances specified in the CREATE DATABASE statement; the absolute maximum is operating system dependent.

For more information, see *Oracle8 Parallel Server Concepts & Administration*.

JOB_QUEUE_INTERVAL

Parameter type:	integer
Parameter class:	static
Default value:	60 (seconds)
Range of values:	1 - 3600 (seconds)
Multiple instances:	can have different values

JOB_QUEUE_INTERVAL specifies the interval between wake-ups for the SNPn background processes of the instance.

For more information on managing table snapshots, see *Oracle8 Server Replication*.

JOB_QUEUE_PROCESSES

Parameter type:	integer
Parameter class:	static
Default value:	0
Range of values:	0 - 36
Multiple instances:	can have different values

JOB_QUEUE_PROCESSES specifies the number of SNPn background processes per instance, where n is 0 to 9 followed by A to Z. If you wish to have your snapshots updated automatically, you must set this parameter to a value of one or higher. One snapshot refresh process will usually be sufficient unless you have many snapshots that refresh simultaneously.

Job Queue processes are also used to process requests created by DBMS_JOB_QUEUE.

For more information on managing table snapshots, see *Oracle8 Server Replication*.

LARGE_POOL_MIN_ALLOC

Parameter type:	string
Parameter class:	static
Default value:	16K
Range of values:	minimum: 16K
	maximum: ~64M

LARGE_POOL_MIN_ALLOC specifies the minimum allocation size from the large pool. The value of the parameter can be specified in megabytes or kilobytes.

LARGE_POOL_MIN_ALLOC can accept a numerical value or a number followed by the suffix "K" or "M" where "K" means "multiply by 1000" and "M" means "multiply by 1000000".

LARGE_POOL_SIZE

Parameter type:	string
Parameter class:	static
Default value:	0
Range of values:	minimum: 300K or LARGE_POOL_MIN_ALLOC, whichever is larger.
	maximum: at least 2GB (maximum is operating system-specific)

The parameter LARGE_POOL_SIZE lets you specify the size of the large pool allocation heap. The default size is 0, and the minimum size is 300K or LARGE_POOL_MIN_ALLOC, whichever is larger. The value of the parameter can be specified in megabytes or kilobytes. If specified, the large pool is used for session memory if running with the multithreaded server. It is also used for IO buffers during backup operations.

LARGE_POOL_SIZE can accept a numerical value or a number followed by the suffix "K" or "M" where "K" means "multiply by 1000" and "M" means "multiply by 1000000".

LGWR_IO_SLAVES

Parameter type:	integer
Parameter class:	static
Default value:	0
Range of values:	0 - system-dependent value

LGWR_IO_SLAVES specifies the number of I/O slaves used by the LGWR process. The LGWR process and its slaves always write to disk. By default the value is 0 and I/O slaves are not used.

Typically I/O slaves are used to "simulate" asynchronous I/O on platforms that do not support asynchronous I/O or implement it inefficiently. However, I/O slaves can be used even when asynchronous I/O is being used. In that case the I/O slaves will use asynchronous I/O.

The default value is almost always adequate.

LICENSE_MAX_SESSIONS

Parameter type:	integer
Parameter class:	dynamic, scope = ALTER SYSTEM
Default value:	0
Range of values:	0 - number of session licenses
Multiple instances:	can have different values

LICENSE_MAX_SESSIONS specifies the maximum number of concurrent user sessions allowed simultaneously. When this limit is reached, only users with the RESTRICTED SESSION privilege can connect to the server. Users who are not able to connect receive a warning message indicating that the system has reached maximum capacity.

A zero value indicates that concurrent usage (session) licensing is not enforced. If you set this parameter to a non-zero number, you might also want to set LICENSE_SESSIONS_WARNING.

Concurrent usage licensing and user licensing should not both be enabled. Either LICENSE_MAX_SESSIONS or LICENSE_MAX_USERS should always be zero.

Multiple instances can have different values, but the total for all instances mounting a database should be less than or equal to the total number of sessions licensed for that database.

For more information, see the *Oracle8 Server Administrator's Guide*.

LICENSE_MAX_USERS

Parameter type:	integer
Parameter class:	dynamic, scope = ALTER SYSTEM
Default value:	0
Range of values:	0 - number of user licenses
Multiple instances:	should have the same values

LICENSE_MAX_USERS specifies the maximum number of users you can create in the database. When you reach this limit, you cannot create more users. You can, however, increase the limit.

Concurrent usage (session) licensing and user licensing should not both be enabled. Either LICENSE_MAX_SESSIONS or LICENSE_MAX_USERS, or both, should be zero.

If different instances specify different values for this parameter, the value of the first instance to mount the database takes precedence.

For more information, see the *Oracle8 Server Administrator's Guide*.

LICENSE_SESSIONS_WARNING

Parameter type:	integer
Parameter class:	dynamic, scope = ALTER SYSTEM
Default value:	0
Range of values:	0 - LICENSE_MAX_SESSIONS
Multiple instances:	can have different values

LICENSE_SESSIONS_WARNING specifies a warning limit on the number of concurrent user sessions. When this limit is reached, additional users can connect, but Oracle writes a message in the ALERT file for each new connection. Users with RESTRICTED SESSION privilege who connect after the limit is reached receive a warning message stating that the system is nearing its maximum capacity.

If this parameter is set to zero, no warning is given when approaching the concurrent usage (session) limit. If you set this parameter to a nonzero number, you should also set LICENSE_MAX_SESSIONS.

For more information, see the *Oracle8 Server Administrator's Guide*.

LM_LOCKS

Parameter type:	integer
Parameter class:	static
Default value:	12000
Range of values:	minimum: 512,
	maximum: limited by
	• the shared memory available in the operating system
	• the maximum size of contiguous shared memory segment; otherwise, it is limited only by the address space
Multiple instances:	must have the same value

LM_LOCKS is a Parallel Server parameter. This parameter specifies the number of locks which will be configured for the lock manager. The number of locks can be represented by the following equation, where R is the number of resources, N is the total number of nodes, and L is the total number of locks.

$$L = R + (R*(N - 1))/N$$

Note that lock configurations are per lock manager instance. Thus the value of LM_LOCKS must be the same for all lock manager instances.

LM_PROCS

Parameter type:	integer
Parameter class:	static
Default value:	64 + the maximum number of instances supported on the port
Range of values:	minimum: 36
	maximum: the result of the following equation:
	PROCESSES + maximum number of instances + safety factor
	Note: This assumes that the PROCESSES parameter has already included the Oracle background processes, including LMON and LMD0. The safety factor should be added to account for temporary overhead or unavailability of some procedure during the clean-up of dead processes.
Multiple instances:	must have the same value

LM_PROCS is a Parallel Server parameter. The value of this parameter represents the value of the PROCESSES parameter plus the maximum number of instances. Note that the processes configurations are per lock manager instance. Thus the value for LM_PROCS must be the same for all lock manager instances.

LM_RESS

Parameter type:	integer
Parameter class:	static
Default value:	6000
Range of values:	minimum: 256
	maximum: limited by
	• the shared memory available in the operating system
	• the maximum size of contiguous shared memory segment; otherwise, it is limited only by the address space
Multiple instances:	must have the same value

LM_RESS is a Parallel Server parameter. This parameter controls the number of resources that can be locked by each lock manager instance. It is recommended that each instance be assigned the same parameter value.

The value specified for LM_RESS should be much less than 2 * DML_LOCKS plus an overhead of about 20 locks.

LM_RESS covers the number of lock resources allocated for DML, DDL (data dictionary locks), data dictionary and library cache locks plus the file and log management locks.

LOCAL_LISTENER

Parameter type:	string
Parameter class:	static
Default value:	"(ADDRESS_LIST = (Address = (Protocol = TCP) (Host=localhost) (Port=1521)) (Address=(Protocol = IPC) (Key= *DBname*)))"

The LOCAL_LISTENER parameter is optional and identifies "local" Net8 listeners so that they can complete client connections to dedicated servers. LOCAL_LISTENER specifies the network name of either a single address or an address list of Net8 listeners. These Net8 listeners need to be running on the same machine as the instance.

The instance and dispatchers register certain information with the listener. This information enables the listener to connect clients to the appropriate dispatchers and dedicated servers. In order to connect clients to dedicated servers, the listener and the instance must be running on the same machine.

When it is present, the LOCAL_LISTENER parameter overrides the MTS_LISTENER_ADDRESS and MTS_MULTIPLE_LISTENERS parameters. For more information on these parameters, see "MTS_LISTENER_ADDRESS" on page 1-71 and "MTS_MULTIPLE_LISTENERS" on page 1-72.

For more information about instances, listener processes, and dispatcher processes, see the *Oracle8 Server Administrator's Guide.* See your operating system-specific Oracle documentation and Net8 documentation for a description of how to specify addresses for the protocols on your system.

LOCK_NAME_SPACE

Parameter type:	string
Parameter class:	static
Range of values:	eight characters maximum, no special characters allowed

LOCK_NAME_SPACE specifies the name space that the distributed lock manager (DLM) uses to generate lock names. This might need to be set if there is a standby or clone database with the same database name on the same cluster.

LOG_ARCHIVE_BUFFER_SIZE

Parameter type:	integer
Parameter class:	static
Default value:	operating system-dependent
Range of values:	1 - operating system-dependent (in operating system blocks)
Multiple instances:	can have different values

LOG_ARCHIVE_BUFFER_SIZE specifies the size of each archival buffer, in redo log blocks (operating system blocks). The default should be adequate for most applications. This parameter, with LOG_ARCHIVE_BUFFERS, can be used to tune archiving.

For more information, see the *Oracle8 Server Administrator's Guide*. See also your operating system-specific Oracle documentation for the default value.

LOG_ARCHIVE_BUFFERS

Parameter type:	integer
Parameter class:	static
Default value:	operating system-dependent
Range of values:	operating system-dependent
Multiple instances:	can have different values

LOG_ARCHIVE_BUFFERS specifies the number of buffers to allocate for archiving. The default should be adequate for most applications.

This parameter, with LOG_ARCHIVE_BUFFER_SIZE, can tune archiving so that it runs as fast as necessary, but not so fast that it reduces system performance.

For more information, see the *Oracle8 Server Administrator's Guide*. See also your operating system-specific Oracle documentation for the default value.

LOG_ARCHIVE_DEST

Parameter type:	string
Parameter class:	static
Default value:	operating system-dependent
Range of values:	any valid path or device name, except raw partitions
Multiple instances:	can have different values

LOG_ARCHIVE_DEST is applicable only if you are using the redo log in ARCHIVELOG mode. Use a text string to specify the default location and root of the disk file or tape device when archiving redo log files. (Archiving to tape is not supported on all operating systems.) The value cannot be a raw partition.

To override the destination that this parameter specifies, either specify a different destination for manual archiving or use the Server Manager command ARCHIVE LOG START *filespec* for automatic archiving, where *filespec* is the new archive destination.

For more information, see the *Oracle8 Server Administrator's Guide*. See also, "LOG_ARCHIVE_DUPLEX_DEST" on page 1-58, "LOG_ARCHIVE_MIN_SUCCEED_DEST" on page 1-60 and "V$ARCHIVE_DEST" on page 3-5

See your Oracle operating system-specific documentation for the default value and for an example of how to specify the destination path or filename using LOG_ARCHIVE_DEST.

LOG_ARCHIVE_DUPLEX_DEST

Parameter type:	string
Parameter class:	dynamic, scope = ALTER SYSTEM
Default value:	a NULL string
Range of values:	Either a NULL string or any valid path or device name, except raw partitions

LOG_ARCHIVE_DUPLEX_DEST is similar to the initialization parameter LOG_ARCHIVE_DEST. This parameter specifies a second archive destination: the duplex archive destination. This duplex archive destination can be either a must-succeed or a best-effort archive destination, depending on how many archive destinations must succeed.

If LOG_ARCHIVE_DUPLEX_DEST is set to be a NULL string ("") or ("), it means there is no duplex archive destination. The default of this parameter is a NULL string.

For more information, see "LOG_ARCHIVE_DEST" on page 1-58, "LOG_ARCHIVE_MIN_SUCCEED_DEST" on page 1-60, and "V$ARCHIVE_DEST" on page 3-5.

LOG_ARCHIVE_FORMAT

Parameter type:	string
Parameter class:	static
Default value:	operating system-dependent (length for uppercase variables is also operating system-dependent)
Range of values:	any valid filename
Multiple instances:	can have different values, but identical values are recommended

LOG_ARCHIVE_FORMAT is applicable only if you are using the redo log in ARCHIVELOG mode. Use a text string and variables to specify the default filename format when archiving redo log files. The string generated from this format is appended to the string specified in the LOG_ARCHIVE_DEST parameter. The following variables can be used in the format:

%s   log sequence number
%t   thread number

Using uppercase letters (for example, %S) for the variables causes the value to be a fixed length padded to the left with zeros.

The following is an example of specifying the archive redo log filename format:

```
LOG_ARCHIVE_FORMAT = "LOG%s_%t.ARC"
```

For more information, see *Oracle8 Server Administrator's Guide*. See also your operating system-specific Oracle documentation for the default value and range of values for LOG_ARCHIVE_FORMAT.

LOG_ARCHIVE_MIN_SUCCEED_DEST

Parameter type:	integer
Parameter class:	dynamic, scope = ALTER SYSTEM
Default value:	1
Range of values:	1 - 2

LOG_ARCHIVE_MIN_SUCCEED_DEST specifies the minimum number of archive log destinations that must succeed. When automatic archiving is enabled, the allowable values are 1 and 2. If this parameter is 1, LOG_ARCHIVE_DEST is a must-succeed destination and LOG_ARCHIVE_DUPLEX_DEST is a best-effort destination. If this parameter is 2, both LOG_ARCHIVE_DEST and LOG_ARCHIVE_DUPLEX_DEST are must-succeed destinations.

For more information, see "LOG_ARCHIVE_DEST" on page 1-58, "LOG_ARCHIVE_DUPLEX_DEST" on page 1-58, and "V$ARCHIVE_DEST" on page 3-5

LOG_ARCHIVE_START

Parameter type:	boolean
Parameter class:	static
Default value:	FALSE
Range of values:	TRUE/FALSE
Multiple instances:	can have different values

LOG_ARCHIVE_START is applicable only when you use the redo log in ARCHIVELOG mode, LOG_ARCHIVE_START indicates whether archiving should be automatic or manual when the instance starts up. TRUE indicates that archiving is automatic. FALSE indicates that the database administrator will archive filled redo log files manually. (The Server Manager command ARCHIVE LOG START or STOP overrides this parameter.)

In ARCHIVELOG mode, if all online redo log files fill without being archived, an error message is issued, and instance operations are suspended until the necessary archiving is performed. This delay is more likely if you use manual archiving. You can reduce its likelihood by increasing the number of online redo log files.

To use ARCHIVELOG mode while creating a database, set this parameter to TRUE. Normally, a database is created in NOARCHIVELOG mode and then altered to ARCHIVELOG mode after creation.

For more information, see the *Oracle8 Server Administrator's Guide*.

LOG_BLOCK_CHECKSUM

Parameter type:	boolean
Parameter class:	static
Default value:	FALSE
Range of values:	TRUE/FALSE

If LOG_BLOCK_CHECKSUM is TRUE, then every log block will be given a checksum before it is written to the current log.

Warning: Setting LOG_BLOCK_CHECKSUM to TRUE can cause performance overhead. Set this parameter to TRUE only under the advice of Oracle Support personnel to diagnose data corruption problems.

LOG_BUFFER

Parameter type:	integer
Parameter class:	static
Default value:	operating system-dependent
Range of values:	operating system-dependent

LOG_BUFFER specifies the amount of memory, in bytes, that is used when buffering redo entries to a redo log file. Redo log entries contain a record of the changes that have been made to the database block buffers. The LGWR process writes redo log entries from the log buffer to a redo log file.

In general, larger values for LOG_BUFFER reduce redo log file I/O, particularly if transactions are long or numerous. In a busy system, the value 65536 or higher would not be unreasonable.

For more information, see the *Oracle8 Server Administrator's Guide*. See also your operating system-specific Oracle documentation for the default value and range of values.

LOG_CHECKPOINT_INTERVAL

Parameter type:	integer
Parameter class:	dynamic, scope = ALTER SYSTEM
Default value:	operating system-dependent
Range of values:	unlimited (operating-system blocks, not database blocks)
Multiple instances:	can have different values

LOG_CHECKPOINT_INTERVAL specifies the frequency of checkpoints in terms of the number of redo log file blocks that are written between consecutive checkpoints.

Regardless of this value, a checkpoint always occurs when switching from one online redo log file to another. If the value exceeds the actual redo log file size, checkpoints occur only when switching logs. The checkpoint frequency is one of the factors which impacts the time required for the database to recover from an unexpected failure.

Extremely frequent checkpointing can cause excessive writes to disk, possibly impacting transaction performance. In addition, if the intervals are so close together that the interval checkpoint requests are arriving at a rate faster than the rate at which Oracle can satisfy these requests, Oracle can choose to ignore some of these requests in order to avoid excessive interval checkpointing activity.

The number of times DBWR has been notified to do a checkpoint for a given instance is shown in the cache statistic **DBWR checkpoints**, which is displayed in the System Statistics Monitor of the Enterprise Manager. For more information about this statistic, see "DBWR checkpoints" on page C-3

Note that specifying a value of 0 (zero) for the interval might cause interval checkpoints to be initiated very frequently since a new request will be started even if a single redo log buffer is written since the last request was initiated. Hence, setting the value to 0 is not recommended.

For more information, see the *Oracle8 Server Administrator's Guide*. See also your operating system-specific Oracle documentation for the default value.

LOG_CHECKPOINT_TIMEOUT

Parameter type:	integer
Parameter class:	dynamic, scope = ALTER SYSTEM
Default value:	0 seconds
Range of values:	0 - unlimited
Multiple instances:	can have different values

LOG_CHECKPOINT_TIMEOUT specifies the maximum amount of time before another checkpoint occurs. The value is specified in seconds. The time begins at the start of the previous checkpoint, then a checkpoint occurs after the amount of time specified by this parameter.

Specifying a value of 0 for the timeout disables time-based checkpoints. Hence, setting the value to 0 is not recommended.

Note: A checkpoint scheduled to occur because of this parameter is delayed until the completion of the previous checkpoint if the previous checkpoint has not yet completed.

For more information, see the *Oracle8 Server Administrator's Guide*.

LOG_CHECKPOINTS_TO_ALERT

Parameter type:	boolean
Parameter class:	static
Default value:	FALSE
Range of values:	TRUE/FALSE

LOG_CHECKPOINTS_TO_ALERT allows you to log your checkpoints to the alert file. This parameter is useful to determine if checkpoints are occurring at the desired frequency.

For more information, see *Oracle8 Server Concepts*.

LOG_FILE_NAME_CONVERT

Parameter type:	string
Parameter class:	dynamic, scope = ALTER SYSTEM
Default value:	none
Range of values:	character strings

The value of LOG_FILE_NAME_CONVERT converts the filename of a new log file on the primary database to the filename of a log file on the standby database. Adding a log file to the primary database necessitates adding a corresponding file to the standby database. When the standby database is updated, this parameter is used to convert the log file name on the primary database to the log file name on the standby database. The file must exist and be writable on the standby database or the recovery process will halt with an error.

Set the value of this parameter to two strings: the first string is the pattern found in the log file names on the primary database; the second string is the pattern found in the log file names on the standby database.

LOG_FILES

Parameter type:	integer
Parameter class:	static
Default value:	255
Range of values:	2 - 255 (must be a minimum of MAXLOGFILES*MAXLOGMEMBERS)
Multiple instances:	must have the same value

LOG_FILES specifies the maximum log group number. This value specifies the maximum number of redo log files that can be opened at runtime for the database. It also gives the upper limit on the group numbers that can be specified when issuing log-related commands. Reduce the value only if you need SGA space and have fewer redo log files.

For more information, see the *Oracle8 Server Administrator's Guide*.

LOG_SIMULTANEOUS_COPIES

Parameter type:	integer
Parameter class:	static
Default value:	CPU_COUNT
Range of values:	0 - unlimited

LOG_SIMULTANEOUS_COPIES specifies the maximum number of redo buffer copy latches available to write log entries simultaneously. For good performance, you can have up to twice as many redo copy latches as CPUs. For a single-processor system, set to zero so that all log entries are copied on the redo allocation latch.

If this parameter is set to 0, redo copy latches are turned off, and the parameters LOG_ENTRY_PREBUILD_THRESHOLD and LOG_SMALL_ENTRY_MAX_SIZE are ignored.

For more information, see the *Oracle8 Server Administrator's Guide*.

LOG_SMALL_ENTRY_MAX_SIZE

Parameter type:	integer
Parameter class:	dynamic, scope = ALTER SESSION
Default value:	operating system-dependent
Range of values:	operating system-dependent

LOG_SMALL_ENTRY_MAX_SIZE specifies the size in bytes of the largest copy to the log buffers that can occur under the redo allocation latch without obtaining the redo buffer copy latch. If the value for LOG_SIMULTANEOUS_COPIES is 0, this parameter is ignored (all writes are "small" and are made without the copy latch).

If the redo entry is copied on the redo allocation latch, the user process releases the latch after the copy. If the redo entry is larger than this parameter, the user process releases the latch after allocating space in the buffer and getting a redo copy latch.

For more information, see the *Oracle8 Server Administrator's Guide*. See also your operating system-specific Oracle documentation for the default value and range of values.

MAX_COMMIT_PROPAGATION_DELAY

Parameter type:	integer
Parameter class:	static
Default value:	90000
Range of values:	0 - 90000
Multiple instances:	must have identical values
OK to change:	no

MAX_COMMIT_PROPAGATION_DELAY is a Parallel Server parameter. This initialization parameter should not be changed except under a limited set of circumstances specific to the Parallel Server. This parameter specifies the maximum amount of time allowed before the System Change Number (SCN) held in the SGA of an instance is refreshed by LGWR. It determines if the local SCN should be refreshed from the lock value when getting the snapshot SCN for a query. Units are in hundredths of seconds. Under very unusual circumstances involving rapid updates and queries of the same data from different instances, the SCN might not be refreshed in a timely manner. Setting the parameter to zero causes the SCN to be refreshed immediately after a commit. The default value of 90,000 hundredths of a second, or fifteen minutes, is an upper bound that allows the preferred existing high performance mechanism to remain in place.

Change this parameter only when it is absolutely necessary to see the most current version of the database when doing a query.

For more information, see *Oracle8 Parallel Server Concepts & Administration*.

MAX_DUMP_FILE_SIZE

Parameter type:	string
Parameter class:	dynamic, scope = ALTER SYSTEM, ALTER SYSTEM DEFERRED, ALTER SESSION
Default value:	10000 blocks
Range of values:	0 - UNLIMITED

MAX_DUMP_FILE_SIZE specifies the maximum size of trace files to be written. Change this limit if you are concerned that trace files may take up too much space.

MAX_DUMP_FILE_SIZE can accept a numerical value or a number followed by the suffix "K", or "M", where "K" means multiply by 1000 and "M" means multiply by 1000000. A numerical value for MAX_DUMP_FILE_SIZE specifies the maximum size in operating system blocks, whereas a number followed by a "K" or "M" suffix specifies the file size in number of bytes. MAX_DUMP_FILE_SIZE can also assume the special value string UNLIMITED. UNLIMITED means that there is no upper limit on trace file size, thus dump files can be as large as the operating system permits.

For more information, see the *Oracle8 Server Administrator's Guide*.

MAX_ENABLED_ROLES

Parameter type:	integer
Parameter class:	static
Default value:	20
Range of values:	0 - 148

MAX_ENABLED_ROLES specifies the maximum number of database roles that a user can enable, including sub-roles.

The actual number of roles a user can enable is 2 plus the value of MAX_ENABLED_ROLES, because each user has two additional roles, PUBLIC, and the user's own role. For example, if MAX_ENABLED_ROLES is set to 5, user SCOTT can have 7 roles enabled, the five enabled by MAX_ENABLED_ROLES plus PUBLIC and SCOTT.

For more information, see the *Oracle8 Server Administrator's Guide*.

MAX_ROLLBACK_SEGMENTS

Parameter type:	integer
Parameter class:	static
Default value:	30
Range of values:	2 - 65535

MAX_ROLLBACK_SEGMENTS specifies the maximum size of the rollback segment cache in the SGA. The number specified signifies the maximum number of rollback segments that can be kept online (that is, status of INUSE) simultaneously by one instance. For more information, see the *Oracle8 Server Administrator's Guide*.

MAX_TRANSACTION_BRANCHES

Parameter type:	integer
Parameter class:	static
Default value:	8
Range of values:	1 - 32

MAX_TRANSACTION_BRANCHES controls the number of branches in a distributed transaction. For example, a certain TP monitor uses one branch per server involved in a distributed transaction. Another TP monitor uses one branch per server group involved in a distributed transaction.

The previously fixed maximum number of branches limited the number of servers or server groups involved in a distributed transaction to 8 per Oracle instance. With the MAX_TRANSACTION_BRANCHES parameter, the maximum number of branches can be increased to 32, allowing for 32 servers or server groups per Oracle instance to work on one distributed transaction.

Setting MAX_TRANSACTION_BRANCHES to a lower value reduces shared pool memory usage slightly according to the following equation:

```
MAX_TRANSACTION_BRANCHES * DISTRIBUTED_TRANSACTIONS * 72 bytes
```

MTS_DISPATCHERS

Parameter type:	string
Parameter class:	dynamic, scope = ALTER SYSTEM
Default value:	NULL

MTS_DISPATCHERS lets the database administrator enable various attributes for each dispatcher. In Oracle 7.3, the database administrator could specify a protocol and an initial number of dispatchers. These attributes are specified in a position-dependent, comma-separated string assigned to MTS_DISPATCHERS. For example:

```
MTS_DISPATCHERS = "TCP, 3"
```

While remaining backwardly compatible with this format, the parsing software in Oracle8 supports a name-value syntax (similar to the syntax used by Net8) to enable the specification of the existing and additional attributes in a position-independent case-insensitive manner. For example:

```
MTS_DISPATCHERS = "(PROTOCOL=TCP)(DISPATCHERS=3)"
```

One and only one of the following attributes is required: ADDRESS, DESCRIPTION, or PROTOCOL.

Attribute	Description
ADDRESS (ADD or ADDR)	The network address (in Net8 syntax) of the end point which the dispatchers will listen on. (Includes the protocol.)
DESCRIPTION (DES or DESC)	The network description (in Net8 syntax) of the end point which the dispatchers will listen on. (Includes the protocol.)
PROTOCOL (PRO or PROT)	The network protocol for which the dispatchers will generate a listening end point.

The ADDRESS and DESCRIPTION attributes provides support for the specification of additional network attributes. (This enables support of multi-homed hosts.)

The attributes CONNECTION, DISPATCHERS, LISTENER, MULTIPLEX, POOL, SERVICE, and TICKS are optional:

Attribute	Description
CONNECTION (CON or CONN)	The maximum number of network connections to allow for each dispatcher. Default is set by Net8 and is platform specific.
DISPATCHERS (DIS or DISP)	The initial number of dispatchers to start. Default is 1.
LISTENER (LIS, LIST)	The network name of an address or address list of the Net8 listeners with which the dispatchers will register. The LISTENER attribute makes it easier to administer multi-homed hosts. This attribute specifies the appropriate listeners with which the dispatchers will register. The LISTENER attribute overrides the LOCAL_LISTENER parameter and the denigrated MTS_LISTENER_ADDRESS and MTS_MULTPLE_LISTENERS parameters. For more information, see "LOCAL_LISTENER" on page 1-56, "MTS_LISTENER_ADDRESS" on page 1-71, and "MTS_MULTIPLE_LISTENERS" on page 1-72.

Attribute	Description
MULTIPLEX (MUL or MULT)	Used to enable the Net8 "Network Session Multiplex" feature.
	If "1", "ON", "YES", "TRUE", or "BOTH" is specified, then "Network Session Multiplex" is enabled for both incoming and outgoing network connections.
	If "IN" is specified, then "Network Session Multiplex" is enabled for incoming network connections.
	If "OUT" is specified, then "Network Session Multiplexing" is enabled for outgoing network connections.
	If "0", "NO", "OFF", or "FALSE" is specified, then "Network Session Multiplexing" is disabled for both incoming and outgoing network connections.
	The default "Network Session Multiplex" is disabled on both incoming and outgoing network connections.
POOL (POO)	Used to enable the Net8 "Connection Pooling" feature.
	If a number is specified, then "Connection Pooling" is enabled for both incoming and outgoing network connections and the number specified is the timeout in ticks for both incoming and outgoing network connections.
	If "ON", "YES", "TRUE", or "BOTH" is specified, then "Connection Pooling" is enabled for both incoming and outgoing network connections and the default timeout (set by Net8) will be used for both incoming and outgoing network connections.
	If "IN" is specified, then "Connection Pooling" is enabled for incoming network connections and the default timeout (set by Net8) will be used for incoming network connections.
	If "OUT" is specified, then "Connection Pooling" is enabled for outgoing network connections and the default timeout (set by Net8) will be used for outgoing network connections.
	If "NO", "OFF", or "FALSE" is specified, then "Connection Pooling" is disabled for both incoming and outgoing network connections.
	POOL can also be assigned a name-value string such as: "(IN=10)", "(OUT=20)", or "((IN=10)(OUT=20))", in which case, if an "IN" numeric value is specified, then "Connection Pooling" is enabled for incoming connections and the number specified is the timeout in ticks for incoming network connections. If an "OUT" numeric value is specified, then "Connection Pooling" is enabled for outgoing network connections and the number specified is the timeout in ticks for outgoing network connections. If the numeric value of a specified timeout is 0, then the default value (set by Net8) will be used.
	The default "Connection Pooling" is disabled on both incoming and outgoing network connections.
SERVICE (SER, SERV)	The service name which the dispatchers register with the Net8 listeners.
	The SERVICE attribute overrides the MTS_SERVICE parameter. This attribute specifies a service name that the dispatchers will use to register. For more information, see "MTS_SERVICE" on page 1-75.
SESSIONS (SES or SESS)	The maximum number of network sessions to allow for each dispatcher.
	Default is set by Net8 and is platform specific.
TICKS (TIC or TICK)	The size of a network tick in seconds. See the *Net8 Administrator's Guide* for more details about what this means. The default is set by Net8 and is platform specific.

For more information, see the *Oracle8 Server Administrator's Guide*. See also the *Net8 Administrator's Guide*.

MTS_LISTENER_ADDRESS

Parameter type:	string
Parameter class:	static
Default value:	NULL

MTS_LISTENER_ADDRESS specifies the configuration of the Listener process. The Listener process requires an address to listen for connection requests for each network protocol that is used on your system. Addresses are specified as the Net8 description of the connection address.

Warning: Each address must be specified with its own parameter. (This differs from the Net8 syntax.) For example, if you use TCP/IP as well as DECNet, you would provide specifications similar to the following in your initialization file:

```
MTS_LISTENER_ADDRESS =      \
    "(ADDRESS=(PROTOCOL=tcp)(HOST=myhost)(PORT=7002))"
    MTS_LISTENER_ADDRESS =     \
    "(ADDRESS=(PROTOCOL=decnet)(NODE=name)(OBJECT=mts))"
```

Note: If you have multiple MTS_LISTENER_ADDRESS parameters, they must be adjacent to each other in your initialization file.

Address specifications for the Listener process are operating system-specific and network protocol-specific.

MTS_LISTENER_ADDRESS is obsolete but is supported for backward compatibility. The functionality of MTS_LISTENER_ADDRESS has been replaced with the LOCAL_LISTENER parameter and LISTENER attribute of the MTS_DISPATCHERS parameter. For more information on these parameters, see "LOCAL_LISTENER" on page 1-56 and "MTS_DISPATCHERS" on page 1-68.

For more information, see the *Oracle8 Server Administrator's Guide*. See your operating system-specific Oracle documentation and Net8 documentation for a description of how to specify addresses for the protocols on your system.

MTS_MAX_DISPATCHERS

Parameter type:	integer
Parameter class:	static
Default value:	if dispatchers are configured, then defaults to whichever is greater: 5 or the number of dispatchers configured
Range of values:	operating system-dependent

MTS_MAX_DISPATCHERS specifies the maximum number of dispatcher processes allowed to be running simultaneously.

For more information, see the *Oracle8 Server Administrator's Guide*. See also your operating system-specific Oracle documentation for the default value and range of values.

MTS_MAX_SERVERS

Parameter type:	integer
Parameter class:	static
Default value:	defaults to whichever is greater: 20 or 2 times the value of MAX_SERVERS
Range of values:	operating system-dependent

MTS_MAX_SERVERS specifies the maximum number of shared server processes allowed to be running simultaneously.

For more information, see the *Oracle8 Server Administrator's Guide*. See also your operating system-specific Oracle documentation for the default value and range of values.

MTS_MULTIPLE_LISTENERS

Parameter type:	boolean
Parameter class:	static
Default value:	FALSE
Range of values:	TRUE/FALSE

If MTS_MULTIPLE_LISTENERS is set to TRUE, the syntax of the MTS_LISTENER_ADDRESS parameter changes to the following:

```
MTS_MULTIPLE_LISTENERS = TRUE
MTS_LISTENER_ADDRESS =
    (ADDRESS_LIST=(ADDRESS=(PROTOCOL=tcp)(PORT=5000)(HOST=zeus))\
    (ADDRESS=(PROTOCOL=decnet)(OBJECT=outa)(NODE=zeus))
```

MTS_MULTIPLE _LISTENERS is obsolete but is supported for backward compatibility. The functionality of MTS_MULTIPLE _LISTENERS has been replaced by the LOCAL_LISTENER parameter and LISTENER attribute of the MTS_DISPATCHERS parameter. For more information, see "LOCAL_LISTENER" on page 1-56 and "MTS_DISPATCHERS" on page 1-68.

MTS_RATE_LOG_SIZE

Parameter type:	string
Parameter class:	static
Default value:	each name-value listed in Table 1-6 defaults to 10
Range of values:	DEFAULTS/EVENT_LOOPS/MESSAGES/SERVER_BUFFERS/CLIENT_BUFFERS/TOTAL_BUFFERS/IN_CONNECTS/OUT_CONNECTS/RECONNECTS

MTS_RATE_LOG_SIZE specifies the sample size used to calculate dispatcher rate statistics. The sample size determines how much memory will be used and the frequency with which maximum rates will be determined. The memory used by each dispatcher is about 8 bytes per statistic multiplied by the sample size specified.

Dispatcher rate statistics themselves are calculated by first logging a sample of events (the size of the sample is specified by MTS_RATE_LOG_SIZE) and the times at which they occur. The rates are then calculated based on this sample.

MTS_RATE_LOG_SIZE accepts a name-value string. Each value defaults to 10. These values are shared among all dispatchers.

The following declaration for MTS_RATE_LOG_SIZE directs each dispatcher to log this many events: 4 inbound connections, 32 buffers to go either to the client or the server, and 16 events for unspecified statistics.

```
MTS_RATE_LOG_SIZE="(IN_CONNECTS=4)(TOTAL_BUFFERS=32)(DEFAULTS=16)"
```

Valid name values for MTS_RATE_LOG_SIZE are listed below.

Table 1-6: Name values for the MTS_RATE_LOG_SIZE Parameter

Name	Description
DEFAULTS	Overrides 10 as the number of events to log for unspecified statistics.
EVENT_LOOPS	Specifies number of event loops to log.
MESSAGES	Specifies number of messages to log.
SERVER_BUFFERS	Specifies number of buffers going to the server to log.
CLIENT_BUFFERS	Specifies number of buffers going to the client to log.
TOTAL_BUFFERS	Specifies number of buffers going in either direction to log.
IN_CONNECTS	Specifies number of inbound connections to log.
OUT_CONNECTS	Specifies number of outbound connections to log.
RECONNECTS	Specifies number of connection pool reconnections to log.

MTS_RATE_SCALE

Parameter type: string

Parameter class: static

Default value: default values for the name-value strings are listed in Table 1-7

Range of values: DEFAULTS/EVENT_LOOPS/MESSAGES/SERVER_BUFFERS/CLIENT_BUFFERS/TOTAL_BUFFERS/IN_CONNECTS/OUT_CONNECTS/RECONNECTS

MTS_RATE_SCALE specifies the scale at which dispatcher rate statistics are reported. The values are specified in 100ths of a second. Thus,

```
MTS_RATE_SCALE = "(EVENT_LOOPS=6000)"
```

means that the event loops statistic will be reported on a once per-minute interval.

MTS_RATE_SCALE accepts a name-value string. Valid names are listed in Table 1-7.

Table 1-7: Name values for the MTS_RATE_SCALE Parameter

Name	Default	Description
DEFAULTS	none	Specifies the scale for statistics not otherwise specified
EVENT_LOOPS	6000	Specifies scale in which to report event loops.

Table 1-7: Name values for the MTS_RATE_SCALE Parameter

Name	Default	Description
MESSAGES	100	Specifies scale in which to report messages.
SERVER_BUFFERS	10	Specifies scale in which to report buffers going to the server.
CLIENT_BUFFERS	10	Specifies scale in which to report buffers going to the client.
TOTAL_BUFFERS	10	Specifies scale in which to report buffers going in either direction. (Default = 10)
IN_CONNECTS	6000	Specifies scale in which to report inbound connections.
OUT_CONNECTS	6000	Specifies scale in which to report outbound connections.
RECONNECTS	6000	Specifies scale in which to report connection pool reconnections.

MTS_SERVERS

Parameter type:	integer
Parameter class:	dynamic, scope = ALTER SYSTEM
Default value:	0
Range of values:	operating system-dependent

MTS_SERVERS specifies the number of server processes that you want to create when an instance is started up.

For more information, see the *Oracle8 Server Administrator's Guide*. See also your operating system-specific Oracle documentation for the default value and range of values.

MTS_SERVICE

Parameter type:	string
Parameter class:	static
Default value:	NULL

MTS_SERVICE specifies the name of the service you want to be associated with the dispatcher. Using this name in the CONNECT string allows users to connect to an instance through a dispatcher. Oracle always checks for such a service before establishing a normal database connection.

The name you specify must be unique. It should *not* be enclosed in quotation marks. It is a good idea for this name to be the same as the instance name. That way, if the dispatcher is unavailable for any reason, the CONNECT string will still connect the user to the database.

If not specified, MTS_SERVICE defaults to the value specified by DB_NAME. If DB_NAME also is not specified, the Oracle Server returns an error at startup indicating that the value for this parameter is missing.

For more information, see the *Oracle8 Server Administrator's Guide*. See also the *Net8 Administrator's Guide*.

NLS_CURRENCY

Parameter type:	string
Parameter class:	dynamic, scope = ALTER SESSION
Default value:	derived
Range of values:	any valid character string, with a maximum of 10 bytes (not including null)

NLS_CURRENCY specifies the string to use as the local currency symbol for the L number format element. The default value of this parameter is determined by NLS_TERRITORY.

For more information, see "NLS_CURRENCY" on page 4-20. See also the *Oracle8 Server Administrator's Guide*.

NLS_DATE_FORMAT

Parameter type:	string
Parameter class:	dynamic, scope = ALTER SESSION
Default value:	derived
Range of values:	any valid date format mask but not exceeding a fixed length

NLS_DATE_FORMAT specifies the default date format to use with the TO_CHAR and TO_DATE functions. The default value of this parameter is determined by NLS_TERRITORY. The value of this parameter can be any valid date format mask, and the value must be surrounded by double quotation marks. For example:

```
NLS_DATE_FORMAT = "MM/DD/YYYY"
```

For more information, see "NLS_DATE_FORMAT" on page 4-21. See also the *Oracle8 Server Administrator's Guide*.

NLS_DATE_LANGUAGE

Parameter type:	string
Parameter class:	dynamic, scope = ALTER SESSION
Default value:	value for NLS_LANGUAGE
Range of values:	any valid NLS_LANGUAGE value

NLS_DATE_LANGUAGE specifies the language to use for the spelling of day and month names and date abbreviations (AM, PM, AD, BC). The default value of this parameter is the language specified by NLS_LANGUAGE.

For more information, see "NLS_DATE_ LANGUAGE" on page 4-22. See also the *Oracle8 Server Administrator's Guide*.

NLS_ISO_CURRENCY

Parameter type:	string
Parameter class:	dynamic, scope = ALTER SESSION
Default value:	derived
Range of values:	any valid NLS_TERRITORY value

NLS_ISO_CURRENCY specifies the string to use as the international currency symbol for the C number format element. The default value of this parameter is determined by NLS_TERRITORY.

For more information, see "NLS_ISO_CURRENCY" on page 4-23. See also the *Oracle8 Server Administrator's Guide*.

NLS_LANGUAGE

Parameter type:	string
Parameter class:	dynamic, scope = ALTER SESSION
Default value:	operating system-dependent
Range of values:	any valid language name

NLS_LANGUAGE specifies the default language of the database. This language is used for messages, the day and month names, the symbols for AD, BC, AM, and PM, and the default sorting mechanism. This parameter has the format:

```
NLS_LANGUAGE = FRENCH
```

Examples of supported languages are American, French, and Japanese.

This parameter determines the default values of the parameters NLS_DATE_LANGUAGE and NLS_SORT. For a complete list of languages, see "Supported Languages" on page 4-41.

For more information, see "NLS_LANGUAGE" on page 4-15. See also the *Oracle8 Server Administrator's Guide*, your country release notes, and operating system-specific Oracle documentation.

NLS_NUMERIC_CHARACTERS

Parameter type:	string
Parameter class:	dynamic, scope = ALTER SESSION
Default value:	derived

NLS_NUMERIC_CHARACTERS specifies the characters to use as the group separator and decimal and overrides those defined implicitly by NLS_TERRITORY. The group separator is the character that separates integer groups (that is, the thousands, millions, billions, and so on). The decimal separates the integer portion of a number from the decimal portion.

Any character can be the decimal or group separator. The two characters specified must be single-byte, and both characters must be different from each other each other. The characters cannot be any numeric character or any of the following characters: plus (+), hyphen (-), less than sign (<), greater than sign (>).

The characters are specified in the following format:

```
NLS_NUMERIC_CHARACTERS = "<decimal_character><group_separator>"
```

For example, if you wish to specify a comma as the decimal character and a space as the group separator, you would set this parameter as follows:

```
NLS_NUMERIC_CHARACTERS = ", "
```

The default value of this parameter is determined by NLS_TERRITORY.

For more information, see "NLS_NUMERIC_CHARACTERS" on page 4-24. See also the *Oracle8 Server Administrator's Guide*.

NLS_SORT

Parameter type:	string
Parameter class:	dynamic, scope = ALTER SESSION
Default value:	derived
Range of values:	BINARY or valid linguistic definition name

NLS_SORT specifies the collating sequence for ORDER BY queries. If the value is BINARY, then the collating sequence for ORDER BY queries is based on the numeric value of characters (a binary sort that requires less system overhead).

If the value is a named linguistic sort, sorting is based on the order of the defined linguistic sort. Most languages supported by the NLS_LANGUAGE parameter also support a linguistic sort with the same name.

Note: Setting NLS_SORT to anything other than BINARY causes a sort to use a full table scan, regardless of the path chosen by the optimizer. BINARY is the exception because indexes are built according to a binary order of keys. Thus the optimizer can use an index to satisfy the ORDER BY clause when NLS_SORT is set to BINARY. If NLS_SORT is set to any linguistic sort, the optimizer must include a full table scan and a full sort into the execution plan.

You must use the NLS_SORT operator with comparison operations if you want the linguistic sort behavior.

The default value of this parameter depends on the value of the NLS_LANGUAGE parameter.

For more information on this parameter, see "NLS_SORT" on page 4-25 and the *Oracle8 Server Administrator's Guide*. For a list of supported linguistic definitions and extended definitions, see "Linguistic Definitions" on page 4-51. See also your operating system-specific Oracle documentation for the sorting rules used by the linguistic sorting mechanisms.

NLS_TERRITORY

Parameter type:	string
Parameter class:	dynamic, scope = ALTER SESSION
Default value:	operating system-dependent
Range of values:	any valid territory name

NLS_TERRITORY specifies the name of the territory whose conventions are to be followed for day and week numbering. Also specifies the default date format, the default decimal character and group separator, and the default ISO and local currency symbols. Supported territories include America, France, Japan, and so on. For a complete list of territories, see "Supported Territories" on page 4-42.

This parameter determines the default values for the following parameters: NLS_CURRENCY, NLS_ISO_CURRENCY, NLS_DATE_FORMAT, and NLS_NUMERIC_CHARACTERS.

For more information, see "NLS_TERRITORY" on page 4-17. See also the *Oracle8 Server Administrator's Guide.* See your operating system-specific Oracle documentation for the territory-dependent default values for these parameters.

OBJECT_CACHE_MAX_SIZE_PERCENT

Parameter type:	integer
Parameter class:	dynamic, scope = ALTER SESSION, ALTER SYSTEM DEFERRED
Default value:	10%
Range of values:	0% to operating system-dependent maximum

OBJECT_CACHE_MAX_SIZE_PERCENT specifies the percentage of the optimal cache size that the session object cache can grow past the optimal size; the maximum size is equal to the optimal size plus the product of this percentage and the optimal size. When the cache size exceeds this maximum size, the system will attempt to shrink the cache to the optimal size.

OBJECT_CACHE_OPTIMAL_SIZE

Parameter type:	integer
Parameter class:	dynamic, scope = ALTER SESSION, ALTER SYSTEM DEFERRED
Default value:	100 Kbytes
Range of values:	10 Kbytes to operating system-dependent maximum

OBJECT_CACHE_OPTIMAL_SIZE specifies the size to which the session object cache is reduced when the size of the cache exceeds the maximum size.

OPEN_CURSORS

Parameter type:	integer
Parameter class:	static
Default value:	50
Range of values:	1 - operating system limit

OPEN_CURSORS specifies the maximum number of open cursors (context areas) a session can have at once. This constrains a session from opening an excessive number of cursors. Assuming that a session does not open the number of cursors specified by OPEN_CURSORS, there is no added overhead by setting this value too high.

It is important to have the value of OPEN_CURSORS set high enough to prevent your application from running out of open cursors. The number will vary from one application to another.

This parameter also constrains the size of the PL/SQL cursor cache which PL/SQL uses to avoid having to reparse as statements are reexecuted by a user.

For more information, see the *Oracle8 Server Administrator's Guide.* See also your operating system-specific Oracle documentation for the range of values.

OPEN_LINKS

Parameter type:	integer
Parameter class:	static
Default value:	4
Range of values:	0 - 255

OPEN_LINKS specifies the maximum number of concurrent open connections to remote databases in one session. The value should equal or exceed the number of databases referred to in a single SQL statement that references multiple databases so that all the databases can be open to execute the statement. Value should be increased if many different databases are accessed over time. Thus, if queries alternately access databases A, B, and C and OPEN_LINKS is set to 2, time would be spent waiting while one connection was broken and another made.

This parameter refers only to connections used for distributed transactions. Direct connections to a remote database specified as an application connects are not counted. For information on migratable open connections for XA transactions, see "OPEN_LINKS_PER_INSTANCE" on page 1-82.

If OPEN_LINKS is set to 0, then no distributed transactions are allowed.

For more information, see the *Oracle8 Server Administrator's Guide* and *Oracle8 Server Distributed Database Systems*.

OPEN_LINKS_PER_INSTANCE

Parameter type:	integer
Parameter class:	static
Default value:	4
Range of values:	0 - UB4MAXVAL
Multiple instances	can be specified for multiple instances. The value need not be same for all instances.
OK to change:	yes, provided a shutdown and restart is performed

OPEN_LINKS_PER_INSTANCE specifies the maximum number of migratable open connections. XA transactions use migratable open connections so that the connections are cached after a transaction is committed. Another transaction can use the connection provided the user that created the connection is the same as the user that owns the transaction.

OPEN_LINKS_PER_INSTANCE is different from the OPEN_LINKS parameter in that OPEN_LINKS indicates the number of connections from a session. The OPEN_LINKS parameter is not applicable to XA applications. For more information, see "OPEN_LINKS" on page 1-82.

OPS_ADMIN_GROUP

Parameter type:	string LIST
Parameter class:	dynamic, scope = ALTER SYSTEM, ALTER SESSION
Default value:	all active instances
Allowable values:	a string representing a group name.

OPS_ADMIN_GROUP is a Parallel Server parameter. OPS_ADMIN_GROUP allows instances to be partitioned in a parallel server environment for monitoring or administration purposes. The database must be mounted in parallel server mode (that is, PARALLEL_SERVER=TRUE).

The value of OPS_ADMIN_GROUP determines which instances return information in a GV$ fixed-view query. For example, assume instances {1,3,4} are active at the time of a GV$ query and the instance group *group1* contains the instances 1 and 4. If OPS_ADMIN_GROUP = *group1*, then a query over GV$*viewname* retrieves information only from instances 1 and 4.

If none of the instances specified for OPS_ADMIN_GROUP are active and a GV$ view is queried, then an error is returned.

If the database is mounted in non-parallel sever mode (that is, PARALLEL_SERVER=FALSE) then the OPS_ADMIN_GROUP parameter has no effect. Every query involving GV$ views will be run on the local instance.

OPTIMIZER_MODE

Parameter type:	integer
Parameter class:	dynamic, scope=ALTER SESSION
Default value:	CHOOSE
Range of values:	RULE/CHOOSE/FIRST_ROWS/ALL_ROWS

OPTIMIZER_MODE specifies the behavior of the optimizer. When set to RULE, this parameter causes rule-based optimization to be used unless hints are specified in the query. When set to CHOOSE, the optimizer uses the cost-based approach for a SQL statement if there are statistics in the dictionary for at least one table accessed in the statement. (Otherwise, the rule-based approach is used.)

You can set the goal for cost-based optimization by setting this parameter to FIRST_ROWS or ALL_ROWS. FIRST_ROWS causes the optimizer to choose execution plans that minimize response time. ALL_ROWS causes the optimizer to choose execution plans that minimize total execution time.

For more information about tuning SQL statements, see *Oracle8 Server Tuning*. For more information about the optimizer, see *Oracle8 Server Concepts* and *Oracle8 Server Tuning*.

OPTIMIZER_PERCENT_PARALLEL

Parameter type:	integer
Parameter class:	dynamic, scope = ALTER SESSION
Default value:	0
Range of values:	0 - 100

OPTIMIZER_PERCENT_PARALLEL specifies the amount of parallelism that the optimizer uses in its cost functions. The default of 0 means that the optimizer chooses the best serial plan. A value of 100 means that the optimizer uses each object's degree of parallelism in computing the cost of a full table scan operation. Low values favor indexes, and high values favor table scans.

Cost-based optimization will always be used for any query that references an object with a nonzero degree of parallelism. For such queries a RULE hint or optimizer mode or goal will be ignored. Use of a FIRST_ROWS hint or optimizer mode will override a nonzero setting of OPTIMIZER_PERCENT_PARALLEL.

OPTIMIZER_SEARCH_LIMIT

Parameter type:	integer
Parameter class:	dynamic, scope = ALTER SESSION
Default value:	5

OPTIMIZER_SEARCH_LIMIT specifies the search limit for the optimizer.

ORACLE_TRACE_COLLECTION_NAME

Parameter type:	string
Parameter class:	static
Default value:	NULL
Range of values:	valid collection name up to 16 characters long

ORACLE_TRACE_COLLECTION_NAME specifies the Oracle Trace collection name. This parameter is also used in the output file names (collection definition file .CDF and data file .DAT).

ORACLE_TRACE_COLLECTION_PATH

Parameter type:	string
Parameter class:	static
Default value:	operating system-specific
Range of values:	full directory pathname

ORACLE_TRACE_COLLECTION_PATH specifies the directory pathname where Oracle Trace collection definition and data files are located. If you accept the default, the complete file specification is generally (may be different for non-UNIX systems) $ORACLE_HOME/rdbms/log/*collection name*.cdf and *collection name*.dat.

ORACLE_TRACE_COLLECTION_SIZE

Parameter type:	integer
Parameter class:	static
Default value:	5242880
Range of values:	0 - 4294967295

ORACLE_TRACE_COLLECTION_SIZE specifies the maximum size, in bytes, of the Oracle Trace collection file. Once the collection file reaches this maximum, the collection is disabled.

ORACLE_TRACE_ENABLE

Parameter type:	boolean
Parameter class:	static
Default value:	FALSE
Range of values:	TRUE, FALSE

In order to enable Oracle Trace collections for the server, ORACLE_TRACE_ENABLE should be set and left at TRUE. When set to TRUE, this does not start an Oracle Trace collection, it allows Oracle Trace to be used for that server. When set to TRUE, Oracle Trace can then be started by using the Oracle Trace Manager application (supplied with the Oracle Enterprise Manager Performance Pack), or including a name in the oracle_trace_collection_name parameter (default = null).

ORACLE_TRACE_FACILITY_NAME

Parameter type:	string
Parameter class:	static
Default value:	operating system-specific
Range of values:	valid facility name up to 16 characters long

ORACLE_TRACE_FACILITY_NAME specifies the Oracle Trace product definition file (.FDF file). The file must be located in the directory pointed to by the ORACLE_TRACE_FACILITY_PATH parameter. The product definition file contains definition information for all the events and data items that can be collected for a product that uses the Oracle Trace data collection API. Products can have multiple product definition files (multiple event sets and data items). The Oracle Server has multiple event sets and therefore multiple product definition files. Oracle recommends that you use the "default" event set for Server collections ORACLED.FDF. See the Oracle Trace documentation for more information on the Server event sets.

ORACLE_TRACE_FACILITY_PATH

Parameter type:	string
Parameter class:	static
Default value:	operating system-specific
Range of values:	full directory pathname

ORACLE_TRACE_FACILITY_PATH specifies the directory pathname where Oracle TRACE facility definition files are located.

OS_AUTHENT_PREFIX

Parameter type:	string
Parameter class:	static
Default value:	operating system-specific (typically "OPS$")

OS_AUTHENT_PREFIX authenticates users attempting to connect to the server with the users' operating system account name and password. The value of this parameter is concatenated to the beginning of every user's operating system account. The prefixed username is compared with the Oracle usernames in the database when a connection request is attempted. The default value of this parameter is OPS$ for backward compatibility with previous versions. However, you might prefer to set the prefix value to "" (a null string), thereby eliminating the addition of any prefix to operating system account names.

Note: The text of the OS_AUTHENT_PREFIX parameter is case sensitive with some operating systems.

For more information, see the *Oracle8 Server Administrator's Guide.* See also your operating system-specific Oracle documentation.

OS_ROLES

Parameter type:	boolean
Parameter class:	static
Default value:	FALSE
Range of values:	TRUE/FALSE

If OS_ROLES is set to TRUE, the database allows the operating system to identify each username's roles. When a user attempts to create a session, the username's security domain is initialized using the roles identified by the operating system. A user can subsequently enable as many roles identified by the operating system as specified by the parameter MAX_OS_ROLES.

If OS_ROLES is set to TRUE, the operating system completely manages the role grants for all database usernames. Any revokes of roles granted by the operating system are ignored, and any previously granted roles are ignored.

The default value, FALSE, causes roles to be identified and managed by the database.

For more information, see the *Oracle8 Server Administrator's Guide*.

PARALLEL_DEFAULT_MAX_INSTANCES

Parameter type:	integer
Parameter class:	static
Default value:	operating system-dependent
Range of values:	0 - number of instances
Multiple instances:	should have the same value

PARALLEL_DEFAULT_MAX_INSTANCES specifies the default number of instances to split a table across for parallel query processing. The value of this parameter is used if the INSTANCES DEFAULT is specified in the PARALLEL clause of a table's definition. This parameter might be desupported in future releases.

For more information, see *Oracle8 Parallel Server Concepts & Administration*.

PARALLEL_INSTANCE_GROUP

Parameter type:	string
Parameter class:	dynamic, scope = ALTER SESSION, ALTER SYSTEM
Default value:	group consisting of all instances currently active
Range of values:	a string representing a group name

PARALLEL_INSTANCE_GROUP is a Parallel Server parameter and can be used in parallel mode only. This parameter identifies the parallel instance group to be used for spawning parallel query slaves. Parallel operations will spawn parallel query slaves only on instances that specify a matching group in their INSTANCE_GROUPS parameter.

If the value assigned to PARALLEL_INSTANCE_GROUP is the name of a group that does not exist, then the operation runs serially. No parallelism is used.

For more information see *Oracle8 Parallel Server Concepts & Administration*.

PARALLEL_MAX_SERVERS

Parameter type:	integer
Parameter class:	static
Default value:	operating system-specific
Range of values:	0 - 256
Multiple instances:	each instance must have either a value of zero or the same value as the other instances

PARALLEL_MAX_SERVERS specifies the maximum number of parallel query servers or parallel recovery processes for an instance. Oracle will increase the number of query servers as demand requires from the number created at instance startup up to this value. The same value should be used for all instances in a parallel server environment.

Proper setting of the PARALLEL_MAX_SERVERS parameter ensures that the number of query servers in use will not cause a memory resource shortage during periods of peak database use.

If PARALLEL_MAX_SERVERS is set too low, some queries may not have a query server available to them during query processing.

Setting PARALLEL_MAX_SERVERS too high leads to memory resource shortages during peak periods, which can degrade performance. For each instance to which you do not want to apply the parallel query option, set this initialization parameter to zero.

For more information, see *Oracle8 Parallel Server Concepts & Administration*.

PARALLEL_MIN_MESSAGE_POOL

Parameter type:	integer
Parameter class:	static
Default value:	cpus*parallel_max_servers*1.5*(OS message buffer size) or cpus*5*1.5*(OS message size)
Range of values:	0 -(SHARED_POOLSIZE*.90)

PARALLEL_MIN_MESSAGE_POOL specifies the minimum permanent amount of memory which will be allocated from the SHARED POOL (see SHARED_POOL_SIZE), to be used for messages in parallel execution.

This memory is allocated at startup time if PARALLEL_MIN_SERVERS is set to a non-zero value, or when the server is first allocated. Setting this parameter is most effective when PARALLEL_MIN_SERVERS is set to a non-zero value, because the memory will be allocated in a contiguous section.

This parameter should only be set if the default formula is known to be significantly inaccurate. setting this parameter too high will lead to a shortage of memory for the shared pool; setting it too low will lead to costlier memory allocation when doing parallel execution. This parameter cannot be set to a number higher than 90% of the shared pool.

PARALLEL_MIN_PERCENT

Parameter type:	integer
Parameter class:	dynamic, scope = ALTER SESSION
Default value:	0
Range of values:	0 - 100
OK to change:	yes
Multiple instances:	can have different values; application dependent

PARALLEL_MIN_PERCENT specifies the minimum percent of threads required for parallel query. Setting this parameter ensures that a parallel query will not be executed sequentially if adequate resources are not available. The default value of 0 means that this parameter is not used.

If too few query slaves are available, an error message is displayed and the query is not executed. Consider the following settings:

```
PARALLEL_MIN_PERCENT = 50
PARALLEL_MIN_SERVERS = 5
PARALLEL_MAX_SERVERS = 10
```

In a system with 20 instances up and running, the system would have a maximum of 200 query slaves available. If 190 slaves are already in use and a new user wants to run a query with 40 slaves (for example, degree 2 instances 20), an error message would be returned because 20 instances (that is, 50% of 40) are not available.

PARALLEL_MIN_SERVERS

Parameter type:	integer
Parameter class:	static
Default value:	0
Range of values:	0 - PARALLEL_MAX_SERVERS
Multiple instances:	can have different values

PARALLEL_MIN_SERVERS specifies the minimum number of query server processes for an instance. This is also the number of query server processes Oracle creates when the instance is started.

For more information, see *Oracle8 Parallel Server Concepts & Administration*.

PARALLEL_SERVER

Parameter type:	boolean
Parameter class:	static
Default value:	FALSE
Range of values:	TRUE/FALSE
Multiple instances:	must have the same value

Set PARALLEL_SERVER to TRUE to enable the Parallel Server option.

For more information, see *Oracle8 Parallel Server Concepts & Administration*.

PARALLEL_SERVER_IDLE_TIME

Parameter type:	integer
Parameter class:	static
Default value:	operating system-specific
Range of values:	0 to the OS-dependent maximum
Multiple instances:	can have different values

PARALLEL_SERVER_IDLE_TIME specifies the amount of idle time after which Oracle terminates a query server process. This value is expressed in minutes.

PARALLEL_TRANSACTION_RESOURCE_TIMEOUT

Parameter type:	integer
Parameter class:	dynamic, scope = ALTER SYSTEM
Default value:	300
Range of values:	0 to the OS-dependent maximum
Multiple instances:	can have different values; however, it is recommended that the same value is used across all instances

PARALLEL_TRANSACTION_RESOURCE_TIMEOUT is a Parallel Server parameter. This parameter specifies the maximum amount of time which can pass before a session, executing a parallel operation (either parallel DDL or parallel DML), times out while waiting for a resource held by another session in an incompatible lock mode. Such timeouts are an indication of potential deadlock involving the parallel transaction and other transactions currently running in the parallel server system.

The value of the parameter is specified in seconds. The time begins when the session starts to wait for a busy resource. Setting the parameter to 0 sets the maximum timeout to an effectively infinite value. Note that this is only the maximum timeout allowed for parallel transactions. For certain resources, a lower timeout value is used by Oracle.

PARTITION_VIEW_ENABLED

Parameter type:	boolean
Parameter class:	dynamic, scope = ALTER SESSION
Default value:	FALSE
Range of values:	TRUE/FALSE
OK to change:	yes

If PARTITION_VIEW_ENABLED is set to TRUE, the optimizer prunes (or skips) unnecessary table accesses in a partition view. This parameter also changes the way the cost-based optimizer computes statistics on a partition view from statistics on underlying tables.

PLSQL_V2_COMPATIBILITY

Parameter type:	boolean
Parameter class:	dynamic, scope = ALTER SESSION, ALTER SYSTEM
Default value:	FALSE
Range of values:	TRUE/FALSE

The PLSQL_V2_COMPATIBILITY initialization parameter is optional and sets the compatibility level for PL/SQL. The default value is FALSE: PL/SQL V3 behavior is enforced and V2 behavior is not allowed.

If PLSQL_V2_COMPATIBILITY=TRUE,then the following PL/SQL V2 behaviors are accepted when you are running PL/SQL V3:

- PL/SQL will allow elements of an index table passed in as an IN parameter to be modified or deleted. For example,

```
function foo (x IN table_t) is
begin
x.delete(2);
end;
```

  In contrast, PL/SQL V3 correctly enforces the read-only semantics of IN parameters and does not let index table methods modify index tables passed in as IN parameters.

- The PL/SQL compiler will allow OUT parameters to be used in expression contexts in some cases (for example, in dot-qualified names on the right-hand side of assignment statements). This behavior is restricted to a few cases - fields of OUT parameters that are record, and OUT parameters referenced in the FROM list of a SELECT statement.

In contrast, PL/SQL V3 does not permit OUT parameters to be used in expression contexts.

- PL/SQL will allow OUT parameters in the FROM clause of a SELECT list, where their value is read.

- PL/SQL will not return an error on the illegal syntax

```
return expression
```

which should be

```
return type
```

In contrast, PL/SQL V3 returns an error.

- PL/SQL will allow the passing of an IN argument into another procedure as an OUT. (This is restricted to fields of IN parameters that are records.)

In contrast, PL/SQL V3 does not allow the passing of an IN argument into another procedure as an OUT.

- PL/SQL will allow a type to be referenced earlier than its definition in the source.

In contrast, PL/SQL V3 requires a type definition to precede its use.

PRE_PAGE_SGA

Parameter type:	boolean
Parameter class:	static
Default value:	FALSE
Range of values:	FALSE/TRUE
OK to change:	no

If PRE_PAGE_SGA is set to TRUE, this parameter touches all the SGA pages, causing them to be brought into memory. As a result, it increases instance start up time and user login time, but it can reduce the number of page faults that occur shortly thereafter. The reduction in page faults allows the instance to reach its maximum performance capability quickly rather than through an incremental build up. It is most useful on systems that have sufficient memory to hold all the SGA pages without degrading performance in other areas.

PROCESSES

Parameter type:	integer
Parameter class:	static
Default value:	30
Range of values:	6 to operating system-dependent
Multiple instances:	can have different values

For a multiple-process operation, PROCESSES specifies the maximum number of operating system user processes that can simultaneously connect to an Oracle Server. This value should allow for all background processes such as LCK processes, Job Queue processes, and Parallel Query processes.

The default values of SESSIONS is derived from PROCESSES. If you alter the value of PROCESSES, you may want to adjust the values of this derived parameters.

For more information, see the *Oracle8 Server Administrator's Guide*. See also your operating system-specific Oracle documentation for the range of values.

RECOVERY_PARALLELISM

Parameter type:	integer
Parameter class:	static
Default value:	operating system-dependent
Range of values:	operating system-dependent, but cannot exceed PARALLEL_MAX_SERVERS

RECOVERY_PARALLELISM specifies the number of processes to participate in instance or media recovery. A value of zero or one indicates that recovery is to be performed serially by one process.

For more information, see *Oracle8 Parallel Server Concepts & Administration*.

REDUCE_ALARM

Parameter type:	boolean
Parameter class:	static
Default value:	FALSE
Range of values:	TRUE/FALSE

REDUCE_ALARM is an initialization parameter.

REMOTE_DEPENDENCIES_MODE

Parameter type:	string
Parameter class:	dynamic, scope = ALTER SESSION, ALTER SYSTEM
Default value:	TIMESTAMP
Range of values:	TIMESTAMP/SIGNATURE

REMOTE_DEPENDENCIES_MODE is used with PL/SQL stored procedures. It specifies how dependencies upon remote stored procedures are to be handled by the database.

If this parameter is set to TIMESTAMP, which is the default setting, the client running the procedure compares the timestamp recorded on the server side procedure with the current timestamp of the local procedure and executes the procedure only if the timestamps match.

If the parameter is set to SIGNATURE, the procedure is allowed to execute as long as the signatures are considered safe. This allows client PL/SQL applications to be run without recompilation.

REMOTE_LOGIN_PASSWORDFILE

Parameter type:	string
Parameter class:	static
Default value:	NONE
Range of values:	NONE/SHARED/EXCLUSIVE
Multiple instances:	should have the same value

REMOTE_LOGIN_PASSWORDFILE specifies whether Oracle checks for a password file and how many databases can use the password file. Setting the parameter to NONE signifies that Oracle should ignore any password file (and therefore privileged users must be authenticated by the operating system). Setting the parameter to EXCLUSIVE signifies that the password file can be used by only one database and the password file can contain names other than SYS and INTERNAL. Setting the parameter to SHARED allows more than one database to use a password file. However, the only users recognized by the password file are SYS and INTERNAL.

For more information about secure connections for privileged users, see the *Oracle8 Server Administrator's Guide*.

REMOTE_OS_AUTHENT

Parameter type:	boolean
Parameter class:	static
Default value:	FALSE
Range of values:	TRUE/FALSE

Setting REMOTE_OS_AUTHENT to TRUE allows authentication of remote clients with the value of OS_AUTHENT_PREFIX.

For more information, see the *Oracle8 Server Administrator's Guide*.

REMOTE_OS_ROLES

Parameter type:	boolean
Parameter class:	static
Default value:	FALSE
Range of values:	TRUE/FALSE

Setting REMOTE_OS_ROLES to TRUE allows operating system roles for remote clients. The default value, FALSE, causes roles to be identified and managed by the database for remote clients.

For more information, see the *Oracle8 Server Administrator's Guide*.

REPLICATION_DEPENDENCY_TRACKING

Parameter type:	boolean
Parameter class:	static
Default value:	TRUE
Range of values:	TRUE/FALSE

Setting REPLICATION_DEPENDENCY_TRACKING to TRUE turns on dependency tracking for read/write operations to the database. Dependency tracking is essential for the Replication Server to propagate changes in parallel. This is the default value. FALSE allows read/write operations to the database to run faster, but does not produce dependency information for the Replication Server to perform parallel propagations. Users should not specify this value unless they are sure that their application will perform absolutely no read/write operations to replicated tables.

RESOURCE_LIMIT

Parameter type:	boolean
Parameter class:	dynamic, scope = ALTER SYSTEM
Default value:	FALSE
Range of values:	TRUE/FALSE

The value of RESOURCE_LIMIT changes the enforcement status of resource limits set in database profiles. A value of FALSE disables the enforcement of resource limits. A value of TRUE enables the enforcement of resource limits.

For more information, see the *Oracle8 Server Administrator's Guide*.

ROLLBACK_SEGMENTS

Parameter type:	string
Parameter class:	static
Default value:	NULL (the instance uses public rollback segments by default if you do not specify this parameter
Range of values:	any rollback segment names listed in DBA_ROLLBACK_SEGS except SYSTEM
Multiple instances:	must have different values (different instances cannot specify the same rollback segment)
OK to change:	yes

ROLLBACK_SEGMENTS specifies one or more rollback segments to allocate by name to this instance. If ROLLBACK_SEGMENTS is set, an instance acquires all of the rollback segments named in this parameter, even if the number of rollback segments exceeds the minimum number required by the instance (calculated from the ratio TRANSACTIONS /TRANSACTIONS_PER_ROLLBACK_SEGMENT).

Note: Never name the SYSTEM rollback segment as a value for the ROLLBACK_SEGMENTS parameter.

This parameter has the following syntax:

```
ROLLBACK_SEGMENTS = (rbseg_name [, rbseg_name] ... )
```

Although this parameter usually specifies private rollback segments, it can also specify public rollback segments if they are not already in use.

Different instances in an Oracle Parallel Server cannot name the same rollback segment for any of the ROLLBACK_SEGMENTS. Query the data dictionary view DBA_ROLLBACK_SEGS to find the name, segment ID number, and status of each rollback segment in the database.

For more information, see the *Oracle8 Server Administrator's Guide*.

ROW_CACHE_CURSORS

Parameter type:	integer
Parameter class:	static
Default value:	10
Range of values:	10 - 3300

ROW_CACHE_CURSORS specifies the maximum number of cached recursive cursors used by the dictionary cache manager for selecting rows from the data dictionary. The default value is sufficient for most systems.

For more information about memory structure and processes, see *Oracle8 Server Concepts*.

ROW_LOCKING

Parameter type:	string
Parameter class:	static
Default value:	ALWAYS
Range of values:	ALWAYS/DEFAULT/INTENT
Multiple instances:	must have the same value

ROW_LOCKING specifies whether row locks are acquired when a table is updated or on update. The default of ALWAYS means that only row locks are acquired when a table is updated. DEFAULT is the same as ALWAYS. INTENT means that only row locks are used on a SELECT FOR UPDATE, but at update time table locks are acquired.

For information about tuning SQL statements, see *Oracle8 Server Tuning*.

SEQUENCE_CACHE_ENTRIES

Parameter type:	integer
Parameter class:	static
Default value:	10
Range of values:	10 - 32000
Multiple instances:	can have different values

SEQUENCE_CACHE_ENTRIES specifies the number of sequences that can be cached in the SGA for immediate access. This cache is managed on a least recently used (LRU) basis, so if a request is made for a sequence that is not in the cache and there are no free entries, the oldest one on the LRU list is deleted and replaced with the newly requested one. Highest concurrency is achieved when this value is set to the highest possible number of sequences that will be used on an instance at one time.

Each entry requires approximately 110 bytes in the SGA for an Oracle Parallel Server. Sequences created with the NOCACHE option do not reside in this cache. They must be written through to the data dictionary on every use.

For more information about managing schema objects, see *Oracle8 Server Administrator's Guide* and *Oracle8 Server Application Developer's Guide*.

SEQUENCE_CACHE_HASH_BUCKET

Parameter type:	integer
Parameter class:	static
Default value:	7
Multiple instances:	can have different values

SEQUENCE_CACHE_HASH_BUCKET specifies the number of sequences that can be cached in the SGA for immediate access. This cache is managed on a least recently used (LRU) basis, so if a request is made for a sequence that is not in the cache and there are no free entries, the oldest one on the LRU list is deleted and replaced with the newly requested one. Highest concurrency is achieved when this value is set to the highest possible number of sequences that will be used on an instance at one time.

Each entry requires approximately 110 bytes in the SGA for an Oracle Parallel Server. Sequences created with the NOCACHE option do not reside in this cache. They must be written through to the data dictionary on every use.

For more information about managing schema objects, see *Oracle8 Server Administrator's Guide* and *Oracle8 Server Application Developer's Guide*.

SERIAL _REUSE

Parameter type:	string LIST
Parameter class:	static
Default Value:	NULL
Range of values:	DISABLE/SELECT/DML/PLSQL/ALL/NULL

This parameter indicates which types of SQL cursors should make use of the serial-reusable memory feature. This feature moves well-structured private cursor memory into the SGA (shared pool) so that it can be reused by sessions executing the same cursor. The default NULL value is equivalent to setting the value to DISABLE. Values include:

Table 1-8: Values for the SERIAL_REUSE Initialization Parameter

Value	Description
DISABLE	disables the option for all SQL statement types. This value overrides any other values included in the list.
SELECT	enables the option for SELECT statements
DML	enables the option for DML statements
PLSQL	currently has no effect (although PLSQL packages do support the serial-reuse memory option using PLSQL Pragmas).
ALL	enables the option for both DML and SELECT statements. Equivalent to setting SELECT, DML, and PLSQL

SESSION_CACHED_CURSORS

Parameter type:	integer
Parameter class:	static
Default:	0
Range of values:	0 to operating system dependent
Multiple instances:	can have different values:

SESSION_CACHED_CURSORS lets you specify the number of session cursors to cache. Repeated parse calls of the same SQL statement cause the session cursor for that statement to be moved into the session cursor cache. Subsequent parse calls will find the cursor in the cache and need not reopen the cursor. The value of this parameter is the maximum number of session cursors to keep in the session cursor cache.

SESSION_MAX_OPEN_FILES

Parameter type:	integer
Parameter class:	static
Default value:	10
Range of values:	1 - the least of (50, MAX_OPEN_FILES defined at the OS level)

SESSION_MAX_OPEN_FILES specifies the maximum number of BFILEs that can be opened in any given session. Once this number is reached, subsequent attempts to open more files in the session using DBMS_LOB.FILEOPEN() or

OCILobFileOpen() will fail. This parameter is also dependent on the equivalent parameter defined for the underlying operating system.

SESSIONS

Parameter type:	integer
Parameter class:	static
Default value:	derived (1.1 * PROCESSES + 5)

SESSIONS specifies the total number of user and system sessions. The default number is greater than PROCESSES to allow for recursive sessions.

The default values of ENQUEUE_RESOURCES and TRANSACTIONS are derived from SESSIONS. If you alter the value of SESSIONS, you might want to adjust the values of ENQUEUE_RESOURCES and TRANSACTIONS.

With the multi-threaded server, you should adjust the value of SESSIONS to approximately 1.1 * (*total number of connections*).

For more information on memory structures and processes, see *Oracle8 Server Concepts*.

SHADOW_CORE_DUMP

Parameter type:	string
Parameter class:	static
Default value:	FULL
Range of values:	FULL/PARTIAL

The value of SHADOW_CORE_DUMP determines whether the SGA will be included in core dumps. By default (FULL), the SGA is included in the core dump. If SHADOW_CORE_DUMP=PARTIAL, the SGA is not dumped.

SHARED_POOL_RESERVED_MIN_ALLOC

Parameter type:	string
Parameter class:	static
Default value:	5000
Range of values:	5000 - SHARED_POOL_RESERVED_SIZE (in bytes)

The value of SHARED_POOL_RESERVED_MIN_ALLOC controls allocation of reserved memory. Memory allocations larger than this value can allocate space from the reserved list if a chunk of memory of sufficient size is not found on the shared pool free lists.

The default value is adequate for most systems. If you increase the value, then the Oracle Server will allow fewer allocations from the reserved list and will request more memory from the shared pool list.

SHARED_POOL_RESERVED_MIN_ALLOC can accept a numerical value or a number followed by the suffix "K" or "M" where "K" means "multiply by 1000" and "M" means "multiply by 1000000".

For more information on this parameter see *Oracle8 Server Tuning*.

SHARED_POOL_RESERVED_SIZE

Parameter type:	string
Parameter class:	static
Default value:	5% of the value of SHARED_POOL_SIZE
Range of values:	from SHARED_POOL_RESERVED_MIN_ALLOC to one half of SHARED_POOL_SIZE (in bytes)

SHARED_POOL_RESERVED_SIZE specifies the shared pool space which is reserved for large contiguous requests for shared pool memory. This parameter, along with the SHARED_POOL_RESERVED_MIN_ALLOC parameter, can be used to avoid performance degradation in the shared pool from situations where pool fragmentation forces Oracle to search for and free chunks of unused pool to satisfy the current request.

The shared pool contains the library cache of shared SQL requests, the dictionary cache, stored procedures, and other cache structures that are specific to a particular instance configuration. For example, in an MTS configuration, the session and private SQL area for each client process is included in the shared pool. When the instance is configured for parallel query, the shared pool includes the parallel query message buffers.

Proper sizing of the shared pool can reduce resource consumption in at least three ways:

- Parse time is avoided if the SQL statement is already in the shared pool. This saves CPU resources.

- Application memory overhead is reduced, since all applications use the same pool of shared SQL statements and dictionary resources.

- I/O resources are saved, since dictionary elements which are in the shared pool do not require disk access.

Default value for SHARED_POOL_RESERVED_SIZE is 5% of the SHARED_POOL_SIZE. This means that, by default, the reserved list will always be configured.

If SHARED_POOL_RESERVED_SIZE > 1/2 SHARED_POOL_SIZE, Oracle signals an error.

Ideally, this parameter should be large enough to satisfy any request scanning for memory on the reserved list without flushing objects from the shared pool. The amount of operating system memory, however, may constrain the size of the shared pool. In general, you should set SHARED_POOL_RESERVED_SIZE to 10% of SHARED_POOL_SIZE. For most systems, this value will be sufficient if you have already tuned the shared pool.

SHARED_POOL_RESERVED_SIZE can accept a numerical value or a number followed by the suffix "K" or "M" where "K" means "multiply by 1000" and "M" means "multiply by 1000000".

For more information on this parameter see *Oracle8 Server Tuning*.

SHARED_POOL_SIZE

Parameter type:	string
Parameter class:	static
Default value:	3,500,000 bytes
Range of values:	300 Kbytes - operating system-dependent

SHARED_POOL_SIZE specifies the size of the shared pool in bytes. The shared pool contains shared cursors and stored procedures. Larger values improve performance in multi-user systems. Smaller values use less memory.

SHARED_POOL_SIZE can accept a numerical value or a number followed by the suffix "K" or "M" where "K" means "multiply by 1000" and "M" means "multiply by 1000000".

For more information, see the *Oracle8 Server Administrator's Guide*.

SORT_AREA_RETAINED_SIZE

Parameter type:	integer
Parameter class:	dynamic, scope= ALTER SESSION, ALTER SYSTEM DEFERRED
Default value:	the value of SORT_AREA_SIZE
Range of values:	from the value equivalent to one database block to the value of SORT_AREA_SIZE

SORT_AREA_RETAINED_SIZE specifies the maximum amount, in bytes, of User Global Area (UGA) memory retained after a sort run completes. The retained size controls the size of the read buffer which is used to maintain a portion of the sort in memory. This memory is released back to the UGA, not to the operating system, after the last row is fetched from the sort space.

If a sort requires more memory, a temporary segment is allocated and the sort becomes an external (disk) sort. The maximum amount of memory to use for the sort is then specified by SORT_AREA_SIZE instead of by this parameter.

Larger values permit more sorts to be performed in memory. However, multiple sort spaces of this size may be allocated. Usually, only one or two sorts occur at one time, even for complex queries. In some cases, though, additional concurrent sorts are required. Each sort occurs in its own memory area, as specified by SORT_AREA_RETAINED_SIZE.

For more information, see *Oracle8 Server Concepts*.

SORT_AREA_SIZE

Parameter type:	integer
Parameter class:	dynamic, scope= ALTER SESSION, ALTER SYSTEM DEFERRED
Default value:	operating system-dependent
Range of values:	0 - system-dependent value

SORT_AREA_SIZE specifies the maximum amount, in bytes, of Program Global Area (PGA) memory to use for a sort. If MTS is enabled, the sort area is allocated from the SGA. After the sort is complete and all that remains to do is to fetch the rows, the memory is released down to the size specified by SORT_AREA_RETAINED_SIZE. After the last row is fetched, all memory is freed. The memory is released back to the PGA, not to the operating system.

Increasing SORT_AREA_SIZE size improves the efficiency of large sorts. Multiple allocations never exist; there is only one memory area of SORT_AREA_SIZE for each user process at any time.

If more space is required to complete the sort than will fit into the memory provided, then temporary segments on disk hold the intermediate sort runs.

The default is usually adequate for most OLTP operations. You might want to adjust this parameter for decision support systems, batch jobs, or large CREATE INDEX operations.

For more information, see *Oracle8 Server Concepts*. See also your operating system-specific Oracle documentation for the default value on your system.

SORT_DIRECT_WRITES

Parameter type:	string
Parameter class:	dynamic, scope= ALTER SESSION, ALTER SYSTEM DEFERRED
Default value:	AUTO
Range of values:	AUTO/TRUE/FALSE

SORT_DIRECT_WRITES can improve sort performance if memory and temporary space are abundant on your system. This parameter controls whether sort data will bypass the buffer cache to write intermediate sort results to disk. When set to the default of AUTO, and the value of the sort area size is greater than ten times the block size, memory is allocated from the sort area to do this. When SORT_DIRECT_WRITES is TRUE, additional buffers are allocated from memory during each sort.

Additional temporary segment space can be required when SORT_DIRECT_WRITES is enabled. The sort allocation mechanism allocates temporary space using fixed-size chunks which are based on the SORT_WRITE_BUFFER_SIZE parameter. Since the values for this parameter are typically an order of magnitude larger than the DB_BLOCK_SIZE chunks used when SORT_DIRECT_WRITES is disabled, unused temporary space in the final sort segment increases the overall space requirements.

When SORT_DIRECT_WRITES is set to FALSE, the sorts that write to disk write through the buffer cache.

For more information, see *Oracle8 Server Tuning*.

SORT_READ_FAC

Parameter type:	integer
Parameter class:	dynamic, scope= ALTER SESSION, ALTER SYSTEM DEFERRED
Default value:	operating system-dependent

SORT_READ_FAC is a unitless ratio that describes the amount of time to read a single database block divided by the block transfer rate. The value is operating system-specific. You can set the value for your specific disk subsystem using the following equation:

$$\text{sort\_read\_fac} = \frac{\text{avg\_seek\_time} + \text{avg\_latency} + \text{blk\_transfer\_time}}{\text{blk\_transfer\_time}}$$

See your operating system-specific Oracle documentation for the default value.

SORT_SPACEMAP_SIZE

Parameter type:	integer
Parameter class:	static
Default value:	operating system-dependent

SORT_SPACEMAP_SIZE specifies the size in bytes of the sort space map. Only if you have very large indexes should you adjust this parameter. A sort automatically increases its space map if necessary, but it does not necessarily do so when it will make best use of disk storage. The sort makes optimal use of disk storage if SORT_SPACEMAP_SIZE is set to

[(*total_sort_bytes*) / (*sort_area_size*)] + 64

where *total_sort_bytes* is

(*number_of_records*) * [*sum_of_average_column_sizes* + (2 * *number_of_col*)]

Here, columns include the SELECT list for the ORDER BY, the SELECT list for the GROUP BY, and the key list for CREATE INDEX. It also includes 10 bytes for ROWID for CREATE INDEX and GROUP BY or ORDER BY columns not mentioned in the SELECT list for these cases.

For more information on memory structures and processes, see *Oracle8 Server Concepts*. See also your operating system-specific Oracle documentation for the default value.

SORT_WRITE_BUFFER_SIZE

Parameter type:	integer
Parameter class:	dynamic, scope= ALTER SESSION, ALTER SYSTEM DEFERRED
Default value:	32768
Range of values:	32Kb, 64Kb

SORT_WRITE_BUFFER_SIZE sets the size of the sort IO buffer when the SORT_DIRECT_WRITES parameter is set to TRUE.
SORT_WRITE_BUFFER_SIZE is recommended for use with symmetric replication.

SORT_WRITE_BUFFERS

Parameter type:	integer
Parameter class:	dynamic, scope= ALTER SESSION, ALTER SYSTEM DEFERRED
Default value:	1
Range of values:	2-8

SORT_WRITE_BUFFERS specifies the number of sort buffers when the SORT_DIRECT_WRITES parameter is set to TRUE. SORT_WRITE_BUFFERS is recommended for use with symmetric replication.

SPIN_COUNT

Parameter type:	integer
Parameter class:	dynamic, scope= ALTER SESSION, ALTER SYSTEM DEFERRED
Default value:	1
Range of values:	1-1,000,000

In multi-processor environments, you can improve performance by tuning the SPIN_COUNT initialization parameter.

A process continues to request a latch until it obtains one. If the number of requests reaches SPIN_COUNT, the process fails to acquire the latch, sleeps, then tries to acquire the latch again. Because a latch is a low-level lock, a process does not hold it long. It is less expensive to use CPU time by spinning a process than it is to make a process sleep.

You can check the contention level of the latch by monitoring the miss rate and sleep rate from the UTLBSTAT and UTLESTAT scripts. Try reducing the sleep rate by tuning the spin count. If the contention level is high, increase the spin count to allow processes to spin more before acquiring latches. However, since increasing the spin count increases CPU usage, system throughput may decline at some point.

The default value is adequate for almost all systems.

See your operating system-specific documentation for more information.

SQL_TRACE

Parameter type:	boolean
Parameter class:	dynamic, scope = ALTER SESSION
Default value:	FALSE
Range of values:	TRUE/FALSE

The value of SQL_TRACE disables or enables the SQL trace facility. Setting this parameter to TRUE provides information on tuning that you can use to improve performance. Because the SQL trace facility causes system overhead, you should run the database with the value TRUE only for the purpose of collecting statistics. The value can also be changed using the DBMS_SYSTEM package.

For more information about performance diagnostic tools, see *Oracle8 Server Tuning*. See also *Oracle8 Server SQL Reference*.

SQL92_SECURITY

Parameter type:	boolean
Parameter class:	static
Default value:	FALSE
Range of values:	TRUE/FALSE

SQL92_SECURITY specifies whether table-level SELECT privileges are required to execute an update or delete that references table column values.

STAR_TRANSFORMATION_ENABLED

Parameter type:	boolean
Parameter class:	dynamic, scope = ALTER SESSION
Default value:	FALSE
Range of values:	TRUE/FALSE

The value of STAR_TRANSFORMATION_ENABLED determines whether a cost-based query transformation will be applied to star queries. If set to TRUE, the optimizer will consider performing a cost-based query transformation on the star query. If set to FALSE, the transformation will not be applied.

For more information, see *Oracle8 Server Concepts*.

TAPE_ASYNCH_IO

Parameter type:	boolean
Parameter class:	static
Default value:	TRUE
Range of values:	TRUE, FALSE

TAPE_ASYNCH_IO can be used to control whether I/O to sequential devices (for example, BACKUP/RESTORE of Oracle data TO/FROM tape) is asynchronous. If a platform supports asynchronous I/O to sequential devices, it is recommended that this parameter is left to its default. However, if the asynchronous I/O implementation is not stable, TAPE_ASYNCH_IO can be used to disable its use. If a platform does not support asynchronous I/O to sequential devices, this parameter has no effect.

TEMPORARY_TABLE_LOCKS

Parameter type:	integer
Parameter class:	static
Default value:	derived (SESSIONS)
Range of values:	0 - operating system-dependent

TEMPORARY_TABLE_LOCKS specifies the number of temporary tables that can be created in the temporary segment space. A temporary table lock is needed any time a sort occurs that is too large too hold in memory, either as the result of a select on a large table with ORDER BY or as a result of sorting a large index. Installations with many users of applications that simultaneously perform several ordered queries on large tables might need to increase this number. Most installations should do well with the default.

For more information, see the *Oracle8 Server Administrator's Guide*. See also your operating system-specific Oracle documentation for the range of values.

THREAD

Parameter type:	integer
Parameter class:	static
Default value:	0
Range of values:	0 - maximum number of enabled threads
Multiple instances:	if specified, must have different values

THREAD is applicable only to instances that intend to run in parallel (shared) mode.

THREAD specifies the number of the redo thread that is to be used by the instance. Any available redo thread number can be used, but an instance cannot use the same thread number as another instance. Also, an instance cannot start when its redo thread is disabled. A value of zero causes an available, enabled public thread to be chosen. An instance cannot mount a database if the thread is used by another instance or if the thread is disabled.

Redo threads are specified with the THREAD option of the ALTER DATABASE ADD LOGFILE command. Redo threads are enabled with the ALTER DATABASE ENABLE [PUBLIC] THREAD command. The PUBLIC keyword signifies that the redo thread may be used by any instance. This is useful when running systems that have faster access to disks from certain nodes.

Thread 1 is the default thread in exclusive mode. An instance running in exclusive mode can specify THREAD to use the redo log files in a thread other than thread 1.

For more information, see *Oracle8 Parallel Server Concepts & Administration* and *Oracle8 Server SQL Reference*.

TIMED_OS_STATISTICS

Parameter type:	string
Parameter class:	dynamic, scope = ALTER SYSTEM
Default value:	OFF
Range of values:	OFF, CALL, LOGOFF

TIMED_OS_STATISTICS can be used by the system administrator to gather operating system statistics when calls are pushed or popped, or when the user logs off. The operating system statistics are gathered only if the TIMED_STATISTICS parameter is set to TRUE. For more information on this parameter, see "TIMED_STATISTICS" on page 1-113.

TIMED_OS_STATISTICS can be assigned one of the following strings:

OFF	do not gather operating system statistics while calls are pushed or popped or when the user logs off. This is the default value
CALL	gather statistics at every push or pop call. Because this option implies significant overhead, it must be used with caution
LOGOFF	gather statistics when the user logs off from an Oracle session

TIMED_STATISTICS

Parameter type:	boolean
Parameter class:	dynamic, scope = ALTER SYSTEM, ALTER SESSION
Default value:	FALSE
Range of values:	TRUE/FALSE

If TIMED_STATISTICS is FALSE, the statistics related to time are always zero and the server can avoid the overhead of requesting the time from the operating system. To turn on statistics, set the value to TRUE. Normally,

TIMED_STATISTICS should be FALSE. On some systems with very fast timer access, timing might be enabled even when the parameter is set to FALSE. On these systems, setting the parameter to TRUE might produce more accurate statistics for long-running operations.

For more information about performance diagnostic tools, see *Oracle8 Server Tuning*.

TRANSACTION_AUDITING

Parameter type:	boolean
Parameter class:	dynamic, scope = ALTER SYSTEM DEFERRED
Default value:	TRUE
Range of values:	TRUE/FALSE

If TRANSACTION_AUDITING is TRUE, the transaction layer generates a special redo record which contains session and user information. This information includes the user logon name, user name, the session ID, some operating system information, and client information. On each successive commit, the transaction layer generates a record that contains only the session ID (which links back to the first record since it also contains the session ID). These records might be useful if using a redo log analysis tool.

If TRANSACTION_AUDITING is FALSE, no redo record is generated.

TRANSACTIONS

Parameter type:	integer
Parameter class:	static
Default value:	derived (1.1 * SESSIONS)
Multiple instances:	can have different values

TRANSACTIONS specifies the maximum number of concurrent transactions. Greater values increase the size of the SGA and can increase the number of rollback segments allocated. The default value is greater than SESSIONS (and, in turn, PROCESSES) to allow for recursive transactions.

For more information about memory structures and processes, see *Oracle8 Server Concepts* and the *Oracle8 Server Administrator's Guide*.

TRANSACTIONS_PER_ROLLBACK_SEGMENT

Parameter type:	integer
Parameter class:	static
Default value:	21
Range of values:	1 - operating system-dependent
Multiple instances:	can have different values

TRANSACTIONS_PER_ROLLBACK_SEGMENT specifies the number of concurrent transactions allowed per rollback segment. The minimum number of rollback segments acquired at startup is TRANSACTIONS divided by the value for this parameter. For example, if TRANSACTIONS is 101 and this parameter is 10, then the minimum number of rollback segments acquired would be the ratio 101/10, rounded up to 11.

More rollback segments can be acquired if they are named in the parameter ROLLBACK_SEGMENTS.

For more information, see the *Oracle8 Server Administrator's Guide*. See also your operating system-specific Oracle documentation for the range of values.

USE_ISM

Parameter type:	boolean
Parameter class:	static
Default value:	TRUE
Range of values:	TRUE/FALSE

If USE_ISM is FALSE, the shared page table is not enabled. By default, the page table is enabled.

USER_DUMP_DEST

Parameter type:	string
Parameter class:	dynamic, scope = ALTER SYSTEM
Default value:	operating system-dependent
Range of values:	valid local pathname, directory, or disk

USER_DUMP_DEST specifies the pathname for a directory where the server will write debugging trace files on behalf of a user process.

For example, this directory might be set to **C:\ORACLE\UTRC** on MS-DOS; to **/oracle/utrc** on UNIX; or to **DISK$UR3:[ORACLE.UTRC]** on VMS.

For more information about performance diagnostic tools, see *Oracle8 Server Tuning*. See also your operating system-specific Oracle documentation for the range of values.

UTL_FILE_DIR

Parameter type:	string
Parameter class:	static
Default value:	none
Range of values:	any valid directory path

UTL_FILE_DIR allows database administrators to specify directories that are permitted for PL/SQL file I/O. Each directory must be specified with a separate UTL_FILE_DIR parameter in the INIT.ORA file.

Note that all users can read or write all files specified in the UTL_FILE_DIR parameter(s). This means that all PL/SQL users must be trusted with the information in the directories specified by the UTL_FILE_DIR parameters.

Static Data Dictionary Views

This chapter contains descriptions of data dictionary tables and views. To see the data dictionary views available to you, query the view DICTIONARY.

See Chapter 3, "Dynamic Performance (V$) Views" for descriptions of the V$ views.

In Trusted Oracle Server, each of the dictionary tables and views contains a column that indicates the label of each row in the table or view. Trusted Oracle also provides some additional dictionary tables and views, and some Oracle8 dictionary tables and views contain columns that support compatibility with Trusted Oracle applications.

See the *Trusted Oracle Server Administrator's Guide* for more information about Trusted Oracle dictionary tables and views.

Data Dictionary Views

The following is an alphabetical reference of the data dictionary views accessible to all users of an Oracle Server. Most views can be accessed by any user with the CREATE_SESSION privilege.

The data dictionary views that begin with DBA_ are restricted. These views can be accessed only by users with the SELECT_ANY_TABLE privilege. This privilege is assigned to the DBA role when the system is initially installed.

ALL_ALL_TABLES

This view describes all of the tables (object tables and relational tables) accessible to the user.

Column	Datatype	NULL	Description
OWNER	VARCHAR2(30)		Owner of the table
TABLE_NAME	VARCHAR2(30)		Name of the table
TABLESPACE_NAME	VARCHAR2(30)		Name of the tablespace containing the table
CLUSTER_NAME	VARCHAR2(30)		Name of the cluster, if any, to which the table belongs
IOT_NAME	VARCHAR2(30)		Name of the index organized table, if any, to which the overflow entry belongs
PCT_FREE	NUMBER		Minimum percentage of free space in a bloc
PCT_USED	NUMBER		Minimum percentage of used space in a block
INI_TRANS	NUMBER		Initial number of transactions
MAX_TRANS	NUMBER		Maximum number of transactions
INITIAL_EXTENT	NUMBER		Size of the initial extent in bytes
NEXT_EXTENT	NUMBER		Size of secondary extents in bytes
MIN_EXTENTS	NUMBER		Minimum number of extents allowed in the segment
MAX_EXTENTS	NUMBER		Maximum number of extents allowed in the segment
PCT_INCREASE	NUMBER		Percentage increase in extent size
FREELISTS	NUMBER		Number of process freelists allocated in this segment
FREELIST_GROUPS	NUMBER		Number of freelist groups allocated in this segment
LOGGING	VARCHAR2(3)		Logging attribute
BACKED_UP	VARCHAR2(1)		Has table been backed up since last modification?
NUM_ROWS	NUMBER		The number of rows in the table
BLOCKS	NUMBER		The number of used blocks in the table
EMPTY_BLOCKS	NUMBER		The number of empty (never used) blocks in the table

Column	Datatype	NULL	Description
AVG_SPACE	NUMBER		The average available free space in the table
CHAIN_CNT	NUMBER		The number of chained rows in the table
AVG_ROW_LEN	NUMBER		The average row length, including row overhead
AVG_SPACE_FREELIST _BLOCKS	NUMBER		The average freespace of all blocks on a freelist
NUM_FREELIST_BLOCKS	NUMBER		The number of blocks on the freelist
DEGREE	VARCHAR2(10)		The number of threads per instance for scanning the table
INSTANCES	VARCHAR2(10)		The number of instances across which the table is to be scanned
CACHE	VARCHAR2(5)		Whether the table is to be cached in the buffer cache
TABLE_LOCK	VARCHAR2(8)		Whether table locking is enabled or disabled
SAMPLE_SIZE	NUMBER		The sample size used in analyzing this table
LAST_ANALYZED	DATE		The date of the most recent time this table was analyzed
PARTITIONED	VARCHAR2(3)		Is this table partitioned? YES or NO
IOT_TYPE	VARCHAR2(12)		If an index organized table, then IOT_TYPE is IOT or IOT_OVERFLOW else NULL
TABLE_TYPE_OWNER	VARCHAR2(30)		Owner of the type of the table if the table is a typed table
TABLE_TYPE	VARCHAR2(30)		Type of the table if the table is a typed table
TEMPORARY	VARCHAR2(1)		Can the current session only see data that it place in this object itself?
NESTED	VARCHAR2(3)		Is the table a nested table?
BUFFER_POOL	VARCHAR2(7)		Name of the default buffer pool for the appropriate object

ALL_ARGUMENTS

This view lists all of the arguments in the object which are accessible to the user.

Column	Datatype	NULL	Description
OWNER	VARCHAR2(30)	NOT NULL	Username of the owner of the object
OBJECT_NAME	VARCHAR2(30)		Procedure or function name
OVERLOAD	VARCHAR2(40)		Overload unique identifier
PACKAGE_NAME	VARCHAR2(30)		Package name
OBJECT_ID	NUMBER	NOT NULL	Object number of the object
ARGUMENT_NAME	VARCHAR2(30)		Argument name

Column	Datatype	NULL	Description
POSITION	NUMBER	NOT NULL	Position in argument list, or NULL for function return value
SEQUENCE	NUMBER	NOT NULL	Argument sequence, including all nesting levels
DATA_LEVEL	NUMBER	NOT NULL	Nesting depth of argument for composite types
DATA_TYPE	VARCHAR2(14)		Datatype of the argument
DEFAULT_VALUE	LONG		Default value for the argument
DEFAULT_LENGTH	NUMBER		Length of default value for the argument
IN_OUT	VARCHAR2(9)		Argument direction (IN, OUT, or IN/OUT)
DATA_LENGTH	NUMBER		Length of the column in bytes
DATA_PRECISION	NUMBER		Length: decimal digits (NUMBER) or binary digits (FLOAT)
DATA_SCALE	NUMBER		Digits to right of decimal point in a number
RADIX	NUMBER		Argument radix for a number
CHARACTER_SET_NAME	VARCHAR2(44)		Character set name for the argument
TYPE_OWNER	VARCHAR2(30)		Owner name of the type
TYPE_NAME	VARCHAR2(30)		Name
TYPE_SUBNAME	VARCHAR2(30)		This is valid only in case of package local types; in such cases, the package name is the name and the type name is the subname
TYPE_LINK	VARCHAR2(128)		Database link valid only in case of package local types, in case the package is remote

ALL_CATALOG

This view lists all tables, views, synonyms, and sequences accessible to the user.

Column	Datatype	NULL	Description
OWNER	VARCHAR2(30)	NOT NULL	Owner of the object
TABLE_NAME	VARCHAR2(30)	NOT NULL	Name of the object
TABLE_TYPE	VARCHAR2(11)		Type of the object

ALL_CLUSTERS

This view list all clusters accessible to the user.

Column	Datatype	NULL	Description
OWNER	VARCHAR2(30)	NOT NULL	Owner of the cluster

Column	Datatype	NULL	Description
CLUSTER_NAME	VARCHAR2(30)	NOT NULL	Name of the tablespace containing the cluster
TABLESPACE_NAME	VARCHAR2(30)	NOT NULL	Name of the tablespace containing the cluster
PCT_FREE	NUMBER		Minimum percentage of free space in a block
PCT_USED	NUMBER	NOT NULL	Minimum percentage of used space in a block
KEY_SIZE	NUMBER		Estimated size of cluster key plus associated rows
INI_TRANS	NUMBER	NOT NULL	Initial number of transactions
MAX_TRANS	NUMBER	NOT NULL	Maximum number of transactions
INITIAL_EXTENT	NUMBER		Size of the initial extent in bytes
NEXT_EXTENT	NUMBER		Size of secondary extents in bytes
MIN_EXTENTS	NUMBER	NOT NULL	Minimum number of extents allowed in the segment
MAX_EXTENTS	NUMBER	NOT NULL	Maximum number of extents allowed in the segment
PCT_INCREASE	NUMBER	NOT NULL	Percentage increase in extent size
FREELISTS	NUMBER		Number of process freelists allocated to this segment
FREELIST_GROUPS	NUMBER		Number of freelist groups allocated to this segment
AVG_BLOCKS_PER_KEY	NUMBER		Number of blocks in the table divided by number of hash keys
CLUSTER_TYPE	VARCHAR2(5)		Type of cluster: B-Tree index or hash
FUNCTION	VARCHAR2(15)		If a hash cluster, the hash function
HASHKEYS	NUMBER		If a hash cluster, the number of hash keys (hash buckets)
DEGREE	VARCHAR2(10)		The number of threads per instance for scanning the cluster
INSTANCES	VARCHAR2(10)		The number of instances across which the cluster is to be scanned
CACHE	VARCHAR2(5)		Whether the cluster is to be cached in the buffer cache
BUFFER_POOL	VARCHAR2(7)		Name of the default buffer pool for the appropriate object

ALL_COL_COMMENTS

This view lists comments on columns of accessible tables and views.

Column	Datatype	NULL	Description
OWNER	VARCHAR2(30)	NOT NULL	Owner of the object
TABLE_NAME	VARCHAR2(30)	NOT NULL	Name of the object
COLUMN_NAME	VARCHAR2(30)	NOT NULL	Name of the column
COMMENTS	VARCHAR2(4000)		Comment on the column

ALL_COL_PRIVS

This view lists grants on columns for which the user or PUBLIC is the grantee.

Column	Datatype	NULL	Description
GRANTOR	VARCHAR2(30)	NOT NULL	Name of the user who performed the grant
GRANTEE	VARCHAR2(30)	NOT NULL	Name of the user to whom access was granted
TABLE_SCHEMA	VARCHAR2(30)	NOT NULL	Schema of the object
TABLE_NAME	VARCHAR2(30)	NOT NULL	Name of the object
COLUMN_NAME	VARCHAR2(30)	NOT NULL	Name of the column
PRIVILEGE	VARCHAR2(40)	NOT NULL	Privilege on the column
GRANTABLE	VARCHAR2(3)		YES if the privileges was granted with ADMIN OPTION; otherwise NO

ALL_COL_PRIVS_MADE

This view lists grants on columns for which the user is owner or grantor.

Column	Datatype	NULL	Description
GRANTEE	VARCHAR2(30)	NOT NULL	Name of the user to whom access was granted
OWNER	VARCHAR2(30)	NOT NULL	Username of the owner of the object
TABLE_NAME	VARCHAR2(30)	NOT NULL	Name of the object
COLUMN_NAME	VARCHAR2(30)	NOT NULL	Name of the column
GRANTOR	VARCHAR2(30)	NOT NULL	Name of the user who performed the grant
PRIVILEGE	VARCHAR2(40)	NOT NULL	Privilege on the column

Column	Datatype	NULL	Description
GRANTABLE	VARCHAR2(3)		YES if the privilege was granted with ADMIN OPTION; otherwise NO

ALL_COL_PRIVS_RECD

This view lists grants on columns for which the user or PUBLIC is the grantee.

Column	Datatype	NULL	Description
GRANTEE	VARCHAR2(30)	NOT NULL	Name of the user to whom access was granted
OWNER	VARCHAR2(30)	NOT NUL	Username of the owner of the object
TABLE_NAME	VARCHAR2(30)	NOT NULL	Name of the object
COLUMN_NAME	VARCHAR2(30)	NOT NULL	Name of the object
GRANTOR	VARCHAR2(30)	NOT NULL	Name of the user who performed the grant
PRIVILEGE	VARCHAR2(40)	NOT NULL	Privilege on the column
GRANTABLE	VARCHAR2(3)		YES if the privilege was granted with ADMIN OPTION; otherwise NO

ALL_COLL_TYPES

This view displays the named collection types accessible to the user.

Column	Datatype	NULL	Description
OWNER	VARCHAR2(30)	NOT NULL	Owner of the type
TYPE_NAME	VARCHAR2(30)	NOT NULL	Name of the type
COLL_TYPE	VARCHAR2(30)	NOT NULL	Collection type
UPPER_BOUND	NUMBER		Maximum size of the VARRAY type
ELEM_TYPE_MOD	VARCHAR2(7)		Type modifier of the element
ELEM_TYPE_OWNER	VARCHAR2(30)		Owner of the type of the element
ELEM_TYPE_NAME	VARCHAR2(30)		Name of the type of the element
LENGTH	NUMBER		Length of the CHAR element or maximum length of the VARCHAR or VARCHAR2 element
PRECISION	NUMBER		Decimal precision of the NUMBER or DECIMAL element or binary precision of the FLOAT element
SCALE	NUMBER		Scale of the NUMBER or DECIMAL element

Column	Datatype	NULL	Description
CHARACTER_SET _NAME	VARCHAR2(44)		The name of the character set: CHAR_CS NCHAR_CS

ALL_CONS_COLUMNS

This view contains information about accessible columns in constraint definitions.

Column	Datatype	NULL	Description
OWNER	VARCHAR2(30)	NOT NULL	Owner of the constraint definition
CONSTRAINT_NAME	VARCHAR2(30)	NOT NULL	Name associated with the constraint definition
TABLE_NAME	VARCHAR2(30)	NOT NULL	Name associated with table with constraint definition
COLUMN_NAME	VARCHAR2(4000)		Name associated with column or attribute of the object type column specified in the constraint definition
POSITION	NUMBER		Original position of column or attribute in definition

ALL_CONSTRAINTS

This view lists constraint definitions on accessible tables.

Column	Datatype	NULL	Description
OWNER	VARCHAR2(30)	NOT NULL	Owner of the constraint definition
CONSTRAINT_NAME	VARCHAR2(30)	NOT NULL	Name associated with the constraint definition
CONSTRAINT_TYPE	VARCHAR2(1)		Type of constraint definition: C (check constraint on a table), P (primary key), U (unique key), R (referential integrity), or V (with check option, on a view), or O (with read only, on a view)
TABLE_NAME	VARCHAR2(30)	NOT NULL	Name associated with table with constraint definition
SEARCH_CONDITION	LONG		Text of search condition for table check
R_OWNER	VARCHAR2(30)		Owner of table used in referential constraint
R_CONSTRAINT_NAME	VARCHAR2(30)		Name of unique constraint definition for referenced table
DELETE_RULE	VARCHAR2(9)		Delete rule for a referential constraint: CASCADE / NO ACTION
STATUS	VARCHAR2(8)		Enforcement status of constraint: ENABLED or DISABLED
DEFERRABLE	VARCHAR2(14)		Indicates whether the constraint is deferrable
DEFERRED	VARCHAR2(9)		Indicates whether the constraint was initially deferred

Column	Datatype	NULL	Description
VALIDATED	VARCHAR2(13)		Indicates whether all data obeys the constraint: VALIDATED, NOT VALIDATED
GENERATED	VARCHAR2(14)		Indicates whether the name system is generated
BAD	VARCHAR2(3)		Creating this constraint should give ORA-02436. Rewrite it before 2000 AD.
LAST_CHANGE	DATE		Indicates when the constraint was last enabled or disabled

ALL_DB_LINKS

This view lists database links accessible to the user.

Column	Datatype	NULL	Description
OWNER	VARCHAR2(30)	NOT NULL	Username of the owner of the database link
DB_LINK	VARCHAR2(128)	NOT NULL	Name of the database link
USERNAME	VARCHAR2(30)		Name of user when logging in
HOST	VARCHAR2(2000)		Net8 string for connect
CREATED	DATE	NOT NULL	Creation time of the database link

ALL_DEF_AUDIT_OPTS

This view contains default object-auditing options that will be applied when objects are created.

Column	Datatype	NULL	Description
ALT	VARCHAR2(3)		Auditing ALTER WHENEVER SUCCESSFUL / UNSUCCESSFUL
AUD	VARCHAR2(3)		Auditing AUDIT WHENEVER SUCCESSFUL / UNSUCCESSFUL
COM	VARCHAR2(3)		Auditing COMMENT WHENEVER SUCCESSFUL / UNSUCCESSFUL
DEL	VARCHAR2(3)		Auditing DELETE WHENEVER SUCCESSFUL / UNSUCCESSFUL
GRA	VARCHAR2(3)		Auditing GRANT WHENEVER SUCCESSFUL / UNSUCCESSFUL
IND	VARCHAR2(3)		Auditing INDEX WHENEVER SUCCESSFUL / UNSUCCESSFUL
INS	VARCHAR2(3)		Auditing INSERT WHENEVER SUCCESSFUL / UNSUCCESSFUL
LOC	VARCHAR2(3)		Auditing LOCK WHENEVER SUCCESSFUL / UNSUCCESSFUL
REN	VARCHAR2(3)		Auditing RENAME WHENEVER SUCCESSFUL / UNSUCCESSFUL
SEL	VARCHAR2(3)		Auditing SELECT WHENEVER SUCCESSFUL / UNSUCCESSFUL
UPD	VARCHAR2(3)		Auditing UPDATE WHENEVER SUCCESSFUL / UNSUCCESSFUL

Column	Datatype	NULL	Description
REF	VARCHAR2(3)		Auditing REFERENCES WHENEVER SUCCESSFUL / UNSUCCESSFUL
EXE	VARCHAR2(3)		Auditing EXECUTE WHENEVER SUCCESSFUL / UNSUCCESSFUL

ALL_DEPENDENCIES

This view lists dependencies between objects accessible to the user.

Column	Datatype	NULL	Description
OWNER	VARCHAR2(30)	NOT NULL	Owner of the object
NAME	VARCHAR2(30)	NOT NULL	Name of object
TYPE	VARCHAR2(12)		Type of object: PROCEDURE, PACKAGE, FUNCTION, PACKAGE BODY, TRIGGER
REFERENCED_OWNER	VARCHAR2(30)		Owner of the parent object
REFERENCED_NAME	VARCHAR2(64)		Type of parent object: PROCEDURE, PACKAGE, FUNCTION, PACKAGE BODY, TRIGGER
REFERENCED_TYPE	VARCHAR2(12)		Type of referenced object
REFERENCED_LINK_NAME	VARCHAR2(128)		Name of the link to the parent object (if remote)
DEPENDENCY_TYPE	VARCHAR2(4)		Two values: REF when the dependency is a REF dependency; HARD otherwise

ALL_DIRECTORIES

This view contains the description of all directories accessible to the user.

Column	Datatype	NULL	Description
OWNER	VARCHAR2(30)	NOT NULL	Owner of the directory (always SYS)
DIRECTORY_NAME	VARCHAR2(30)	NOT NULL	Name of the directory
DIRECTORY_PATH	VARCHAR2(4000)		Operating system pathname for the directory

ALL_ERRORS

This view lists current errors on all objects accessible to the user.

Column	Datatype	NULL	Description
OWNER	VARCHAR2(30)	NOT NULL	Owner of the object
NAME	VARCHAR2(30)	NOT NULL	Name of object
TYPE	VARCHAR2(12)		Type of object: VIEW, PROCEDURE, PACKAGE, FUNCTION, PACKAGE BODY
SEQUENCE	NUMBER	NOT NULL	Sequence number, for ordering
LINE	NUMBER	NOT NULL	Line number at which this error occurs
POSITION	NUMBER	NOT NULL	Position in the line at which this error occurs
TEXT	VARCHAR2(4000)	NOT NULL	Text of the error

ALL_IND_COLUMNS

This view lists columns of the indexes on accessible tables.

Column	Datatype	NULL	Description
INDEX_OWNER	VARCHAR2(30)	NOT NULL	Index owner
INDEX_NAME	VARCHAR2(30)	NOT NULL	Index name
TABLE_OWNER	VARCHAR2(30)	NOT NULL	Table or cluster owner
TABLE_NAME	VARCHAR2(30)	NOT NULL	Table or cluster name
COLUMN_NAME	VARCHAR2(4000)		Column name or attribute of object type column
COLUMN_POSITION	NUMBER	NOT NULL	Position of column or attribute within index
COLUMN_LENGTH	NUMBER	NOT NULL	Indexed length of the column

ALL_IND_PARTITIONS

This view describes, for each index partition, the partition level partitioning information, the storage parameters for the partition, and various partition statistics determined by ANALYZE that the current user can access.

Column	Datatype	NULL	Description
INDEX_OWNER	VARCHAR2(30)	NOT NULL	Index owner
INDEX_NAME	VARCHAR2(30)	NOT NULL	Index name
PARTITION_NAME	VARCHAR2(30)		Partition name
HIGH_VALUE	LONG		Partition bound value expression
HIGH_VALUE_LENGTH	NUMBER	NOT NULL	Length of partition bound value expression

Column	Datatype	NULL	Description
PARTITION_POSITION	NUMBER	NOT NULL	Position of the partition within the index
STATUS	VARCHAR2(8)		Indicates whether index partition is usable or not
TABLESPACE_NAME	VARCHAR2(30)	NOT NULL	Name of the tablespace containing the partition
PCT_FREE	NUMBER	NOT NULL	Minimum percentage of free space in a block
INI_TRANS	NUMBER	NOT NULL	Initial number of transactions
MAX_TRANS	NUMBER	NOT NULL	Maximum number of transactions
INITIAL_EXTENT	NUMBER		Size of the initial extent in bytes
NEXT_EXTENT	NUMBER		Size of secondary extents in bytes
MIN_EXTENT	NUMBER	NOT NULL	Minimum number of extents allowed in the segment
MAX_EXTENT	NUMBER	NOT NULL	Maximum number of extents allowed in the segment
PCT_INCREASE	NUMBER	NOT NULL	Percentage increase in extent size
FREELISTS	NUMBER		Number of process freelists allocated in this segment
LOGGING	VARCHAR2(3)		Logging attribute of partition
BLEVEL	NUMBER		B-Tree level
LEAF_BLOCKS	NUMBER		Number of leaf blocks in the index partition
DISTINCT_KEYS	NUMBER		Number of distinct keys in the index partition
AVG_LEAF_BLOCKS _PER_KEY	NUMBER		Average number of leaf blocks per key
AVG_DATA_BLOCKS _PER_KEY	NUMBER		Average number of data blocks per key
CLUSTERING_FACTOR	NUMBER		Measurement of the amount of (dis)order of the table this index partition is for
NUM_ROWS	NUMBER		Number of rows returned by the ANALYZE command
SAMPLE_SIZE	NUMBER		Sample size used in analyzing this partition
LAST_ANALYZED	DATE		Date of the most recent time this partition was analyzed
BUFFER_POOL	VARCHAR2(7)		The actual buffer pool for the partition

ALL_INDEXES

This view contains descriptions of indexes on tables accessible to the user. To gather statistics for this view, use the SQL command ANALYZE. This view supports parallel partitioned index scans.

Column	Datatype	NULL	Description
OWNER	VARCHAR2(30)	NOT NULL	Username of the owner of the index
INDEX_NAME	VARCHAR2(30)	NOT NULL	Name of the index

Column	Datatype	NULL	Description
INDEX_TYPE	VARCHAR2(12)		Type of index
TABLE_OWNER	VARCHAR2(30)	NOT NULL	Owner of the indexed object
TABLE_NAME	VARCHAR2(30)	NOT NULL	Name of the indexed object
TABLE_TYPE	CHAR(5)		Type of the indexed object
UNIQUENESS	VARCHAR2(9)		Uniqueness status of the index: UNIQUE or NONUNIQUE
TABLESPACE_NAME	VARCHAR2(30)		Name of the tablespace containing the index
INI_TRANS	NUMBER		Initial number of transactions
MAX_TRANS	NUMBER		Maximum number of transactions
INITIAL_EXTENT	NUMBER		Size of the initial extent
NEXT_EXTENT	NUMBER		Size of secondary extents
MIN_EXTENTS	NUMBER		Minimum number of extents allowed in the segment
MAX_EXTENTS	NUMBER		Maximum number of extents allowed in the segment
PCT_INCREASE	NUMBER		Percentage increase in extent size
PCT_THRESHOLD	NUMBER		Threshold percentage of block space allowed per index entry
INCLUDE_COLUMN	NUMBER		User column-id for last column to be included in index organized table top index
FREELISTS	NUMBER		Number of process freelists allocated to this segment
FREELIST_GROUPS	NUMBER		Number of freelist groups allocated to this segment
PCT_FREE	NUMBER		Minimum percentage of free space in a block
LOGGING	VARCHAR(2(3)		Logging information
BLEVEL	NUMBER		B-Tree level: depth of the index from its root block to its leaf blocks. A depth of 0 indicates that the root block and leaf block are the same.
LEAF_BLOCKS	NUMBER		Number of leaf blocks in the index
DISTINCT_KEYS	NUMBER		Number of distinct indexed values. For indexes that enforce UNIQUE and PRIMARY KEY constraints, this value is the same as the number of rows in the table (USER_TABLES.NUM_ROWS)
AVG_LEAF_BLOCKS _PER_KEY	NUMBER		Average number of leaf blocks in which each distinct value in the index appears. This statistic is rounded to the nearest integer. For indexes that enforce UNIQUE and PRIMARY KEY constraints, this value is always 1.
AVG_DATA_BLOCKS _PER_KEY	NUMBER		Average number of data blocks in the table that are pointed to by a distinct value in the index. This statistic is the average number of data blocks that contain rows that contain a given value for the indexed columns. This statistic is rounded to the nearest integer.

Column	Datatype	NULL	Description
CLUSTERING_FACTOR	NUMBER		Statistic that represents the amount of order of the rows in the table based on the values of the index. If its value is near the number of blocks, then the table is very well ordered. In such a case, the index entries in a single leaf block tend to point to rows in the same data blocks. If its value is near the number of rows, then the table is very randomly ordered. In such a case, it is unlikely that index entries in the same leaf block point to rows in the same data blocks.
STATUS	VARCHAR2(8)		Sate of the index: DIRECT LOAD or VALID
NUM_ROWS	NUMBER		Number of rows in this index
SAMPLE_SIZE	NUMBER		Size of the sample used to analyze this index
LAST_ANALYZED	DATE		Timestamp for when this index was last analyzed
DEGREE	VARCHAR2(40)		Number of threads per instance for scanning the index, NULL if PARTITIONED=NO.
INSTANCES	VARCHAR2(40)		Number of instances across which the indexes to be scanned. NULL if PARTITIONED=NO.
PARTITIONED	VARCHAR2(40)		Indicates whether this index is partitioned. Set to 'YES' if it is partitioned
TEMPORARY	VARCHAR2(1)		Can the current session only see data that it places in this object itself?
GENERATED	VARCHAR2(1)		Was the name of this index system generated?
BUFFER_POOL	VARCHAR2(7)		Name of the default buffer pool for the appropriate object

ALL_LABELS

This is a Trusted Oracle Server view that lists system labels. For more information, see the *Trusted Oracle Server Administrator's Guide.*

ALL_LIBRARIES

This new data view lists all the libraries that a user can access.

Column	Datatype	NULL	Description
OWNER	VARCHAR2(30)	NOT NULL	Owner of the library
LIBRARY_NAME	VARCHAR2(30)	NOT NULL	Library name
FILE_SPEC	VARCHAR2(2000)		Operating system file specification associated with the library
DYNAMIC	VARCHAR2(1)		Is the library dynamically loadable? (YES or NO)
STATUS	VARCHAR2(7)		Status of the library

ALL_LOBS

This view displays the LOBs contained in tables accessible to the user.

Column	Datatype	NULL	Description
OWNER	VARCHAR2(30)	NOT NULL	Owner of the table containing the LOB
TABLE_NAME	VARCHAR2(30)	NOT NULL	Name of the table containing the LOB
COLUMN_NAME	VARCHAR2(4000)		Name of the LOB column or attribute
SEGMENT_NAME	VARCHAR2(30)	NOT NULL	Name of the LOB segment
INDEX_NAME	VARCHAR2(30)	NOT NULL	Name of the LOB index
CHUNK	NUMBER		Size of the LOB chunk as a unit of allocation/manipulation in bytes
PCTVERSION	NUMBER	NOT NULL	Maximum percentage of the LOB space used for versioning
CACHE	VARCHAR2(3)		Indicates whether the LOB is accessed through the buffer cache
LOGGING	VARCHAR2(3)		Indicates whether the changes to the LOB are logged
IN_ROW	VARCHAR2(3)		Are some of the LOBs stored with the base row?

ALL_METHOD_PARAMS

This view is a description view of method parameters of types accessible to the user.

Column	Datatype	NULL	Description
OWNER	VARCHAR2(30)	NOT NULL	Owner of the type
TYPE_NAME	VARCHAR2(30)	NOT NULL	Name of the type
METHOD_NAME	VARCHAR2(30)	NOT NULL	Name of the method
METHOD_NO	NUMBER	NOT NULL	Method number for distinguishing overloaded method (not to be used as ID number)
PARAM_NAME	VARCHAR2(30)	NOT NULL	Name of the parameter
PARAM_NO	NUMBER	NOT NULL	Parameter number or position
PARAM_MODE	VARCHAR2(6)		Mode of the parameter

Column	Datatype	NULL	Description
PARAM_TYPE_MOD	VARCHAR2(7)		Type modifier of the parameter
PARAM_TYPE_OWNER	VARCHAR2(30)		Owner of the type of the parameter
PARAM_TYPE_NAME	VARCHAR2(30)		Name of the type of the parameter
CHARACTER_SET_NAME	VARCHAR2(44)		The name of the character set: CHAR_CS or NCHAR_CS

ALL_METHOD_RESULTS

This view is a description view of method results of types accessible to the user.

Column	Datatype	NULL	Description
OWNER	VARCHAR2(30)	NOT NULL	Owner of the type
TYPE_NAME	VARCHAR2(30)	NOT NULL	Name of the type
METHOD_NAME	VARCHAR2(30)	NOT NULL	Name of the method
METHOD_NO	NUMBER	NOT NULL	Method number for distinguishing overloaded method (not to be used as ID number)
RESULT_TYPE_MOD	VARCHAR2(7)	NOT NULL	Type modifier of the result
RESULT_TYPE_OWNER	VARCHAR2(30)		Owner of the type of the result
RESULT_TYPE_NAME	VARCHAR2(30)		Name of the type of the result
CHARACTER_SET_NAME	VARCHAR2(44		The name of the character set: CHAR_CS or NCHAR_CS

ALL_NESTED_TABLES

This view describes the nested tables in tables accessible to the user

Column	Datatype	Null	Description
OWNER	VARCHAR2(30)		Owner of the nested table
TABLE_NAME	VARCHAR2(30)		Name of the nested table

Column	Datatype	Null	Description
TABLE_TYPE_OWNER	VARCHAR2(30)		Owner of the type of which the nested table was created
TABLE_TYPE_NAME	VARCHAR2(30)		Name of the type of the nested table
PARENT_TABLE_NAME	VARCHAR2(30)		Name of the parent table containing the nested table
PARENT_TABLE_COLUMN	VARCHAR2(4000)		Column name of the parent table that corresponds to the nested table

ALL_OBJECT_TABLES

This view contains descriptions of the object tables accessible to the user.

Column	Datatype	NULL	Description
OWNER	VARCHAR2(30)	NOT NULL	Owner of the table
TABLE_NAME	VARCHAR2(30)	NOT NULL	Name of the table
TABLESPACE_NAME	VARCHAR2(30)	NOT NULL	Name of the tablespace containing the table
CLUSTER_NAME	VARCHAR2(30)		Name of the cluster, if any, to which the table belongs
IOT_NAME	VARCHAR2(30)		Name of the index organized table, if any, to which the overflow entry belongs
PCT_FREE	NUMBER		Minimum percentage of free space in a block
PCT_USED	NUMBER		Minimum percentage of used space in a block
INI_TRANS	NUMBER		Initial number of transactions
MAX_TRANS	NUMBER		Maximum number of transactions
INITIAL_EXTENT	NUMBER		Size of the initial extent in bytes
NEXT_EXTENT	NUMBER		Size of secondary extents in bytes
MIN_EXTENTS	NUMBER		Minimum number of extents allowed in the segment
MAX_EXTENTS	NUMBER		Maximum number of extents allowed in the segment
PCT_INCREASE	NUMBER		Percentage increase in extent size

Column	Datatype	NULL	Description
FREELISTS	NUMBER		Number of process freelists allocated in this segment
FREELIST_GROUPS	NUMBER		Number of freelist groups allocated in this segment
LOGGING	VARCHAR2(3)		Logging attribute
BACKED_UP	VARCHAR2(1)		Has table been backed up since last modification?
NUM_ROWS	NUMBER		The number of rows in the table
BLOCKS	NUMBER		The number of used blocks in the table
EMPTY_BLOCKS	NUMBER		The number of empty (never used) blocks in the table
AVG_SPACE	NUMBER		The average available free space in the table
CHAIN_CNT	NUMBER		The number of chained rows in the table
AVG_ROW_LEN	NUMBER		The average row length, including row overhead
AVG_SPACE_FREELIST _BLOCKS	NUMBER		The average freespace of all blocks on a freelist
NUM_FREELIST_BLOCKS	NUMBER		The number of blocks on the freelist
DEGREE	VARCHAR2(10)		The number of threads per instance for scanning the table
INSTANCES	VARCHAR2(10)		The number of instances across which the table is to be scanned
CACHE	VARCHAR2(5)		Whether the table is to be cached in the buffer cache
TABLE_LOCK	VARCHAR2(8)		Whether table locking is enabled or disabled
SAMPLE_SIZE	NUMBER		The sample size used in analyzing this table
LAST_ANALYZED	DATE		The date of the most recent time this table was analyzed
PARTITIONED	VARCHAR2(3)		Is this table partitioned? YES or NO
IOT_TYPE	VARCHAR2(12)		If index organized table, then IOT_TYPE is IOT or IOT_OVERFLOW else NULL
TABLE_TYPE_OWNER	VARCHAR2(30)	NOT NULL	Owner of the type of the table if the table is a typed table

Column	Datatype	NULL	Description
TABLE_TYPE	VARCHAR2(30)	NOT NULL	Type of the table if the table is a typed table
TEMPORARY	VARCHAR2(1)		Can the current session only see data that it place in this object itself?
NESTED	VARCHAR2(3)		Is the table a nested table?
BUFFER_POOL	VARCHAR2(7)		The default buffer pool to be used for table blocks

ALL_OBJECTS

This view lists objects accessible to the user.

Column	Datatype	NULL	Description
OWNER	VARCHAR2(30)	NOT NULL	Username of the owner of the object
OBJECT_NAME	VARCHAR2(30)	NOT NULL	Name of the object
SUBOBJECT_NAME	VARCHAR2(30)		Name of the sub-object (for example, partition)
OBJECT_ID	NUMBER	NOT NULL	Object number of the object
DATA_OBJECT_ID	NUMBER		Object number of the segment which contains the object
OBJECT_TYPE	VARCHAR2(15)		Type and type body of the object: INDEX PARTITION, TABLE PARTITION, PACKAGE, PACKAGE BODY, TRIGGER
CREATED	DATE	NOT NULL	Timestamp for the creation of the object
LAST_DDL_TIME	DATE	NOT NULL	Timestamp for the last modification of the object resulting from a DDL command (including grants and revokes)
TIMESTAMP	VARCHAR2(20)		Timestamp for the creation of the object (character data)
STATUS	VARCHAR2(7)		Status of the object: VALID, INVALID, or N/A
TEMPORARY	VARCHAR2(1)		Can the current session only see data that it placed in this object itself?
GENERATED	VARCHAR2(1)		Was the name of this object system generated?

ALL_PART_COL_STATISTICS

This view contains column statistics and histogram information for table partitions that the current user can access.

Column	Datatype	NULL	Description
OWNER	VARCHAR2(30)	NOT NULL	Owner name
TABLE_NAME	VARCHAR2(30)	NOT NULL	Table name
PARTITION_NAME	VARCHAR2(30)		Table partition name
COLUMN_NAME	VARCHAR2(30)	NOT NULL	Column name
NUM_DISTINCT	NUMBER		Number of distinct values in the column
LOW_VALUE	RAW(32)		Low value in the column
HIGH_VALUE	RAW(32)		High value in the column
DENSITY	NUMBER		Density of the column
NUM_NULLS	NUMBER		Number of nulls in the column
NUM_BUCKETS	NUMBER		Number of buckets in histogram for the column
SAMPLE_SIZE	NUMBER		Sample size used in analyzing this column
LAST_ANALYZED	DATE		Date of the most recent time this column was analyzed

ALL_PART_HISTOGRAMS

This view contains the histogram data (end-points per histogram) for histograms on table partitions that the current user can access.

Column	Datatype	NULL	Description
OWNER	VARCHAR2(30)		Owner name
TABLE_NAME	VARCHAR2(30)		Table name
PARTITION_NAME	VARCHAR2(30)		Table partition name
COLUMN_NAME	VARCHAR2(30)		Column name
BUCKET_NUMBER	NUMBER		Bucket number
ENDPOINT_VALUE	NUMBER		Normalized endpoint values for this bucket

ALL_PART_INDEXES

This view lists the object level partitioning information for all partitioned indexes that the current user can access.

Column	Datatype	NULL	Description
OWNER	VARCHAR2(30)	NOT NULL	Owner of this partitioned index

Column	Datatype	NULL	Description
INDEX_NAME	VARCHAR2(30)	NOT NULL	Name of this partitioned index
PARTITIONING_TYPE	VARCHAR2(7)		Partitioning algorithm: RANGE
PARTITION_COUNT	NUMBER	NOT NULL	Number of partitions in this index
PARTITIONING_KEY _COUNT	NUMBER	NOT NULL	Number of columns in the partitioning key
LOCALITY	VARCHAR2(6)		Indicates whether this partitioned index is LOCAL or GLOBAL
ALIGNMENT	VARCHAR2(12)		Indicates whether this partitioned index is PREFIXED or NON-PREFIXED
DEF_TABLESPACE _NAME	VARCHAR2(30)		Default TABLESPACE, for LOCAL index, for ADD/ SPLIT TABLE partition
DEF_PCT_FREE	NUMBER	NOT NULL	Default PCTFREE, for LOCAL index, for ADD TABLE partition
DEF_INI_TRANS	NUMBER	NOT NULL	Default INITRANS, for LOCAL index, for ADD TABLE partition
DEF_MAX_TRANS	NUMBER	NOT NULL	Default MAXTRANS, for LOCAL index, for ADD TABLE partition
DEF_INITIAL_EXTENT	NUMBER	NOT NULL	Default INITIAL, for LOCAL index, for ADD TABLE partition
DEF_NEXT_EXTENT	NUMBER	NOT NULL	Default NEXT, for LOCAL index, for ADD TABLE partition
DEF_MIN_EXTENTS	NUMBER	NOT NULL	Default MINEXTENTS, for LOCAL index, for ADD TABLE partition
DEF_MAX_EXTENTS	NUMBER	NOT NULL	Default MAXEXTENTS, for LOCAL index, for ADD TABLE partition
DEF_PCT_INCREASE	NUMBER	NOT NULL	Default PCTINCREASE, for LOCAL index, for ADD TABLE partition
DEF_FREELISTS	NUMBER	NOT NULL	Default FREELISTS, for LOCAL index, for ADD TABLE partition
DEF_LOGGING	VARCHAR2(7)		Default LOGGING, for LOCAL index, for ADD TABLE PARTITION
DEF_BUFFER_POOL	VARCHAR2(7)		Default buffer pool for LOCAL index, for ADD TABLE PARTITION

ALL_PART_KEY_COLUMNS

This view describes the partitioning key columns for partitioned objects that the current user access.

Column	Datatype	NULL	Description
OWNER	VARCHAR2(30)		Partitioned table or index owner
NAME	VARCHAR2(30)		Partitioned table or index name

Column	Datatype	NULL	Description
COLUMN_NAME	VARCHAR2(30)		Column name
COLUMN_POSITION	NUMBER		Position of the column within the partitioning key

ALL_PART_TABLES

This view lists the object level partitioning information for partitioned tables the current user access.

Column	Datatype	NULL	Description
OWNER	VARCHAR2(30)	NOT NULL	Owner of this partitioned table
TABLE_NAME	VARCHAR2(30)	NOT NULL	Name of this partitioned table
PARTITIONING_TYPE	VARCHAR2(7)		Partitioning algorithm: 'RANGE'
PARTITION_COUNT	NUMBER	NOT NULL	Number of partitions in this table
PARTITIONING_KEY_COUNT	NUMBER	NOT NULL	Number of columns in the partitioning key
DEF_TABLESPACE_NAME	VARCHAR2(30)	NOT NULL	Default TABLESPACE, used for add partition
DEF_PCT_FREE	NUMBER	NOT NULL	Default PCTFREE, used for add partition
DEF_PCT_USED	NUMBER	NOT NULL	Default PCTUSED, used for add partition
DEF_INI_TRANS	NUMBER	NOT NULL	Default INITRANS, used for add partition
DEF_MAX_TRANS	NUMBER	NOT NULL	Default MAXTRANS, used for add partition
DEF_INITIAL_EXTENT	NUMBER	NOT NULL	Default INITIAL, used for add partition
DEF_NEXT_EXTENT	NUMBER	NOT NULL	Default NEXT, used for add partition
DEF_MIN_EXTENTS	NUMBER	NOT NULL	Default MINEXTENTS, used for add partition
DEF_MAX_EXTENTS	NUMBER	NOT NULL	Default MAXEXTENTS, used for add partition
DEF_PCT_INCREASE	NUMBER	NOT NULL	Default PCTINCREASE, used for add partition
DEF_FREELISTS	NUMBER	NOT NULL	Default FREELISTS, used for add partition
DEF_FREELIST_GROUPS	NUMBER	NOT NULL	Default FREELIST GROUPS, used for add partition
DEF_LOGGING	VARCHAR2(7)		Default LOGGING attribute, used for add partition
DEF_BUFFER_POOL	VARCHAR2(7)		Default buffer pool for the given object, used for add partition

ALL_REFRESH

This view lists all the refresh groups that the user can access.

Column	Datatype	NULL	Description
ROWNER	VARCHAR2(30)	NOT NULL	Name of the owner of the refresh group
RNAME	VARCHAR2(30)	NOT NULL	Name of the refresh group
REFGROUP	NUMBER		Internal identifier of refresh group
IMPLICIT_DESTROY	VARCHAR2(1)		Y or N; if Y, then destroy the refresh group when its last item is subtracted
PUSH_DEFERRED_RPC	VARCHAR2(1)		Y or N; if Y then push changes from snapshot to master before refresh
REFRESH_AFTER_ERRORS	VARCHAR2(1)		If Y, proceed with refresh despite error when pushing deferred RPCs
ROLLBACK_SEG	VARCHAR2(30)		Name of the rollback segment to use while refreshing
JOB	NUMBER		Identifier of job used to refresh the group automatically
NEXT_DATE	DATE		Date that this job will next be refreshed automatically, if not broken
INTERVAL	VARCHAR2(200)		A date function used to compute the next NEXT_DATE
BROKEN	VARCHAR2(1)		Y or N; Y means the job is broken and will never be run
PURGE_OPTION	NUMBER(38)		The method for purging the transaction queue after each push
PARALLELISM	NUMBER(38)		The level of parallelism for transaction propagation
HEAP_SIZE	NUMBER(38)		The size of the heap.

ALL_REFRESH_CHILDREN

This view lists all the objects in refresh groups, where the user can access the group.

Column	Datatype	NULL	Description
OWNER	VARCHAR2(30)	NOT NULL	Owner of the object in the refresh group

Column	Datatype	NULL	Description
NAME	VARCHAR2(30)	NOT NULL	Name of the object in the refresh group
TYPE	VARCHAR2(30)		Type of the object in the refresh group
ROWNER	VARCHAR2(30)	NOT NULL	Name of the owner of the refresh group
RNAME	VARCHAR2(30)	NOT NULL	Name of the refresh group
REFGROUP	NUMBER		Internal identifier of refresh group
IMPLICIT_DESTROY	VARCHAR2(1)		Y or N; if Y, then destroy the refresh group when its last item is subtracted
PUSH_DEFERRED_RPC	VARCHAR2(1)		Y or N; if Y then push changes from snapshot to master before refresh
REFRESH_AFTER _ERRORS	VARCHAR2(1)		If Y, proceed with refresh despite error when pushing deferred RPCs
ROLLBACK_SEG	VARCHAR2(30)		Name of the rollback segment to use while refreshing
JOB	NUMBER		Identifier of job used to refresh the group automatically
NEXT_DATE	DATE		Date that this job will next be refreshed automatically, if not broken
INTERVAL	VARCHAR2(200)		A date function used to compute the next NEXT_DATE
BROKEN	VARCHAR2(1)		Y or N; Y means the job is broken and will never be run
PURGE_OPTION	NUMBER(38)		The method for purging the transaction queue after each push
PARALLELISM	NUMBER(38)		The level of parallelism for transaction propagation
HEAP_SIZE	NUMBER(38)		The size of the heap.

ALL_REFS

This view describes the REF columns and REF attributes in object type columns accessible to the user.

Column	Datatype	NULL	Description
OWNER	VARCHAR2(30)	NOT NULL	Name of the owner
TABLE_NAME	VARCHAR2(30)	NOT NULL	Name of the table

Column	Datatype	NULL	Description
COLUMN_NAME	VARCHAR2(4000)		Name of the REF column or attribute. If it is not a top-level attribute, the value of COLUMN_NAME should be a path name starting with the column name.
WITH_ROWID	VARCHAR2(3)		Is the REF value stored with ROWID (YES or NO)?
IS_SCOPED	VARCHAR2(3)		Is the REF column scoped (YES or NO)?
SCOPE_TABLE_OWNER	VARCHAR2(30)		Name of the owner of the scope table, if it exists and is accessible by the user
SCOPE_TABLE_NAME	VARCHAR2(30)		Name of the scope table, if it exists and is accessible by the user

ALL_REGISTERED_SNAPSHOTS

This view lists all registered snapshots.

Column	Datatype	NULL	Description
OWNER	VARCHAR2(30)	NOT NULL	Owner of the snapshot
NAME	VARCHAR2(30)	NOT NULL	Name of the snapshot
SNAPSHOT_SITE	VARCHAR2(128)	NOT NULL	Global name of the snapshot site.
CAN_USE_LOG	VARCHAR2(3)		YES if this snapshot can use a snapshot log, NO if this snapshot is too complex to use a log
UPDATABLE	VARCHAR2(3)		Specifies whether the snapshot is updatable. YES if it is, NO if it is not. If set to NO, the snapshot is read only.
REFRESH_METHOD	VARCHAR2(11)		Whether the snapshot uses rowids or primary key for fast refresh
SNAPSHOT_ID	NUMBER(38)		Identifier for the snapshot used by the master for fast refresh
VERSION	VARCHAR2(17)		Version of snapshot
QUERY_TXT	LONG		Original query of which this snapshot is an instantiation

ALL_REPCATLOG

This view is used with Advanced Replication. For more information, see *Oracle8 Server Replication*.

ALL_REPCOLUMN

This view is used with Advanced Replication. For more information, see *Oracle8 Server Replication*.

ALL_REPCOLUMN_GROUP

This view is used with Advanced Replication. For more information, see *Oracle8 Server Replication*.

ALL_REPCONFLICT

This view is used with Advanced Replication. For more information, see *Oracle8 Server Replication*.

ALL_REPDDL

This view is used with Advanced Replication. For more information, see *Oracle8 Server Replication*.

ALL_REPGENERATED

This view is used with Advanced Replication. For more information, see *Oracle8 Server Replication*.

ALL_REPGROUP

This view is used with Advanced Replication. For more information, see *Oracle8 Server Replication*.

ALL_REPGROUPED_COLUMN

This view is used with Advanced Replication. For more information, see *Oracle8 Server Replication*.

ALL_REPKEY_COLUMNS

This view is used with Advanced Replication. For more information, see *Oracle8 Server Replication*.

ALL_REPOBJECT

This view is used with Advanced Replication. For more information, see *Oracle8 Server Replication*.

ALL_REPPARAMETER_COLUMN

This view is used with Advanced Replication. For more information, see *Oracle8 Server Replication*.

ALL_REPPRIORITY

This view is used with Advanced Replication. For more information, see *Oracle8 Server Replication*.

ALL_REPPRIORITY_GROUP

This view is used with Advanced Replication. For more information, see *Oracle8 Server Replication*.

ALL_REPPROP

This view is used with Advanced Replication. For more information, see *Oracle8 Server Replication*.

ALL_REPRESOLUTION

This view is used with Advanced Replication. For more information, see *Oracle8 Server Replication*.

ALL_REPRESOL_STATS_CONTROL

This view is used with Advanced Replication. For more information, see *Oracle8 Server Replication*.

ALL_REPRESOLUTION_METHOD

This view is used with Advanced Replication. For more information, see *Oracle8 Server Replication*.

ALL_REPRESOLUTION_STATISTICS

This view is used with Advanced Replication. For more information, see *Oracle8 Server Replication*.

ALL_REPSITES

This view is used with Advanced Replication. For more information, see *Oracle8 Server Replication*.

ALL_SEQUENCES

This view lists descriptions of sequences accessible to the user.

Column	Datatype	NULL	Description
SEQUENCE_OWNER	VARCHAR2(30)	NOT NULL	Name of the owner of the sequence
SEQUENCE_NAME	VARCHAR2(30)	NOT NULL	Sequence name
MIN_VALUE	NUMBER		Minimum value of the sequence
MAX_VALUE	NUMBER		Maximum value of the sequence
INCREMENT_BY	NUMBER	NOT NULL	Value by which sequence is incremented
CYCLE_FLAG	VARCHAR2(1)		Does sequence wrap around on reaching limit
ORDER_FLAG	VARCHAR2(1)		Are sequence numbers generated in order
CACHE_SIZE	NUMBER	NOT NULL	Number of sequence numbers to cache
LAST_NUMBER	NUMBER	NOT NULL	Last sequence number written to disk. If a sequence uses caching, the number written to disk is the last number placed in the sequence cache. This number is likely to be greater than the last sequence number that was used.

ALL_SNAPSHOT_LOGS

This view lists all snapshot logs.

Column	Datatype	NULL	Description
LOG_OWNER	VARCHAR2(30)	NOT NULL	Owner of the log
MASTER	VARCHAR2(30)	NOT NULL	Name of the master table whose changes are logged
LOG_TABLE	VARCHAR2(30)	NOT NULL	Name of the table where the changes to the master table are recorded
LOG_TRIGGER	VARCHAR2(30)		Obsolete with the release of Oracle8 Server. Set to NULL. Formerly, this parameter was an after-row trigger on the master which inserts rows into the log
ROWIDS	VARCHAR2(3)		If YES, records ROWID information
PRIMARY_KEY	VARCHAR2(3)		If YES, records primary key information
FILTER_COLUMNS	VARCHAR2(3)		If YES, snapshot log records filter columns
CURRENT_SNAPSHOTS	DATE		One date per snapshot; the date the snapshot of the master was last refreshed

Column	Datatype	NULL	Description
SNAPSHOT_ID	NUMBER(38)		Unique identifier of the snapshot

ALL_SNAPSHOTS

This view lists all snapshots accessible to the user.

Column	Datatype	NULL	Description
OWNER	VARCHAR2(30)	NOT NULL	Owner of the snapshot
NAME	VARCHAR2(30)	NOT NULL	Name of the view used by users and applications for viewing the snapshot
TABLE_NAME	VARCHAR2(30)	NOT NULL	Table the snapshot is stored in. This table may have additional columns.
MASTER_VIEW	VARCHAR2(30)		View of the master table, owned by the snapshot owner, used for refreshes. This is obsolete in Oracle8 and is set to NULL.
MASTER_OWNER	VARCHAR2(30)		Owner of the master table
MASTER	VARCHAR2(30)		Name of the master table of which this snapshot is a copy
MASTER_LINK	VARCHAR2(128)		Database link name to the master site
CAN_USE_LOG	VARCHAR2(3)		YES if this snapshot can use a snapshot log, NO if this snapshot is too complex to use a log
UPDATABLE	VARCHAR2(3)		Specifies whether the snapshot is updatable. YES if it is, NO if it is not. If set to YES, the snapshot is read only.
REFRESH_METHOD	VARCHAR2(11)		Values used to drive a fast refresh of the snapshot (Primary Key/RowID). If Primary key, then snapshot is a primary snapshot. If RowID, then it uses RowIDs to refresh.
LAST_REFRESH	DATE		Date and time at the master site of the last refresh
ERROR	NUMBER		The number of failed automatic refreshes since last successful refresh
FR_OPERATIONS	VARCHAR2(10)		Status of generated fast refresh operations: (REGENERATE, VALID)
CR_OPERATIONS	VARCHAR2(10)		Status of generated complete refresh operations: (REGENERATE, VALID)
TYPE	VARCHAR2(8)		Type of refresh for all automatic refreshes: COMPLETE, FAST, FORCE
NEXT	VARCHAR2(200)		Date function used to compute next refresh dates
START_WITH	DATE		Date function used to compute next refresh dates
REFRESH_GROUP	NUMBER		All snapshots in a given refresh group get refreshed in the same transaction

Column	Datatype	NULL	Description
UPDATE_TRIG	VARCHAR2(30)		Obsolete. It is NULL for Oracle8 snapshots. Formerly, the name of the trigger that fills the UPDATE_LOG
UPDATE_LOG	VARCHAR2(30)		The table that logs changes made to an updatable snapshots
QUERY	LONG		Original query of which this snapshot is an instantiation
MASTER_ROLLBACK _SEG	VARCHAR2(30)		Rollback segment to use at the master site

ALL_SOURCE

This view lists the text source of all stored objects accessible to the user.

Column	Datatype	NULL	Description
OWNER	VARCHAR2(30)	NOT NULL	Owner of the object
NAME	VARCHAR2(30)	NOT NULL	Name of the object
TYPE	VARCHAR2(12)		Type of object: PROCEDURE, PACKAGE, FUNCTION, PACKAGE BODY, TRIGGER, TYPE, TYPE BODY
LINE	NUMBER	NOT NULL	Line number of this line of source
TEXT	VARCHAR2(4000)		Text source of the stored object

ALL_SYNONYMS

This view lists all synonyms accessible to the user.

Column	Datatype	NULL	Description
OWNER	VARCHAR2(30)	NOT NULL	Owner of the synonym
SYNONYM_NAME	VARCHAR2(30)	NOT NULL	Name of the synonym
TABLE_OWNER	VARCHAR2(30)		Owner of the object referenced by the synonym
TABLE_NAME	VARCHAR2(30)	NOT NULL	Name of the object referenced by the synonym
DB_LINK	VARCHAR2(128)		Name of the database link referenced, if any

ALL_TAB_COL_STATISTICS

This view contains column statistics and histogram information which is in the USER_TAB_COLUMNS view. For more information, see "USER_TAB_COLUMNS" on page 2-157.

Column	Datatype	NULL	Description
TABLE_NAME	VARCHAR2(30)	NOT NULL	Table name
COLUMN_NAME	VARCHAR2(30)	NOT NULL	Column name
NUM_DISTINCT	NUMBER		Number of distinct values in the column
LOW_VALUE	RAW(32)		Low value in the column
HIGH_VALUE	RAW(32)		High value in the column
DENSITY	NUMBER		Density of the column
NUM_NULLS	NUMBER		Number of nulls in the column
NUM_BUCKETS	NUMBER		Number of buckets in histogram for the column
LAST_ANALYZED	DATE		Date of the most recent time this column was analyzed
SAMPLE_SIZE	NUMBER		Sample size used in analyzing this column

ALL_TAB_COLUMNS

This view lists the columns of all tables, views, and clusters accessible to the user. To gather statistics for this view, use the SQL command ANALYZE.

Column	Datatype	NULL	Description
OWNER	VARCHAR2(30)	NOT NULL	Owner of the table, view or cluster
TABLE_NAME	VARCHAR2(30)	NOT NULL	Table, view, or cluster name
COLUMN_NAME	VARCHAR2(30)	NOT NULL	Column name
DATA_TYPE	VARCHAR2(30)		Datatype of the column
DATA_TYPE_MOD	VARCHAR2(3)		Datatype modifier of the column
DATA_TYPE_OWNER	VARCHAR2(30)		Owner of the datatype of the column
DATA_LENGTH	NUMBER	NOT NULL	Length of the column in bytes
DATA_PRECISION	NUMBER		Decimal precision for NUMBER datatype; binary precision for FLOAT datatype, NULL for all other datatypes
DATA_SCALE	NUMBER		Digits to right of decimal point in a number
NULLABLE	VARCHAR2(1)		Specifies whether a column allows NULLs. Value is N if there is a NOT NULL constraint on the column or if the column is part of a PRIMARY KEY.
COLUMN_ID	NUMBER	NOT NULL	Sequence number of the column as created

Column	Datatype	NULL	Description
DEFAULT_LENGTH	NUMBER		Length of default value for the column
DATA_DEFAULT	LONG		Default value for the column
NUM_DISTINCT	NUMBER		These columns remain for backward compatibility with Oracle7. This information is now in the {TAB|PART}_COL_STATISTICS views. This view now picks up these values from HIST_HEAD$ rather than COL$.
LOW_VALUE	RAW(32)		
HIGH_VALUE	RAW(32)		
DENSITY	NUMBER		
NUM_NULLS	NUMBER		The number of nulls in the column
NUM_BUCKETS	NUMBER		The number of buckets in histogram for the column
LAST_ANALYZED	DATE		The date of the most recent time this column was analyzed
SAMPLE_SIZE			The sample size used in analyzing this column
CHARACTER_SET _NAME	VARCHAR2(44)		The name of the character set: CHAR_CS or NCHAR_CS

ALL_TAB_COMMENTS

This view lists comments on tables and views accessible to the user.

Column	Datatype	NULL	Description
OWNER	VARCHAR2(30)	NOT NULL	Owner of the object
TABLE_NAME	VARCHAR2(30)	NOT NULL	Name of the object
TABLE_TYPE	VARCHAR2(11)		Type of the object
COMMENTS	VARCHAR2(4000)		Comment on the object

ALL_TAB_HISTOGRAMS

This view lists histograms on tables and views accessible to the user.

Column	Datatype	NULL	Description
OWNER	VARCHAR2(30)		Owner of table
TABLE_NAME	VARCHAR2(30)		Table name
COLUMN_NAME	VARCHAR2(4000)		Column name or attribute of the object type column
BUCKET_NUMBER	NUMBER		Bucket number
ENDPOINT_VALUE	NUMBER		Normalized endpoint values for this bucket

ALL_TAB_PARTITIONS

This view describes, for each table partition, the partition level partitioning information, the storage parameters for the partition, and various partition statistics determined by ANALYZE that the current user can access.

Column	Datatype	NULL	Description
TABLE_OWNER	VARCHAR2(30)	NOT NULL	Table owner
TABLE_NAME	VARCHAR2(30)	NOT NULL	Table name
PARTITION_NAME	VARCHAR2(30)		Partition name
HIGH_VALUE	LONG		Partition bound value expression
HIGH_VALUE_LENGTH	NUMBER	NOT NULL	Length of partition bound value expression
PARTITION_POSITION	NUMBER	NOT NULL	Position of the partition within the table
TABLESPACE_NAME	VARCHAR2(30)	NOT NULL	Name of the tablespace containing the partition
PCT_FREE	NUMBER	NOT NULL	Minimum percentage of free space in a block
PCT_USED	NUMBER	NOT NULL	Minimum percentage of used space in a block
INI_TRANS	NUMBER	NOT NULL	Initial number of transactions
MAX_TRANS	NUMBER	NOT NULL	Maximum number of transactions
INITIAL_EXTENT	NUMBER		Size of the initial extent in bytes
NEXT_EXTENT	NUMBER		Size of secondary extents in bytes
MIN_EXTENT	NUMBER	NOT NULL	Minimum number of extents allowed in the segment
MAX_EXTENT	NUMBER	NOT NULL	Maximum number of extents allowed in the segment
PCT_INCREASE	NUMBER	NOT NULL	Percentage increase in extent size
FREELISTS	NUMBER		Number of process freelists allocated in this segment
FREELIST_GROUPS	NUMBER		Number of freelist groups allocated in this segment
LOGGING	VARCHAR2(3)		Logging attribute of partition
NUM_ROWS	NUMBER		Number of rows in the partition
BLOCKS	NUMBER		Number of used blocks in the partition
EMPTY_BLOCKS	NUMBER		Number of empty (never used) blocks in the partition
AVG_SPACE	NUMBER		Average available free space in the partition
CHAIN_CNT	NUMBER		Number of chained rows in the partition
AVG_ROW_LEN	NUMBER		Average row length, including row overhead
SAMPLE_SIZE	NUMBER		Sample size used in analyzing this partition
LAST_ANALYZED	DATE		Date of the most recent time this partition was analyzed
BUFFER_POOL	VARCHAR2(7)		The actual buffer pool for this partition

ALL_TAB_PRIVS

This view lists the grants on objects for which the user or PUBLIC is the grantee.

Column	Datatype	NULL	Description
GRANTOR	VARCHAR2(30)	NOT NULL	Name of the user who performed the grant
GRANTEE	VARCHAR2(30)	NOT NULL	Name of the user to whom access is granted
TABLE_SCHEMA	VARCHAR2(30)	NOT NULL	Schema of the object
TABLE_NAME	VARCHAR2(30)	NOT NULL	Name of the object
PRIVILEGE	VARCHAR2(40)	NOT NULL	Privilege on the object
GRANTABLE	VARCHAR2(3)		YES if the privilege was granted with ADMIN OPTION; otherwise NO

ALL_TAB_PRIVS_MADE

This view lists the user's grants and grants on the user's objects.

Column	Datatype	NULL	Description
GRANTEE	VARCHAR2(30)	NOT NULL	Name of the user to whom access was granted
OWNER	VARCHAR2(30)	NOT NULL	Owner of the object
TABLE_NAME	VARCHAR2(30)	NOT NULL	Name of the object
GRANTOR	VARCHAR2(30)	NOT NULL	Name of the user who performed the grant
PRIVILEGE	VARCHAR2(40)	NOT NULL	Privilege on the object
GRANTABLE	VARCHAR2(3)		YES if the privilege was granted with ADMIN OPTION; otherwise NO

ALL_TAB_PRIVS_RECD

This view lists grants on objects for which the user or PUBLIC is the grantee.

Column	Datatype	NULL	Description
GRANTEE	VARCHAR2(30)	NOT NULL	Name of the user to whom access was granted
OWNER	VARCHAR2(30)	NOT NULL	Owner of the object
TABLE_NAME	VARCHAR2(30)	NOT NULL	Name of the object
GRANTOR	VARCHAR2(30)	NOT NULL	Name of the user who performed the grant
PRIVILEGE	VARCHAR2(40)	NOT NULL	Privilege on the object
GRANTABLE	VARCHAR2(3)		YES if the privilege was granted with ADMIN OPTION; otherwise NO

ALL_TABLES

This view contains descriptions of relational tables accessible to the user. To gather statistics for this view, use the SQL command ANALYZE.

Column	Datatype	NULL	Description
OWNER	VARCHAR2(30)		Owner of the table
TABLE_NAME	VARCHAR2(30)		Name of the table
TABLESPACE_NAME	VARCHAR2(30)		Name of the tablespace containing the table
CLUSTER_NAME	VARCHAR2(30)		Name of the cluster, if any, to which the table belongs
IOT_NAME	VARCHAR2(30)		Name of the index organized table, if any, to which the overflow entry belongs
PCT_FREE	NUMBER		Minimum percentage of free space in a block
PCT_USED	NUMBER		Minimum percentage of used space in a block
INI_TRANS	NUMBER		Initial number of transactions
MAX_TRANS	NUMBER		Maximum number of transactions
INITIAL_EXTENT	NUMBER		Size of the initial extent in bytes
NEXT_EXTENT	NUMBER		Size of the secondary extension bytes
MIN_EXTENTS	NUMBER		Minimum number of extents allowed in the segment
MAX_EXTENTS	NUMBER		Maximum number of extents allowed in the segment
PCT_INCREASE	NUMBER		Percentage increase in extent size
FREELISTS	NUMBER		Number of process freelists allocated to this segment
FREELIST_GROUPS	NUMBER		Number of freelist groups allocated to this segment
LOGGING	VARCHAR2(3)		Logging attribute
BACKED_UP	VARCHAR2(1)		Has table been backed up since last change
NUM_ROWS	NUMBER		Number of rows in the table
BLOCKS	NUMBER		Number of used data blocks in the table
EMPTY_BLOCKS	NUMBER		Number of empty (never used) data blocks in the table
AVG_SPACE	NUMBER		Average amount of free space, in bytes, in a data block allocated to the table
CHAIN_CNT	NUMBER		Number of rows in the table that are chained from one data block to another, or which have migrated to a new block, requiring a link to preserve the old ROWID
AVG_ROW_LEN	NUMBER		Average length of a row in the table in bytes

Column	Datatype	NULL	Description
AVG_SPACE_FREELIST _BLOCKS	NUMBER		The average freespace of all blocks on a freelist
NUM_FREELIST_BLOCKS	NUMBER		The number of blocks on the freelist
DEGREE	VARCHAR2(10)		The number of threads per instance for scanning the table
INSTANCES	VARCHAR2(10)		The number of instances across which the table is to be scanned
CACHE	VARCHAR2(5)		Whether the table is to be cached in the buffer cache
TABLE_LOCK	VARCHAR2(8)		Whether table locking is enabled or disabled
SAMPLE_SIZE	NUMBER		Sample size used in analyzing this table
LAST_ANALYZED	DATE		Date of the most recent time this table was analyzed
PARTITIONED	VARCHAR2(3)		Indicates whether this table is partitioned. Set to YES if it is partitioned
IOT_TYPE	VARCHAR2(12)		If this is an index organized table, then IOT_TYPE is IOT or IOT_OVERFLOW. If this is not an index organized table, then IOT_TYPE is NULL
TEMPORARY	VARCHAR2(1)		Can the current session only see data that it place in this object itself?
NESTED	VARCHAR2(3)		Is the table a nested table?
BUFFER_POOL	VARCHAR2(7)		Name of the default buffer pool for the appropriate object

ALL_TRIGGERS

This view lists trigger information for triggers owned by the user, triggers on tables owned by the user, or all triggers if the user has the CREATE ANY TRIGGER privilege.

Column	Datatype	NULL	Description
OWNER	VARCHAR2(30)	NOT NULL	Owner of the trigger
TRIGGER_NAME	VARCHAR2(30)	NOT NULL	Name of the trigger
TRIGGER_TYPE	VARCHAR2(16)		When the trigger fires: BEFORE EACH ROW, AFTER EACH ROW, BEFORE STATEMENT, AFTER STATEMENT
TRIGGERING_EVENT	VARCHAR2(26)		Statement that fires the trigger: INSERT, UPDATE, DELETE
TABLE_OWNER	VARCHAR2(30)	NOT NULL	Owner of the table on which the trigger is defined
TABLE_NAME	VARCHAR2(30)	NOT NULL	Table on which the trigger is defined

Column	Datatype	NULL	Description
REFERENCING_NAME	VARCHAR2(87)		Names used for referencing OLD and NEW column values from within the trigger
WHEN_CLAUSE	VARCHAR2(4000)		WHEN clause. Must evaluate to TRUE for TRIGGER_BODY to execute.
STATUS	VARCHAR2(8)		Whether the trigger is enabled: ENABLED or DISABLED
DESCRIPTION	VARCHAR2(4000)		Trigger description. Useful for re-creating a trigger creation statement.
TRIGGER_BODY	LONG		Statement(s) executed by the trigger when it fires

ALL_TRIGGER_COLS

This view displays the usage of columns in triggers owned by user, on tables owned by user, or on all triggers if the user has the CREATE ANY TRIGGER privilege.

Column	Datatype	NULL	Description
TRIGGER_OWNER	VARCHAR2(30)	NOT NULL	Owner of the triggers
TRIGGER_NAME	VARCHAR2(30)	NOT NULL	Name of the trigger
TABLE_OWNER	VARCHAR2(30)	NOT NULL	Owner of the table on which the trigger is defined
TABLE_NAME	VARCHAR2(30)	NOT NULL	Table on which the trigger is defined
COLUMN_NAME	VARCHAR2(4000)		Name of the column used in the trigger
COLUMN_LIST	VARCHAR2(3)		Column specified in UPDATE clause: Y/N
COLUMN_USAGE	VARCHAR2(17)		How the column is used in the trigger. All applicable combinations of NEW, OLD, IN, OUT, and IN OUT.

ALL_TYPE_ATTRS

This view displays the attributes of types accessible to the user.

Column	Datatype	NULL	Description
OWNER	VARCHAR2(30)		Owner of the type
TYPE_NAME	VARCHAR2(30)	NOT NULL	Name of the type
ATTR_NAME	VARCHAR2(30)	NOT NULL	Name of the attribute
ATTR_TYPE_MOD	VARCHAR2(7)		Type modifier of the attribute
ATTR_TYPE_OWNER	VARCHAR2(30)		Owner of the type of the attribute

Column	Datatype	NULL	Description
ATTR_TYPE_NAME	VARCHAR2(30)		Name of the type of the attribute
LENGTH	NUMBER		Length of the CHAR attribute or maximum length of the VARCHAR or VARCHAR2 attribute
PRECISION	NUMBER		Decimal precision of the NUMBER or DECIMAL attribute or binary precision of the FLOAT attribute
SCALE	NUMBER		Scale of the NUMBER or DECIMAL attribute
CHARACTER_SET_NAME	VARCHAR2(44)		The name of the character set: CHAR_CS or NCHAR_CS

ALL_TYPE_METHODS

This view is a description of methods of types accessible to the user.

Column	Datatype	NULL	Description
OWNER	VARCHAR2(30)	NOT NULL	Owner of the type
TYPE_NAME	VARCHAR2(30)	NOT NULL	Name of the type
METHOD_NAME	VARCHAR2(30)	NOT NULL	Name of the method
METHOD_NO	NUMBER	NOT NULL	Method number for distinguishing overloaded method (not to be used as ID number)
METHOD_TYPE	VARCHAR2(6)		Type of the method
PARAMETERS	NUMBER	NOT NULL	Number of parameters to the method
RESULTS	NUMBER	NOT NULL	Number of results returned by the method

ALL_TYPES

This view displays the types accessible to the user.

Column	Datatype	NULL	Description
OWNER	VARCHAR2(30)		Owner of the type
TYPE_NAME	VARCHAR2(30)	NOT NULL	Name of the type
TYPE_OID	RAW(16)	NOT NULL	Object identifier (OID) of the type
TYPECODE	VARCHAR2(30)		Typecode of the type

Column	Datatype	NULL	Description
ATTRIBUTES	NUMBER		Number of attributes in the type
METHODS	NUMBER		Number of methods in the type
PREDEFINED	VARCHAR2(3)		Indicates whether the type is a predefined type
INCOMPLETE	VARCHAR2(3)		Indicates whether the type is an incomplete type

ALL_UPDATABLE_COLUMNS

This view contains a description of all columns that are updatable in a join view.

Column	Datatype	NULL	Description
OWNER	VARCHAR2(30)	NOT NULL	Table owner
TABLE_NAME	VARCHAR2(30)	NOT NULL	Table name
COLUMN_NAME	VARCHAR2(30)	NOT NULL	Column name
UPDATABLE	VARCHAR2(3)		Indicates whether the column updatable
INSERTABLE	VARCHAR2(3)		Indicates the column insertable
DELETABLE	VARCHAR2(3)		Indicates the column deletable

ALL_USERS

This view contains information about all users of the database.

Column	Datatype	NULL	Description
USERNAME	VARCHAR2(30)	NOT NULL	Name of the user
USER_ID	NUMBER	NOT NULL	ID number of the user
CREATED	DATE	NOT NULL	User creation date

ALL_VIEWS

This view lists the text of views accessible to the user.

Column	Datatype	NULL	Description
OWNER	VARCHAR2(30)	NOT NULL	Owner of the view
VIEW_NAME	VARCHAR2(30)	NOT NULL	Name of the view
TEXT_LENGTH	NUMBER		Length of the view text

Column	Datatype	NULL	Description
TEXT	LONG		View text
TYPE_TEXT_LENGTH	NUMBER		Length of the type clause of the typed view
TYPE_TEXT	VARCHAR2(4000)		Type clause of the typed view
OID_TEXT_LENGTH	NUMBER		Length of the WITH OID clause of the typed view
OID_TEXT	VARCHAR2(4000)		WITH OID clause of the typed view
VIEW_TYPE_OWNER	VARCHAR2(30)		Owner of the type of the view if the view is a typed view
VIEW_TYPE	VARCHAR2(30)		Type of the view if the view is a typed view

AUDIT_ACTIONS

This view contains descriptions for audit trail action type codes.

Column	Datatype	NULL	Description
ACTION	NUMBER	NOT NULL	Numeric audit trail action type code
NAME	VARCHAR2(27)	NOT NULL	Name of the type of audit trail action

CATALOG

This view is included for compatibility with Oracle version 5. Use of this view is not recommended.

CAT

This is a synonym for USER_CATALOG. For more information, see "USER_CATALOG" on page 2-128.

CHAINED_ROWS

This view is the default table for the ANALYZE LIST CHAINED ROWS command.

Column	Description
OWNER_NAME	Table owner
TABLE_NAME	Table name
CLUSTER_NAME	Cluster the table is in, if any
HEAD_ROWID	ROWID the chained row is accessed by
TIMESTAMP	Date/time that the ANALYZE command was issued

CLU

This is a synonym for USER_CLUSTERS. For more information, see "USER_CLUSTERS" on page 2-128.

CODE_PIECES

This view is accessed to create the DBA_OBJECT_SIZE and USER_OBJECT_SIZE views. For more information, see "DBA_OBJECT_SIZE" on page 2-67 and "USER_OBJECT_SIZE" on page 2-143.

CODE_SIZE

This view is accessed to create the DBA_OBJECT_SIZE and USER_OBJECT_SIZE views. For more information, see "DBA_OBJECT_SIZE" on page 2-67 and "USER_OBJECT_SIZE" on page 2-143.

COL

This view is included for compatibility with Oracle version 5. Use of this view is not recommended.

COLS

This is a synonym for USER_TAB_COLUMNS. For more information, see "USER_TAB_COLUMNS" on page 2-157.

COLUMN_PRIVILEGES

This view lists grants on columns for which the user is the grantor, grantee, or owner, or PUBLIC is the grantee.

This view is included for compatibility with Oracle version 6. Use of this view is not recommended.

Column	Description
GRANTEE	Name of the user to whom access was granted
OWNER	Username of the object's owner
TABLE_NAME	Name of the object

Column	Description
COLUMN_NAME	Name of the column
GRANTOR	Name of the user who performed the grant
INSERT_PRIV	Permission to insert into the column
UPDATE_PRIV	Permission to update the column
REFERENCES_PRIV	Permission to reference the column
CREATED	Timestamp for the grant

DBA_2PC_NEIGHBORS

This view contains information about incoming and outgoing connections for pending transactions.

Column	Datatype	NULL	Description
LOCAL_TRAN_ID	VARCHAR2(22)		Local identifier of a transaction
IN_OUT	VARCHAR2(3)		IN for incoming connections, OUT for outgoing
DATABASE	VARCHAR2(128)		IN: client database name; OUT: outgoing database link
DBUSER_OWNER	VARCHAR2(30)		IN: name of local user; OUT: owner of database link
INTERFACE	VARCHAR2(1)		"C" for request commit, otherwise "N" for prepare or request readonly commit
DBID	VARCHAR2(16)		The database ID at the other end of the connection
SESS#	NUMBER		Session number of the connection at this database
BRANCH	VARCHAR2(128)		Transaction branch ID of the connection at this database

DBA_2PC_PENDING

This view contains information about distributed transactions awaiting recovery.

Column	Datatype	NULL	Description
LOCAL_TRAN_ID	VARCHAR2(22)	NOT NULL	String of form: n.n.n; n is a number
GLOBAL_TRAN_ID	VARCHAR2(169)		Globally unique transaction ID
STATE	VARCHAR2(16)	NOT NULL	Collecting, prepared, committed, forced commit, or forced rollback
MIXED	VARCHAR2(3)		YES = part of the transaction committed and part rolled back
ADVICE	VARCHAR2(1)		C for commit, R for rollback, else NULL
TRAN_COMMENT	VARCHAR2(2000)		Text for commit work comment text

Column	Datatype	NULL	Description
FAIL_TIME	DATE	NOT NULL	Value of SYSDATE when the row was inserted (tx or system recovery)
FORCE_TIME	DATE		Time of manual force decision (null if not forced locally)
RETRY_TIME	DATE	NOT NULL	Time automatic recovery (RECO) last tried to recover the transaction
OS_USER	VARCHAR2(2000)		Time automatic recovery (RECO) last tried to recover the transaction
OS_TERMINAL	VARCHAR2(2000)		Time automatic recovery (RECO) last tried to recover the transaction
HOST	VARCHAR2(2000)		Name of the host machine for the end-user
DB_USER	VARCHAR2(30)		Name of the host machine for the end-user
COMMIT#	VARCHAR2(16)		Name of the host machine for the end-user

DBA_ALL_TABLES

This view displays descriptions of all tables (object tables and relational tables) in the database.

Column	Datatype	NULL	Description
OWNER	VARCHAR2(30)		Owner of the table
TABLE_NAME	VARCHAR2(30)		Name of the table
TABLESPACE_NAME	VARCHAR2(30)		Name of the tablespace containing the table
CLUSTER_NAME	VARCHAR2(30)		Name of the cluster, if any, to which the table belongs
IOT_NAME	VARCHAR2(30)		Name of the index organized table, if any, to which the overflow entry belongs
PCT_FREE	NUMBER		Minimum percentage of free space in a block
PCT_USED	NUMBER		Minimum percentage of used space in a block
INI_TRANS	NUMBER		Initial number of transactions
MAX_TRANS	NUMBER		Maximum number of transactions
INITIAL_EXTENT	NUMBER		Size of the initial extent in bytes
NEXT_EXTENT	NUMBER		Size of secondary extents in bytes
MIN_EXTENTS	NUMBER		Minimum number of extents allowed in the segment

Column	Datatype	NULL	Description
MAX_EXTENTS	NUMBER		Maximum number of extents allowed in the segment
PCT_INCREASE	NUMBER		Percentage increase in extent size
FREELISTS	NUMBER		Number of process freelists allocated in this segment
FREELIST_GROUPS	NUMBER		Number of freelist groups allocated in this segment
LOGGING	VARCHAR2(3)		Logging attribute
BACKED_UP	VARCHAR2(1)		Has table been backed up since last modification?
NUM_ROWS	NUMBER		The number of rows in the table
BLOCKS	NUMBER		The number of used blocks in the table
EMPTY_BLOCKS	NUMBER		The number of empty (never used) blocks in the table
AVG_SPACE	NUMBER		The average available free space in the table
CHAIN_CNT	NUMBER		The number of chained rows in the table
AVG_ROW_LEN	NUMBER		The average row length, including row overhead
AVG_SPACE_FREELIST _BLOCKS	NUMBER		The average freespace of all blocks on a freelist
NUM_FREELIST _BLOCKS	NUMBER		The number of blocks on the freelist
DEGREE	VARCHAR2(10)		The number of threads per instance for scanning the table
INSTANCES	VARCHAR2(10)		The number of instances across which the table is to be scanned
CACHE	VARCHAR2(5)		Whether the table is to be cached in the buffer cache
TABLE_LOCK	VARCHAR2(8)		Whether table locking is enabled or disabled
SAMPLE_SIZE	NUMBER		The sample size used in analyzing this table
LAST_ANALYZED	DATE		The date of the most recent time this table was analyzed
PARTITIONED	VARCHAR2(3)		Is this table partitioned? YES or NO
IOT_TYPE	VARCHAR2(12)		If an index organized table, then IOT_TYPE is IOT or IOT_OVERFLOW else NULL
TABLE_TYPE_OWNER	VARCHAR2(30)		Owner of the type of the table if the table is a typed table

Column	Datatype	NULL	Description
TABLE_TYPE	VARCHAR2(30)		Type of the table if the table is a typed table
TEMPORARY	VARCHAR2(1)		Can the current session only see data that it place in this object itself?
NESTED	VARCHAR2(3)		Is the table a nested table?
BUFFER_POOL	VARCHAR2(7)		The default buffer pool to be used for table blocks

DBA_ANALYZE_OBJECTS

This view lists all the objects that have been analyzed.

Column	Datatype	NULL	Description
OWNER	VARCHAR2(30)	NOT NULL	Owner of the object
OBJECT_NAME	VARCHAR2(30)	NOT NULL	Name of the object
OBJECT_TYPE	VARCHAR2(7)		Type of the object

DBA_AUDIT_EXISTS

This view lists audit trail entries produced by AUDIT NOT EXISTS and AUDIT EXISTS.

Column	Datatype	NULL	Description
OS_USERNAME	VARCHAR2(255)		Operating system login username of the user whose actions were audited
USERNAME	VARCHAR2(30)		Name (not ID number) of the user whose actions were audited
USERHOST	VARCHAR2(2000)		Numeric instance ID for the Oracle instance from which the user is accessing the database
TERMINAL	VARCHAR2(2000)		Identifier of the user's terminal
TIMESTAMP	DATE	NOT NULL	Timestamp for the creation of the audit trail entry
OWNER	VARCHAR2(30)		Intended creator of the non-existent object
OBJ_NAME	VARCHAR2(128)		Name of the object affected by the action
ACTION_NAME	VARCHAR2(27)		Name of the action type corresponding to the numeric code in the ACTION column in DBA_AUDIT_TRAIL
NEW_OWNER	VARCHAR2(30)		Owner of the object named in the NEW_NAME column
NEW_NAME	VARCHAR2(128)		New name of an object after a RENAME or the name of the underlying object

Column	Datatype	NULL	Description
OBJ_PRIVILEGE	VARCHAR2(16)		Object privileges granted or revoked by a GRANT or REVOKE statement
SYS_PRIVILEGE	VARCHAR2(40)		System privileges granted or revoked by a GRANT or REVOKE statement
GRANTEE	VARCHAR2(30)		Name of grantee specified in a GRANT or REVOKE statement
SESSIONID	NUMBER	NOT NULL	Numeric ID for each Oracle session
ENTRYID	NUMBER	NOT NULL	Numeric ID for each audit trail entry in the session
STATEMENTID	NUMBER	NOT NULL	Numeric ID for each statement run
RETURNCODE	NUMBER	NOT NULL	Oracle Server message code generated by the action. Some useful values: • zero: the action succeeded • 2004: security violation

DBA_AUDIT_OBJECT

This view contains audit trail records for all objects in the system.

Column	Datatype	NULL	Description
OS_USERNAME	VARCHAR2(255)		Operating system login username of the user whose actions were audited
USERNAME	VARCHAR2(30)		Name (not ID number) of the user whose actions were audited
USERHOST	VARCHAR2(2000)		Numeric instance ID for the Oracle instance from which the user is accessing the database
TERMINAL	VARCHAR2(2000)		Identifier of the user's terminal
TIMESTAMP	DATE	NOT NULL	Timestamp for the creation of the audit trail entry or login time for the CONNECT statement
OWNER	VARCHAR2(30)		Creator of the object affected by the action
OBJ_NAME	VARCHAR2(128)		Name of the object affected by the action
ACTION_NAME	VARCHAR2(27)		Name of the action type corresponding to the numeric code in the ACTION column in DBA_AUDIT_TRAIL
NEW_OWNER	VARCHAR2(30)		Owner of the object named in the NEW_NAME column
NEW_NAME	VARCHAR2(128)		New name of an object after a RENAME or the name of the underlying object

Column	Datatype	NULL	Description
SES_ACTIONS	VARCHAR2(19)		Session summary (a string of 16 characters, one for each action type in the order ALTER, AUDIT, COMMENT, DELETE, GRANT, INDEX, INSERT, LOCK, RENAME, SELECT, UPDATE, REFERENCES, and EXECUTE. Positions 14, 15, and 16 are reserved for future use. The characters are: - for none, S for success, F for failure, and B for both)
COMMENT_TEXT	VARCHAR2(4000		Text comment on the audit trail, inserted by the application
SESSIONID	NUMBER	NOT NULL	Numeric ID for each Oracle session
ENTRYID	NUMBER	NOT NULL	Numeric ID for each audit trail entry in the session
STATEMENTID	NUMBER	NOT NULL	Numeric ID for each statement run
RETURNCODE	NUMBER	NOT NULL	Oracle Server message code generated by the action. Some useful values: • zero: the action succeeded • 2004: security violation
PRIV_USED	VARCHAR2(40)		System privilege used to execute the action
OBJECT_LABEL	MLSLABEL		Label associated with the object being audited. Applies to Trusted Oracle Server only.
SESSION_LABEL	MLSLABEL		Label associated with the session. Applies to Trusted Oracle Server only.

DBA_AUDIT_SESSION

This view lists all audit trail records concerning CONNECT and DISCONNECT.

Column	Datatype	NULL	Description
OS_USERNAME	VARCHAR2(255)		Operating system login username of the user whose actions were audited
USERNAME	VARCHAR2(30)		Name (not ID number) of the user whose actions were audited
USERHOST	VARCHAR2(2000)		Numeric instance ID for the Oracle instance from which the user is accessing the database
TERMINAL	VARCHAR2(2000)		Identifier of the user's terminal
TIMESTAMP	DATE	NOT NULL	Timestamp for the creation of the audit trail entry or login time for the CONNECT statement
ACTION_NAME	VARCHAR2(27)		Name of the action type corresponding to the numeric code in the ACTION column in DBA_AUDIT_TRAIL
LOGOFF_TIME	DATE		Timestamp for user log off
LOGOFF_LREAD	NUMBER		Logical reads for the session

Column	Datatype	NULL	Description
LOGOFF_PREAD	NUMBER		Physical reads for the session
LOGOFF_LWRITE	NUMBER		Logical writes for the session
LOGOFF_DLOCK	VARCHAR2(40)		Deadlocks detected during the session
SESSIONID	NUMBER	NOT NULL	Numeric ID for each Oracle session
RETURNCODE	NUMBER	NOT NULL	Oracle Server message code generated by the action. Some useful values: • zero: the action succeeded • 2004: security violation
SESSION_LABEL	MLSLABEL		Label associated with the session. Applies to Trusted Oracle Server only.

DBA_AUDIT_STATEMENT

This view lists audit trail records concerning GRANT, REVOKE, AUDIT, NOAUDIT, and ALTER SYSTEM statements.

Column	Datatype	NULL	Description
OS_USERNAME	VARCHAR2(255)		Operating system login username of the user whose actions were audited
USERNAME	VARCHAR2(30)		Name (not ID number) of the user whose actions were audited
USERHOST	VARCHAR2(2000)		Numeric instance ID for the Oracle instance from which the user is accessing the database
TERMINAL	VARCHAR2(2000)		Identifier of the user's terminal
TIMESTAMP	DATE	NOT NULL	Timestamp for the creation of the audit trail entry or login time for the CONNECT statement
OWNER	VARCHAR2(30)		Creator of the object affected by the action
OBJ_NAME	VARCHAR2(128)		Name of object affected by the action
ACTION_NAME	VARCHAR2(27)		Name of the action type corresponding to the numeric code in the ACTION column in DBA_AUDIT_TRAIL
NEW_NAME	VARCHAR2(128)		New name of an object after a RENAME or the name of the underlying object
OBJ_PRIVILEGE	VARCHAR2(16)		Object privileges granted or revoked by a GRANT or REVOKE statement
SYS_PRIVILEGE	VARCHAR2(40)		System privileges granted or revoked by a GRANT or REVOKE statement
ADMIN_OPTION	VARCHAR2(1)		Signifies the role or system privilege was granted with ADMIN option
GRANTEE	VARCHAR2(30)		Name of grantee specified in a GRANT or REVOKE statement

Column	Datatype	NULL	Description
AUDIT_OPTION	VARCHAR2(40)		Auditing option set with the AUDIT statement
SES_ACTIONS	VARCHAR2(19)		Session summary (a string of 16 characters, one for each action type in the order ALTER, AUDIT, COMMENT, DELETE, GRANT, INDEX, INSERT, LOCK, RENAME, SELECT, UPDATE, REFERENCES, and EXECUTE. Positions 14, 15, and 16 are reserved for future use. The characters are: - for none, S for success, F for failure, and B for both)
COMMENT_TEXT	VARCHAR2(4000)		Text comment on the audit trail, inserted by the application
SESSIONID	NUMBER	NOT NULL	Numeric ID for each Oracle session
ENTRYID	NUMBER	NOT NULL	Numeric ID for each audit trail entry in the session
STATEMENTID	NUMBER	NOT NULL	Numeric ID for each statement run
RETURNCODE	NUMBER	NOT NULL	Oracle Server message code generated by the action. Some useful values: • zero: the action succeeded • 2004: security violation
PRIV_USED	VARCHAR2(40)		System privilege used to execute the action
SESSION_LABEL	MLSLABEL		Label associated with the session. Applies to Trusted Oracle Server only.

DBA_AUDIT_TRAIL

This view lists all audit trail entries.

Column	Datatype	NULL	Description
OS_USERNAME	VARCHAR2(255)		Operating system login username of the user whose actions were audited
USERNAME	VARCHAR2(30)		Name (not ID number) of the user whose actions were audited
USERHOST	VARCHAR2(2000)		Numeric instance ID for the Oracle instance from which the user is accessing the database
TERMINAL	VARCHAR2(2000)		Identifier of the user's terminal
TIMESTAMP	DATE	NOT NULL	Timestamp for the creation of the audit trail entry or login time for the CONNECT statement
OWNER	VARCHAR2(30)		Creator of the object affected by the action
OBJ_NAME	VARCHAR2(128)		Name of the object affected by the action
ACTION	NUMBER	NOT NULL	Numeric type code corresponding to the action
ACTION_NAME	VARCHAR2(27)		Name of the action type corresponding to the numeric code in the ACTION column
NEW_OWNER	VARCHAR2(30)		Owner of the object named in the NEW_NAME column

Column	Datatype	NULL	Description
NEW_NAME	VARCHAR2(128)		New name of an object after a RENAME or the name of the underlying object
OBJ_PRIVILEGE	VARCHAR2(16)		Object privileges granted or revoked by a GRANT or REVOKE statement
SYS_PRIVILEGE	VARCHAR2(40)		System privileges granted or revoked by a GRANT or REVOKE statement
ADMIN_OPTION	VARCHAR2(1)		Signifies the role or system privilege was granted with ADMIN option
GRANTEE	VARCHAR2(30)		Name of grantee specified in a GRANT or REVOKE statement
AUDIT_OPTION	VARCHAR2(40)		Auditing option set with the AUDIT statement
SES_ACTIONS	VARCHAR2(19)		Session summary (a string of 16 characters, one for each action type in the order ALTER, AUDIT, COMMENT, DELETE, GRANT, INDEX, INSERT, LOCK, RENAME, SELECT, UPDATE, REFERENCES, and EXECUTE. Positions 14, 15, and 16 are reserved for future use. The characters are: - for none, S for success, F for failure, and B for both)
LOGOFF_TIME	DATE		Timestamp for user log off
LOGOFF_LREAD	NUMBER		Logical reads for the session
LOGOFF_PREAD	NUMBER		Physical reads for the session
LOGOFF_LWRITE	NUMBER		Logical writes for the session
LOGOFF_DLOCK	VARCHAR2(40)		Deadlocks detected during the session
COMMENT_TEXT	VARCHAR2(4000)		Text comment on the audit trail entry, providing more information about the statement audited
SESSIONID	NUMBER	NOT NULL	Numeric ID for each Oracle session
ENTRYID	NUMBER	NOT NULL	Numeric ID for each audit trail entry in the session
STATEMENTID	NUMBER	NOT NULL	Numeric ID for each statement run
RETURNCODE	NUMBER	NOT NULL	Oracle Server message code generated by the action. Some useful values: • zero: the action succeeded • 2004: security violation
PRIV_USED	VARCHAR2(40)		System privilege used to execute the action
OBJECT_LABEL	MLSLABEL		Label associated with the object being audited. Applies to Trusted Oracle Server only.
SESSION_LABEL	MLSLABEL		Label associated with the session. Applies to Trusted Oracle Server only.

DBA_BLOCKERS

This view lists all sessions that have someone waiting on a lock they hold that are not themselves waiting on a lock.

Column	Datatype	NULL	Description
HOLDING_SESSION	NUMBER		Session holding a lock

DBA_CATALOG

This view lists all database tables, views, synonyms, and sequences.

Column	Datatype	NULL	Description
OWNER	VARCHAR2(30)	NOT NULL	Owner of the object
TABLE_NAME	VARCHAR2(30)	NOT NULL	Name of the object
TABLE_TYPE	VARCHAR2(11)		Type of the object

DBA_CLU_COLUMNS

This view lists mappings of table columns to cluster columns.

Column	Datatype	NULL	Description
OWNER	VARCHAR2(30)	NOT NULL	Owner of the cluster
CLUSTER_NAME	VARCHAR2(30)	NOT NULL	Cluster name
CLU_COLUMN_NAME	VARCHAR2(30)	NOT NULL	Key column in the cluster
TABLE_NAME	VARCHAR2(30)	NOT NULL	Clustered table name
TAB_COLUMN_NAME	VARCHAR2(4000)		Key column or attribute of the object type column

DBA_CLUSTERS

This view contains description of all clusters in the database.

Column	Datatype	NULL	Description
OWNER	VARCHAR2(30)	NOT NULL	Owner of the cluster
CLUSTER_NAME	VARCHAR2(30)	NOT NULL	Name of the tablespace containing the cluster
TABLESPACE_NAME	VARCHAR2(30)	NOT NULL	Name of the tablespace containing the cluster
PCT_FREE	NUMBER		Minimum percentage of free space in a block
PCT_USED	NUMBER	NOT NULL	Minimum percentage of used space in a block
KEY_SIZE	NUMBER		Estimated size of cluster key plus associated rows

Column	Datatype	NULL	Description
INI_TRANS	NUMBER	NOT NULL	Initial number of transactions
MAX_TRANS	NUMBER	NOT NULL	Maximum number of transactions
INITIAL_EXTENT	NUMBER		Size of the initial extent in bytes
NEXT_EXTENT	NUMBER		Size of secondary extents in bytes
MIN_EXTENTS	NUMBER	NOT NULL	Minimum number of extents allowed in the segment
MAX_EXTENTS	NUMBER	NOT NULL	Maximum number of extents allowed in the segment
PCT_INCREASE	NUMBER	NOT NULL	Percentage increase in extent size
FREELIST_GROUPS	NUMBER		Number of freelist groups allocated to this segment
AVG_BLOCKS_PER_KEY	NUMBER		Average number of blocks containing rows with a given cluster key
CLUSTER_TYPE	VARCHAR2(5)		Type of cluster: B-Tree index or hash
FUNCTION	VARCHAR2(15)		If a hash cluster, the hash function
HASHKEYS	NUMBER		If a hash cluster, the number of hash keys (hash buckets)
DEGREE	VARCHAR2(10)		The number of threads per instance for scanning the table
INSTANCES	VARCHAR2(10)		The number of instances across which the table is to be scanned
CACHE	VARCHAR2(5)		Whether the table is to be cached in the buffer cache
BUFFER_POOL	VARCHAR2(7)		Name of the default buffer pool for the appropriate object

DBA_COL_COMMENTS

This view lists comments on columns of all tables and views.

Column	Datatype	NULL	Description
OWNER	VARCHAR2(30)	NOT NULL	Name of the owner of the object
TABLE_NAME	VARCHAR2(30)	NOT NULL	Name of the object
COLUMN_NAME	VARCHAR2(30)	NOT NULL	Name of the column
COMMENTS	VARCHAR2(4000)		Comment on the object

DBA_COL_PRIVS

This view lists all grants on columns in the database.

Column	Datatype	NULL	Description
GRANTEE	VARCHAR2(30)	NOT NULL	Name of the user to whom access was granted
OWNER	VARCHAR2(30)	NOT NULL	Username of the owner of the object
TABLE_NAME	VARCHAR2(30)	NOT NULL	Name of the object
COLUMN_NAME	VARCHAR2(30)	NOT NULL	Name of the column
GRANTOR	VARCHAR2(30)	NOT NULL	Name of the user who performed the grant
PRIVILEGE	VARCHAR2(40)	NOT NULL	Column privilege
GRANTABLE	VARCHAR2(3)		Privilege is Grantable

DBA_COLL_TYPES

This view displays all named collection types in the database such as VARRAYs, nested tables, object tables, and so on.

Column	Datatype	NULL	Description
OWNER	VARCHAR2(30)	NOT NULL	Owner of the type
TYPE_NAME	VARCHAR2(30)	NOT NULL	Name of the type
COLL_TYPE	VARCHAR2(30)	NOT NULL	Collection type
UPPER_BOUND	NUMBER		Maximum size of the VARRAY type
ELEM_TYPE_MOD	VARCHAR2(7)		Type modifier of the element
ELEM_TYPE_OWNER	VARCHAR2(30)		Owner of the type of the element
ELEM_TYPE_NAME	VARCHAR2(30)		Name of the type of the element
LENGTH	NUMBER		Length of the CHAR element or maximum length of the VARCHAR or VARCHAR2 element
PRECISION	NUMBER		Decimal precision of the NUMBER or DECIMAL element or binary precision of the FLOAT element
SCALE	NUMBER		Scale of the NUMBER or DECIMAL element
CHARACTER_SET_NAME	VARCHAR2(44)		The name of the character set: CHAR_CS NCHAR_CS

DBA_CONSTRAINTS

This view contains constraint definitions on all tables.

Column	Datatype	NULL	Description
OWNER	VARCHAR2(30)	NOT NULL	Owner of the table
CONSTRAINT_NAME	VARCHAR2(30)	NOT NULL	Name associated with constraint definition
CONSTRAINT_TYPE	VARCHAR2(1)		Type of constraint definition: C (check constraint on a table) P (primary key) U (unique key) R (referential integrity) V (with check option on a view) O (with read only, on a view)
TABLE_NAME	VARCHAR2(30)	NOT NULL	Name associated with table with constraint definition
SEARCH_CONDITION	LONG		Text of search condition for table check
R_OWNER	VARCHAR2(30)		Owner of table used in referential constraint
R_CONSTRAINT_NAME	VARCHAR2(30)		Owner of table used in referential constraint
DELETE_RULE	VARCHAR2(9)		The delete rule for a referential constraint
STATUS	VARCHAR2(8)		Enforcement status of constraint: ENABLED or DISABLED
DEFERRABLE	VARCHAR2(14)		Indicates whether the constraint is deferrable
DEFERRED	VARCHAR2(9)		Indicates whether the constraint was initially deferred
GENERATED	VARCHAR2(14)		Indicates whether the name system is generated
LAST_CHANGE	DATE		Indicates when the constraint was last enabled or disabled
BAD	VARCHAR2(3)		Creating this constraint should give ORA-02436. Rewrite it before 2000 AD.
VALIDATED	VARCHAR2(13)		Indicates whether all data obeys the constraint: VALIDATED, NOT VALIDATED

DBA_CONS_COLUMNS

This view contains information about accessible columns in constraint definitions.

Column	Datatype	NULL	Description
OWNER	VARCHAR2(30)	NOT NULL	Owner of the constraint definition
CONSTRAINT_NAME	VARCHAR2(30)	NOT NULL	Name associated with the constraint definition
TABLE_NAME	VARCHAR2(30)	NOT NULL	Name associated with table with constraint definition
COLUMN_NAME	VARCHAR2(4000)		Name associated with column or attribute of the object type column specified in the constraint definition
POSITION	NUMBER		Original position of column or attribute in definition

DBA_DATA_FILES

This view contains information about database files.

Column	Datatype	NULL	Description
FILE_NAME	VARCHAR2(513)		Name of the database file
FILE_ID	NUMBER	NOT NULL	ID of the database file
TABLESPACE_NAME	VARCHAR2(30)	NOT NULL	Name of the tablespace to which the file belongs
BYTES	NUMBER		Size of the file in bytes
BLOCKS	NUMBER	NOT NULL	Size of the file in Oracle blocks
STATUS	VARCHAR2(9)		File status: AVAILABLE or INVALID (INVALID means that the file number is not in use, for example, a file in a tablespace that was dropped)
RELATIVE_FNO	NUMBER		Relative file number
AUTOEXTENSIBLE	VARCHAR2(3)		Autoextensible indicator
MAXBYTES	NUMBER		Maximum file size in bytes
MAXBLOCKS	NUMBER		Maximum file size in blocks
INCREMENT_BY	NUMBER		Autoextension increment

DBA_DB_LINKS

This view lists all database links in the database.

Column	Datatype	NULL	Description
OWNER	VARCHAR2(30)	NOT NULL	Owner of the database link
DB_LINK	VARCHAR2(128)	NOT NULL	Name of the database link
USERNAME	VARCHAR2(3)		Name of user to log in as

Column	Datatype	NULL	Description
HOST	VARCHAR2(2000)		Connect string
CREATED	DATE	NOT NULL	Creation time of the database link

DBA_DDL_LOCKS

This view lists all DDL locks held in the database and all outstanding requests for a DDL lock.

Column	Datatype	NULL	Description
SESSION_ID	NUMBER		Session identifier
OWNER	VARCHAR2(30)		Owner of the lock
NAME	VARCHAR2(30)		Name of the lock
TYPE	VARCHAR2(40)		Lock type: CURSOR, TABLE/PROCEDURE/ TYPE, BODY, TRIGGER, INDEX, CLUSTER
MODE_HELD	VARCHAR2(9)		Lock mode: NONE, NULL, SHARE, EXCLUSIVE
MODE_REQUESTED	VARCHAR2(9)		Lock request type: NONE, NULL, SHARE, EXCLUSIVE

DBA_DEPENDENCIES

This view lists dependencies to and from objects.

Column	Datatype	NULL	Description
OWNER	VARCHAR2(30)	NOT NULL	Owner of the object
NAME	VARCHAR2(3)	NOT NULL	Name of the object
TYPE	VARCHAR2(12)		Type of the object
REFERENCED_OWNER	VARCHAR2(30)		Owner of referenced object (remote owner if remote object)
REFERENCED_NAME	VARCHAR2(64)		Name of referenced object
REFERENCED_TYPE	VARCHAR2(12)		Type of referenced object
REFERENCED_LINK _NAME	VARCHAR2(128)		Name of dblink if this is a remote object
DEPENDENCY_TYPE	VARCHAR2(4)		Two values: REF when the dependency is a REF dependency; HARD otherwise

DBA_DIRECTORIES

This view provides information on all directory objects in the database.

Column	Datatype	NULL	Description
OWNER	VARCHAR2(30)	NOT NULL	Owner of the directory (always SYS)
DIRECTORY_NAME	VARCHAR2(30)	NOT NULL	Name of the directory
DIRECTORY_PATH	VARCHAR2(4000)		Operating system pathname for the directory

DBA_DML_LOCKS

This view lists all DML locks held in the database and all outstanding requests for a DML lock.

Column	Datatype	NULL	Description
SESSION_ID	NUMBER		Session holding or acquiring the lock
OWNER	VARCHAR2(30)	NOT NULL	Owner of the lock
NAME	VARCHAR2(30)	NOT NULL	Name of the lock
MODE_HELD	VARCHAR2(13)		Lock mode: see Table 2-1: *Lock Modes for the DBA_DML_LOCKS View*
MODE_REQUESTED	VARCHAR2(13)		Lock request type: see Table 2-1: *Lock Modes for the DBA_DML_LOCKS View*
LAST_CONVERT	NUMBER		The last convert
BLOCKING_OTHERS	VARCHAR2(40)		Blocking others

Table 2-1: *Lock Modes for the DBA_DML_LOCKS View* describes DML lock mode values that are valid for the MODE_HELD column.

Table 2-1: Lock Modes for the DBA_DML_LOCKS View

Lock Mode	Description
ROWS-S (SS)	Row share
ROW-X (SX)	Row exclusive
SHARE (S)	Share
S/ROW-X (SSX)	Exclusive
NONE	MODE_HELD: Lock requested, not yet obtained MODE_REQUESTED: Lock identifier obtained, lock not held or requested

DBA_ERRORS

This view lists current errors on all stored objects in the database.

Column	Datatype	NULL	Description
OWNER	VARCHAR2(30)	NOT NULL	The owner of the object
NAME	VARCHAR2(30)	NOT NULL	Name of the object
TYPE	VARCHAR2(12)		Type of object: VIEW, PROCEDURE, FUNCTION, PACKAGE, TYPE, TYPE BODY, PACKAGE BODY, or TRIGGER
SEQUENCE	NUMBER	NOT NULL	Sequence number used for ordering purposes
LINE	NUMBER	NOT NULL	Line number at which this error occurs
POSITION	NUMBER	NOT NULL	Position in the line at which this error occurs
TEXT	VARCHAR2(4000)	NOT NULL	Text of the error

DBA_EXP_FILES

This view contains a description of export files.

Column	Datatype	NULL	Description
EXP_VERSION	NUMBER(3)	NOT NULL	Version number of the export session
EXP_TYPE	VARCHAR2(11)		Type of export file: complete, cumulative, or incremental
FILE_NAME	VARCHAR2(100)	NOT NULL	Name of the export file
USER_NAME	VARCHAR2(30)	NOT NULL	Name of user who executed export
TIMESTAMP	DATE	NOT NULL	Timestamp of the export session

DBA_EXP_OBJECTS

This view lists objects that have been incrementally exported.

Column	Datatype	NULL	Description
OWNER	VARCHAR2(30)	NOT NULL	Owner of exported object
OBJECT_NAME	VARCHAR2(30)	NOT NULL	Name of exported object
OBJECT_TYPE	VARCHAR2(12)		Type of exported object
CUMULATIVE	DATE		Timestamp of last cumulative export
INCREMENTAL	DATE	NOT NULL	Timestamp of last incremental export
EXPORT_VERSION	NUMBER(3)	NOT NULL	The ID of the export session

DBA_EXP_VERSION

This view contains the version number of the last export session.

Column	Datatypes	NULL	Description
EXP_VERSION	NUMBER(3)	NOT NULL	Version number of the last export session

DBA_EXTENTS

This view lists the extents comprising all segments in the database.

Column	Datatype	NULL	Description
OWNER	VARCHAR2(30)		Owner of the segment associated with the extent
SEGMENT_NAME	VARCHAR2(81)		Name of the segment associated with the extent
SEGMENT_TYPE	VARCHAR2(17)		Type of the segment: INDEX PARTITION, TABLE PARTITION
TABLESPACE_NAME	VARCHAR2(30)		Name of the tablespace containing the extent
EXTENT_ID	NUMBER	NOT NULL	Extent number in the segment
FILE_ID	NUMBER	NOT NULL	Name of the file containing the extent
BLOCK_ID	NUMBER	NOT NULL	Starting block number of the extent
BYTES	NUMBER		Size of the extent in bytes
BLOCKS	NUMBER	NOT NULL	Size of the extent in Oracle blocks
RELATIVE_FNO	NUMBER	NOT NULL	Relative file number of the first extent block
PARTITION_NAME	VARCHAR2(30)		Object Partition Name (Set to NULL for non-partitioned objects).

DBA_FREE_SPACE

This view lists the free extents in all tablespaces.

Column	Datatype	NULL	Description
TABLESPACE_NAME	VARCHAR2(30)	NOT NULL	Name of the tablespace containing the extent
FILE_ID	NUMBER	NOT NULL	ID number of the file containing the extent
BLOCK_ID	NUMBER	NOT NULL	Starting block number of the extent
BYTES	NUMBER		Size of the extent in bytes
BLOCKS	NUMBER	NOT NULL	Size of the extent in Oracle blocks
RELATIVE_FNO	NUMBER	NOT NULL	Relative file number of the first extent block

DBA_FREE_SPACE_COALESCED

This view contains statistics on coalesced space in tablespaces.

Column	Datatype	NULL	Description
TABLESPACE_NAME	VARCHAR2(30)	NOT NULL	Name of tablespace
TOTAL_EXTENTS	NUMBER		Total number of free extents in tablespace
EXTENTS_COALESCED	NUMBER		Total number of coalesced free extents in tablespace
PERCENT_EXTENTS _COALESCED	NUMBER		Percentage of coalesced free extents in tablespace
TOTAL_BYTES	NUMBER		Total number of free bytes in tablespace
BYTES_COALESCED	NUMBER		Total number of coalesced free bytes in tablespace
TOTAL_BLOCKS	NUMBER		Total number of free Oracle blocks in tablespace
BLOCKS_COALESCED	NUMBER		Total number of coalesced free Oracle blocks in tablespace
PERCENT_BLOCKS _COALESCED	NUMBER		Percentage of coalesced free Oracle blocks in tablespace

DBA_INDEXES

This view contains descriptions for all indexes in the database. To gather statistics for this view, use the SQL command ANALYZE. This view supports parallel partitioned index scans.

Column	Datatype	NULL	Description
OWNER	VARCHAR2(30)	NOT NULL	Username of the owner of the index
INDEX_NAME	VARCHAR2(30)	NOT NULL	Name of the index
INDEX_TYPE	VARCHAR2(12)		Type of index
TABLE_OWNER	VARCHAR2(30)		Owner of the indexed object
TABLE_NAME	VARCHAR2(30)	NOT NULL	Name of the indexed object
TABLE_TYPE	VARCHAR2(11)	NOT NULL	Type of the indexed object
UNIQUENESS	VARCHAR2(9)		Uniqueness status of the index: UNIQUE or NONUNIQUE
TABLESPACE_NAME	VARCHAR2(30)		Name of the tablespace containing the index
INI_TRANS	NUMBER		Initial number of transactions
MAX_TRANS	NUMBER		Maximum number of transactions
INITIAL_EXTENT	NUMBER		Size of initial extent
NEXT_EXTENT	NUMBER		Size of secondary extents
MIN_EXTENTS	NUMBER		Minimum number of extents allowed in the segment

Column	Datatype	NULL	Description
MAX_EXTENTS	NUMBER		Maximum number of extents allowed in the segment
PCT_INCREASE	NUMBER		Percentage increase in extent size
PCT_THRESHOLD	NUMBER		Threshold percentage of block space allowed per index entry
INCLUDE_COLUMN	NUMBER		User column-id for last column to be included in index organized table top index
FREELISTS	NUMBER		Number of process freelists allocated to this segment
FREELIST_GROUPS	NUMBER		Number of freelist groups allocated to this segment
PCT_FREE	NUMBER		Minimum percentage of free space in a block
LOGGING	VARCHAR2(3)		Logging attribute
BLEVEL	NUMBER		B-Tree level: depth of the index from its root block to its leaf blocks. A depth of 0 indicates that the root block and leaf block are the same.
LEAF_BLOCKS	NUMBER		The number of leaf blocks in the index
DISTINCT_KEYS	NUMBER		The number of distinct keys in the index
AVG_LEAF_BLOCKS _PER_KEY	NUMBER		The average number of leaf blocks per key
AVG_DATA_BLOCKS _PER_KEY	NUMBER		The average number of data blocks per key
CLUSTERING_FACTOR	NUMBER		A measurement of the amount of (dis)order of the table this index is for
STATUS	VARCHAR2(8)		Whether index is in Direct Load State
NUM_ROWS	NUMBER		Number of rows in this index
SAMPLE_SIZE	NUMBER		Size of the sample used to analyze this index
LAST_ANALYZED	DATE		Timestamp for when this index was last analyzed
DEGREE	VARCHAR2(40)		Number of threads per instance for scanning the index. NULL if PARTITIONED=NO.
INSTANCES	VARCHAR2(40)		Number of instances across which the indexes are to be scanned. NULL if PARTITIONED=NO.
PARTITIONED	VARCHAR2(3)		Indicates whether this index is partitioned. Set to YES if it is partitioned
TEMPORARY	VARCHAR2(1)		Can the current session only see data that it place in this object itself?
GENERATED	VARCHAR2(1)		Was the name of this index system generated?
BUFFER_POOL	VARCHAR2(7)		Name of the default buffer pool for the appropriate object

DBA_IND_COLUMNS

This view contains descriptions of the columns comprising the indexes on all tables and clusters.

Column	Datatype	NULL	Description
INDEX_OWNER	VARCHAR2(30)	NOT NULL	Index owner
INDEX_NAME	VARCHAR2(30)	NOT NULL	Index name
TABLE_OWNER	VARCHAR2(30)	NOT NULL	Table or cluster owner
TABLE_NAME	VARCHAR2(30)	NOT NULL	Table or cluster name
COLUMN_NAME	VARCHAR2(4000)		Column name or attribute of the object type column
COLUMN_POSITION	NUMBER	NOT NULL	Position of column or attribute within index
COLUMN_LENGTH	NUMBER	NOT NULL	Indexed length of the column or attribute

DBA_IND_PARTITIONS

This view describes, for each index partition, the partition level partitioning information, the storage parameters for the partition, and various partition statistics determined by ANALYZE.

Column	Datatype	NULL	Description
INDEX_OWNER	VARCHAR2(30)	NOT NULL	Index owner
INDEX_NAME	VARCHAR2(30)	NOT NULL	Index name
PARTITION_NAME	VARCHAR2(30)		Partition name
HIGH_VALUE	LONG		Partition bound value expression
HIGH_VALUE_LENGTH	NUMBER	NOT NULL	Length of partition bound value expression
PARTITION_POSITION	NUMBER	NOT NULL	Position of the partition within the index
STATUS	VARCHAR2(8)		Indicates whether index partition is usable or not
TABLESPACE_NAME	VARCHAR2(30)	NOT NULL	Name of the tablespace containing the partition
PCT_FREE	NUMBER	NOT NULL	Minimum percentage of free space in a block
INI_TRANS	NUMBER	NOT NULL	Initial number of transactions
MAX_TRANS	NUMBER	NOT NULL	Maximum number of transactions
INITIAL_EXTENT	NUMBER		Size of the initial extent in bytes
NEXT_EXTENT	NUMBER		Size of secondary extents in bytes
MIN_EXTENT	NUMBER	NOT NULL	Minimum number of extents allowed in the segment
MAX_EXTENT	NUMBER	NOT NULL	Maximum number of extents allowed in the segment

Column	Datatype	NULL	Description
PCT_INCREASE	NUMBER	NOT NULL	Percentage increase in extent size
FREELISTS	NUMBER		Number of process freelists allocated in this segment
LOGGING	VARCHAR2(3)		Logging attribute of partition
BLEVEL	NUMBER		B-Tree level
LEAF_BLOCKS	NUMBER		Number of leaf blocks in the index partition
DISTINCT_KEYS	NUMBER		Number of distinct keys in the index partition
AVG_LEAF_BLOCKS _PER_KEY	NUMBER		Average number of leaf blocks per key
AVG_DATA_BLOCKS _PER_KEY	NUMBER		Average number of data blocks per key
CLUSTERING_FACTOR	NUMBER		Measurement of the amount of (dis)order of the table this index partition is for
NUM_ROWS	NUMBER		Number of rows in this index partition
SAMPLE_SIZE	NUMBER		Sample size used in analyzing this partition
LAST_ANALYZED	DATE		Date of the most recent time this partition was analyzed
BUFFER_POOL	VARCHAR2(7)		The buffer pool for this partition

DBA_JOBS

This view lists all jobs in the database.

Column	Datatype	NULL	Description
JOB	NUMBER	NOT NULL	Identifier of job. Neither import/export nor repeated executions change it.
LOG_USER	VARCHAR2(30)	NOT NULL	USER who was logged in when the job was submitted
PRIV_USER	VARCHAR2(30)	NOT NULL	USER whose default privileges apply to this job
SCHEMA_USER	VARCHAR2(30)	NOT NULL	Default schema used to parse the job For example, if the SCHEMA_USER is SCOTT and you submit the procedure HIRE_EMP as a job, Oracle looks for SCOTT.HIRE_EMP.
LAST_DATE	DATE		Date that this job last successfully executed
LAST_SEC	VARCHAR2(8)		Same as LAST_DATE. This is when the last successful execution started.
THIS_DATE	DATE		Date that this job started executing (usually NULL if not executing)
THIS_SEC	VARCHAR2(8)		Same as THIS_DATE. This is when the last successful execution started.
NEXT_DATE	DATE	NOT NULL	Date that this job will next be executed

Column	Datatype	NULL	Description
NEXT_SEC	VARCHAR2(8))		Same as NEXT_DATE. The job becomes due for execution at this time.
TOTAL_TIME	NUMBER		Total wall clock time spent by the system on this job, in seconds
BROKEN	VARCHAR2(1)		If Y, no attempt is made to run this job.
INTERVAL	VARCHAR2(200)	NOT NULL	A date function, evaluated at the start of execution, becomes next NEXT_DATE
FAILURES	NUMBER		How many times has this job started and failed since its last success?
WHAT	VARCHAR2(4000)		Body of the anonymous PL/SQL block that this job executes
CURRENT_SESSION_LABEL	MLSLABEL		Trusted Oracle Server label of the current session as seen by the job. Applies to Trusted Oracle Server only.
CLEARANCE_HI	MLSLABEL		Highest level of clearance available to the job. Applies to Trusted Oracle Server only.
CLEARANCE_LO	MLSLABEL		Lowest level of clearance available to the job. Applies to Trusted Oracle Server only.
NLS_ENV	VARCHAR2(4000)		ALTER SESSION parameters describing the NLS environment of the job
MISC_ENV	RAW(32)		Other session parameters that apply to this job

DBA_JOBS_RUNNING

This view lists all jobs in the database that are currently running.

Column	Datatype	NULL	Description
SID	NUMBER		Identifier of process that is executing the job. See "V$LOCK" on page 3-51.
JOB	NUMBER		Identifier of job. This job is currently executing.
FAILURES	NUMBER		Number of times this job started and failed since its last success
LAST_DATE	DATE		Date that this job last successfully executed
LAST_SEC	VARCHAR2(8)		Same as LAST_DATE. This is when the last successful execution started.
THIS_DATE	DATE		Date that this job started executing (usually null if not executing)
THIS_SEC	VARCHAR2(8)		Same as THIS_DATE. This is when the last successful execution started.

DBA_LIBRARIES

This view lists all the libraries in the database.

Column	Datatype	NULL	Description
OWNER	VARCHAR2(30)	NOT NULL	Owner of the library
LIBRARY_NAME	VARCHAR2(30)	NOT NULL	Library name
FILE_SPEC	VARCHAR2(2000)		Operating system file specification associated with the library
DYNAMIC	VARCHAR2(1)		Is the library dynamically loadable? (YES or NO)
STATUS	VARCHAR2(7)		Status of the library

DBA_LOBS

This view displays the LOBs contained in all tables.

Column	Datatype	NULL	Description
OWNER	VARCHAR2(30)	NOT NULL	Owner of the table containing the LOB
TABLE_NAME	VARCHAR2(30)	NOT NULL	Name of the table containing the LOB
COLUMN_NAME	VARCHAR2(30)		Name of the LOB column or attribute
SEGMENT_NAME	VARCHAR2(30)	NOT NULL	Name of the LOB segment
INDEX_NAME	VARCHAR2(30)	NOT NULL	Name of the LOB index
CHUNK	NUMBER		Size of the LOB chunk as a unit of allocation/manipulation in bytes
PCTVERSION	NUMBER	NOT NULL	Maximum percentage of the LOB space used for versioning
CACHE	VARCHAR2(3)		Indicates whether the LOB is accessed through the buffer cache
LOGGING	VARCHAR2(3)		Indicates whether the changes to the LOB are logged
IN_ROW	VARCHAR2(3)		Are some of the LOBs stored with the base row?

DBA_LOCKS

This view lists all locks or latches held in the database, and all outstanding requests for a lock or latch.

Column	Datatype	NULL	Description
SESSION_ID	NUMBER		Session holding or acquiring the lock
LOCK_TYPE	VARCHAR2(26)		Lock type
MODE HELD	VARCHAR2(40)		Lock mode

Column	Datatype	NULL	Description
MODE REQUESTED	VARCHAR2(40)		Lock mode requested
LOCK_ID1	VARCHAR2(40)		Type-specific lock identifier, part 1
LOCK_ID2	VARCHAR2(40)		Type-specific lock identifier, part 2
LAST_CONVERT	NUMBER		The last convert
BLOCKING_OTHERS	VARCHAR2(40)		Blocking others

DBA_METHOD_PARAMS

This view is a description of method parameters of types in the database.

Column	Datatype	NULL	Description
OWNER	VARCHAR2(30)	NOT NULL	Owner of the type
TYPE_NAME	VARCHAR2(30)	NOT NULL	Name of the type
METHOD_NAME	VARCHAR2(30)	NOT NULL	Name of the method
METHOD_NO	NUMBER	NOT NULL	Method number for distinguishing overloaded method (not to be used as ID number)
PARAM_NAME	VARCHAR2(30)	NOT NULL	Name of the parameter
PARAM_NO	NUMBER	NOT NULL	Parameter number or position
PARAM_MODE	VARCHAR2(6)		Mode of the parameter
PARAM_TYPE_MOD	VARCHAR2(7)		Type modifier of the parameter
PARAM_TYPE_OWNER	VARCHAR2(30)		Owner of the type of the parameter
PARAM_TYPE_NAME	VARCHAR2(30)		Name of the type of the parameter
CHARACTER_SET_NAME	VARCHAR2(44)		The name of the character set: CHAR_CS NCHAR_CS

DBA_METHOD_RESULTS

This view is a description of method results of all types in the database.

Column	Datatype	NULL	Description
OWNER	VARCHAR2(30)	NOT NULL	Owner of the type
TYPE_NAME	VARCHAR2(30)	NOT NULL	Name of the type
METHOD_NAME	VARCHAR2(30)	NOT NULL	Name of the method
METHOD_NO	NUMBER	NOT NULL	The method number
RESULT_TYPE_MOD	VARCHAR2(7)		Type modifier of the result
RESULT_TYPE_OWNER	VARCHAR2(30)		Owner of the type of the result
RESULT_TYPE_NAME	VARCHAR2(30)		Name of the type of the result

Column	Datatype	NULL	Description
CHARACTER_SET_NAME	VARCHAR2(44)		The name of the character set: CHAR_CS, NCHAR_CS

DBA_NESTED_TABLES

This view displays descriptions of the nested tables contained in all tables.

Column	Datatype	NULL	Description
OWNER	VARCHAR2(30)		Owner of the nested table
TABLE_NAME	VARCHAR2(30)		Name of the nested table
TABLE_TYPE_OWNER	VARCHAR2(30)		Owner of the type of which the nested table was created
TABLE_TYPE_NAME	VARCHAR2(30)		Name of the type of the nested table
PARENT_TABLE_NAME	VARCHAR2(30)		Name of the parent table containing the nested table
PARENT_TABLE_COLUMN	VARCHAR2(4000)		Column name of the parent table that corresponds to the nested table

DBA_OBJECT_SIZE

This view lists the sizes, in bytes, of various PL/SQL objects.

Column	Datatype	NULL	Description
OWNER	VARCHAR2(30)	NOT NULL	Owner of the object
NAME	VARCHAR2(30)	NOT NULL	Name of the object
TYPE	VARCHAR2(12)		Type of the object: TABLE, VIEW, SYNONYM, SEQUENCE, PROCEDURE, FUNCTION, PACKAGE, or PACKAGE BODY
SOURCE_SIZE	NUMBER		Size of the source in bytes
PARSED_SIZE	NUMBER		Size of the parsed form of the object in bytes
CODE_SIZE	NUMBER		Code size in bytes
ERROR_SIZE	NUMBER		Size of error messages in bytes

DBA_OBJECT_TABLES

This view displays descriptions of all object tables in the database.

Column	Datatype	NULL	Description
OWNER	VARCHAR2(30)	NOT NULL	Owner of the table
TABLE_NAME	VARCHAR2(30)	NOT NULL	Name of the table
TABLESPACE_NAME	VARCHAR2(30)	NOT NULL	Name of the tablespace containing the table
CLUSTER_NAME	VARCHAR2(30)		Name of the cluster, if any, to which the table belongs
IOT_NAME	VARCHAR2(30)		Name of the index organized table, if any, to which the overflow entry belongs
PCT_FREE	NUMBER		Minimum percentage of free space in a block
PCT_USED	NUMBER		Minimum percentage of used space in a block
INI_TRANS	NUMBER		Initial number of transactions
MAX_TRANS	NUMBER		Maximum number of transactions
INITIAL_EXTENT	NUMBER		Size of the initial extent in bytes
NEXT_EXTENT	NUMBER		Size of secondary extents in bytes
MIN_EXTENTS	NUMBER		Minimum number of extents allowed in the segment
MAX_EXTENTS	NUMBER		Maximum number of extents allowed in the segment
PCT_INCREASE	NUMBER		Percentage increase in extent size
FREELISTS	NUMBER		Number of process freelists allocated in this segment
FREELIST_GROUPS	NUMBER		Number of freelist groups allocated in this segment
LOGGING	VARCHAR2(3)		Logging attribute
BACKED_UP	VARCHAR2(1)		Has table been backed up since last modification?
NUM_ROWS	NUMBER		The number of rows in the table
BLOCKS	NUMBER		The number of used blocks in the table
EMPTY_BLOCKS	NUMBER		The number of empty (never used) blocks in the table
AVG_SPACE	NUMBER		The average available free space in the table

Column	Datatype	NULL	Description
CHAIN_CNT	NUMBER		The number of chained rows in the table
AVG_ROW_LEN	NUMBER		The average row length, including row overhead
AVG_SPACE_FREELIST _BLOCKS	NUMBER		The average freespace of all blocks on a freelist
NUM_FREELIST_BLOCKS	NUMBER		The number of blocks on the freelist
DEGREE	VARCHAR2(10)		The number of threads per instance for scanning the table
INSTANCES	VARCHAR2(10)		The number of instances across which the table is to be scanned
CACHE	VARCHAR2(5)		Whether the table is to be cached in the buffer cache
TABLE_LOCK	VARCHAR2(8)		Whether table locking is enabled or disabled
SAMPLE_SIZE	NUMBER		The sample size used in analyzing this table
LAST_ANALYZED	DATE		The date of the most recent time this table was analyzed
PARTITIONED	VARCHAR2(3)		Is this table partitioned? YES or NO
IOT_TYPE	VARCHAR2(12)		If an index organized table, then IOT_TYPE is IOT or IOT_OVERFLOW else NULL
TABLE_TYPE_OWNER	VARCHAR2(30)	NOT NULL	Owner of the type of the table if the table is a typed table
TABLE_TYPE	VARCHAR2(30)	NOT NULL	Type of the table if the table is a typed table
TEMPORARY	VARCHAR2(1)		Can the current session only see data that it place in this object itself?
NESTED	VARCHAR2(3)		Is the table a nested table?
BUFFER_POOL	VARCHAR2(7)		The default buffer pool to be used for table blocks

DBA_OBJECTS

This view lists all objects in the database.

Column	Datatype	NULL	Description
OWNER	VARCHAR2(30)		Username of the owner of the object
OBJECT_NAME	VARCHAR2(128)		Name of the object
SUBOBJECT_NAME	VARCHAR2(30)		Name of the sub-object (for example, partition)

Column	Datatype	NULL	Description
OBJECT_ID	NUMBER		Object number of the object
DATA_OBJECT_ID	NUMBER		Object number of the segment which contains the object
OBJECT_TYPE	VARCHAR2(15)		Type and type body of the object: INDEX PARTITION, TABLE PARTITION, PACKAGE, PACKAGE BODY, or TRIGGER
CREATED	DATE		Timestamp for the creation of the object
LAST_DDL_TIME	DATE		Timestamp for the last DDL change (including GRANT and REVOKE) to the object
TIMESTAMP	VARCHAR2(20)		Timestamp for the specification of the object
STATUS	VARCHAR2(7)		Status of the object
TEMPORARY	VARCHAR2(1)		Can the current session only see data that it place in this object itself?
GENERATED	VARCHAR2(1)		Was the name of this object system generated?

DBA_OBJ_AUDIT_OPTS

This view lists auditing options for all tables and views.

Column	Datatype	NULL	Description
OWNER	VARCHAR2(30)		Owner of the object
OBJECT_NAME	VARCHAR2(30)		Name of the object
OBJECT_TYPE	VARCHAR2(9)		Type of the object
ALT	VARCHAR2(3)		Auditing ALTER WHENEVER SUCCESSFUL/UNSUCCESSFUL
AUD	VARCHAR2(3)		Auditing AUDIT WHENEVER SUCCESSFUL/UNSUCCESSFUL
COM	VARCHAR2(3)		Auditing COMMENT WHENEVER SUCCESSFUL/UNSUCCESSFUL
DEL	VARCHAR2(3)		Auditing DELETE WHENEVER SUCCESSFUL/UNSUCCESSFUL
GRA	VARCHAR2(3)		Auditing GRANT WHENEVER SUCCESSFUL/UNSUCCESSFUL
IND	VARCHAR2(3)		Auditing INDEX WHENEVER SUCCESSFUL/UNSUCCESSFUL
INS	VARCHAR2(3)		Auditing INSERT WHENEVER SUCCESSFUL/UNSUCCESSFUL
LOC	VARCHAR2(3)		Auditing LOCK WHENEVER SUCCESSFUL/UNSUCCESSFUL
REN	VARCHAR2(3)		Auditing RENAME WHENEVER SUCCESSFUL/UNSUCCESSFUL
SEL	VARCHAR2(3)		Auditing SELECT WHENEVER SUCCESSFUL/UNSUCCESSFUL
UPD	VARCHAR2(3)		Auditing UPDATE WHENEVER SUCCESSFUL/UNSUCCESSFUL
REF	VARCHAR2(3)		Auditing REFERENCE WHENEVER SUCCESSFUL/UNSUCCESSFUL (not used)
EXE	VARCHAR2(3)		Auditing EXE WHENEVER SUCCESSFUL/UNSUCCESSFUL
CRE	VARCHAR2(3)		Auditing CRE WHENEVER SUCCESSFUL/UNSUCCESSFUL

Column	Datatype	NULL	Description
REA	VARCHAR2(3)		Auditing REA WHENEVER SUCCESSFUL/UNSUCCESSFUL
WRI	VARCHAR2(3)		Auditing WRI WHENEVER SUCCESSFUL/UNSUCCESSFUL

DBA_PART_COL_STATISTICS

This view contains column statistics and histogram information for all table partitions.

Column	Datatype	NULL	Description
OWNER	VARCHAR2(30)	NOT NULL	Owner name
TABLE_NAME	VARCHAR2(30)	NOT NULL	Table name
PARTITION_NAME	VARCHAR2(30)		Table partition name
COLUMN_NAME	VARCHAR2(30)	NOT NULL	Column name
NUM_DISTINCT	NUMBER		Number of distinct values in the column
LOW_VALUE	RAW(32)		Low value in the column
HIGH_VALUE	RAW(32)		High value in the column
DENSITY	NUMBER		Density of the column
NUM_NULLS	NUMBER		Number of nulls in the column
NUM_BUCKETS	NUMBER		Number of buckets in histogram for the column
SAMPLE_SIZE	NUMBER		Sample size used in analyzing this column
LAST_ANALYZED	DATE		Date of the most recent time this column was analyzed

DBA_PART_HISTOGRAMS

This view contains the histogram data (end-points per histogram) for histograms on all table partitions.

Column	Datatype	NULL	Description
OWNER	VARCHAR2(30)		Owner name
TABLE_NAME	VARCHAR2(30)		Table name
PARTITION_NAME	VARCHAR2(30)		Table partition name
COLUMN_NAME	VARCHAR2(30)		Column name
BUCKET_NUMBER	NUMBER		Bucket number
ENDPOINT_VALUE	NUMBER		Normalized endpoint values for this bucket

DBA_PART_INDEXES

This view lists the object level partitioning information for all partitioned indexes.

Column	Datatype	NULL	Description
OWNER	VARCHAR2(30)	NOT NULL	Owner of this partitioned index
INDEX_NAME	VARCHAR2(30)	NOT NULL	Name of this partitioned index
PARTITIONING_TYPE	VARCHAR2(7)		Partitioning algorithm: RANGE
PARTITION_COUNT	NUMBER	NOT NULL	Number of partitions in this index
PARTITIONING_KEY_COUNT	NUMBER	NOT NULL	Number of columns in the partitioning key
LOCALITY	VARCHAR2(6)		Indicates whether this partitioned index is LOCAL or GLOBAL
ALIGNMENT	VARCHAR2(12)		Indicates whether this partitioned index is PREFIXED or NON-PREFIXED
DEF_TABLESPACE_NAME	VARCHAR2(30)		Default TABLESPACE, used for LOCAL index, for ADD/SPLIT TABLE PARTITION
DEF_PCT_FREE	NUMBER	NOT NULL	Default PCTFREE, used for LOCAL index, for ADD TABLE PARTITION
DEF_INI_TRANS	NUMBER	NOT NULL	Default INITRANS, used for LOCAL index, for ADD TABLE PARTITION
DEF_MAX_TRANS	NUMBER	NOT NULL	Default MAXTRANS, used for LOCAL index, for ADD TABLE PARTITION
DEF_INITIAL_EXTENT	NUMBER	NOT NULL	Default INITIAL, used for LOCAL index, for ADD TABLE PARTITION
DEF_NEXT_EXTENT	NUMBER	NOT NULL	Default NEXT, used for LOCAL index, for ADD TABLE PARTITION
DEF_MIN_EXTENTS	NUMBER	NOT NULL	Default MINEXTENTS, used for LOCAL index, for ADD TABLE PARTITION
DEF_MAX_EXTENTS	NUMBER	NOT NULL	Default MAXEXTENTS, used for LOCAL index, for ADD TABLE PARTITION
DEF_PCT_INCREASE	NUMBER	NOT NULL	Default PCTINCREASE, used for LOCAL index, for ADD TABLE PARTITION
DEF_FREELISTS	NUMBER	NOT NULL	Default FREELISTS, used for LOCAL index, for ADD TABLE PARTITION
DEF_LOGGING	VARCHAR2(7)		Default LOGGING, for LOCAL index, for ADD TABLE PARTITION
DEF_BUFFER_POOL	VARCHAR2(7)		Default buffer pool for the index, for ADD TABLE PARTITION

DBA_PART_KEY_COLUMNS

This view describes the partitioning key columns for all partitioned objects.

Column	Datatype	NULL	Description
OWNER	VARCHAR2(30)		Partitioned table or index owner
NAME	VARCHAR2(30)		Partitioned table or index name
COLUMN_NAME	VARCHAR2(30)		Column name
COLUMN_POSITION	NUMBER		Position of the column within the partitioning key

DBA_PART_TABLES

This view lists the object level partitioning information for all the partitioned tables.

Column	Datatype	NULL	Description
OWNER	VARCHAR2(30)	NOT NULL	Owner of this partitioned table
TABLE_NAME	VARCHAR2(30)	NOT NULL	Name of this partitioned table
PARTITIONING_TYPE	VARCHAR2(7)		Partitioning algorithm: RANGE
PARTITION_COUNT	NUMBER	NOT NULL	Number of partitions in this table
PARTITIONING_KEY _COUNT	NUMBER	NOT NULL	Number of columns in the partitioning key
DEF_TABLESPACE _NAME	VARCHAR2(30)	NOT NULL	Default TABLESPACE, used for ADD partition
DEF_PCT_FREE	NUMBER	NOT NULL	Default PCTFREE, used for ADD partition
DEF_PCT_USED	NUMBER	NOT NULL	Default PCTUSED, used for ADD partition
DEF_INI_TRANS	NUMBER	NOT NULL	Default INITRANS, used for ADD partition
DEF_MAX_TRANS	NUMBER	NOT NULL	Default MAXTRANS, used for ADD partition
DEF_INITIAL_EXTENT	NUMBER	NOT NULL	Default INITIAL, used for ADD partition
DEF_NEXT_EXTENT	NUMBER	NOT NULL	Default NEXT, used for ADD partition
DEF_MIN_EXTENTS	NUMBER	NOT NULL	Default MINEXTENTS, used for ADD partition
DEF_MAX_EXTENTS	NUMBER	NOT NULL	Default MAXEXTENTS, used for ADD partition
DEF_PCT_INCREASE	NUMBER	NOT NULL	Default PCTINCREASE, used for ADD partition
DEF_FREELISTS	NUMBER	NOT NULL	Default FREELISTS, used for ADD partition
DEF_FREELIST _GROUPS	NUMBER	NOT NULL	Default FREELIST GROUPS, used for ADD partition
DEF_LOGGING	VARCHAR2(7)		Default LOGGING attribute, used for ADD partition
DEF_BUFFER_POOL	VARCHAR2(7)		Default buffer pool for the given object, used for ADD partition

DBA_PRIV_AUDIT_OPTS

This view describes current system privileges being audited across the system and by user.

Column	Datatype	NULL	Description
USER_NAME	VARCHAR2(30)		User name if by user auditing, else NULL for system-wide auditing
PRIVILEGE	VARCHAR2(40)	NOT NULL	Name of the system privilege being audited
SUCCESS	VARCHAR2(10)		Mode for WHENEVER SUCCESSFUL system auditing
FAILURE	VARCHAR2(10)		Mode for WHENEVER NOT SUCCESSFUL system auditing

DBA_PROFILES

This view displays all profiles and their limits.

Column	Datatype	NULL	Description
PROFILE	VARCHAR2(30)	NOT NULL	Profile name
RESOURCE_NAME	VARCHAR2(32)	NOT NULL	Resource name
RESOURCE_TYPE	VARCHAR2(8)		Indicates whether the resource profile is a KERNEL or a PASSWORD parameter
LIMIT	VARCHAR2(40)		Limit placed on this resource for this profile

DBA_QUEUE_TABLES

This view describes the names and types of the queues in all of the queue tables created in the database. For more information about this view and Advanced Queuing, see the *Oracle8 Server Application Developer's Guide*.

Column	Datatype	NULL	Description
OWNER	VARCHAR2(30)		Schema of the queue table
QUEUE_TABLE	VARCHAR2(30)		Name of the queue table
TYPE	VARCHAR2(7)		Type of user data: RAW: raw type OBJECT: user-defined object type VARIANT: variant type (internal use only)
OBJECT_TYPE	VARCHAR2(61)		Object type of the payload when TYPE is OBJECT
SORT_ORDER	VARCHAR2(22)		User specified sort order
RECIPIENTS	VARCHAR2(8)		SINGLE or MULTIPLE recipients
MESSAGE_GROUPING	VARCHAR2(13)		NONE or TRANSACTIONAL

Column	Datatype	NULL	Description
USER_COMMENT	VARCHAR2(50)		Comment supplied by the user

DBA_QUEUES

This view describes the operational characteristics for every queue in a database. For more information about this view and Advanced Queuing, see the *Oracle8 Server Application Developer's Guide*.

Column	Datatypes	NULL	Description
OWNER	VARCHAR2(30)	NOT NULL	Name of the queue schema
NAME	VARCHAR2(30)	NOT NULL	Name of the queue
QUEUE_TABLE	VARCHAR2(30)	NOT NULL	The name of the queue table where this queue resides
QID	NUMBER	NOT NULL	Unique queue identifier
QUEUE_TYPE	VARCHAR2(15)		Queue type: NORMAL_QUEUE - Normal queue EXCEPTION_QUEUE - Exception queue
MAX_RETRIES	NUMBER		Number of dequeue attempts allowed
RETRY_DELAY	NUMBER		Time lapse in seconds before retry takes place
ENQUEUE_ENABLED	VARCHAR2(7)		YES/NO
DEQUEUE_ENABLED	VARCHAR2(7)		YES/NO
RETENTION	VARCHAR2(40)		Number of seconds message is retained after dequeue FOREVER - messages stay in the queue permanently
USER_COMMENT	VARCHAR2(50)		User comment about the table

DBA_RCHILD

This view lists all the children in any refresh group.

Column	Datatype	NULL	Description
REFGROUP	NUMBER		Internal identifier of refresh group
OWNER	VARCHAR2(30)	NOT NULL	Owner of the object in the refresh group
NAME	VARCHAR2(30)	NOT NULL	Name of the object in the refresh group
TYPE#	VARCHAR2(30)		Type of the object in the refresh group

DBA_REFRESH

This view lists all the refresh groups.

Column	Datatype	NULL	Description
ROWNER	VARCHAR2(30)	NOT NULL	Name of the owner of the refresh group
RNAME	VARCHAR2(30)	NOT NULL	Name of the refresh group
REFGROUP	NUMBER		Internal identifier of refresh group
IMPLICIT_DESTROY	VARCHAR2(1)		Y or N; if Y, then destroy the refresh group when its last item is removed
PUSH_DEFERRED_RPC	VARCHAR2(1)		Y or N; if Y, then push changes from snapshot to master before refresh
REFRESH_AFTER _ERRORS	VARCHAR2(1)		Y or N; if Y, proceed with refresh despite error when pushing deferred RPC's
ROLLBACK_SEG	VARCHAR2(30)		Name of the rollback segment to use while refreshing
JOB	NUMBER		Identifier of job used to refresh the group automatically
NEXT_DATE	DATE		Date that this job will next be refreshed automatically, if not broken
INTERVAL	VARCHAR2(200)		A date function used to compute the next NEXT_DATE
BROKEN	VARCHAR2(1)		Y or N; Y means the job is broken and will never be run
PURGE_OPTION	NUMBER(38)		The method for purging the transaction queue after each push
PARALLELISM	NUMBER(38)		The level of parallelism for transaction propagation
HEAP_SIZE	NUMBER(38)		The size of the heap.

DBA_REFRESH_CHILDREN

This view lists all of the objects in refresh groups.

Column	Datatype	NULL	Description
OWNER	VARCHAR2(30)	NOT NULL	Owner of the object in the refresh group
NAME	VARCHAR2(30)	NOT NULL	Name of the object in the refresh group
TYPE	VARCHAR2(30)		Type of the object in the refresh group
ROWNER	VARCHAR2(30)	NOT NULL	Name of the owner of the refresh group
RNAME	VARCHAR2(30)	NOT NULL	Name of the refresh group
REFGROUP	NUMBER		Internal identifier of refresh group
IMPLICIT_DESTROY	VARCHAR2(1)		Y or N; if Y, then destroy the refresh group when its last item is removed
PUSH_DEFERRED_RPC	VARCHAR2(1)		Y or N; if Y, then push changes from snapshot to master before refresh
REFRESH_AFTER _ERRORS	VARCHAR2(1)		Y or N; if Y, proceed with refresh despite error when pushing deferred RPC's
ROLLBACK_SEG	VARCHAR2(30)		Name of the rollback segment to use while refreshing
JOB	NUMBER		Identifier of job used to refresh the group automatically
NEXT_DATE	DATE		Date that this job will next be refreshed automatically, if not broken
INTERVAL	VARCHAR2(200)		A date function used to compute the next NEXT_DATE
BROKEN	VARCHAR2(1)		Y or N; Y means the job is broken and will never be run
PURGE_OPTION	NUMBER(38)		The method for purging the transaction queue after each push
PARALLELISM	NUMBER(38)		The level of parallelism for transaction propagation
HEAP_SIZE	NUMBER(38)		The size of the heap.

DBA_REFRESH_TIMES

This view is used with Advanced Replication. For more information, see *Oracle8 Server Replication*.

DBA_REFS

This view describes the REF columns and REF attributes in object type columns of all the tables in the database.

Column	Datatype	NULL	Description
OWNER	VARCHAR2(30)	NOT NULL	Name of the owner
TABLE_NAME	VARCHAR2(30)	NOT NULL	Name of the table
COLUMN_NAME	VARCHAR2 (4000)		Name of the REF column or attribute. If it is not a top-level attribute, the value of COLUMN_NAME should be a path name starting with the column name.
WITH_ROWID	VARCHAR2(3)		Is the REF value stored with ROWID? (YES or NO)
IS_SCOPED	VARCHAR2(3)		Is the REF column scoped? (YES or NO)
SCOPE_TABLE _OWNER	VARCHAR2(30)		Name of the owner of the scope table, if it exists
SCOPE_TABLE _NAME	VARCHAR2(30)		Name of the scope table, if it exists

DBA_REGISTERED_SNAPSHOT_GROUPS

This view lists all the snapshot repgroups at this site.

Column	Datatype	NULL	Description
NAME	VARCHAR2(30)	NOT NULL	Name of the snapshot replication group
SNAPSHOT_SITE	VARCHAR2(128)	NOT NULL	Site of the master of the snapshot repgroup
GROUP_COMMENT	VARCHAR2(80)		Description of the snapshot repgroup
VERSION	VARCHAR2(8)		Version of the snapshot repgroup

DBA_REGISTERED_SNAPSHOTS

This view is used to get information about remote snapshots of local tables.

Column	Datatype	NULL	Description
OWNER	VARCHAR2(30)	NOT NULL	Owner of the snapshot
NAME	VARCHAR2(30)	NOT NULL	Name of the snapshot
SNAPSHOT_SITE	VARCHAR2(128)	NOT NULL	Global name of the snapshot site
CAN_USE_LOG	VARCHAR2(3)		If set to NO, this snapshot is complex and cannot fast refresh
UPDATABLE	VARCHAR2(3)		If set to NO, the snapshot is read only
REFRESH_METHOD	VARCHAR2(11)		Indicates whether the snapshot uses ROWIDs or primary key for fast refresh

Column	Datatype	NULL	Description
SNAPSHOT_ID	NUMBER(38)		Identifier for the snapshot used by the master for fast refresh
VERSION	VARCHAR2(17)		Version of snapshot
QUERY_TXT	LONG		Query defining the snapshot

DBA_REPCATLOG

This view is used with Advanced Replication. For more information, see *Oracle8 Server Replication*.

DBA_REPCOLUMN

This view is used with Advanced Replication. For more information, see *Oracle8 Server Replication*.

DBA_REPCOLUMN_GROUP

This view is used with Advanced Replication. For more information, see *Oracle8 Server Replication*.

DBA_REPCONFLICT

This view is used with Advanced Replication. For more information, see *Oracle8 Server Replication*.

DBA_REPDDL

This view is used with Advanced Replication. For more information, see *Oracle8 Server Replication*.

DBA_REPGENERATED

This view is used with Advanced Replication. For more information, see *Oracle8 Server Replication*.

DBA_REPGROUP

This view is used with Advanced Replication. For more information, see *Oracle8 Server Replication*.

DBA_REPGROUPED_COLUMN

This view is used with Advanced Replication. For more information, see *Oracle8 Server Replication*.

DBA_REPKEY_COLUMNS

This view is used with Advanced Replication. For more information, see *Oracle8 Server Replication*.

DBA_REPOBJECT

This view is used with Advanced Replication. For more information, see *Oracle8 Server Replication*.

DBA_REPPARAMETER_COLUMN

This view is used with Advanced Replication. For more information, see *Oracle8 Server Replication*.

DBA_REPPRIORITY

This view is used with Advanced Replication. For more information, see *Oracle8 Server Replication*.

DBA_REPPRIORITY_GROUP

This view is used with Advanced Replication. For more information, see *Oracle8 Server Replication*.

DBA_REPPROP

This view is used with Advanced Replication. For more information, see *Oracle8 Server Replication*.

DBA_REPRESOLUTION

This view is used with Advanced Replication. For more information, see *Oracle8 Server Replication*.

DBA_REPRESOLUTION_METHOD

This view is used with Advanced Replication. For more information, see *Oracle8 Server Replication.*

DBA_REPRESOL_STATS_CONTROL

This view is used with Advanced Replication. For more information, see *Oracle8 Server Replication.*

DBA_REPSITES

This view is used with Advanced Replication. For more information, see *Oracle8 Server Replication.*

DBA_RGROUP

This view lists all refresh groups.

Column	Datatype	NULL	Description
REFGROUP	NUMBER		Internal identifier of refresh group
OWNER	VARCHAR2(30)	NOT NULL	Owner of the object in the refresh group
NAME	VARCHAR2(30)	NOT NULL	Name of the object in the refresh group
IMPLICIT_DESTROY	VARCHAR2(1)		Y or N; if Y, then destroy the refresh group when its last item is removed
PUSH_DEFERRED_RPC	VARCHAR2(1)		Y or N; if Y, then push changes from snapshot to master before refresh
REFRESH_AFTER _ERRORS	VARCHAR2(1)		Y or N; if Y, proceed with refresh despite error when pushing deferred RPC's
ROLLBACK_SEG	VARCHAR2(30)		Name of the rollback segment to use while refreshing
JOB	NUMBER	NOT NULL	Identifier of job used to refresh the group automatically
PURGE_OPTION	NUMBER(38)		The method for purging the transaction queue after each push
PARALLELISM	NUMBER(38)		The level of parallelism for transaction propagation
HEAP_SIZE	NUMBER(38)		The size of the heap.

DBA_ROLES

This view lists all roles that exist in the database.

Column	Datatype	NULL	Description
ROLE	VARCHAR2(30)	NOT NULL	Role name
PASSWORD_REQUIRED	VARCHAR2(8)		Indicates if the role requires a password to be enabled

DBA_ROLE_PRIVS

This view lists roles granted to users and roles.

Column	Datatype	NULL	Description
GRANTEE	VARCHAR2(30)		Grantee name, user or role receiving the grant
GRANTED_ROLE	VARCHAR2(30)	NOT NULL	Granted role name
ADMIN_OPTION	VARCHAR2(3)		Whether the grant was with the ADMIN option: YES/NO
DEFAULT_ROLE	VARCHAR2(3)		Whether the role is designated as a DEFAULT ROLE for the user: YES/NO

DBA_ROLLBACK_SEGS

This view contains descriptions of rollback segments.

Column	Datatype	NULL	Description
SEGMENT_NAME	VARCHAR2(30)	NOT NULL	Name of the rollback segment
OWNER	VARCHAR2(6)		Owner of the rollback segment
TABLESPACE_NAME	VARCHAR2(30)	NOT NULL	Name of the tablespace containing the rollback segment
SEGMENT_ID	NUMBER	NOT NULL	ID number of the rollback segment
FILE_ID	NUMBER	NOT NULL	ID number of the file containing the segment head
BLOCK_ID	NUMBER	NOT NULL	ID number of the block containing the segment header
INITIAL_EXTENT	NUMBER		Initial extent size in bytes
NEXT_EXTENT	NUMBER		Secondary extent size in bytes
MIN_EXTENTS	NUMBER	NOT NULL	Minimum number of extents
MAX_EXTENTS	NUMBER	NOT NULL	Maximum number of extent
PCT_INCREASE	NUMBER	NOT NULL	Percent increase for extent size
STATUS	VARCHAR2(16)		Rollback segment status

Column	Datatype	NULL	Description
INSTANCE_NUM	VARCHAR2(40)		Rollback segment owning parallel server instance number
RELATIVE_FNO	NUMBER	NOT NULL	Relative file number of the segment header

DBA_SEGMENTS

This view contains information about storage allocated for all database segments.

Column	Datatype	NULL	Description
OWNER	VARCHAR2(30)		Username of the segment owner
SEGMENT_NAME	VARCHAR2(81)		Name, if any, of the segment
PARTITION_NAME	VARCHAR2(30)		Object Partition Name (Set to NULL for non-partitioned objects).
SEGMENT_TYPE	VARCHAR2(17)		Type of segment: INDEX PARTITION, TABLE PARTITION, TABLE, CLUSTER, INDEX, ROLLBACK, DEFERRED ROLLBACK, TEMPORARY, or CACHE
TABLESPACE_NAME	VARCHAR2(30)		Name of the tablespace containing the segment
HEADER_FILE	NUMBER		ID of the file containing the segment header
HEADER_BLOCK	NUMBER		ID of the block containing the segment header
BYTES	NUMBER		Size in bytes, of the segment
BLOCKS	NUMBER		Size, in Oracle blocks, of the segment
EXTENTS	NUMBER		Number of extents allocated to the segment
INITIAL_EXTENT	NUMBER		Size in bytes of the initial extent of the segment
NEXT_EXTENT	NUMBER		Size in bytes of the next extent to be allocated to the segment
MIN_EXTENTS	NUMBER		Minimum number of extents allowed in the segment
MAX_EXTENTS	NUMBER		Maximum number of extents allowed in the segment
PCT_INCREASE	NUMBER		Percent by which to increase the size of the next extent to be allocated
FREELISTS	NUMBER		Number of process freelists allocated to this segment
FREELIST_GROUPS	NUMBER		Number of freelist groups allocated to this segment
RELATIVE_FNO	NUMBER		Relative file number of the segment header
BUFFER_POOL	VARCHAR2(7)		Name of the default buffer pool for the appropriate object

DBA_SEQUENCES

This view contains descriptions of all sequences in the database.

Column	Datatype	NULL	Description
SEQUENCE_OWNER	VARCHAR2(30)	NOT NULL	Name of the owner of the sequence
SEQUENCE_NAME	VARCHAR2(30)	NOT NULL	Sequence name
MIN_VALUE	NUMBER		Minimum value of the sequence
MAX_VALUE	NUMBER		Maximum value of the sequence
INCREMENT_BY	NUMBER	NOT NULL	Value by which sequence is incremented
CYCLE_FLAG	VARCHAR2(1)		Does sequence wrap around on reaching limit?
ORDER_FLAG	VARCHAR2(1)		Are sequence numbers generated in order?
CACHE_SIZE	NUMBER	NOT NULL	Number of sequence numbers to cache
LAST_NUMBER	NUMBER	NOT NULL	Last sequence number written to disk

DBA_SNAPSHOT_LOGS

This view lists all snapshot logs in the database.

Column	Datatype	NULL	Description
LOG_OWNER	VARCHAR2(30)	NOT NULL	Owner of the snapshot log
MASTER	VARCHAR2(30)	NOT NULL	Name of the master table of which the log logs changes
LOG_TABLE	VARCHAR2(30)	NOT NULL	Log table; holds timestamps and changes made to the master table
LOG_TRIGGER	VARCHAR2(30)		Obsolete with the release of Oracle8 Server. Set to NULL. Formerly, this parameter was an after-row trigger on the master which inserts rows into the log
FILTER_COLUMNS	VARCHAR2(3)		If set to YES, the snapshot log records filter column information
ROWIDS	VARCHAR2(3)		If set to YES, the snapshot log records ROWID information
PRIMARY_KEY	VARCHAR2(3)		If set to YES, the snapshot log records primary key information
CURRENT_SNAPSHOTS	DATE		One date per snapshot; the date the snapshot of the master last refreshed
SNAPSHOT_ID	NUMBER(38)		Unique identifier of the snapshot

DBA_SNAPSHOTS

This view lists all snapshots in the database.

Column	Datatype	NULL	Description
OWNER	VARCHAR2(30)	NOT NULL	Owner of the snapshot
NAME	VARCHAR2(30)	NOT NULL	The view used by users and applications for viewing the snapshot
TABLE_NAME	VARCHAR2(30)	NOT NULL	Table the snapshot is stored in.
MASTER_VIEW	VARCHAR2(30)		View of the master table, owned by the snapshot owner, used for refreshes. This is obsolete in Oracle8 and is set to NULL.
MASTER_OWNER	VARCHAR2(30)		Owner of the master table
MASTER	VARCHAR2(30)		Name of the master table of which this snapshot is a copy
MASTER_LINK	VARCHAR2(128)		Database link name to the master site
CAN_USE_LOG	VARCHAR2(3)		If NO, this snapshot is complex and will never use a log
UPDATABLE	VARCHAR2(3)		If NO, the snapshot is read only
LAST_REFRESH	DATE		SYSDATE from the master site at the time of the last refresh
ERROR	NUMBER		The number of failed automatic refreshes since last successful refresh
TYPE	VARCHAR2(8)		The type of refresh (complete, fast, force) for all automatic refreshes
NEXT	VARCHAR2(200)		The date function used to compute next refresh dates
START_WITH	DATE		The date expression for the first automatic refresh time.
REFRESH_GROUP	NUMBER		All snapshots in a given refresh group get refreshed in the same transaction
REFRESH_METHOD	VARCHAR2(11)		Values used to drive a fast refresh of the snapshot
UPDATE_TRIG	VARCHAR2(30)		Obsolete with the release of Oracle8 Server. Set to NULL. Formerly, this parameter was the name of the trigger that fills the UPDATE_LOG
UPDATE_LOG	VARCHAR2(30)		The table that logs changes made to an updatable snapshots
QUERY	LONG		The original query of which this snapshot is an instantiation
FR_OPERATIONS	VARCHAR2(10)		Status of generated fast refresh operations: (REGENERATE, VALID)
CR_OPERATIONS	VARCHAR2(10)		Status of generated complete refresh operations: (REGENERATE, VALID)
MASTER_ROLLBACK _SEG	VARCHAR2(30)		The rollback segment used at the master site

DBA_SOURCE

This view contains source of all stored objects in the database.

Column	Datatype	NULL	Description
OWNER	VARCHAR2(30)	NOT NULL	Owner of the object
NAME	VARCHAR2(30)	NOT NULL	Name of the object
TYPE	VARCHAR2(12)		Type of the object: PROCEDURE, FUNCTION, PACKAGE, TYPE, TYPE BODY, or PACKAGE BODY
LINE	NUMBER	NOT NULL	Line number of this line of source
TEXT	VARCHAR2(4000)		Source text

DBA_STMT_AUDIT_OPTS

This view contains information which describes current system auditing options across the system and by user.

Column	Datatype	NULL	Description
USER_NAME	VARCHAR2(30)		User name if by user auditing, else NULL for system-wide auditing
AUDIT_OPTION	VARCHAR2(40)	NOT NULL	Name of the system auditing option
SUCCESS	VARCHAR2(10)		Mode for WHENEVER SUCCESSFUL system auditing
FAILURE	VARCHAR2(10)		Mode for WHENEVER NOT SUCCESSFUL system auditing

DBA_SYNONYMS

This view lists all synonyms in the database.

Column	Datatype	NULL	Description
OWNER	VARCHAR2(30)	NOT NULL	Username of the owner of the synonym
SYNONYM_NAME	VARCHAR2(30)	NOT NULL	Name of the synonym
TABLE_OWNER	VARCHAR2(30)		Owner of the object referenced by the synonym
TABLE_NAME	VARCHAR2(30)	NOT NULL	Name of the object referenced by the synonym
DB_LINK	VARCHAR2(128)		Name of the database link referenced in a remote synonym

DBA_SYS_PRIVS

This view lists system privileges granted to users and roles.

Column	Datatype	NULL	Description
GRANTEE	VARCHAR2(30)	NOT NULL	Grantee name, user, or role receiving the grant
PRIVILEGE	VARCHAR2(40)	NOT NULL	System privilege
ADMIN_OPTION	VARCHAR2(3)		Grant was with the ADMIN option

DBA_TAB_COL_STATISTICS

This view contains column statistics and histogram information which is in the DBA_TAB_COLUMNS view. For more information, see "DBA_TAB_COLUMNS" on page 2-87.

Column	Datatype	NULL	Description
TABLE_NAME	VARCHAR2(30)	NOT NULL	Table name
COLUMN_NAME	VARCHAR2(30)	NOT NULL	Column name
NUM_DISTINCT	NUMBER		Number of distinct values in the column
LOW_VALUE	RAW(32)		Low value in the column
HIGH_VALUE	RAW(32)		High value in the column
DENSITY	NUMBER		Density of the column
NUM_NULLS	NUMBER		Number of nulls in the column
NUM_BUCKETS	NUMBER		Number of buckets in histogram for the column
SAMPLE_SIZE	NUMBER		Sample size used in analyzing this column
LAST_ANALYZED	DATE		Date of the most recent time this column was analyzed

DBA_TAB_COLUMNS

This view contains information which describes columns of all tables, views, and clusters. To gather statistics for this view, use the SQL command ANALYZE.

Column	Datatype	NULL	Description
OWNER	VARCHAR2(30)	NOT NULL	Owner of the table, view, or cluster
TABLE_NAME	VARCHAR2(30)	NOT NULL	Table, view, or cluster name
COLUMN_NAME	VARCHAR2(30)	NOT NULL	Column name
DATA_TYPE	VARCHAR2(30)		Datatype of the column
DATA_TYPE_MOD	VARCHAR2(3)		Datatype modifier of the column

Column	Datatype	NULL	Description
DATA_TYPE_OWNER	VARCHAR2(30)		Owner of the datatype of the column
DATA_LENGTH	NUMBER	NOT NULL	Length of the column in bytes
DATA_PRECISION	NUMBER		Decimal precision for NUMBER datatype; binary precision for FLOAT datatype; NULL for all other datatypes
DATA_SCALE	NUMBER		Digits to right of decimal point in a number
NULLABLE	VARCHAR2(1)		Does column allow NULL values?
COLUMN_ID	NUMBER	NOT NULL	Sequence number of the column as created
DEFAULT_LENGTH	NUMBER		Length of default value for the column
DATA_DEFAULT	LONG		
NUM_DISTINCT	NUMBER		These columns remain for backward compatibility with Oracle7. This information is now in the {TAB|PART}_COL_STATISTICS views.
LOW_VALUE	RAW(32)		
HIGH_VALUE	RAW(32)		
DENSITY	NUMBER		
NUM_NULLS	NUMBER		
NUM_BUCKETS	NUMBER		
LAST_ANALYZED	DATE		
SAMPLE_SIZE	SAMPLE_SIZE		
CHARACTER_SET _NAME	VARCHAR2(44)		The name of the character set: CHAR_CS, NCHAR_CS

DBA_TAB_COMMENTS

This view contains comments on all tables and views in the database.

Column	Datatype	NULL	Description
OWNER	VARCHAR2(30)	NOT NULL	Owner of the object
TABLE_NAME	VARCHAR2(30)	NOT NULL	Name of the object
TABLE_TYPE	VARCHAR2(11)		Type of the object.
COMMENTS	VARCHAR2(4000)		Comment on the object

DBA_TAB_HISTOGRAMS

This view lists histograms on columns of all tables.

Column	Datatype	NULL	Description
ENDPOINT_VALUE	VARCHAR2(30)		Owner of Table
TABLE_NAME	VARCHAR2(30)		Table name

Column	Datatype	NULL	Description
COLUMN_NAME	VARCHAR2(30)		Column name or attribute of the object type column
BUCKET_NUMBER	NUMBER		Bucket number
ENDPOINT_VALUE	NUMBER		Normalized endpoint values for this bucket

DBA_TAB_PARTITIONS

This view describes, for each table partition, the partition level partitioning information, the storage parameters for the partition, and various partition statistics determined by ANALYZE.

Column	Datatype	NULL	Description
TABLE_OWNER	VARCHAR2(30)	NOT NULL	Table owner
TABLE_NAME	VARCHAR2(30)	NOT NULL	Table name
PARTITION_NAME	VARCHAR2(30)		Partition name
HIGH_VALUE	LONG		Partition bound value expression
HIGH_VALUE_LENGTH	NUMBER	NOT NULL	Length of partition bound value expression
PARTITION_POSITION	NUMBER	NOT NULL	Position of the partition within the table
TABLESPACE_NAME	VARCHAR2(30)	NOT NULL	Name of the tablespace containing the partition
PCT_FREE	NUMBER	NOT NULL	Minimum percentage of free space in a block
PCT_USED	NUMBER	NOT NULL	Minimum percentage of used space in a block
INI_TRANS	NUMBER	NOT NULL	Initial number of transactions
MAX_TRANS	NUMBER	NOT NULL	Maximum number of transactions
INITIAL_EXTENT	NUMBER		Size of the initial extent in bytes
NEXT_EXTENT	NUMBER		Size of secondary extents in bytes
MIN_EXTENT	NUMBER	NOT NULL	Minimum number of extents allowed in the segment
MAX_EXTENT	NUMBER	NOT NULL	Maximum number of extents allowed in the segment
PCT_INCREASE	NUMBER	NOT NULL	Percentage increase in extent size
FREELISTS	NUMBER		Number of process freelists allocated in this segment
FREELIST_GROUPS	NUMBER		Number of freelist groups allocated in this segment
LOGGING	VARCHAR2(3)		Logging attribute of partition
NUM_ROWS	NUMBER		Number of rows in the partition
BLOCKS	NUMBER		Number of used blocks in the partition
EMPTY_BLOCKS	NUMBER		Number of empty (never used) blocks in the partition
AVG_SPACE	NUMBER		Average available free space in the partition
CHAIN_CNT	NUMBER		Number of chained rows in the partition
AVG_ROW_LEN	NUMBER		Average row length, including row overhead

Column	Datatype	NULL	Description
SAMPLE_SIZE	NUMBER		Sample size used in analyzing this partition
LAST_ANALYZED	DATE		Date of the most recent time this partition was analyzed
BUFFER_POOL	VARCHAR2(7)	NOT NULL	The buffer pool for the partition

DBA_TAB_PRIVS

This view lists all grants on objects in the database.

Column	Datatype	NULL	Description
GRANTEE	VARCHAR2(30)	NOT NULL	User to whom access was granted
OWNER	VARCHAR2(30)	NOT NULL	Owner of the object
TABLE_NAME	VARCHAR2(30)	NOT NULL	Name of the object
GRANTOR	VARCHAR2(30)	NOT NULL	Name of the user who performed the grant
PRIVILEGE	VARCHAR2(40)	NOT NULL	Table Privilege
GRANTABLE	VARCHAR2(3)		Privilege is grantable

DBA_TABLES

This view contains descriptions of all relational tables in the database. To gather statistics for this view, use the SQL command ANALYZE.

Column	Datatype	NULL	Description
OWNER	VARCHAR2(30)	NOT NULL	Owner of the table
TABLE_NAME	VARCHAR2(30)	NOT NULL	Name of the table
TABLESPACE_NAME	VARCHAR2(30)		Name of the tablespace containing the table
CLUSTER_NAME	VARCHAR2(30)		Name of the cluster, if any, to which the table belongs
IOT_NAME	VARCHAR2(30)		Name of the index organized table, if any, to which the overflow entry belongs
PCT_FREE	NUMBER		Minimum percentage of free space in a block
PCT_USED	NUMBER		Minimum percentage of used space in a block
INI_TRANS	NUMBER		Initial number of transactions
MAX_TRANS	NUMBER		Maximum number of transactions
INITIAL_EXTENT	NUMBER		Size of the initial extent in bytes
NEXT_EXTENT	NUMBER		Size of secondary extents in bytes
MIN_EXTENTS	NUMBER		Minimum number of extents allowed in the segment
MAX_EXTENTS	NUMBER		Maximum number of extents allowed in the segment

Column	Datatype	NULL	Description
PCT_INCREASE	NUMBER		Percentage increase in extent size
FREELISTS	NUMBER		Number of process freelists allocated to this segment
FREELIST_GROUPS	NUMBER		Number of freelist groups allocated to this segment
LOGGING	VARCHAR2(3)		Whether logging is enabled (YES or NO)
BACKED_UP	VARCHAR2(1)		Has table been backed up since last modification?
NUM_ROWS	NUMBER		Number of rows returned by the ANALYZE command
BLOCKS	NUMBER		The number of used data blocks in the table
EMPTY_BLOCKS	NUMBER		The number of empty (never used) data blocks in the table
AVG_SPACE	NUMBER		The average available free space in the table
CHAIN_CNT	NUMBER		The number of chained rows in the table
AVG_ROW_LEN	NUMBER		The average row length, including row overhead
AVG_SPACE_FREELIST _BLOCKS	NUMBER		The average freespace of all blocks on a freelist
NUM_FREELIST_BLOCKS	NUMBER		The number of blocks on the freelist
DEGREE	VARCHAR2(10)		Number of query servers used for a full-table scan
INSTANCES	VARCHAR2(10)		The number of instances across which the table is to be scanned
CACHE	VARCHAR2(5)		Whether the table is to be cached in the buffer cache
TABLE_LOCK	VARCHAR2(8)		Whether table locking is enabled or disabled
SAMPLE_SIZE	NUMBER		Sample size used in analyzing this table
LAST_ANALYZED	DATE		Date of the most recent time this table was analyzed
PARTITIONED	VARCHAR2(3)		Indicates whether this table is partitioned. Set to YES if it is partitioned
IOT_TYPE	VARCHAR2(12)		If this is an index organized table, then IOT_TYPE is IOT or IOT_OVERFLOW. If this is not an index organized table, then IOT_TYPE is NULL
TABLE_TYPE_OWNER	VARCHAR2(0)		Owner of the type of the table if the table is a typed table
TABLE_TYPE	VARCHAR2(0)		Type of the table if the table is a typed table
PACKED	VARCHAR2(0)		If the table is a typed table, does it store objects in packed format?
TEMPORARY	VARCHAR2(1)		Whether the table is temporary (Y or N)
NESTED	VARCHAR2(3)		Is the table a nested table?
BUFFER_POOL	VARCHAR2(7)		Name of the default buffer pool for the appropriate object

DBA_TABLESPACES

This view contains descriptions of all tablespaces.

Column	Datatype	NULL	Description
TABLESPACE_NAME	VARCHAR2(30)	NOT NULL	Tablespace name
INITIAL_EXTENT	NUMBER		Default initial extent size
NEXT_EXTENT	NUMBER		Default incremental extent size
MIN_EXTENTS	NUMBER	NOT NULL	Default minimum number of extents
MAX_EXTENTS	NUMBER	NOT NULL	Default maximum number of extents
PCT_INCREASE	NUMBER	NOT NULL	Default percent increase for extent size
MIN_EXTLEN	NUMBER		Minimum extent size for the tablespace
STATUS	VARCHAR2(9)		Tablespace status: ONLINE, OFFLINE, or READ ONLY
CONTENTS	VARCHAR2(9)		Tablespace contents: "PERMANENT", or "TEMPORARY"
LOGGING	VARCHAR2(9)		Default logging attribute

DBA_TRIGGERS

This view lists all triggers in the database.

Column	Datatype	NULL	Description
OWNER	VARCHAR2(30)	NOT NULL	Owner of the trigger
TRIGGER_NAME	VARCHAR2(30)	NOT NULL	Name of the trigger
TRIGGER_TYPE	VARCHAR2(16)		When the trigger fires: BEFORE EACH ROW, AFTER EACH ROW, BEFORE STATEMENT, AFTER STATEMENT
TRIGGERING_EVENT	VARCHAR2(26)		Statement that will fire the trigger: INSERT, UPDATE, and/or DELETE
TABLE_OWNER	VARCHAR2(30)	NOT NULL	Owner of the table with which this trigger is associated
TABLE_NAME	VARCHAR2(30)	NOT NULL	Name of the table
REFERENCING _NAMES	VARCHAR2(87)		Names used for referencing OLD and NEW values within the trigger
WHEN_CLAUSE	VARCHAR2(4000)		WHEN clause must evaluate to true in order for triggering body to execute
STATUS	VARCHAR2(8)		If DISABLED, then trigger will not fire
DESCRIPTION	VARCHAR2(4000)		Trigger description, useful for re-creating trigger creation statement
TRIGGER_BODY	LONG		Action taken by this trigger when it fires

DBA_TRIGGER_COLS

This view lists column usage in all triggers.

Column	Datatype	NULL	Description
TRIGGER_OWNER	VARCHAR2(30)	NOT NULL	Owner of the trigger
TRIGGER_NAME	VARCHAR2(30)	NOT NULL	Name of the trigger
TABLE_OWNER	VARCHAR2(30)	NOT NULL	Owner of the table
TABLE_NAME	VARCHAR2(30)	NOT NULL	Name of the table on which the trigger is defined
COLUMN_NAME	VARCHAR2(4000)		Name of the column used in trigger definition
COLUMN_LIST	VARCHAR2(3)		Is column specified in UPDATE OF clause?
COLUMN_USAGE	VARCHAR2(17)		Usage of column within trigger body

DBA_TS_QUOTAS

This view lists tablespace quotas for all users.

Column	Datatype	NULL	Description
TABLESPACE_NAME	VARCHAR2(30)	NOT NULL	Tablespace name
USERNAME	VARCHAR2(30)	NOT NULL	User with resource rights on the tablespace
BYTES	NUMBER		Number of bytes charged to the user
MAX_BYTES	NUMBER		User's quota in bytes, or -1 if no limit.
BLOCKS	NUMBER	NOT NULL	Number of Oracle blocks charged to the user
MAX_BLOCKS	NUMBER		User's quota in Oracle blocks, or -1 if no limit.

DBA_TYPE_ATTRS

This view displays the attributes of types in the database.

Column	Datatype	NULL	Description
OWNER	VARCHAR2(30)		Owner of the type
TYPE_NAME	VARCHAR2(30)	NOT NULL	Name of the type
ATTR_NAME	VARCHAR2(30)	NOT NULL	Name of the attribute
ATTR_TYPE_MOD	VARCHAR2(7)		Type modifier of the attribute
ATTR_TYPE_OWNER	VARCHAR2(30)		Owner of the type of the attribute
ATTR_TYPE_NAME	VARCHAR2(30)		Name of the type of the attribute
LENGTH	NUMBER		Length of the CHAR attribute or maximum length of the VARCHAR or VARCHAR2 attribute

Column	Datatype	NULL	Description
PRECISION	NUMBER		Decimal precision of the NUMBER or DECIMAL attribute or binary precision of the FLOAT attribute
SCALE	NUMBER		Scale of the NUMBER or DECIMAL attribute
CHARACTER_SET_NAME	VARCHAR2(44)		The name of the character set: CHAR_CS NCHAR_CS

DBA_TYPE_METHODS

This view is a description of methods of all types in the database.

Column	Datatype	NULL	Description
OWNER	VARCHAR2(30)	NOT NULL	Owner of the type
TYPE_NAME	VARCHAR2(30)	NOT NULL	Name of the type
METHOD_NAME	VARCHAR2(30)	NOT NULL	Name of the method
METHOD_NO	NUMBER	NOT NULL	Method number for distinguishing overloaded method (not to be used as the ID number
METHOD_TYPE	VARCHAR2(6)		Type of the method
PARAMETERS	NUMBER	NOT NULL	Number of parameters to the method
RESULTS	NUMBER	NOT NULL	Number of results returned by the method

DBA_TYPES

This view displays all abstract datatypes in the database.

Column	Datatype	NULL	Description
OWNER	VARCHAR2(30)		Owner of the type
TYPE_NAME	VARCHAR2(30)	NOT NULL	Name of the type
TYPE_OID	RAW(16)	NOT NULL	Object identifier (OID) of the type
TYPECODE	VARCHAR2(30)		Typecode of the type
ATTRIBUTES	NUMBER		Number of attributes in the type
METHODS	NUMBER		Number of methods in the type
PREDEFINED	VARCHAR2(3)		Indicates whether the type is a predefined type
INCOMPLETE	VARCHAR2(3)		Indicates whether the type is an incomplete type

DBA_UPDATABLE_COLUMNS

This view contains a description of columns that are updatable by the database administrator in a join view. See *Oracle8 Server Concepts* for information on updatable join views.

Column	Datatype	NULL	Description
OWNER	VARCHAR2(30)	NOT NULL	Table owner
TABLE_NAME	VARCHAR2(30)	NOT NULL	Table name
COLUMN_NAME	VARCHAR2(30)	NOT NULL	Column name
UPDATABLE	VARCHAR2(3)		Indicates whether the column is updatable
INSERTABLE	VARCHAR2(3)		Indicates whether the column is insertable
DELETABLE	VARCHAR2(3)		Indicates whether the column is deletable

DBA_USERS

This view lists information about all users of the database.

Column	Datatype	NULL	Description
USERNAME	VARCHAR2(30)	NOT NULL	Name of the user
USER_ID	NUMBER	NOT NULL	ID number of the user
PASSWORD	VARCHAR2(30)		Encrypted password
DEFAULT_TABLESPACE	VARCHAR2(30)	NOT NULL	Default tablespace for data
TEMPORARY _TABLESPACE	VARCHAR2(30)	NOT NULL	Default tablespace for temporary table
CREATED	DATE	NOT NULL	User creation date
PROFILE	VARCHAR2(30)	NOT NULL	User resource profile name
ACCOUNT_STATUS	VARCHAR2(30)	NOT NULL	Indicates if the account is locked, expired, or unlocked
LOCK_DATE	DATE		Date the account was locked if account status was locked
EXPIRY_DATE	DATE		Date of expiration of the account
EXTERNAL_NAME	VARCHAR2(4000)		User external name

DBA_VIEWS

This view contains the text of all views in the database.

Column	Datatype	NULL	Description
OWNER	VARCHAR2(30)	NOT NULL	Owner of the view
VIEW_NAME	VARCHAR2(30)	NOT NULL	Name of the view
TEXT_LENGTH	NUMBER		Length of the view text
TEXT	LONG		View text
TYPE_TEXT_LENGTH	NUMBER		Length of the type clause of the typed view
TYPE_TEXT	VARCHAR2(4000)		Type clause of the typed view
OID_TEXT_LENGTH	NUMBER		Length of the WITH OID clause of the typed view
OID_TEXT	VARCHAR2(4000)		WITH OID clause of the typed view
VIEW_TYPE_OWNER	VARCHAR2(30)		Owner of the type of the view if the view is a typed view
VIEW_TYPE	VARCHAR2(30)		Type of the view if the view is a typed view

DBMS_ALERT_INFO

This view lists registered alerts.

Column	Datatype	NULL	Description
NAME	VARCHAR2(30)	NOT NULL	Name of the alert
SID	VARCHAR2(30)	NOT NULL	Session ID of a session waiting for this alert
CHANGED	VARCHAR2(1)		Boolean flag to indicate that an alert has been signaled. Y: Alert signaled N: No alert.
MESSAGE	VARCHAR2(1800)		Optional message passed by signaler

DBMS_LOCK_ALLOCATED

This view lists user-allocated locks.

Column	Datatype	NULL	Description
NAME	VARCHAR2(128)	NOT NULL	Name of the lock
LOCKID	NUMBER(38)		Lock identifier number
EXPIRATION	DATE		Planned lock expiration date (updates whenever the allocation procedure is run)

DEFCALL

This view is used with Advanced Replication. For more information, see *Oracle8 Server Replication*.

DEFCALLDEST

This view is used with Advanced Replication. For more information, see *Oracle8 Server Replication*.

DEFDEFAULTDEST

This view is used with Advanced Replication. For more information, see *Oracle8 Server Replication*.

DEFERRCOUNT

This view is used with Advanced Replication. For more information, see *Oracle8 Server Replication*.

DEFERROR

This view is used with Advanced Replication. For more information, see *Oracle8 Server Replication*.

DEFLOB

This view is used with Advanced Replication. For more information, see *Oracle8 Server Replication*.

DEFPROPAGATOR

This view is used with Advanced Replication. For more information, see *Oracle8 Server Replication*.

DEFSCHEDULE

This view is used with Advanced Replication. For more information, see *Oracle8 Server Replication*.

DEFTRAN

This view is used with Advanced Replication. For more information, see *Oracle8 Server Replication*.

DEFTRANDEST

This view is used with Advanced Replication. For more information, see *Oracle8 Server Replication*.

DEPTREE

This view, created by UTLDTREE.SQL, contains information on the object dependency tree. For user SYS, this view displays shared cursors (and only shared cursors) that depend on the object. For all other users, it displays objects other than shared cursors. Other users can access SYS.DEPTREE for information on shared cursors.

Column	Datatype	NULL	Description
NESTED_LEVEL	NUMBER		Nesting level in the dependency tree
TYPE	VARCHAR2(15)		Object type
OWNER	VARCHAR2(30)		Object owner
NAME	VARCHAR2(1002)		Object name
SEQ#	NUMBER		Sequence number in the dependency tree. Used for ordering queries. (See also: "IDEPTREE" on page 2-108.)

DICT

This is a synonym for DICTIONARY. For more information, see "DICTIONARY" on page 2-98.

DICTIONARY

This view contains descriptions of data dictionary tables and views.

Column	Datatype	NULL	Description
TABLE_NAME	VARCHAR2(30)		Name of the object
COMMENTS	VARCHAR2(4000)		Text comment on the object

DICT_COLUMNS

This view contains descriptions of columns in data dictionary tables and views.

Column	Datatype	NULL	Description
TABLE_NAME	VARCHAR2(30)		Name of the object that contains the column
COLUMN_NAME	VARCHAR2(30)		Name of the column
COMMENTS	VARCHAR2(4000)		Text comment on the column

ERROR_SIZE

This view is accessed to create the DBA_OBJECT_SIZE and USER_OBJECT_SIZE views. For more information, see "DBA_OBJECT_SIZE" on page 2-67 and "USER_OBJECT_SIZE" on page 2-143.

EXCEPTIONS

This view contains information on violations of integrity constraints. This view is created by the UTLEXCPT.SQL script.

Column	Datatype	NULL	Description
ROW_ID	ROWID		Row that caused the violation
OWNER	VARCHAR2(30)		Owner of the table
TABLE_NAME	VARCHAR2(30)		Name of the table
CONSTRAINT	VARCHAR2(30)		Integrity constraint that was violated

FILE_LOCK

This is a Parallel Server view. This view displays the mapping of PCM locks to datafiles as specified in initialization parameter GC_FILES_TO_LOCKS. For more information on this parameter, see "GC_FILES_TO_LOCK" on page 1-44.

Column	Datatype	NULL	Description
FILE_ID	NUMBER	NOT NULL	Datafile identifier number (to find file name, query DBA_DATA_FILES or V$DBFILES)
FILE_NAME	VARCHAR2(513)		The datafile name
TS_NAME	VARCHAR2(30)	NOT NULL	The tablespace name for the datafile
START_LK	NUMBER		The first lock corresponding to the datafile

Column	Datatype	NULL	Description
NLOCKS	NUMBER		The number of PCM locks allocated to the datafile
BLOCKING	NUMBER		The number of blocks protected by a PCM lock on the datafile

For more information on this view, see *Oracle8 Parallel Server Concepts & Administration*.

FILE_PING

This is a Parallel Server view. This view displays the number of blocks pinged per datafile. You can use this information to determine access usage of existing datafiles for better settings of GC_FILES_TO_LOCKS. For more information on this parameter, see "GC_FILES_TO_LOCK" on page 1-44.

For more information, see *Oracle8 Parallel Server Concepts & Administration*.

Column	Datatype	NULL	Description
FILE_ID	NUMBER	NOT NULL	Datafile identifier number (to find file name, query DBA_DATA_FILES or V$DBFILES)
FILE_NAME	NUMBER		The file name
TS_NAME	VARCHAR2(30)	NOT NULL	Datafile identifier number (to find file name, query DBA_DATA_FILES or V$DBFILES)
FREQUENCY	NUMBER		The ping count.
X_2_NULL	NUMBER		Number of lock conversions from Exclusive-to-NULL for all blocks in the file
X_2_NULL_FORCED_WRITE	NUMBER		Number of forced writes that occur for blocks of the specified file due to Exclusive-to-NULL conversions
X_2_NULL_FORCED_STALE	NUMBER		Number of times a block in the file was made STALE due to Exclusive-to-NULL conversions
X_2_S	NUMBER		Number of lock conversions from Exclusive-to-Shared for all blocks in the file
X_2_S_FORCED_WRITE	NUMBER		Number of forced writes that occur for blocks of the specified file due to Exclusive-to-Shared conversions
X_2_SSX	NUMBER		Number of lock conversions from Exclusive-to-Sub Shared Exclusive for all blocks in the file

Column	Datatype	NULL	Description
X_2_SSX_FORCED_WRITE	NUMBER		Number of forced writes that occur for blocks of the specified file due to Exclusive-to-Sub Shared Exclusive conversions
S_2_NULL	NUMBER		Number of lock conversions from Shared-to-NULL for all blocks in the file
S_2_NULL_FORCED_STALE	NUMBER		Number of times a block in the file was made STALE due to Shared-to-NULL conversions
SS_2_NULL	NUMBER		Number of lock conversions from Sub Shared-to-NULL for all blocks in the file
WRB	NUMBER		Number of times the instance received a write single buffer cross instance call for this file
WRB_FORCED_WRITE	NUMBER		Number of blocks written due to write single buffer cross instance calls for this file
RBR	NUMBER		Number of times the instance received a reuse block range cross instance call for this file
RBR_FORCED_WRITE	NUMBER		Number of blocks written due to resuse block range cross instance calls for this file
RBR_FORCED_STALE	NUMBER		Number of times a block in this file was made STALE due to resuse block range cross instance calls
CBR	NUMBER		Number of times the instance received a checkpoint block range cross instance call for this file
CBR_FORCED_WRITE	NUMBER		Number of blocks in this file which were written due to checkpoint cross range cross instance calls
NULL_2_X	NUMBER		Number of lock conversions from NULL-to-Exclusive for all blocks of the specified file
S_2_X	NUMBER		Number of lock conversions from Shared-to-Exclusive for all blocks of the specified file
SSX_2_X	NUMBER		Number of lock conversions from Sub Shared Exclusive-to-Exclusive for all blocks of the specified file
NULL_2_S	NUMBER		Number of lock conversions from NULL-to-Shared for all blocks of the specified file
NULL_2_SS	NUMBER		Number of lock conversions from NULL-to-Sub Shared for all blocks of the specified file

FILEXT$

This view is the equivalent of DBA_DATA_FILES. Oracle recommends you use DBA_DATA_FILES instead of FILEXT$. For more information, see "DBA_DATA_FILES" on page 2-55.

Column	Datatype	NULL	Description
FILE#	NUMBER	NOT NULL	Absolute file number
MAXEXTEND	NUMBER		Maximum file size
INC	NUMBER		Increment amount

GLOBAL_NAME

This view contains one row that displays the global name of the current database.

Column	Datatype	NULL	Description
GLOBAL_NAME	VARCHAR2(4000)		Global name of the database

HS_ALL_CAPS

This view contains information about all of the capabilities (that is, features) associated with non-Oracle (FDS) data stores.

Column	Datatype	NULL	Description
CAP_NUMBER	NUMBER		Capability number
CONTEXT	NUMBER		Context in which this capability is applicable
TRANSLATION	VARCHAR2(255)		Valid for functions; contains translation to FDS dialect
ADDITIONAL_INFO	NUMBER		Flag for internal use
FDS_CLASS_NAME	VARCHAR2(30)		Name of the FDS Class
FDS_INST_NAME	VARCHAR2(30)		Name of the FDS instance

HS_ALL_DD

This view contains data dictionary information about non-Oracle (FDS) data stores.

Column	Datatype	NULL	Description
DD_TABLE_NAME	VARCHAR2(30)		Data dictionary table name

Column	Datatype	NULL	Description
TRANSLATION_TYPE	CHAR(1)		T = Translation, M = Mimic
TRANSLATION_TEXT	VARCHAR2(4000)		SQL statement containing the mapping
FDS_CLASS_NAME	VARCHAR2(30)		Name of the FDS Class
FDS_INST_NAME	VARCHAR2(30)		Name of the FDS instance
DD_TABLE_DESC	VARCHAR2(255)		Description of the ORACLE data dictionary table

HS_ALL_INITS

This view contains initialization parameter information about non-Oracle (FDS) data stores.

Column	Datatype	NULL	Description
INIT_VALUE_NAME	VARCHAR2(64)		Name of the initialization parameter
INIT_VALUE	VARCHAR2(255)		Value of the initialization parameter
INIT_VALUE_TYPE	VARCHAR2(1)		Environment variable (T or F). T= this is an environment variable, F= do not set as an environment variable
FDS_CLASS_NAME	VARCHAR2(30)		Name of the FDS Class
FDS_INST_NAME	VARCHAR2(30)		Name of the FDS instance

HS_BASE_CAPS

This view contains information about base capability (that is, base features) of the non-Oracle (FDS) data store.

Column	Datatype	NULL	Description
CAP_NUMBER	NUMBER	NOT NULL	Capability number
CAP_DESCRIPTION	VARCHAR2(255)		Description of the capability

HS_BASE_DD

This view displays information from the base data dictionary translation table.

Column	Datatype	NULL	Description
DD_TABLE_ID	NUMBER	NOT NULL	Sequence - a counter which is incremented for every row inserted (used internally)
DD_TABLE_NAME	VARCHAR2(30)	NOT NULL	Name of the Oracle data dictionary table
DD_TABLE_DESC	VARCHAR2(255)		Description of the Oracle data dictionary table

HS_CLASS_CAPS

This view contains information about the class-specific (driver) capabilities belonging to the non-Oracle (FDS) data store.

Column	Datatype	NULL	Description
CAP_NUMBER	NUMBER	NOT NULL	Capability number
CAP_DESCRIPTION	VARCHAR2(255)		Capability description
CONTEXT	NUMBER		Flag indicating the context in which the capability is enabled
TRANSLATION	VARCHAR2(255)		Valid for functions; contains translation to FDS dialect
ADDITIONAL_INFO	NUMBER		Additional flags for internal use
FDS_CLASS_NAME	VARCHAR2(30)	NOT NULL	Name of the FDS Class
FDS_CLASS_ID	NUMBER	NOT NULL	Sequence - a counter which is incremented for every row inserted (used internally)

HS_CLASS_DD

This view displays information from the non-Oracle data store (FDS) class-specific data dictionary translations.

Column	Datatype	NULL	Description
DD_TABLE_NAME	VARCHAR2(30)	NOT NULL	Name of the Oracle data dictionary table
DD_TABLE_DESC	VARCHAR2(255)		Description of the Oracle data dictionary table
TRANSLATION_TYPE	CHAR(1)	NOT NULL	T = Translation, M = Mimic
TRANSLATION_TEXT	VARCHAR2(4000)		SQL statement containing the mapping
FDS_CLASS_ID	NUMBER	NOT NULL	Sequence - a counter which is incremented for every row inserted (used internally)
FDS_CLASS_NAME	VARCHAR2(30)	NOT NULL	Name of the FDS Class
DD_TABLE_ID	NUMBER	NOT NULL	Sequence - a counter which is incremented for every row inserted (used internally)

HS_CLASS_INIT

This view displays information about the non-Oracle (FDS) class-specific initialization parameters.

Column	Datatype	NULL	Description
INIT_VALUE_NAME	VARCHAR2(64)	NOT NULL	Name of the initialization parameter
INIT_VALUE	VARCHAR2(255)	NOT NULL	Value of the initialization parameter

Column	Datatype	NULL	Description
INIT_VALUE_TYPE	VARCHAR2(1)	NOT NULL	Environment variable (T or F). T= this is an environment variable, F= do not set as an environment variable
FDS_CLASS_NAME	VARCHAR2(30)	NOT NULL	Name of the FDS Class
FDS_CLASS_INIT_ID	NUMBER	NOT NULL	Sequence - a counter which is incremented for every row inserted (used internally)
FDS_CLASS_ID	NUMBER	NOT NULL	Sequence - a counter which is incremented for every row inserted (used internally)

HS_EXTERNAL_OBJECT_PRIVILEGES

This view contains information about the privileges on objects that are granted to users.

Column	Datatype	NULL	Description
OBJECT_NAME	VARCHAR2(30)	NOT NULL	Name of the object. Name is unique for each instance.
PRIVILEGE_NAME	VARCHAR2(30)	NOT NULLI	Name of the privilege that was granted
GRANTEE	VARCHAR2(30)	NOT NULL	ID of the user that was granted the privilege
FDS_CLASS_NAME	VARCHAR2(30)	NOT NULLI	Name of the FDS Class
FDS_INST_NAME	VARCHAR2(30)	NOT NULLI	Name of the FDS instance

HS_EXTERNAL_OBJECTS

This view contains information about all of the distributed external objects accessible from the Oracle Server.

Column	Datatype	NULL	Description
FDS_CLASS_NAME	VARCHAR2(30)	NOT NULL	Name of the FDS Class
FDS_INST_NAME	VARCHAR2(30)	NOT NULL	Name of the FDS instance
OWNER	VARCHAR(30)	NOT NULL	Name of the user who created the object
OBJECT_NAME	VARCHAR2(30)	NOT NULL	Name of the object. Name is unique for each instance.
OBJECT_TYPE	VARCHAR2(13)	NOT NULL	Type of object: FUNCTION, PROCEDURE, PACKAGE, or LIBRARY
OBJECT_TEXT	LONG	NOT NULL	SQL text used to create the object.

HS_EXTERNAL_USER_PRIVILEGES

This view contains information about all of the granted privileges that are not tied to any particular object.

Column	Datatype	NULL	Description
PRIVILEGE_NAME	VARCHAR2(30)	NOT NULL	Name of the privilege that was granted
GRANTEE	VARCHAR2(30)	NOT NULL	ID of the user that was granted the privilege
FDS_CLASS_NAME	VARCHAR2(30)	NOT NULL	Name of the FDS Class
FDS_INST_NAME	VARCHAR2(30)	NOT NULL	Name of the FDS instance

HS_FDS_CLASS

This view contains information about legal non-Oracle (FDS) classes.

Column	Datatype	NULL	Description
FDS_CLASS_NAME	VARCHAR2(30)	NOT NULL	Name of the FDS class (i.e ODBC, DB2)
FDS_CLASS _COMMENTS	VARCHAR2(255)		Text description of the non-Oracle class
FDS_CLASS_ID	NUMBER	NOT NULL	Sequence - a counter which is incremented for every row inserted (used internally)

HS_FDS_INST

This view contains information about non-Oracle (FDS) instances.

Column	Datatype	NULL	Description
FDS_INST_NAME	VARCHAR2(30)	NOT NULL	Name of the FDS instance
FDS_INST_COMMENTS	VARCHAR2(255)		Text description of the non-Oracle instance
FDS_CLASS_NAME	VARCHAR2(30)	NOT NULL	Name of the FDS class
FDS_INST_ID	NUMBER	NOT NULL	Sequence - a counter which is incremented for every row inserted (used internally)
FDS_CLASS_ID	NUMBER	NOT NULL	Sequence - a counter which is incremented for every row inserted (used internally)

HS_INST_CAPS

This view contains information about instance-specific capabilities (that is, features).

Column	Datatype	NULL	Description
CAP_NUMBER	NUMBER	NOT NULL	Capability number
CAP_DESCRIPTION	VARCHAR2(255)		Capability description
CONTEXT	NUMBER		Context in which this capability is applicable
TRANSLATION	VARCHAR2(255)		Valid for functions; contains translation to FDS dialect
ADDITIONAL_INFO	NUMBER		Additional flags for internal use
FDS_CLASS_NAME	VARCHAR2(30)	NOT NULL	Name of the FDS class (i.e ODBC, DB2)
FDS_INST_NAME	VARCHAR2(30)	NOT NULL	Name of the FDS instance
FDS_CLASS_ID	NUMBER	NOT NULL	Sequence - a counter which is incremented for every row inserted (used internally)
FDS_INST_ID	NUMBER	NOT NULL	Sequence - a counter which is incremented for every row inserted (used internally)

HS_INST_DD

This view displays information from the non-Oracle (FDS) instance-specific data dictionary translations.

Column	Datatype	NULL	Description
DD_TABLE_NAME	VARCHAR2(30)	NOT NULL	Name of the Oracle data dictionary table
DD_TABLE_DESC	VARCHAR2(255)		Description of the Oracle data dictionary table
TRANSLATION_TYPE	CHAR(1)	NOT NULL	T = Translation, M = Mimic
TRANSLATION_TEXT	VARCHAR2(4000)		SQL statement containing the mapping
FDS_CLASS_NAME	VARCHAR2(30)	NOT NULL	Name of the FDS class (that is, ODBC, DB2)
FDS_INST_NAME	VARCHAR2(30)	NOT NULL	Name of the FDS instance
DD_TABLE_ID	NUMBER	NOT NULL	Sequence - a counter which is incremented for every row inserted (used internally)
FDS_CLASS_ID	NUMBER	NOT NULL	Sequence - a counter which is incremented for every row inserted (used internally)
FDS_INST_ID	NUMBER	NOT NULL	Sequence - a counter which is incremented for every row inserted (used internally)

HS_INST_INIT

This view contains information about the non-Oracle (FDS) instance-specific initialization parameters.

Column	Datatype	NULL	Description
INIT_VALUE_NAME	VARCHAR2(64)	NOT NULL	Name of the initialization parameter
INIT_VALUE	VARCHAR2(255)	NOT NULL	Value of the initialization parameter
INIT_VALUE_TYPE	VARCHAR2(1)	NOT NULL	Environment variable (T or F). T= this is an environment variable, F= do not set as an environment variable
FDS_CLASS_NAME	VARCHAR2(30)	NOT NULL	Name of the FDS class (for example: ODBC, DB2)
FDS_INST_NAME	VARCHAR2(30)	NOT NULL	Name of the FDS instance
FDS_INST_INIT_ID	NUMBER	NOT NULL	Sequence - a counter which is incremented for every row inserted (used internally)
FDS_CLASS_ID	NUMBER	NOT NULL	Sequence - a counter which is incremented for every row inserted (used internally)
FDS_INST_ID	NUMBER	NOT NULL	Sequence - a counter which is incremented for every row inserted (used internally)

IDEPTREE

This view, created by UTLDTREE.SQL, lists the indented dependency tree. It is a pre-sorted, pretty-print version of DEPTREE.

Column	Datatype	NULL	Description
NESTED_LEVEL	NUMBER		Nesting level in the dependency tree
TYPE	VARCHAR2(15)		Object type
OWNER	VARCHAR2(30)		Object owner
NAME	VARCHAR2(1002)		Object name

IND

This is a synonym for USER_INDEXES. For more information, see "USER_INDEXES" on page 2-135.

INDEX_HISTOGRAM

This view contains information from the VALIDATE INDEX command.

Column	Datatype	NULL	Description
REPEAT_COUNT	NUMBER		Number of times that one or more index keys is repeated in the table
KEYS_WITH_REPEAT _COUNT	NUMBER		Number of index keys that are repeated that many times

INDEX_STATS

This view stores information from the last VALIDATE INDEX command.

Column	Datatype	NULL	Description
HEIGHT	NUMBER		Height of the B-Tree
BLOCKS	NUMBER	NOT NULL	Blocks allocated to the segment
NAME	VARCHAR2(30)	NOT NULL	Name of the index
PARTITION_NAME	VARCHAR2(30)		Name of the partition of the index which was analyzed. If the index is not partitioned, a NULL is returned
LF_ROWS	NUMBER		Number of leaf rows (values in the index)
LF_BLKS	NUMBER		Number of leaf blocks in the B-Tree
LF_ROWS_LEN	NUMBER		Sum of the lengths of all the leaf rows
LF_BLK_LEN	NUMBER		Usable space in a leaf block
BR_ROWS	NUMBER		Number of branch rows in the B-Tree
BR_BLKS	NUMBER		Number of branch blocks in the B-Tree
BR_ROWS_LEN	NUMBER		Sum of the lengths of all the branch blocks in the B-Tree
BR_BLK_LEN	NUMBER		Usable space in a branch block
DEL_LF_ROWS	NUMBER		Number of deleted leaf rows in the index
DEL_LF_ROWS_LEN	NUMBER		Total length of all deleted rows in the index
DISTINCT_KEYS	NUMBER		Number of distinct keys in the index (may include rows that have been deleted)
MOST_REPEATED_KEY	NUMBER		How many times the most repeated key is repeated (may include rows that have been deleted)
BTREE_SPACE	NUMBER		Total space currently allocated in the B-Tree
USED_SPACE	NUMBER		Total space that is currently being used in the B-Tree
PCT_USED	NUMBER		Percent of space allocated in the B-Tree that is being used
ROWS_PER_KEY	NUMBER		Average number of rows per distinct key (this figure is calculated without consideration of deleted rows)

Column	Datatype	NULL	Description
BLKS_GETS_PER _ACCESS	NUMBER		Expected number of consistent mode block reads per row, assuming that a randomly chosen row is accessed using the index. Used to calculate the number of consistent reads that will occur during an index scan.

LOADER_CONSTRAINT_INFO

This is a SQL*LOADER view used for direct loads. For more information, see *Oracle8 Server Utilities*.

LOADER_FILE_TS

This is a SQL*LOADER view used for direct loads. For more information, see *Oracle8 Server Utilities*.

LOADER_PART_INFO

This is a SQL*LOADER view used for direct loads. For more information, see *Oracle8 Server Utilities*.

LOADER_PARAM_INFO

This is a SQL*LOADER view used for direct loads. For more information, see *Oracle8 Server Utilities*.

LOADER_TAB_INFO

This is a SQL*LOADER view used for direct loads. For more information, see *Oracle8 Server Utilities*.

LOADER_TRIGGER_INFO

This is a SQL*LOADER view used for direct loads. For more information, see *Oracle8 Server Utilities*.

NLS_DATABASE_PARAMETERS

This view lists permanent NLS parameters of the database.

Column	Datatype	NULL	Description
PARAMETER	VARCHAR2(30)	NOT NULL	Parameter name
VALUE	VARCHAR2(30)		Parameter value

NLS_INSTANCE_PARAMETERS

This view lists NLS parameters of the instance.

Column	Datatype	NULL	Description
PARAMETER	VARCHAR2(30)		Parameter name
VALUE	VARCHAR2(30)		Parameter value

NLS_SESSION_PARAMETERS

This view lists NLS parameters of the user session.

Column	Datatype	NULL	Description
PARAMETER	VARCHAR2(30)		Parameter name
VALUE	VARCHAR2(30)		Parameter value

OBJ

This is a synonym for USER_VIEWS. For more information, see "USER_OBJECTS" on page 2-142.

PARSED_PIECES

This view is accessed to create the DBA_OBJECT_SIZE and USER_OBJECT_SIZE views. For more information, see "DBA_OBJECT_SIZE" on page 2-67 and "USER_OBJECT_SIZE" on page 2-143.

PARSED_SIZE

This view is accessed to create the DBA_OBJECT_SIZE and USER_OBJECT_SIZE views. For more information, see "DBA_OBJECT_SIZE" on page 2-67 and "USER_OBJECT_SIZE" on page 2-143.

PLAN_TABLE

This view is the default table for results of the EXPLAIN PLAN statement. It is created by UTLXPLAN.SQL, and it contains one row for each step in the execution plan.

Column	Datatype	NULL	Description
STATEMENT_ID	VARCHAR2(30)		Optional statement identifier specified in the EXPLAIN PLAN statement
TIMESTAMP	DATE		Date and time that the EXPLAIN PLAN statement was issued
REMARKS	VARCHAR2(80)		Place for Comments that can be added to the steps of the execution plan
OPERATION	VARCHAR2(30)		Name of the operation performed at this step
OPTIONS	VARCHAR2(30)		Options used for the operation performed at this step
OBJECT_NODE	VARCHAR2(128)		Name of the database link used to reference the object
OBJECT_OWNER	VARCHAR2(30)		Owner of the object
OBJECT_NAME	VARCHAR2(30)		Name of the object
OBJECT_INSTANCE	NUMBER(38)		Numbered position of the object name in the original SQL statement
OBJECT_TYPE	VARCHAR2(30)		Descriptive modifier that further describes the type of object
OPTIMIZER	VARCHAR2(255)		The current mode of the optimizer
SEARCH_COLUMNS	NUMBER		Not currently used
ID	NUMBER(38)		Identification number for this step in the execution plan
PARENT_ID	NUMBER(38)		ID of the next step that operates on the results of this step
POSITION	NUMBER(38)		Order of processing for steps with the same parent ID. For cost-based optimization, the value in the first row of the plan is the statement's execution cost. For rule-based optimization, the value is null in the first row.
COST	NUMBER(38)		The cost of the current operation estimated by the cost-based optimizer (CBO)
CARDINALITY	NUMBER(38)		The number of rows returned by the current operation (estimated by the CBO)
BYTES	NUMBER(38)		The number of bytes returned by the current operation

Column	Datatype	NULL	Description
OTHER_TAG	VARCHAR2(255)		OTHER_TAG, describes the function of the SQL text in the OTHER column. Values for OTHER_TAG are: • SERIAL - the SQL is the text of a locally-executed, serial query plan. Currently, SQL is not loaded in OTHER for this case. • SERIAL_FROM_REMOTE - the SQL text shown in the OTHER column will be executed at a remote site. • PARALLEL_COMBINED_WITH_PARENT - the parent of this operation is a DFO that performs both operations in the parallel execution plan. • PARALLEL_COMBINED_WITH_CHILD - the child of this operation is a DFO that performs both operations in the parallel execution plan. • PARALLEL_TO_SERIAL - the SQL text shown in the OTHER column is the top-level of the parallel plan. • PARALLEL_TO_PARALLEL - the SQL text shown in the OTHER column is executed and output in parallel. • PARALLEL_FROM_SERIAL - this operation consumes data from a serial operation and outputs it in parallel.
PARTITION_START	VARCHAR2(255)		The start partition of a range of accessed partitions
PARTITION_STOP	VARCHAR2(255)		The stop partition of a range of accessed partitions
PARTITION_ID	NUMBER(38)		The step that has computed the pair of values of the PARTITION_START and PARTITION_STOP columns
OTHER	LONG		Holds SQL text for remote cursors and parallel query slaves

PRODUCT_COMPONENT_VERSION

This view contains version and status information for component products.

Column	Datatype	NULL	Description
PRODUCT	VARCHAR2(64)		Product name
VERSION	VARCHAR2(64)		Version number
STATUS	VARCHAR2(64)		Status of release

PSTUBTBL

This table contains information on stubs generated by the PSTUB utility so that an Oracle Forms 3.0 client can call stored procedures in an Oracle database.

Note: The contents of this table are intended only for use by the PSTUB utility.

Column	Datatype	NULL	Description
USERNAME	VARCHAR2(30)		Schema part of the identifier of a stored procedure
DBNAME	VARCHAR2(128)		Database link part of the identifier of a stored procedure
LUN	VARCHAR2(30)		Library unit name part of the identifier of a stored procedure
LUTYPE	VARCHAR2(3)		Type of the stored procedure
LINENO	NUMBER		Line number of the stub
LINE	VARCHAR2(1800)		Text of the stub

PUBLICSYN

This view contains information on public synonyms.

Column	Datatype	NULL	Description
SNAME	VARCHAR2(30)		Name of the synonym
CREATOR	VARCHAR2(30)		Owner of the synonym
TNAME	VARCHAR2(30)		Table of which this is a synonym
DATABASE	VARCHAR2(128)		Database in which the table resides
TABTYPE	VARCHAR2(9)		Type of table

PUBLIC_DEPENDENCY

This view lists dependencies to and from objects, by object number.

Column	Datatype	NULL	Description
OBJECT_ID	NUMBER	NOT NULL	Object number
REFERENCED_OBJECT_ID	NUMBER	NOT NULL	Referenced object (the parent object)

RESOURCE_COST

This view lists the cost for each resource.

Column	Datatype	NULL	Description
RESOURCE_NAME	VARCHAR2(32)	NOT NULL	Name of the resource
UNIT_COST	NUMBER	NOT NULL	Cost of the resource

RESOURCE_MAP

This view contains descriptions for resources. It maps the resource name to the resource number.

Column	Datatype	NULL	Description
RESOURCE#	NUMBER	NOT NULL	Numeric resource code
TYPE#	NUMBER	NOT NULL	Name of type
NAME	VARCHAR2(32)	NOT NULL	Name of resource

ROLE_ROLE_PRIVS

This view contains information about roles granted to other roles.
(Information is only provided about roles to which the user has access.)

Column	Datatype	NULL	Description
ROLE	VARCHAR2(30)	NOT NULL	Name of the role
GRANTED_ROLE	VARCHAR2(30)	NOT NULL	Role that was granted
ADMIN_OPTION	VARCHAR2(3)		Signifies that the role was granted with ADMIN option

ROLE_SYS_PRIVS

This view contains information about system privileges granted to roles. Information is provided only about roles to which the user has access.

Column	Datatype	NULL	Description
ROLE	VARCHAR2(30)	NOT NULL	Name of the role
PRIVILEGE	VARCHAR2(40)	NOT NULL	System privilege granted to the role
ADMIN_OPTION	VARCHAR2(3)		Signifies the grant was with the ADMIN option

ROLE_TAB_PRIVS

This view contains information about table privileges granted to roles. Information is provided only about roles to which the user has access.

Column	Datatype	NULL	Description
ROLE	VARCHAR2(30)	NOT NULL	Name of the role
OWNER	VARCHAR2(30)	NOT NULL	Owner of the object
TABLE_NAME	VARCHAR2(30)	NOT NULL	Name of the object
COLUMN_NAME	VARCHAR2(30)		Name of the column, if applicable
PRIVILEGE	VARCHAR2(40)	NOT NULL	Object privilege granted to the role
GRANTABLE	VARCHAR2(3)		YES if the role was granted with ADMIN OPTION; otherwise NO

SEQ

This is a synonym for USER_SEQUENCES. For more information see "USER_SEQUENCES" on page 2-154.

SESSION_PRIVS

This view lists the privileges that are currently available to the user.

Column	Datatype	NULL	Description
PRIVILEGE	VARCHAR2(40)	NOT NULL	Name of the privilege

SESSION_ROLES

This view lists the roles that are currently enabled to the user.

Column	Datatype	NULL	Description
ROLE	VARCHAR2(30)	NOT NULL	Name of the role

SOURCE_SIZE

This view is accessed to create the DBA_OBJECT_SIZE and USER_OBJECT_SIZE views. For more information, see "DBA_OBJECT_SIZE" on page 2-67, and "USER_OBJECT_SIZE" on page 2-143.

STMT_AUDIT_OPTION_MAP

This view contains information about auditing option type codes.

Column	Datatype	NULL	Description
OPTION#	NUMBER	NOT NULL	Numeric auditing option type code
NAME	VARCHAR2(40)	NOT NULL	Name of the auditing option

SYN

This is a synonym for USER_SYNONYMS. For more information, see "USER_SYNONYMS" on page 2-156.

SYNONYMS

This view is included for compatibility with Oracle version 5. Use of this view is not recommended.

SYSCATALOG

This view is included for compatibility with Oracle version 5. Use of this view is not recommended.

SYSFILES

This view is included for compatibility with Oracle version 5. Use of this view is not recommended.

SYSSEGOBJ

This view is included for compatibility with Oracle version 5. Use of this view is not recommended.

SYSTEM_PRIVILEGE_MAP

This view contains information about system privilege codes.

Column	Datatype	NULL	Description
PRIVILEGE	NUMBER	NOT NULL	Numeric privilege type code
NAME	VARCHAR2(40)	NOT NULL	Name of the type of privilege

SYS_OBJECTS

This view maps object IDs to object types and segment data block addresses.

Column	Datatype	NULL	Description
OBJECT_TYPE	VARCHAR2(15)		Type of the object
OBJECT_TYPE_ID	NUMBER		Type ID of the object
SEGMENT_TYPE_ID	NUMBER		Type of segment: TABLE, CLUSTER, INDEX, ROLLBACK, DEFERRED ROLLBACK, TEMPORARY, CACHE
OBJECT_ID	NUMBER		Object identifier
HEADER_FILE	NUMBER		ID of the file containing the segment header
HEADER_BLOCK	NUMBER		ID of the block containing the segment header
TS_NUMBER	NUMBER		The tablespace number

TAB

This view is included for compatibility with Oracle version 5. Use of this view is not recommended.

TABLE_PRIVILEGES

This view contains information on grants on objects for which the user is the grantor, grantee, or owner, or PUBLIC is the grantee. This view is included for compatibility with Oracle version 6. Use of this view is not recommended.

Column	Datatype	NULL	Description
GRANTEE	VARCHAR2(30)	NOT NULL	Name of the user to whom access is granted
OWNER	VARCHAR2(30)	NOT NULL	Owner of the object
TABLE_NAME	VARCHAR2(30)	NOT NULL	Name of the object
GRANTOR	VARCHAR2(30)	NOT NULL	Name of the user who performed the grant
SELECT_PRIV	VARCHAR2(1)		Permission to select from the object
INSERT_PRIV	VARCHAR2(1)		Permission to insert into the object
DELETE_PRIV	VARCHAR2(1)		Permission to delete from the object
UPDATE_PRIV	VARCHAR2(1)		Permission to update the object
REFERENCES_PRIV	VARCHAR2(1)		Permission to reference the object
ALTER_PRIV	VARCHAR2(1)		Permission to alter the object
INDEX_PRIV	VARCHAR2(1)		Permission to create or drop an index on the object
CREATED	VARCHAR2(0)		Timestamp for the grant

TABLE_PRIVILEGE_MAP

This view contains information about access privilege codes.

Column	Datatype	NULL	Description
PRIVILEGE	NUMBER	NOT NULL	Numeric privilege (auditing option) type code
NAME	VARCHAR2(40)	NOT NULL	Name of the type of privilege (auditing option)

TABS

This is a synonym for USER_TABLES. For more information, see "USER_TABLES" on page 2-161.

TABQUOTAS

This view is included for compatibility with Oracle version 5. Use of this view is not recommended.

TRUSTED_SERVERS

This view displays whether a server is trusted or untrusted.

Column	Datatype	NULL	Description
TRUST	VARCHAR2(9)		Trustedness of the server listed. Values can be TRUSTED or UNTRUSTED Servers which are not listed in the NAME column have opposite trustedness. See the examples below.
NAME	VARCHAR2(128)		Server name. Can be a specific server name or "ALL" for all servers.

For example:

If all servers are trusted, then TRUSTED_SERVERS returns:

```
TRUST         NAME
-------       ------
Trusted       ALL
```

If none of the servers are trusted, then TRUSTED_SERVERS returns:

```
TRUST         NAME
-------       ------
Untrusted     ALL
```

If all servers are trusted, except DB1, then TRUSTED_SERVERS returns:

```
TRUST          NAME
-------        ------
Untrusted      DB1
```

If all servers are untrusted, except DB1, then TRUSTED_SERVERS returns:

```
TRUST          NAME
-------        ------
Trusted        DB1
```

For more information on this view see *Oracle8 Server Distributed Systems*.

TS_PITR_CHECK

This view, created by CATPITR.SQL provides information on any dependencies or restrictions which might prevent tablespace point-in-time recovery from proceeding. This view applies only to the tablespace point-in-time recovery feature. For more information, see *Oracle8 Server Backup and Recovery Guide*.

Column	Datatype	NULL	Description
OBJ1_OWNER	VARCHAR2(30)	NOT NULL	The owner of the object preventing tablespace point-in-time recovery. See the REASON column for details.
OBJ1_NAME	VARCHAR2(30)	NOT NULL	The name of the object preventing tablespace point-in-time recovery
OBJ1_TYPE	VARCHAR2(15)		The object type for the object preventing tablespace point-in-time recovery
OBJ1_SUBNAME	VARCHAR2(30)		Subordinate to OBJ1_NAME
TS1_NAME	VARCHAR2(30)	NOT NULL	Name of the tablespace containing the object preventing tablespace point-in-time recovery
OBJ2_NAME	VARCHAR2(30)		The name of a second object which may be preventing tablespace point-in-time recovery. If NULL, object 1 is the only object preventing recovery
OBJ2_TYPE	VARCHAR2(15)		The object type for the second object (will be NULL if OBJ2_NAME is NULL)
OBJ2_OWNER	VARCHAR2(30)		The owner of the second object (will be NULL if OBJ2_NAME is NULL)
OBJ2_SUBNAME	VARCHAR2(30)		Subordinate to OBJ2_NAME
TS2_NAME	VARCHAR2(30)		Name of the tablespace containing second object which may be preventing tablespace point-in-time recovery (-1 indicates not applicable)
CONSTRAINT_NAME	VARCHAR2(30)		Name of the constraint

Column	Datatype	NULL	Description
REASON	VARCHAR2(78)		Reason why tablespace point-in-time recovery cannot proceed

TS_PITR_OBJECTS_TO_BE_DROPPED

This view lists all objects lost as a result of performing tablespace point-in-time recovery. This view applies only to the tablespace point-in-time recovery feature.

Column	Datatype	NULL	Description
OWNER	VARCHAR2(30)	NOT NULL	The owner of the object
NAME	VARCHAR2(30)	NOT NULL	The name of the object that will be lost as a result of undergoing tablespace point-in-time recovery
CREATION_TIME	DATE	NOT NULL	Creation timestamp of the object
TABLESPACE_NAME	VARCHAR2(30)		Name of the tablespace containing the object

USER_ALL_TABLES

This table contains descriptions of the tables (object tables and relational tables) available to the user.

Column	Datatype	NULL	Description
TABLE_NAME	VARCHAR2(30)		Name of the table
TABLESPACE_NAME	VARCHAR2(30)		Name of the tablespace containing the table
CLUSTER_NAME	VARCHAR2(30)		Name of the cluster, if any, to which the table belongs
IOT_NAME	VARCHAR2(30)		Name of the index organized table, if any, to which the overflow entry belongs
PCT_FREE	NUMBER		Minimum percentage of free space in a block
PCT_USED	NUMBER		Minimum percentage of used space in a block
INI_TRANS	NUMBER		Initial number of transactions
MAX_TRANS	NUMBER		Maximum number of transactions
INITIAL_EXTENT	NUMBER		Size of the initial extent in bytes
NEXT_EXTENT	NUMBER		Size of secondary extents in bytes

Column	Datatype	NULL	Description
MIN_EXTENTS	NUMBER		Minimum number of extents allowed in the segment
MAX_EXTENTS	NUMBER		Maximum number of extents allowed in the segment
PCT_INCREASE	NUMBER		Percentage increase in extent size
FREELISTS	NUMBER		Number of process freelists allocated in this segment
FREELIST_GROUPS	NUMBER		Number of freelist groups allocated in this segment
LOGGING	VARCHAR2(3)		Logging attribute
BACKED_UP	VARCHAR2(1)		Has table been backed up since last modification?
NUM_ROWS	NUMBER		The number of rows in the table
BLOCKS	NUMBER		The number of used blocks in the table
EMPTY_BLOCKS	NUMBER		The number of empty (never used) blocks in the table
AVG_SPACE	NUMBER		The average available free space in the table
CHAIN_CNT	NUMBER		The number of chained rows in the table
AVG_ROW_LEN	NUMBER		The average row length, including row overhead
AVG_SPACE_FREELIST _BLOCKS	NUMBER		The average freespace of all blocks on a freelist
NUM_FREELIST_BLOCKS	NUMBER		The number of blocks on the freelist
DEGREE	VARCHAR2(10)		The number of threads per instance for scanning the table
INSTANCES	VARCHAR2(10)		The number of instances across which the table is to be scanned
CACHE	VARCHAR2(5)		Whether the table is to be cached in the buffer cache
TABLE_LOCK	VARCHAR2(8)		Whether table locking is enabled or disabled
SAMPLE_SIZE	NUMBER		The sample size used in analyzing this table
LAST_ANALYZED	DATE		The date of the most recent time this table was analyzed
PARTITIONED	VARCHAR2(3)		Is this table partitioned? YES or NO
IOT_TYPE	VARCHAR2(12)		If index organized table, then IOT_TYPE is IOT or IOT_OVERFLOW else NULL
TABLE_TYPE_OWNER	VARCHAR2(30)		Owner of the type of the table if the table is a typed table

Column	Datatype	NULL	Description
TABLE_TYPE	VARCHAR2(30)		Type of the table if the table is a typed table
PACKED	VARCHAR2(1)		If the table is a typed table, does it store objects in packed format?
TEMPORARY	VARCHAR2(1)		Can the current session only see data that it place in this object itself?
NESTED	VARCHAR2(3)		Is the table a nested table?
BUFFER_POOL	VARCHAR2(7)		The default buffer pool to be used for table blocks

USER_ARGUMENTS

This view lists the arguments in the object which are accessible to the user.

Column	Datatype	NULL	Description
OBJECT_NAME	VARCHAR2(30)		Procedure or function name
PACKAGE_NAME	VARCHAR2(30)		Package name
OBJECT_ID	NUMBER	NOT NULL	Object number of the object
OVERLOAD	VARCHAR2(40)		Overload unique identifier
ARGUMENT_NAME	VARCHAR2(30)		Argument name
POSITION	NUMBER	NOT NULL	Position in argument list, or null for function return value
SEQUENCE	NUMBER	NOT NULL	Argument sequence, including all nesting levels
DATA_LEVEL	NUMBER	NOT NULL	Nesting depth of argument for composite types
DATA_TYPE	VARCHAR2(14)		Datatype of the argument
DEFAULT_VALUE	LONG		Default value for the argument
DEFAULT_LENGTH	NUMBER		Length of default value for the argument
IN_OUT	VARCHAR2(9)		Argument direction (IN, OUT, or IN/OUT)
DATA_LENGTH	NUMBER		Length of the column in bytes
DATA_PRECISION	NUMBER		Length: decimal digits (NUMBER) or binary digits (FLOAT)
DATA_SCALE	NUMBER		Digits to right of decimal point in a number
RADIX	NUMBER		Argument radix for a number
CHARACTER_SET_NAME	VARCHAR2(44)		Character set name for the argument
TYPE_OWNER	VARCHAR2(30)		Owner name of the type
TYPE_NAME	VARCHAR2(30)		Name

Column	Datatype	NULL	Description
TYPE_SUBNAME	VARCHAR2(30)		This is valid only in case of package local types; in such cases, the package name is the name and the type name is the subname
TYPE_LINK	VARCHAR2(128)		Database link valid only in case of package local types, in case the package is remote

USER_AUDIT_OBJECT

This view, created by CATAUDIT.SQL, lists audit trail records for statements concerning objects.

Column	Datatype	NULL	Description
OS_USERNAME	VARCHAR2(255)		Operating system login username of the user whose actions were audited
USERNAME	VARCHAR2(30)		Name (not ID number) of the user whose actions were audited
USERHOST	VARCHAR2(2000)		Numeric instance ID for the Oracle instance from which the user is accessing the database
TERMINAL	VARCHAR2(2000)		Identifier for the user's terminal
TIMESTAMP	DATE	NOT NULL	Timestamp for the creation of the audit trail entry or login time for the CONNECT statement
OWNER	VARCHAR2(30)		Creator of object affected by the action
OBJ_NAME	VARCHAR2(128)		Name of the object affected by the action
ACTION_NAME	VARCHAR2(27)		Name of the action type corresponding to the numeric code in ACTION
NEW_OWNER	VARCHAR2(30)		Owner of the object named in the NEW_NAME column
NEW_NAME	VARCHAR2(128)		New name of an object renamed by a RENAME statement
SES_ACTIONS	VARCHAR2(19)		Session summary (a string of 11 characters, one for each action type, in the order ALTER, AUDIT, COMMENT, DELETE, GRANT, INDEX, INSERT, LOCK, RENAME, SELECT, and UPDATE; coded: for none, S for success, F for failure, and B for both)
COMMENT_TEXT	VARCHAR2(4000)		Text Comment on the audit trail entry (inserted by an application program)
SESSIONID	NUMBER	NOT NULL	Numeric ID for each Oracle session
ENTRYID	NUMBER	NOT NULL	Numeric ID for each audit trail entry in the session
STATEMENTID	NUMBER	NOT NULL	Numeric ID for each statement run (a statement may cause many actions)
RETURNCODE	NUMBER	NOT NULL	Oracle message code generated by the action (zero if the action succeeded)
PRIV_USED	VARCHAR2(40)		System privilege used to execute the action

Column	Datatype	NULL	Description
OBJECT_LABEL	MLSLABEL		Label associated with the object being audited. Applies to Trusted Oracle Server only.
SESSION_LABEL	MLSLABEL		Label associated with the user's session. Applies to Trusted Oracle Server only.

USER_AUDIT_SESSION

This view, created by CATAUDIT.SQL, lists all audit trail records concerning connections and disconnections for the user.

Column	Datatype	NULL	Description
OS_USERNAME	VARCHAR2(255)		Operating system log on user name of the user whose actions were audited
USERNAME	VARCHAR2(30)		Name (not ID number) of the user whose actions were audited
USERHOST	VARCHAR2(2000)		Numeric instance ID for the Oracle instance from which the user is accessing the database
TERMINAL	VARCHAR2(2000)		Identifier for the user's terminal
TIMESTAMP	DATE	NOT NULL	Timestamp for the creation of the audit trail entry or login time for the CONNECT statement
ACTION_NAME	VARCHAR2(27)		Name of the action type corresponding to the numeric code in ACTION
LOGOFF_TIME	DATE		Timestamp for user log off
LOGOFF_LREAD	NUMBER		Logical reads for the session
LOGOFF_PREAD	NUMBER		Physical reads for the session
LOGOFF_LWRITE	NUMBER		Logical writes for the session
LOGOFF_DLOCK	VARCHAR2(40)		Deadlocks detected during the session
SESSIONID	NUMBER	NOT NULL	Numeric ID for each Oracle session
RETURNCODE	NUMBER	NOT NULL	Oracle message code generated by the action (zero if the action succeeded)
SESSION_LABEL	MLSLABEL		Label associated with the user's session. Applies to Trusted Oracle Server only.

USER_AUDIT_STATEMENT

This view, created by CATAUDIT.SQL, lists audit trail entries for the following statements issued by the user: GRANT, REVOKE, AUDIT, NOAUDIT, and ALTER SYSTEM.

Column	Datatype	NULL	Description
OS_USERNAME	VARCHAR2(255)		Operating system log on username of the user whose actions were audited
USERNAME	VARCHAR2(30)		Name (not ID number) of the user whose actions were audited
USERHOST	VARCHAR2(2000)		Numeric instance ID for the Oracle instance from which the user is accessing the database
TERMINAL	VARCHAR2(2000)		Identifier for the user's terminal
TIMESTAMP	DATE	NOT NULL	Timestamp for the creation of the audit trail entry or login time for the CONNECT statement
OWNER	VARCHAR2(30)		Creator of object affected by the action
OBJ_NAME	VARCHAR2(128)		Name of the object affected by the action
ACTION_NAME	VARCHAR2(27)		Name of the action type corresponding to the numeric code in ACTION
NEW_NAME	VARCHAR2(128)		New name of an object after a RENAME
OBJ_PRIVILEGE	VARCHAR2(16)		Object privileges granted/revoked by a GRANT/ REVOKE statement
SYS_PRIVILEGE	VARCHAR2(40)		System privileges granted/revoked by a GRANT/ REVOKE statement
ADMIN_OPTION	VARCHAR2(1)		Signifies the role or system privilege was granted with ADMIN option
GRANTEE	VARCHAR2(30)		Username of the grantee specified in a GRANT/ REVOKE statement
AUDIT_OPTION	VARCHAR2(40)		Auditing option set with the AUDIT statement
SES_ACTIONS	VARCHAR2(19)		Session summary (a string of 11 characters, one for each action type, in the order ALTER, AUDIT, COMMENT, DELETE, GRANT, INDEX, INSERT, LOCK, RENAME, SELECT, and UPDATE; coded: for none, S for success, F for failure, and B for both)
COMMENT_TEXT	VARCHAR2(4000)		Text Comment on the audit trail entry (inserted by an application program)
SESSIONID	NUMBER	NOT NULL	Numeric ID for each Oracle session
ENTRYID	NUMBER	NOT NULL	Numeric ID for each audit trail entry in the session
STATEMENTID	NUMBER	NOT NULL	Numeric ID for each statement run (a statement may cause many actions)
RETURNCODE	NUMBER	NOT NULL	Oracle message code generated by the action (zero if the action succeeded)

Column	Datatype	NULL	Description
PRIV_USED	VARCHAR2(40)		System privilege used to execute the action
SESSION_LABEL	MLSLABEL		Label associated with the user's session. Applies to Trusted Oracle Server only.

USER_AUDIT_TRAIL

This view, created by CATAUDIT.SQL, lists audit trail entries relevant to the user.

Column	Datatype	NULL	Description
OS_USERNAME	VARCHAR2(255)		Operating system log on username of the user whose actions were audited
USERNAME	VARCHAR2(30)		Name (not ID number) of the user whose actions were audited
USERHOST	VARCHAR2(2000)		Numeric instance ID for the Oracle instance from which the user is accessing the database
TERMINAL	VARCHAR2(2000)		Identifier for the user's terminal
TIMESTAMP	DATE	NOT NULL	Timestamp for the creation of the audit trail entry or login time for the CONNECT statement
OWNER	VARCHAR2(30)		Creator of object affected by the action
OBJ_NAME	VARCHAR2(128)		Name of object affected by the action
ACTION	NUMBER	NOT NULL	Numeric type code corresponding to the action name
ACTION_NAME	VARCHAR2(27)		Name of the action type corresponding to the numeric code in ACTION
NEW_OWNER	VARCHAR2(30)		Owner of the object named in the NEW_NAME column
NEW_NAME	VARCHAR2(128)		New name of an object renamed by a RENAME statement
OBJ_PRIVILEGE	VARCHAR2(16)		Object privileges granted/revoked by a GRANT/ REVOKE statement
SYS_PRIVILEGE	VARCHAR2(40)		System privileges granted/revoked by a GRANT/ REVOKE statement
ADMIN_OPTION	VARCHAR2(1)		Signifies the role or system privilege was granted with ADMIN option
GRANTEE	VARCHAR2(30)		Username of the grantee specified in a GRANT/ REVOKE statement
AUDIT_OPTION	VARCHAR2(40)		Auditing option set with the AUDIT statement

Column	Datatype	NULL	Description
SES_ACTIONS	VARCHAR2(19)		Session summary (a string of 16 characters, one for each action type in the order ALTER, AUDIT, COMMENT, DELETE, GRANT, INDEX, INSERT, LOCK, RENAME, SELECT, UPDATE, REFERENCES, and EXECUTE. Positions 14, 15, and 16 are reserved for future use. The characters are: - for none, S for success, F for failure, and B for both)
LOGOFF_TIME	DATE		Timestamp for user log off
LOGOFF_LREAD	NUMBER		Logical reads for the session
LOGOFF_PREAD	NUMBER		Physical reads for the session
LOGOFF_LWRITE	NUMBER		Logical writes for the session
LOGOFF_DLOCK	VARCHAR2(40)		Deadlocks detected during the session
COMMENT_TEXT	VARCHAR2(4000)		Text Comment on the audit trail entry, providing more information about the statement audited
SESSIONID	NUMBER	NOT NULL	Numeric ID for each Oracle session
ENTRYID	NUMBER	NOT NULL	Numeric ID for each audit trail entry in the session
STATEMENTID	NUMBER	NOT NULL	Numeric ID for each statement run (a statement can cause many actions)
RETURNCODE	NUMBER	NOT NULL	Oracle message code generated by the action (zero if the action succeeded)
PRIV_USED	VARCHAR2(40)		System privilege used to execute the action
OBJECT_LABEL	MLSLABEL		Label associated with the object being audited. Applies to Trusted Oracle Server only.
SESSION_LABEL	MLSLABEL		Label associated with the user's session. Applies to Trusted Oracle Server only.

USER_CATALOG

This view lists tables, views, synonyms, and sequences owned by the user.

Column	Datatype	NULL	Description
TABLE_NAME	VARCHAR2(30)	NOT NULL	Name of the object
TABLE_TYPE	VARCHAR2(11)		Type of the object

USER_CLUSTERS

This view contains descriptions of user's own clusters.

Column	Datatype	NULL	Description
CLUSTER_NAME	VARCHAR2(30)	NOT NULL	Name of the cluster

Column	Datatype	NULL	Description
TABLESPACE_NAME	VARCHAR2(30)	NOT NULL	Name of the tablespace containing the cluster
PCT_FREE	NUMBER		Minimum percentage of free space in a block
PCT_USED	NUMBER	NOT NULL	Minimum percentage of used space in a block
KEY_SIZE	NUMBER		Estimated size of cluster key plus associated rows
INI_TRANS	NUMBER	NOT NULL	Initial number of transactions
MAX_TRANS	NUMBER	NOT NULL	Maximum number of transactions
INITIAL_EXTENT	NUMBER		Size of the initial extent in bytes
NEXT_EXTENT	NUMBER		Size of secondary extents in bytes
MIN_EXTENTS	NUMBER	NOT NULL	Minimum number of extents allowed in the segment
MAX_EXTENTS	NUMBER	NOT NULL	Maximum number of extents allowed in the segment
PCT_INCREASE	NUMBER	NOT NULL	Percentage increase in extent size
FREELISTS	NUMBER		Number of process freelists allocated to this segment
FREELIST_GROUPS	NUMBER		Number of freelist groups allocated to this segment
AVG_BLOCKS_PER_KEY	NUMBER		Number of blocks in the table divided by number of hash keys
CLUSTER_TYPE	VARCHAR2(5)		Type of cluster: B-Tree index or hash
FUNCTION	VARCHAR2(15)		If a hash cluster, the hash function
HASHKEYS	NUMBER		If a hash cluster, the number of hash keys (hash buckets)
DEGREE	VARCHAR2(10)		The number of threads per instance for scanning the cluster
INSTANCES	VARCHAR2(10)		The number of instances across which the cluster is to be scanned
CACHE	VARCHAR2(5)		Whether the cluster is to be cached in the buffer cache
BUFFER_POOL	VARCHAR2(7)		Name of the default buffer pool for the appropriate object

USER_CLU_COLUMNS

This view contains a mapping of columns in user's tables to cluster columns.

Column	Datatype	NULL	Description
CLUSTER_NAME	VARCHAR2(30)	NOT NULL	Cluster name
CLU_COLUMN_NAME	VARCHAR2(30)	NOT NULL	Key column in the cluster
TABLE_NAME	VARCHAR2(30)	NOT NULL	Clustered table name
TAB_COLUMN_NAME	VARCHAR2(4000)		Key column or attribute of the object type column

USER_COL_COMMENTS

This view lists comments on columns of user's tables and views.

Column	Datatype	NULL	Description
TABLE_NAME	VARCHAR2(30)	NOT NULL	Object name
COLUMN_NAME	VARCHAR2(30)	NOT NULL	Column name
COMMENTS	VARCHAR2(4000)		Comment on the column

USER_COL_PRIVS

This view lists grants on columns for which the user is the owner, grantor, or grantee.

Column	Datatype	NULL	Description
GRANTEE	VARCHAR2(30)	NOT NULL	Name of the user to whom access was granted
OWNER	VARCHAR2(30)	NOT NULL	Owner of the object
TABLE_NAME	VARCHAR2(30)	NOT NULL	Name of the object
COLUMN_NAME	VARCHAR2(30)	NOT NULL	Name of the column
GRANTOR	VARCHAR2(30)	NOT NULL	Name of the user who performed the grant
PRIVILEGE	VARCHAR2(40)	NOT NULL	Privilege on the column
GRANTABLE	VARCHAR2(3)		YES if the privilege was granted with ADMIN OPTION; otherwise NO

USER_COL_PRIVS_MADE

This view lists all grants on columns of objects owned by the user.

Column	Datatype	NULL	Description
GRANTEE	VARCHAR2(30)	NOT NULL	Name of the user to whom access was granted
TABLE_NAME	VARCHAR2(30)	NOT NULL	Name of the object
COLUMN_NAME	VARCHAR2(30)	NOT NULL	Name of the column
GRANTOR	VARCHAR2(30)	NOT NULL	Name of the user who performed the grant
PRIVILEGE	VARCHAR2(40)	NOT NULL	Privilege on the column
GRANTABLE	VARCHAR2(3)		YES if the privilege was granted with ADMIN OPTION; otherwise NO

USER_COL_PRIVS_RECD

This view lists grants on columns for which the user is the grantee.

Column	Datatype	NULL	Description
GRANTEE	VARCHAR2(30)	NOT NULL	Name of the user to whom access was granted
TABLE_NAME	VARCHAR2(30)	NOT NULL	Name of the object
COLUMN_NAME	VARCHAR2(30)	NOT NULL	Name of the column
GRANTOR	VARCHAR2(30)	NOT NULL	Name of the user who performed the grant
PRIVILEGE	VARCHAR2(40)	NOT NULL	Privilege on the column
GRANTABLE	VARCHAR2(3)		YES if the privilege was granted with ADMIN OPTION; otherwise NO

USER_COLL_TYPES

This new data dictionary view displays the user's named collection types.

Column	Datatype	NULL	Description
TYPE_NAME	VARCHAR2(30)	NOT NULL	Name of the type
COLL_TYPE	VARCHAR2(30)	NOT NULL	Collection type
UPPER_BOUND	NUMBER		Maximum size of the VARYING ARRAY type
ELEM_TYPE_MOD	VARCHAR2(7)		Type modifier of the element
ELEM_TYPE_OWNER	VARCHAR2(30)		Owner of the type of the element
ELEM_TYPE_NAME	VARCHAR2(30)		Name of the type of the element
LENGTH	NUMBER		Length of the CHAR element or maximum length of the VARCHAR or VARCHAR2 element
PRECISION	NUMBER		Decimal precision of the NUMBER or DECIMAL element or binary precision of the FLOAT element
SCALE	NUMBER		Scale of the NUMBER or DECIMAL element
CHARACTER_SET_NAME	VARCHAR2(44)		The name of the character set: CHAR_CS, NCHAR_CS

USER_CONSTRAINTS

This view lists constraint definitions on user's tables.

Column	Datatype	NULL	Description
OWNER	VARCHAR2(30)	NOT NULL	Owner of the constraint definition

Column	Datatype	NULL	Description
CONSTRAINT_NAME	VARCHAR2(30)	NOT NULL	Name associated with the constraint definition
CONSTRAINT_TYPE	VARCHAR2(1)		Type of constraint definition: C (check constraint on a table) P (primary key) U (unique key) R (referential integrity) V (with check option on a view)
TABLE_NAME	VARCHAR2(30)	NOT NULL	Name associated with table with constraint definition
SEARCH_CONDITION	LONG		Text of search condition for table check
R_OWNER	VARCHAR2(30)		Owner of table used in referential constraint
R_CONSTRAINT_NAME	VARCHAR2(30)		Name of unique constraint definition for referenced table
DELETE_RULE	VARCHAR2(9)		The delete rule for a referential constraint: CASCADE, NO ACTION
STATUS	VARCHAR2(8)		Enforcement status of constraint: ENABLED or DISABLED
DEFERRABLE	VARCHAR2(14)		Indicates whether the constraint is deferrable
DEFERRED	VARCHAR2(9)		Indicates whether the constraint was initially deferred
GENERATED	VARCHAR2(14)		Indicates whether the name system is generated
LAST_CHANGE	VARCHAR2(3)		Indicates when the constraint was last enabled or disabled
VALIDATED	DATE		Indicates whether all data obeys the constraint: VALIDATED, NOT VALIDATED

USER_CONS_COLUMNS

This view contains information about columns in constraint definitions owned by the user.

Column	Datatype	NULL	Description
OWNER	VARCHAR2(30)	NOT NULL	Owner of the constraint definition
CONSTRAINT_NAME	VARCHAR2(30)	NOT NULL	Name associated with the constraint definition
TABLE_NAME	VARCHAR2(30)	NOT NULL	Name associated with table with constraint definition
COLUMN_NAME	VARCHAR2(4000)		Name associated with column or attribute of the object type column specified in the constraint definition

Column	Datatype	NULL	Description
POSITION	NUMBER		Original position of column or attribute in definition

USER_DB_LINKS

This view contains information on database links owned by the user.

Column	Datatype	NULL	Description
DB_LINK	VARCHAR2(128)	NOT NULL	Name of the database link
USERNAME	VARCHAR2(30)		Name of user to log in as
PASSWORD	VARCHAR2(30)		Password for login
HOST	VARCHAR2(2000)		Net8 string for connect
CREATED	DATE	NOT NULL	Creation time of the database link

USER_DEPENDENCIES

This view lists dependencies to and from a user's objects.

Column	Datatype	NULL	Description
NAME	VARCHAR2(30)	NOT NULL	Name of the object
TYPE	VARCHAR2(12)		Type of object: PROCEDURE, PACKAGE, FUNCTION, PACKAGE BODY
REFERENCED_OWNER	VARCHAR2(64)		Owner of the parent object
REFERENCED_NAME	VARCHAR2(30)		Name of the parent object
REFERENCED_TYPE	VARCHAR2(12)		Type of the parent object: PROCEDURE, PACKAGE, FUNCTION, PACKAGE BODY
REFERENCED_LINK_NAME	VARCHAR2(128)		Name of the link to the parent object (if remote)
SCHEMAID	NUMBER		The schema ID
DEPENDENCY_TYPE	VARCHAR2(4)		Two values: REF when the dependency is a REF dependency; HARD otherwise

USER_ERRORS

This view lists current errors on all a user's stored objects.

Column	Datatype	NULL	Description
NAME	VARCHAR2(30)	NOT NULL	Name of the object
TYPE	VARCHAR2(12)		Type of object: PROCEDURE, PACKAGE, FUNCTION, PACKAGE BODY
SEQUENCE	NUMBER	NOT NULL	Sequence number, for ordering
LINE	NUMBER	NOT NULL	Line number at which this error occurs
POSITION	NUMBER	NOT NULL	Position in the line at which this error occurs
TEXT	VARCHAR2(4000)	NOT NULL	Text of the error

USER_EXTENTS

This view lists extents of the segments belonging to a user's objects.

Column	Datatype	NULL	Description
SEGMENT_NAME	VARCHAR2(81)		Name of the segment associated with the extent
SEGMENT_TYPE	VARCHAR2(17)		Type of the segment: INDEX PARTITION, TABLE PARTITION
TABLESPACE_NAME	VARCHAR2(30)		Name of the tablespace containing the extent
PARTITION_NAME	VARCHAR2(30)		Object Partition Name (Set to NULL for non-partitioned objects).
EXTENT_ID	NUMBER	NOT NULL	Extent number in the segment
BYTES	NUMBER		Size of the extent in bytes
BLOCKS	NUMBER	NOT NULL	Size of the extent in Oracle blocks

USER_FREE_SPACE

This view lists the free extents in tablespaces accessible to the user.

Column	Datatype	NULL	Description
TABLESPACE_NAME	VARCHAR2(30)	NOT NULL	Name of the tablespace containing the extent
FILE_ID	NUMBER	NOT NULL	ID number of the file containing the extent
BLOCK_ID	NUMBER	NOT NULL	Starting block number of the extent
BYTES	NUMBER		Size of the extent in bytes
BLOCKS	NUMBER	NOT NULL	Size of the extent in Oracle blocks
RELATIVE_FNO	NUMBER	NOT NULL	Relative file number of the first extent block

USER_ INDEXES

This view contains descriptions of the user's own indexes. To gather statistics for this view, use the SQL command ANALYZE. This view supports parallel partitioned index scans.

Column	Datatype	NULL	Description
INDEX_NAME	VARCHAR2(30)	NOT NULL	Name of the index
INDEX_TYPE	VARCHAR2(12)		Type of index
TABLE_OWNER	VARCHAR2(30)	NOT NULL	Owner of the indexed object
TABLE_NAME	VARCHAR2(30)	NOT NULL	Name of the indexed object
TABLE_TYPE	VARCHAR2(11)		Type of the indexed object
UNIQUENESS	VARCHAR2(9)		Uniqueness status of the index: UNIQUE or NONUNIQUE
TABLESPACE_NAME	VARCHAR2(30)		Name of the tablespace containing the index
INI_TRANS	NUMBER		Initial number of transactions
MAX_TRANS	NUMBER		Maximum number of transactions
INITIAL_EXTENT	NUMBER		Size of the initial extent in bytes
NEXT_EXTENT	NUMBER		Size of secondary extents in bytes
MIN_EXTENTS	NUMBER		Minimum number of extents allowed in the segment
MAX_EXTENTS	NUMBER		Maximum number of extents allowed in the segment
PCT_INCREASE	NUMBER		Percentage increase in extent size
PCT_THRESHOLD	NUMBER		Threshold percentage of block space allowed per index entry
INCLUDE_COLUMN	NUMBER		User column-id for last column to be included in index organized table top index
FREELISTS	NUMBER		Number of process freelists allocated in this segment
FREELIST_GROUPS	NUMBER		Number of freelist groups allocated to this segment
PCT_FREE	NUMBER		Minimum percentage of free space in a block
LOGGING	VARCHAR2(3)		Logging attribute
BLEVEL	NUMBER		B-Tree level: depth of the index from its root block to its leaf blocks. A depth of 0 indicates that the root block and leaf block are the same.
LEAF_BLOCKS	NUMBER		Number of leaf blocks in the index.
DISTINCT_KEYS	NUMBER		Number of distinct indexed values. For indexes that enforce UNIQUE and PRIMARY KEY constraints, this value is the same as the number of rows in the table USER_TABLES.NUM_ROWS.
AVG_LEAF_BLOCKS _PER_KEY	NUMBER		Average number of leaf blocks in which each distinct value in the index appears. This statistic is rounded to the nearest integer. For indexes that enforce UNIQUE and PRIMARY KEY constraints, this value is always 1.

Column	Datatype	NULL	Description
AVG_DATA_BLOCKS _PER_KEY	NUMBER		Average number of data blocks in the table that are pointed to by a distinct value in the index. This statistic is the average number of data blocks that contain rows that contain a given value for the indexed column(s). This statistic is rounded to the nearest integer.
CLUSTERING_FACTOR	NUMBER		This statistic represents the amount of order of the rows in the table based on the values of the index. If its value is near the number of blocks, then the table is well ordered. In such a case, the index entries in a single leaf block tend to point to rows in the same data blocks. If its value is near the number of rows, then the table is randomly ordered. In such a case, it is unlikely that index entries in the same leaf block point to rows in the same data blocks.
STATUS	VARCHAR2(8)		State of the index: DIRECT LOAD or VALID
NUM_ROWS	NUMBER		Number of rows in this index
SAMPLE_SIZE	NUMBER		Size of the sample used to analyze this index
LAST_ANALYZED	DATE		Timestamp for when this index was last analyzed
DEGREE	VARCHAR2(40)		Number of threads per instance for scanning the index. NULL if PARTITIONED=NO.
INSTANCES	VARCHAR2(40)		The number of instances across which the partitioned index is to be scanned
PARTITIONED	VARCHAR2(3)		Indicates whether this index is partitioned. Set to YES if it is partitioned
TEMPORARY	VARCHAR2(1)		Can the current session only see data that it place in this object itself?
GENERATED	VARCHAR2(1)		Was the name of this index system generated?
BUFFER_POOL	VARCHAR2(7)		Name of the default buffer pool for the appropriate object

USER_IND_COLUMNS

This view lists columns of the user's indexes or on user's tables.

Column	Datatype	NULL	Description
INDEX_NAME	VARCHAR2(30)	NOT NULL	Index name
TABLE_NAME	VARCHAR2(30)	NOT NULL	Table or cluster name
COLUMN_NAME	VARCHAR2(4000)		Column name or attribute of the object type column
COLUMN_POSITION	NUMBER	NOT NULL	Position of column or attribute within index
COLUMN_LENGTH	NUMBER	NOT NULL	Indexed length of the column or attribute

USER_IND_PARTITIONS

This view describes, for each index partition that the current user owns, the partition level partitioning information, the storage parameters for the partition, and various partition statistics determined by ANALYZE.

Column	Datatype	NULL	Description
INDEX_NAME	VARCHAR2(30)	NOT NULL	Index name
PARTITION_NAME	VARCHAR2(30)		Partition name
HIGH_VALUE	LONG		Partition bound value expression
HIGH_VALUE_LENGTH	NUMBER	NOT NULL	Length of partition bound value expression
PARTITION_POSITION	NUMBER	NOT NULL	Position of the partition within the index
STATUS	VARCHAR2(8)		Indicates whether index partition is usable or not
TABLESPACE_NAME	VARCHAR2(30)	NOT NULL	Name of the tablespace containing the partition
PCT_FREE	NUMBER	NOT NULL	Minimum percentage of free space in a block
INI_TRANS	NUMBER	NOT NULL	Initial number of transactions
MAX_TRANS	NUMBER	NOT NULL	Maximum number of transactions
INITIAL_EXTENT	NUMBER		Size of the initial extent in bytes
NEXT_EXTENT	NUMBER		Size of secondary extents in bytes
MIN_EXTENT	NUMBER	NOT NULL	Minimum number of extents allowed in the segment
MAX_EXTENT	NUMBER	NOT NULL	Maximum number of extents allowed in the segment
PCT_INCREASE	NUMBER	NOT NULL	Percentage increase in extent size
FREELISTS	NUMBER		Number of process freelists allocated in this segment
LOGGING	VARCHAR2(3)		Logging attribute of partition
BLEVEL	NUMBER		B-Tree level
LEAF_BLOCKS	NUMBER		Number of leaf blocks in the index partition
DISTINCT_KEYS	NUMBER		Number of distinct keys in the index partition
AVG_LEAF_BLOCKS _PER_KEY	NUMBER		Average number of leaf blocks per key
AVG_DATA_BLOCKS _PER_KEY	NUMBER		Average number of data blocks per key
CLUSTERING_FACTOR	NUMBER		Measurement of the amount of (dis)order of the table this index partition is for
NUM_ROWS	NUMBER		Number of rows in this index partition
SAMPLE_SIZE	NUMBER		Sample size used in analyzing this partition
LAST_ANALYZED	DATE		Date of the most recent time this partition was analyzed
BUFFER_POOL	VARCHAR2(7)		The buffer pool for the partition

USER_JOBS

This view lists all jobs owned by the user. For more information, see the *Oracle8 Server Administrator's Guide.*

Column	Datatype	NULL	Description
JOB	NUMBER	NOT NULL	Identifier of job. Neither import/export nor repeated executions change it.
LOG_USER	VARCHAR2(30)	NOT NULL	USER who was logged in when the job was submitted
PRIV_USER	VARCHAR2(30)	NOT NULL	USER whose default privileges apply to this job
SCHEMA_USER	VARCHAR2(30)	NOT NULL	Default schema used to parse the job For example, if the SCHEMA_USER is SCOTT and you submit the procedure HIRE_EMP as a job, Oracle looks for SCOTT.HIRE_EMP.
LAST_DATE	DATE		Date this job last successfully executed
LAST_SEC	VARCHAR2(8)		Same as LAST_DATE. This is when the last successful execution started.
THIS_DATE	DATE		Date that this job started executing (usually null if not executing)
THIS_SEC	VARCHAR2(8)		Same as THIS_DATE. This is when the last successful execution started.
NEXT_DATE	DATE	NOT NULL	Date that this job will next be executed
NEXT_SEC	VARCHAR2(8)		Same as NEXT_DATE. The job becomes due for execution at this time.
TOTAL_TIME	NUMBER		Total wall clock time spent by the system on this job, in seconds
BROKEN	VARCHAR2(1)		If Y, no attempt is being made to run this job. See DBMS_JOB.BROKEN (JOB).
INTERVAL	VARCHAR2(200)	NOT NULL	A date function, evaluated at the start of execution, becomes next NEXT_DATE
FAILURES	NUMBER		How many times has this job started and failed since its last success?
WHAT	VARCHAR2(4000)		Body of the anonymous PL/SQL block that this job executes
CURRENT_SESSION _LABEL	MLSLABEL		Trusted Oracle Server label of the current session as seen by the job. Applies to Trusted Oracle Server only.
CLEARANCE_HI	MLSLABEL		Highest level of clearance available to the job. Applies to Trusted Oracle Server only.
CLEARANCE_LO	MLSLABEL		Lowest level of clearance available to the job. Applies to Trusted Oracle Server only.
NLS_ENV	VARCHAR2(4000)		ALTER SESSION parameters describing the NLS environment of the job
MISC_ENV	RAW(32)		Other session parameters that apply to this job

USER_LIBRARIES

This view lists all the libraries that a user owns.

Column	Datatype	NULL	Description
LIBRARY_NAME	VARCHAR2(30)	NOT NULL	Library name
FILE_SPEC	VARCHAR2(2000)		File specification associated with the library
DYNAMIC	VARCHAR2(1)		Is the library dynamically loadable? (YES or NO)
STATUS	VARCHAR2(7)		Status of the library

USER_LOBS

This view displays the user's LOBs contained in the user's tables.

Column	Datatype	NULL	Description
TABLE_NAME	VARCHAR2(30)	NOT NULL	Name of the table containing the LOB
COLUMN_NAME	VARCHAR2(30)	NOT NULL	Name of the LOB column or attribute
SEGMENT_NAME	VARCHAR2(30)	NOT NULL	Name of the LOB segment
INDEX_NAME	VARCHAR2(30)	NOT NULL	Name of the LOB index
CHUNK	NUMBER		Size of the LOB chunk as a unit of allocation/manipulation in bytes
PCTVERSION	NUMBER	NOT NULL	Maximum percentage of the LOB space used for versioning
CACHE	VARCHAR2(3)		Indicates whether the LOB is accessed through the buffer cache
LOGGING	VARCHAR2(3)		Indicates whether the changes to the LOB are logged
IN_ROW	VARCHAR2(3)		Are some of the LOBs stored with the base row?

USER_METHOD_PARAMS

This view is a description of method parameters of the user's types.

Column	Datatype	NULL	Description
TYPE_NAME	VARCHAR2(30)	NOT NULL	Name of the type
METHOD_NAME	VARCHAR2(30)	NOT NULL	Name of the method
METHOD_NO	NUMBER	NOT NULL	Method number for distinguishing overloaded method (not to be used as ID number)
PARAM_NAME	VARCHAR2(30)	NOT NULL	Name of the parameter
PARAM_NO	NUMBER	NOT NULL	Parameter number or position
PARAM_MODE	VARCHAR2(6)		Mode of the parameter

Column	Datatype	NULL	Description
PARAM_TYPE_MOD	VARCHAR2(7)		Type modifier of the parameter
PARAM_TYPE_OWNER	VARCHAR2(30)		Owner of the type of the parameter
PARAM_TYPE_NAME	VARCHAR2(30)		Name of the type of the parameter
CHARACTER_SET_NAME	VARCHAR2(44)		The name of the character set: CHAR_CS NCHAR_CS

USER_METHOD_RESULTS

This view is a description of method results of the user's types.

Column	Datatype	NULL	Description
TYPE_NAME	VARCHAR2(30)	NOT NULL	Name of the type
METHOD_NAME	VARCHAR2(30)	NOT NULL	Name of the method
METHOD_NO	NUMBER	NOT NULL	Method number for distinguishing overloaded method (not to be used as ID number)
RESULT_TYPE_MOD	VARCHAR2(7)		Type modifier of the result
RESULT_TYPE_OWNER	VARCHAR2(30)		Owner of the type of the result
RESULT_TYPE_NAME	VARCHAR2(30)		Name of the type of the result
CHARACTER_SET_NAME	VARCHAR2(44)		The name of the character set: CHAR_CS NCHAR_CS

USER_NESTED_TABLES

This view describes the nested tables contained in the user's own tables.

Column	Datatype	NULL	Description
TABLE_NAME	VARCHAR2(30)		Name of the nested table
TABLE_TYPE_OWNER	VARCHAR2(30)		Owner of the type of which the nested table was created
TABLE_TYPE_NAME	VARCHAR2(30)		Name of the type of the nested table
PARENT_TABLE_NAME	VARCHAR2(30)		Name of the parent table containing the nested table
PARENT_TABLE_COLUMN	VARCHAR2(4000)		Column name of the parent table that corresponds to the nested table

USER_OBJECT_TABLES

This view contains descriptions of the object tables available to the user.

Column	Datatype	NULL	Description
TABLE_NAME	VARCHAR2(30)	NOT NULL	Name of the table
TABLESPACE_NAME	VARCHAR2(30)		Name of the tablespace containing the table
CLUSTER_NAME	VARCHAR2(30)		Name of the cluster, if any, to which the table belongs
IOT_NAME	VARCHAR2(30)		Name of the index organized table, if any, to which the overflow entry belongs
PCT_FREE	NUMBER		Minimum percentage of free space in a block
PCT_USED	NUMBER		Minimum percentage of used space in a block
INI_TRANS	NUMBER		Initial number of transactions
MAX_TRANS	NUMBER		Maximum number of transactions
INITIAL_EXTENT	NUMBER		Size of the initial extent in bytes
NEXT_EXTENT	NUMBER		Size of secondary extents in bytes
MIN_EXTENTS	NUMBER		Minimum number of extents allowed in the segment
MAX_EXTENTS	NUMBER		Maximum number of extents allowed in the segment
PCT_INCREASE	NUMBER		Percentage increase in extent size
FREELISTS	NUMBER		Number of process freelists allocated in this segment
FREELIST_GROUPS	NUMBER		Number of freelist groups allocated in this segment
LOGGING	VARCHAR2(3)		Logging attribute
BACKED_UP	VARCHAR2(1)		Has table been backed up since last modification?
NUM_ROWS	NUMBER		The number of rows in the table
BLOCKS	NUMBER		The number of used blocks in the table
EMPTY_BLOCKS	NUMBER		The number of empty (never used) blocks in the table
AVG_SPACE	NUMBER		The average available free space in the table
CHAIN_CNT	NUMBER		The number of chained rows in the table
AVG_ROW_LEN	NUMBER		The average row length, including row overhead

Column	Datatype	NULL	Description
AVG_SPACE_FREELIST _BLOCKS	NUMBER		The average freespace of all blocks on a freelist
NUM_FREELIST_BLOCKS	NUMBER		The number of blocks on the freelist
DEGREE	VARCHAR2(10)		The number of threads per instance for scanning the table
INSTANCES	VARCHAR2(10)		The number of instances across which the table is to be scanned
CACHE	VARCHAR2(5)		Whether the table is to be cached in the buffer cache
TABLE_LOCK	VARCHAR2(8)		Whether table locking is enabled or disabled
SAMPLE_SIZE	NUMBER		The sample size used in analyzing this table
LAST_ANALYZED	DATE		The date of the most recent time this table was analyzed
PARTITIONED	VARCHAR2(3)		Is this table partitioned? YES or NO
IOT_TYPE	VARCHAR2(12)		If an index organized table, then IOT_TYPE is IOT or IOT_OVERFLOW else NULL
TABLE_TYPE_OWNER	VARCHAR2(30)	NOT NULL	Owner of the type of the table if the table is a typed table
TABLE_TYPE	VARCHAR2(30)	NOT NULL	Type of the table if the table is a typed table
PACKED	VARCHAR2(1)		If the table is a typed table, does it store objects in packed format?
TEMPORARY	VARCHAR2(1)		Can the current session only see data that it place in this object itself?
NESTED	VARCHAR2(3)		Is the table a nested table?
BUFFER_POOL	VARCHAR2(7)		The default buffer pool to be used for table blocks

USER_OBJECTS

This view lists objects owned by the user.

Column	Datatype	NULL	Description
OBJECT_NAME	VARCHAR2(128)		Name of the object
SUBOBJECT_NAME	VARCHAR2(30)		Name of the sub-object (for example, partition)
OBJECT_ID	NUMBER		Object number of the object

Column	Datatype	NULL	Description
DATA_OBJECT_ID	NUMBER		Object number of the segment which contains the object
OBJECT_TYPE	VARCHAR2(15)		Type and type body of the object: INDEX PARTITION, TABLE PARTITION, PACKAGE, PACKAGE BODY, or TRIGGER
CREATED	DATE		Timestamp for the creation of the object
LAST_DDL_TIME	DATE		Timestamp of the last DDL command applied to the object (including grants and revokes)
TIMESTAMP	VARCHAR2(19)		Timestamp for the creation of the object (character data)
STATUS	VARCHAR2(7)		Status of the object: VALID, INVALID
TEMPORARY	VARCHAR2(1)		Can the current session only see data that it place in this object itself?
GENERATED	VARCHAR2(1)		Was the name of this object system generated?

USER_OBJECT_SIZE

This view lists the PL/SQL objects owned by the user.

Column	Datatype	NULL	Description
NAME	VARCHAR2(30)	NOT NULL	Name of the object
TYPE	VARCHAR2(12)		Type of the object: PROCEDURE, PACKAGE, or PACKAGE BODY
SOURCE_SIZE	NUMBER		Size of source code in bytes
PARSED_SIZE	NUMBER		Size of parsed code in bytes
CODE_SIZE	NUMBER		Size of compiled code in bytes
ERROR_SIZE	NUMBER		Size of error messages in bytes

USER_OBJ_AUDIT_OPTS

This view, created by CATAUDIT.SQL, lists auditing options for the user's tables and views.

Column	Datatype	NULL	Description
OBJECT_NAME	VARCHAR2(30)		Name of the object
OBJECT_TYPE	VARCHAR2(9)		Type of the object: TABLE or VIEW
ALT	VARCHAR2(3)		Auditing ALTER WHENEVER SUCCESSFUL/UNSUCCESSFUL
AUD	VARCHAR2(3)		Auditing AUDIT WHENEVER SUCCESSFUL/UNSUCCESSFUL
COM	VARCHAR2(3)		Auditing COMMENT WHENEVER SUCCESSFUL/ UNSUCCESSFUL
DEL	VARCHAR2(3)		Auditing DELETE WHENEVER SUCCESSFUL/UNSUCCESSFUL
GRA	VARCHAR2(3)		Auditing GRANT WHENEVER SUCCESSFUL/UNSUCCESSFUL
IND	VARCHAR2(3)		Auditing INDEX WHENEVER SUCCESSFUL/UNSUCCESSFUL
INS	VARCHAR2(3)		Auditing INSERT WHENEVER SUCCESSFUL/UNSUCCESSFUL
LOC	VARCHAR2(3)		Auditing LOCK WHENEVER SUCCESSFUL/UNSUCCESSFUL
REN	VARCHAR2(3)		Auditing RENAME WHENEVER SUCCESSFUL/ UNSUCCESSFUL
SEL	VARCHAR2(3)		Auditing SELECT WHENEVER SUCCESSFUL/UNSUCCESSFUL
UPD	VARCHAR2(3)		Auditing UPDATE WHENEVER SUCCESSFUL/UNSUCCESSFUL
REF	VARCHAR2(3)		Auditing REFERENCES WHENEVER SUCCESSFUL/ UNSUCCESSFUL
EXE	VARCHAR2(3)		Auditing EXECUTE WHENEVER SUCCESSFUL/ UNSUCCESSFUL
CRE	VARCHAR2(3)		Auditing CREATE WHENEVER SUCCESSFUL/UNSUCCESSFUL
REA	VARCHAR2(3)		Auditing READ WHENEVER SUCCESSFUL/UNSUCCESSFUL
WRI	VARCHAR2(3)		Auditing WRITE WHENEVER SUCCESSFUL/UNSUCCESSFUL

USER_PART_COL_STATISTICS

This view contains column statistics and histogram information for table partitions that the current user owns.

Column	Datatype	NULL	Description
TABLE_NAME	VARCHAR2(30)	NOT NULL	Table name
PARTITION_NAME	VARCHAR2(30)		Table partition name
COLUMN_NAME	VARCHAR2(30)	NOT NULL	Column name
NUM_DISTINCT	NUMBER		Number of distinct values in the column
LOW_VALUE	RAW(32)		Low value in the column

Column	Datatype	NULL	Description
HIGH_VALUE	RAW(32)		High value in the column
DENSITY	NUMBER		Density of the column
NUM_NULLS	NUMBER		Number of nulls in the column
NUM_BUCKETS	NUMBER		Number of buckets in histogram for the column
SAMPLE_SIZE	NUMBER		Sample size used in analyzing this column
LAST_ANALYZED	DATE		Date of the most recent time this column was analyzed

USER_PART_HISTOGRAMS

This view contains the histogram data (end-points per histogram) for histograms on table partitions that the current user can access.

Column	Datatype	NULL	Description
TABLE_NAME	VARCHAR2(30)		Table name
PARTITION_NAME	VARCHAR2(30)		Table partition name
COLUMN_NAME	VARCHAR2(30)		Column name
BUCKET_NUMBER	NUMBER		Bucket number
ENDPOINT_VALUE	NUMBER		Normalized endpoint values for this bucket

USER_PART_KEY_COLUMNS

This view describes the partitioning key columns for partitioned objects that the current user owns.

Column	Datatype	NULL	Description
NAME	VARCHAR2(30)		Partitioned table or index name
COLUMN_NAME	VARCHAR2(30)		Column name
COLUMN_POSITION	NUMBER		Position of the column within the partitioning key

USER_PART_INDEXES

This view lists the object level partitioning information for all partitioned indexes that the user owns.

Column	Datatype	NULL	Description
INDEX_NAME	VARCHAR2(30)	NOT NULL	Name of this partitioned index
PARTITIONING_TYPE	VARCHAR2(7)		Partitioning algorithm: RANGE

Column	Datatype	NULL	Description
PARTITION_COUNT	NUMBER	NOT NULL	Number of partitions in this index
PARTITIONING_KEY _COUNT	NUMBER	NOT NULL	Number of columns in the partitioning key
LOCALITY	VARCHAR2(6)		Indicates whether this partitioned index is LOCAL or GLOBAL
ALIGNMENT	VARCHAR2(12)		Indicates whether this partitioned index is PREFIXED or NON-PREFIXED
DEF_TABLESPACE _NAME	VARCHAR2(30)		Default TABLESPACE, for LOCAL index, for ADD/ SPLIT TABLE partition
DEF_PCT_FREE	NUMBER	NOT NULL	Default PCTFREE, for LOCAL index, for ADD TABLE partition
DEF_INI_TRANS	NUMBER	NOT NULL	Default INITRANS, for LOCAL index, for ADD TABLE partition
DEF_MAX_TRANS	NUMBER	NOT NULL	Default MAXTRANS, for LOCAL index, for ADD TABLE partition
DEF_INITIAL_EXTENT	NUMBER	NOT NULL	Default INITIAL, for LOCAL index, for ADD TABLE partition
DEF_NEXT_EXTENT	NUMBER	NOT NULL	Default NEXT, for LOCAL index, for ADD TABLE partition
DEF_MIN_EXTENTS	NUMBER	NOT NULL	Default MINEXTENTS, for LOCAL index, for ADD TABLE partition
DEF_MAX_EXTENTS	NUMBER	NOT NULL	Default MAXEXTENTS, for LOCAL index, for ADD TABLE partition
DEF_PCT_INCREASE	NUMBER	NOT NULL	Default PCTINCREASE, for LOCAL index, for ADD TABLE partition
DEF_FREELISTS	NUMBER	NOT NULL	Default FREELISTS, for LOCAL index, for ADD TABLE partition
DEF_LOGGING	VARCHAR2(7)		Default LOGGING, for LOCAL index, for ADD TABLE PARTITION
DEF_BUFFER_POOL	VARCHAR2(7)		Default buffer pool, for LOCAL index, for ADD TABLE PARTITION

USER_PART_TABLES

This view describes the object level partitioning information for partitioned tables that the current user owns.

Column	Datatype	NULL	Description
TABLE_NAME	VARCHAR2(30)	NOT NULL	Name of this partitioned table
PARTITIONING_TYPE	VARCHAR2(7)		Partitioning algorithm: RANGE
PARTITION_COUNT	NUMBER	NOT NULL	Number of partitions in this table
PARTITIONING_KEY_COUNT	NUMBER	NOT NULL	Number of columns in the partitioning key

Column	Datatype	NULL	Description
DEF_TABLESPACE_NAME	VARCHAR2(30)	NOT NULL	Default TABLESPACE, used for ADD partition
DEF_PCT_FREE	NUMBER	NOT NULL	Default PCTFREE, used for ADD partition
DEF_PCT_USED	NUMBER	NOT NULL	Default PCTUSED, used for ADD partition
DEF_INI_TRANS	NUMBER	NOT NULL	Default INITRANS, used for ADD partition
DEF_MAX_TRANS	NUMBER	NOT NULL	Default MAXTRANS, used for ADD partition
DEF_INITIAL_EXTENT	NUMBER	NOT NULL	Default INITIAL, used for ADD partition
DEF_NEXT_EXTENT	NUMBER	NOT NULL	Default NEXT, used for ADD partition
DEF_MIN_EXTENTS	NUMBER	NOT NULL	Default MINEXTENTS, used for ADD partition
DEF_MAX_EXTENTS	NUMBER	NOT NULL	Default MAXEXTENTS, used for ADD partition
DEF_PCT_INCREASE	NUMBER	NOT NULL	Default PCTINCREASE, used for ADD partition
DEF_FREELISTS	NUMBER	NOT NULL	Default FREELISTS, used for ADD partition
DEF_FREELIST_GROUPS	NUMBER	NOT NULL	Default FREELIST GROUPS, used for ADD partition
DEF_LOGGING	VARCHAR2(7)		Default LOGGING attribute, used for ADD PARTITION
DEF_BUFFER_POOL	VARCHAR2(7)		The default buffer pool for the given object

USER_PASSWORD_LIMITS

This view describes the password profile parameters that are assigned to the user.

Column	Datatype	NULL	Description
RESOURCE_NAME	VARCHAR2(32)	NOT NULL	Name of the password resource
LIMIT	VARCHAR2(40)		Value of the resource limit

USER_QUEUE_TABLES

This view describes only the queues in the queue tables created in the user's schema. For more information about this view and Advanced Queuing, see the *Oracle8 Server Application Developer's Guide*.

Column	Datatype	NULL	Description
QUEUE_TABLE	VARCHAR2(30)		Name of the queue table
TYPE	VARCHAR2(7)		Type of payload: RAW: raw type OBJECT: user-defined object type VARIANT: variant type (internal use only)
OBJECT_TYPE	VARCHAR2(61)		Object type of the payload when TYPE is OBJECT

Column	Datatype	NULL	Description
SORT_ORDER	VARCHAR2(22)		User specified sort order
RECIPIENTS	VARCHAR2(8)		SINGLE or MULTIPLE recipients
MESSAGE_GROUPING	VARCHAR2(13)		NONE or TRANSACTIONAL
USER_COMMENT	VARCHAR2(50)		Comment supplied by the user

USER_QUEUES

This view describes the operational characteristics for every queue in the user's schema. For more information about this view and Advanced Queuing, see the *Oracle8 Server Application Developer's Guide.*

Column	Datatype	NULL	Description
NAME	VARCHAR2(30)	NOT NULL	Name of the queue
QUEUE_TABLE	VARCHAR2(30)	NOT NULL	The name of the queue table where this queue resides
QID	NUMBER	NOT NULL	Unique queue identifier
QUEUE_TYPE	VARCHAR2(15)		Queue type: NORMAL_QUEUE - Normal queue EXCEPTION_QUEUE - Exception queue
MAX_RETRIES	NUMBER		Number of dequeue attempts allowed
RETRY_DELAY	NUMBER		Time lapse in seconds before retry takes place
ENQUEUE_ENABLED	VARCHAR2(7)		YES/NO
DEQUEUE_ENABLED	VARCHAR2(7)		YES/NO
RETENTION	VARCHAR2(40)		Number of seconds message is retained after dequeue. FOREVER - messages stay in the queue permanently
USER_COMMENT	VARCHAR2(50)		Comment supplied by the user

USER_REFRESH

This view lists all the refresh groups.

Column	Datatype	NULL	Description
ROWNER	VARCHAR2(30)	NOT NULL	Name of the owner of the refresh group
RNAME	VARCHAR2(30)	NOT NULL	Name of the refresh group
REFGROUP	NUMBER		Internal identifier of refresh group
IMPLICIT_DESTROY	VARCHAR2(1)		Y or N; if Y, then destroy the refresh group when its last item is removed
PUSH_DEFERRED _RPC	VARCHAR2(1)		Y or N, if Y then push changes from snapshot to master before refresh

Column	Datatype	NULL	Description
REFRESH_AFTER _ERRORS	VARCHAR2(1)		If Y, proceed with refresh despite error when pushing deferred RPCs
ROLLBACK_SEG	VARCHAR2(30)		Name of the rollback segment to use while refreshing
JOB	NUMBER		Identifier of job used to refresh the group automatically
NEXT_DATE	DATE		Date that this job will next be refreshed automatically, if not broken
INTERVAL	VARCHAR2(200)		A date function used to compute the next NEXT_DATE
BROKEN	VARCHAR2(1)		Y or N; Y means the job is broken and will never be run
PURGE_OPTION	NUMBER(38)		The method for purging the transaction queue after each push
PARALLELISM	NUMBER(38)		The level of parallelism for transaction propagation
HEAP_SIZE	NUMBER(38)		The size of the heap.

USER_REFRESH_CHILDREN

This view lists all the objects in refresh groups, where the user owns the refresh group.

Column	Datatype	NULL	Description
OWNER	VARCHAR2(30)	NOT NULL	Owner of the object in the refresh group
NAME	VARCHAR2(30)	NOT NULL	Name of the object in the refresh group
TYPE	VARCHAR2(30)		Type of the object in the refresh group
ROWNER	VARCHAR2(30)	NOT NULL	Name of the owner of the refresh group
RNAME	VARCHAR2(30)	NOT NULL	Name of the refresh group
REFGROUP	NUMBER		Internal identifier of refresh group
IMPLICIT_DESTROY	VARCHAR2(1)		Y or N; if Y, then destroy the refresh group when its last item is removed
PUSH_DEFERRED_RPC	VARCHAR2(1)		Y or N, if Y then push changes from snapshot to master before refresh
REFRESH_AFTER _ERRORS	VARCHAR2(1)		If Y, proceed with refresh despite error when pushing deferred RPCs
ROLLBACK_SEG	VARCHAR2(30)		Name of the rollback segment to use while refreshing
JOB	NUMBER		Identifier of job used to refresh the group automatically
NEXT_DATE	DATE		Date that this job will next be refreshed automatically, if not broken
INTERVAL	VARCHAR2(200)		A date function used to compute the next NEXT_DATE

Column	Datatype	NULL	Description
BROKEN	VARCHAR2(1)		Y or N; Y means the job is broken and will never be run
PURGE_OPTION	NUMBER(38)		The method for purging the transaction queue after each push
PARALLELISM	NUMBER(38)		The level of parallelism for transaction propagation
HEAP_SIZE	NUMBER(38)		The size of the heap.

USER_REFS

This view describes the REF columns and REF attributes in the object type columns of the user's tables.

Column	Datatype	NULL	Description
TABLE_NAME	VARCHAR2(30)	NOT NULL	Name of the table
COLUMN_NAME	VARCHAR2(4000)		Name of the REF column or attribute. If it is not a top-level attribute, the value of COLUMN_NAME should be a path name starting with the column name.
WITH_ROWID	VARCHAR2(3)		Is the REF value stored with ROWID? (YES or NO)
IS_SCOPED	VARCHAR2(3)		Is the REF column scoped? (YES or NO)
SCOPE_TABLE_OWNER	VARCHAR2(30)		Name of the owner of the scope table, if it exists and is accessible by the user
SCOPE_TABLE_NAME	VARCHAR2(30)		Name of the scope table, if it exists and is accessible by the user

USER_REPCATLOG

This view is used with Advanced Replication. For more information, see *Oracle8 Server Replication*.

USER_REPCOLUMN

This view is used with Advanced Replication. For more information, see *Oracle8 Server Replication*.

USER_REPCOLUMN_GROUP

This view is used with Advanced Replication. For more information, see *Oracle8 Server Replication*.

USER_REPCONFLICT

This view is used with Advanced Replication. For more information, see *Oracle8 Server Replication*.

USER_REPDDL

This view is used with Advanced Replication. For more information, see *Oracle8 Server Replication*.

USER_REPGENERATED

This view is used with Advanced Replication. For more information, see *Oracle8 Server Replication*.

USER_REPGROUP

This view is used with Advanced Replication. For more information, see *Oracle8 Server Replication*.

USER_REPGROUPED_COLUMN

This view is used with Advanced Replication. For more information, see *Oracle8 Server Replication*.

USER_REPKEY_COLUMNS

This view is used with Advanced Replication. For more information, see *Oracle8 Server Replication*.

USER_REPOBJECT

This view is used with Advanced Replication. For more information, see *Oracle8 Server Replication*.

USER_REPPARAMETER_COLUMN

This view is used with Advanced Replication. For more information, see *Oracle8 Server Replication*.

USER_REPPRIORITY

> This view is used with Advanced Replication. For more information, see *Oracle8 Server Replication*.

USER_REPPRIORITY_GROUP

> This view is used with Advanced Replication. For more information, see *Oracle8 Server Replication*.

USER_REPPROP

> This view is used with Advanced Replication. For more information, see *Oracle8 Server Replication*.

USER_REPRESOLUTION

> This view is used with Advanced Replication. For more information, see *Oracle8 Server Replication*.

USER_REPRESOL_STATS_CONTROL

> This view is used with Advanced Replication. For more information, see *Oracle8 Server Replication*.

USER_REPRESOLUTION_METHOD

> This view is used with Advanced Replication. For more information, see *Oracle8 Server Replication*.

USER_REPRESOLUTION_STATISTICS

> This view is used with Advanced Replication. For more information, see *Oracle8 Server Replication*.

USER_REPSITES

> This view is used with Advanced Replication. For more information, see *Oracle8 Server Replication*.

USER_RESOURCE_LIMITS

This view displays the resource limits for the current user.

Column	Datatype	NULL	Description
RESOURCE_NAME	VARCHAR2(32)	NOT NULL	Name of the resource
LIMIT	VARCHAR2(40)		Limit placed on this resource

USER_ROLE_PRIVS

This view lists roles granted to the user.

Column	Datatype	NULL	Description
USERNAME	VARCHAR2(30)		Name of the user, or PUBLIC
GRANTED_ROLE	VARCHAR2(30)		Name of the role granted to the user
ADMIN_OPTION	VARCHAR2(3)		Granted with ADMIN option: YES/NO
DEFAULT_ROLE	VARCHAR2(3)		Role is designated as the user's default role: YES/NO
OS_GRANTED	VARCHAR2(3)		Granted by the operating system: Y/N (occurs if configuration parameter OS_ROLES = TRUE)

USER_SEGMENTS

This view lists information about storage allocation for database segments belonging to a user's objects.

Column	Datatype	NULL	Description
SEGMENT_NAME	VARCHAR2(81)		Name of the segment, if any
PARTITION_NAME	VARCHAR2(30)		Object Partition Name (Set to NULL for non-partitioned objects).
SEGMENT_TYPE	VARCHAR2(17)		Type of segment: INDEX PARTITION, TABLE PARTITION, TABLE, CLUSTER, INDEX, ROLLBACK, DEFERRED ROLLBACK, TEMPORARY, CACHE
TABLESPACE_NAME	VARCHAR2(30)		Name of the tablespace containing the segment
BYTES	NUMBER		Size of the segment in bytes
BLOCKS	NUMBER		Size of the segment in Oracle blocks
EXTENTS	NUMBER		Number of extents allocated to the segment
INITIAL_EXTENT	NUMBER		Size of the initial extent in Oracle blocks
NEXT_EXTENT	NUMBER		Size of the next extent to be allocated in Oracle blocks
MIN_EXTENTS	NUMBER		Minimum number of extents allowed in the segment
MAX_EXTENTS	NUMBER		Maximum number of extents allowed in the segment

Column	Datatype	NULL	Description
PCT_INCREASE	NUMBER		Percent by which to increase the size of the next extent to be allocated
FREELISTS	NUMBER		Number of process freelists allocated to this segment
FREELIST_GROUPS	NUMBER		Number of freelist groups allocated to this segment
BUFFER_POOL	VARCHAR2(7)		Name of the default buffer pool for the appropriate object

USER_SEQUENCES

This view lists descriptions of the user's sequences.

Column	Datatype	NULL	Description
SEQUENCE_NAME	VARCHAR2(30)	NOT NULL	SEQUENCE name
MIN_VALUE	NUMBER		Minimum value of the sequence
MAX_VALUE	NUMBER		Maximum value of the sequence
INCREMENT_BY	NUMBER	NOT NULL	Value by which the sequence is incremented
CYCLE_FLAG	VARCHAR2(1)		Does sequence wraparound on reaching limit
ORDER_FLAG	VARCHAR2(1)		Are sequence numbers generated in order
CACHE_SIZE	NUMBER	NOT NULL	Number of sequence numbers to cache
LAST_NUMBER	NUMBER	NOT NULL	Last sequence number written to disk. If a sequence uses caching, the number written to disk is the last number placed in the sequence cache. This number is likely to be greater than the last sequence number that was actually used. This value is *not* continuously updated during database operation. It is intended for use after a warm start or import.

USER_SNAPSHOTS

This view lists snapshots that the user can view.

Column	Datatype	NULL	Description
OWNER	VARCHAR2(30)	NOT NULL	Owner of the snapshot
NAME	VARCHAR2(30)	NOT NULL	Name of the view used by users and applications for viewing the snapshot
TABLE_NAME	VARCHAR2(30)	NOT NULL	The table name
MASTER_VIEW	VARCHAR2(30)		View of the master table, owned by the snapshot owner, used for refreshes. this is obsolete in Oracle8 and is NULL.
MASTER_OWNER	VARCHAR2(30)		Owner of the master table
MASTER	VARCHAR2(30)		Name of the master table of which this snapshot is a copy

Column	Datatype	NULL	Description
MASTER_LINK	VARCHAR2(128)		Database link name to the master site
CAN_USE_LOG	VARCHAR2(3)		YES if this snapshot can use a snapshot log, NO if this snapshot is too complex to use a log
UPDATABLE	VARCHAR2(3)		If YES, then snapshot is updatable snapshot. If NO, then is a read-only snapshot.
LAST_REFRESH	DATE		Date and time at the master site of the last refresh
ERROR	NUMBER		The number of failed automatic refreshes since last successful refresh
TYPE	VARCHAR2(8)		Type of refresh for all automatic refreshes: COMPLETE, FAST, FORCE
NEXT	VARCHAR2(200)		Date function used to compute next refresh dates
START_WITH	DATE		Date function used to compute next refresh dates
REFRESH_GROUP	NUMBER		All snapshots in a given refresh group get refreshed in the same transaction
REFRESH_METHOD	VARCHAR2(11)		Values used to drive a fast refresh of the snapshot
FR_OPERATIONS	VARCHAR2(10)		Status of generated fast refresh operations: (REGENERATE, VALID)
CR_OPERATIONS	VARCHAR2(10)		Status of generated complete refresh operations: (REGENERATE, VALID)
UPDATE_TRIG	VARCHAR2(30)		Obsolete. It is NULL for Oracle8 snapshots.
UPDATE_LOG	VARCHAR2(30)		The table that logs changes made to an updatable snapshots
QUERY	LONG		Original query of which this snapshot is an instantiation
MASTER_ROLLBACK_SEG	VARCHAR2(30		Rollback segment used at the main site.

USER_SNAPSHOT_LOGS

This view lists all snapshot logs owned by the user.

Column	Datatype	NULL	Description
LOG_OWNER	VARCHAR2(30)	NOT NULL	Owner of the snapshot log
MASTER	VARCHAR2(30)	NOT NULL	Name of the master table for which the log records changes
LOG_TABLE	VARCHAR2(30)	NOT NULL	Log table that holds the ROWIDs and timestamps of rows that changed in the master table
LOG_TRIGGER	VARCHAR2(30)		Obsolete. It is NULL for Oracle8 snapshots.
ROWIDS	VARCHAR2(3)		If YES, the snapshot log records rowid information
PRIMARY_KEY	VARCHAR2(3)		If YES, the snapshot log records primary_key information

Column	Datatype	NULL	Description
FILTER_COLUMNS	VARCHAR2(3)		If YES, the snapshot log records filter column information
CURRENT_SNAPSHOTS	DATE		Date and time when the snapshot of the master was last refreshed
SNAPSHOT_ID	NUMBER(38)		Unique snapshot identifier.

USER_SOURCE

This view contains text source of all stored objects belonging to the user.

Column	Datatype	NULL	Description
NAME	VARCHAR2(30)	NOT NULL	Name of the object
TYPE	VARCHAR2(12)		Type of object: PROCEDURE, PACKAGE, FUNCTION, TYPE, TYPE BODY, or PACKAGE BODY
LINE	NUMBER	NOT NULL	Line number of this line of source
TEXT	VARCHAR2(4000)		Text source of the stored object

USER_SYNONYMS

This view lists the user's private synonyms.

Column	Datatype	NULL	Description
SYNONYM_NAME	VARCHAR2(30)	NOT NULL	Name of the synonym
TABLE_OWNER	VARCHAR2(30)		Owner of the object referenced by the synonym
TABLE_NAME	VARCHAR2(30)	NOT NULL	Name of the object referenced by the synonym
DB_LINK	VARCHAR2(128)		Database link referenced in a remote synonym

USER_SYS_PRIVS

This view lists system privileges granted to the user.

Column	Datatype	NULL	Description
USERNAME	VARCHAR2(30)		Name of the user, or PUBLIC
PRIVILEGE	VARCHAR2(40)	NOT NULL	System privilege granted to the user
ADMIN_OPTION	VARCHAR2(3)		Signifies the privilege was granted with ADMIN option

USER_TAB_COL_STATISTICS

This view contains column statistics and histogram information which is in the USER_TAB_COLUMNS view. For more information, see "USER_TAB_COLUMNS" on page 2-157.

Column	Datatype	NULL	Description
TABLE_NAME	VARCHAR2(30)	NOT NULL	Table name
COLUMN_NAME	VARCHAR2(30)	NOT NULL	Column name
NUM_DISTINCT	NUMBER		Number of distinct values in the column
LOW_VALUE	RAW(32)		Low value in the column
HIGH_VALUE	RAW(32)		High value in the column
DENSITY	NUMBER		Density of the column
NUM_NULLS	NUMBER		Number of nulls in the column
NUM_BUCKETS	NUMBER		Number of buckets in histogram for the column
SAMPLE_SIZE	NUMBER		Sample size used in analyzing this column
LAST_ANALYZED	DATE		Date of the most recent time this column was analyzed

USER_TAB_COLUMNS

his view contains information about columns of user's tables, views, and clusters. To gather statistics for this view, use the SQL command ANALYZE.

Column	Datatype	NULL	Description
TABLE_NAME	VARCHAR2(30)	NOT NULL	Table, view, or cluster name
COLUMN_NAME	VARCHAR2(30)	NOT NULL	Column name
DATA_LENGTH	NUMBER	NOT NULL	Maximum length of the column in bytes
DATA_TYPE	VARCHAR2(30)		Datatype of the column
DATA_TYPE_MOD	VARCHAR2(3)		Datatype modifier of the column
DATA_TYPE_OWNER	VARCHAR2(30)		Owner of the datatype of the column
DATA_PRECISION	NUMBER		Decimal precision for NUMBER datatype; binary precision for FLOAT datatype; NULL for all other datatypes
DATA_SCALE	NUMBER		Digits to right of decimal point in a number
NULLABLE	VARCHAR2(1)		Does column allow NULLs? Value is N if there is a NOT NULL constraint on the column or if the column is part of a PRIMARY KEY.
COLUMN_ID	NUMBER	NOT NULL	Sequence number of the column as created
DEFAULT_LENGTH	NUMBER		Length of default value for the column

Column	Datatype	NULL	Description
DATA_DEFAULT	LONG		Default value for the column
NUM_DISTINCT	NUMBER		These columns remain for backward compatibility with Oracle7. This information is now in the {TABIPART}_COL_STATISTICS views. This view now picks up these values from HIST_HEAD$ rather than COL$.
LOW_VALUE HIGH_VALUE	RAW(32)		
DENSITY	NUMBER		
NUM_NULLS	NUMBER		The number of NULLs in the column
NUM_BUCKETS	NUMBER		The number of buckets in histogram for the column
LAST_ANALYZED	DATE		The date of the most recent time this column was analyzed
SAMPLE_SIZE	NUMBER		The sample size used in analyzing this column
PACKED	VARCHAR2(1)		Does column store values in packed format?
CHARACTER_SET _NAME	VARCHAR2(44)		The name of the character set: CHAR_CS, NCHAR_CS

USER_TAB_COMMENTS

This view contains comments on the tables and views owned by the user.

Column	Datatype	NULL	Description
TABLE_NAME	VARCHAR2(30)	NOT NULL	Name of the object
TABLE_TYPE	VARCHAR2(11)		Type of the object: TABLE (indicating the value for object tables and regular tables) or VIEW
COMMENTS	VARCHAR2(4000)		Comment on the object

USER_TAB_HISTOGRAMS

This view lists histograms on columns of user's tables.

Column	Datatype	NULL	Description
TABLE_NAME	VARCHAR2(30)		Table name
COLUMN_NAME	VARCHAR2(4000)		Column name or attribute of the object type column
BUCKET_NUMBER	NUMBER		Bucket number
ENDPOINT_VALUE	NUMBER		Normalized endpoint values for this bucket

USER_TAB_PARTITIONS

This view describes, for each table partition, the partition level partitioning information, the storage parameters for the partition, and various partition statistics determined by ANALYZE that the current user owns.

Column	Datatype	NULL	Description
TABLE_NAME	VARCHAR2(30)	NOT NULL	Table name
PARTITION_NAME	VARCHAR2(30)		Partition name
HIGH_VALUE	LONG		Partition bound value expression
HIGH_VALUE_LENGTH	NUMBER	NOT NULL	Length of partition bound value expression
PARTITION_POSITION	NUMBER	NOT NULL	Position of the partition within the table
TABLESPACE_NAME	VARCHAR2(30)	NOT NULL	Name of the tablespace containing the partition
PCT_FREE	NUMBER	NOT NULL	Minimum percentage of free space in a block
PCT_USED	NUMBER	NOT NULL	Minimum percentage of used space in a block
INI_TRANS	NUMBER	NOT NULL	Initial number of transactions
MAX_TRANS	NUMBER	NOT NULL	Maximum number of transactions
INITIAL_EXTENT	NUMBER		Size of the initial extent in bytes
NEXT_EXTENT	NUMBER		Size of secondary extents in bytes
MIN_EXTENT	NUMBER	NOT NULL	Minimum number of extents allowed in the segment
MAX_EXTENT	NUMBER	NOT NULL	Maximum number of extents allowed in the segment
PCT_INCREASE	NUMBER	NOT NULL	Percentage increase in extent size
FREELISTS	NUMBER		Number of process freelists allocated in this segment
FREELIST_GROUPS	NUMBER		Number of freelist groups allocated in this segment
LOGGING	VARCHAR2(3)		Logging attribute of partition
NUM_ROWS	NUMBER		Number of rows in the partition
BLOCKS	NUMBER		Number of used blocks in the partition
EMPTY_BLOCKS	NUMBER		Number of empty (never used) blocks in the partition
AVG_SPACE	NUMBER		Average available free space in the partition
CHAIN_CNT	NUMBER		Number of chained rows in the partition
AVG_ROW_LEN	NUMBER		Average row length, including row overhead
SAMPLE_SIZE	NUMBER		Sample size used in analyzing this partition
LAST_ANALYZED	DATE		Date of the most recent time this partition was analyzed
BUFFER_POOL	VARCHAR2(7)		Actual buffer pool of the given object

USER_TAB_PRIVS

This view contains information on grants on objects for which the user is the owner, grantor, or grantee.

Column	Datatype	NULL	Description
GRANTEE	VARCHAR2(30)	NOT NULL	Name of the user to whom access was granted
OWNER	VARCHAR2(30)	NOT NULL	Owner of the object
TABLE_NAME	VARCHAR2(30)	NOT NULL	Name of the object
GRANTOR	VARCHAR2(30)	NOT NULL	Name of the user who performed the grant
PRIVILEGE	VARCHAR2(40)	NOT NULL	Privilege on the object
GRANTABLE	VARCHAR2(3)		YES if the privileges was granted with ADMIN OPTION; otherwise NO

USER_TAB_PRIVS_MADE

This view contains information about all grants on objects owned by the user.

Column	Datatype	NULL	Description
GRANTEE	VARCHAR2(30)	NOT NULL	Name of the user to whom access was granted
TABLE_NAME	VARCHAR2(30)	NOT NULL	Name of the object
GRANTOR	VARCHAR2(30)	NOT NULL	Name of the user who performed the grant
PRIVILEGE	VARCHAR2(40)	NOT NULL	Privilege on the object
GRANTABLE	VARCHAR2(3)		YES if the privilege was granted with ADMIN OPTION; otherwise NO

USER_TAB_PRIVS_RECD

This view contains information about grants on objects for which the user is the grantee.

Column	Datatype	NULL	Description
OWNER	VARCHAR2(30)	NOT NULL	Owner of the object
TABLE_NAME	VARCHAR2(30)	NOT NULL	Name of the object
GRANTOR	VARCHAR2(30)	NOT NULL	Name of the user who performed the grant
PRIVILEGE	VARCHAR2(40)	NOT NULL	Privilege on the object
GRANTABLE	VARCHAR2(3)		YES if the privilege was granted with ADMIN OPTION; otherwise NO

USER_TABLES

This view contains a description of the user's own relational tables. To gather statistics for this view, use the SQL command ANALYZE.

Column	Datatype	NULL	Description
TABLE_NAME	VARCHAR2(30)	NOT NULL	Name of the table
TABLESPACE_NAME	VARCHAR2(30)		Name of the tablespace containing the table
CLUSTER_NAME	VARCHAR2(30)		Name of the cluster, if any, to which the table belongs
IOT_NAME	VARCHAR2(30)		Name of the index organized table, if any, to which the overflow entry belongs
PCT_FREE	NUMBER		Minimum percentage of free space in a block
PCT_USED	NUMBER		Minimum percentage of used space in a block
INI_TRANS	NUMBER		Initial number of transactions
MAX_TRANS	NUMBER		Maximum number of transactions
INITIAL_EXTENT	NUMBER		Size of the initial extent in bytes
NEXT_EXTENT	NUMBER		Size of secondary extents in bytes
MIN_EXTENTS	NUMBER		Minimum number of extents allowed in the segment
MAX_EXTENTS	NUMBER		Maximum number of extents allowed in the segment
PCT_INCREASE	NUMBER		Percentage increase in extent size
FREELISTS	NUMBER		Number of process freelists allocated to this segment
FREELIST_GROUPS	NUMBER		Number of freelist groups allocated to this segment
LOGGING	VARCHAR2(3)		Logging attribute
BACKED_UP	VARCHAR2(1)		Has table been backed up since last modification
NUM_ROWS	NUMBER		Number of rows returned by the ANALYZE command
BLOCKS	NUMBER		Number of used data blocks in the table
EMPTY_BLOCKS	NUMBER		Number of empty (never used) data blocks in the table
AVG_SPACE	NUMBER		Average amount of free space (in bytes) in a data block allocated to the table
CHAIN_CNT	NUMBER		Number of rows in the table that are chained from one data block to another or that have migrated to a new block, requiring a link to preserve the old ROWID
AVG_ROW_LEN	NUMBER		Average length of a row in the table in bytes
AVG_SPACE_FREELIST _BLOCKS	NUMBER		The average freespace of all blocks on a freelist
NUM_FREELIST _BLOCKS	NUMBER		The number of blocks on the freelist
DEGREE	VARCHAR2(10)		The number of threads per instance for scanning the table
INSTANCES	VARCHAR2(10)		The number of instances across which the table is to be scanned

Column	Datatype	NULL	Description
CACHE	VARCHAR2(5)		Whether the table is to be cached in the buffer cache
TABLE_LOCK	VARCHAR2(8)		Whether table locking is enabled or disabled
SAMPLE_SIZE	NUMBER		Sample size used in analyzing this table
LAST_ANALYZED	DATE		Date of the most recent time this table was analyzed
PARTITIONED	VARCHAR2(3)		Indicates whether this table is partitioned. Set to 'YES' if it is partitioned
IOT_TYPE	VARCHAR2(12)		If this is an index organized table, then IOT_TYPE is IOT or IOT_OVERFLOW. If this is not an index organized table, IOT_TYPE is NULL
TABLE_TYPE_OWNER	VARCHAR2(0)		Owner of the type of the table if the table is a typed table
TABLE_TYPE	VARCHAR2(0)		Type of the table if the table is a typed table
PACKED	VARCHAR2(0)		If the table is a typed table, does it store objects in packed format?
TEMPORARY	VARCHAR2(1)		Can the current session see only the data that it places in this object itself?
NESTED	VARCHAR2(3)		Is the table a nested table?
BUFFER_POOL	VARCHAR2(7)		Name of the default buffer pool for the appropriate object

USER_TABLESPACES

This view contains descriptions of accessible tablespaces.

Column	Datatype	NULL	Description
TABLESPACE_NAME	VARCHAR2(30)	NOT NULL	Tablespace name
INITIAL_EXTENT	NUMBER		Default initial extent size
NEXT_EXTENT	NUMBER		Default incremental extent size
MIN_EXTENTS	NUMBER	NOT NULL	Default minimum number of extents
MAX_EXTENTS	NUMBER	NOT NULL	Default maximum number of extents
PCT_INCREASE	NUMBER	NOT NULL	Default percent increase for extent size
MIN_EXTLEN	NUMBER		Minimum extent size for the tablespace
STATUS	VARCHAR2(9)		Tablespace status: ONLINE, OFFLINE, or INVALID (tablespace has been dropped)
CONTENTS	VARCHAR2(9)		Tablespace contents: "PERMANENT", or "TEMPORARY"
LOGGING	VARCHAR2(9)		Default logging attribute

USER_TRIGGERS

This view contains descriptions of the user's triggers.

Column	Datatype	NULL	Description
TRIGGER_NAME	VARCHAR2(30)	NOT NULL	Name of the trigger
TRIGGER_TYPE	VARCHAR2(16)		When the trigger fires: BEFORE EACH ROW, AFTER EACH ROW, BEFORE STATEMENT, AFTER STATEMENT
TRIGGERING_EVENT	VARCHAR2(26)		Statement that fires the trigger: INSERT, UPDATE, DELETE
TABLE_OWNER	VARCHAR2(30)	NOT NULL	Owner of the table on which the trigger is defined
TABLE_NAME	VARCHAR2(30)	NOT NULL	Table on which the trigger is defined
REFERENCING_NAMES	VARCHAR2(87)		Names used for referencing to OLD and NEW values within the trigger
WHEN_CLAUSE	VARCHAR2(4000)		WHEN clause. Must evaluate to TRUE for TRIGGER_BODY to execute.
STATUS	VARCHAR2(8)		Whether the trigger is enabled: ENABLED or DISABLED
DESCRIPTION	VARCHAR2(4000)		Trigger description. Useful for re-creating a trigger creation statement.
TRIGGER_BODY	LONG		Statement(s) executed by the trigger when it fires

USER_TRIGGER_COLS

This view displays the usage of columns in triggers owned by the user or on one of the user's tables.

Column	Datatype	NULL	Description
TRIGGER_OWNER	VARCHAR2(30)	NOT NULL	Owner of the trigger
TRIGGER_NAME	VARCHAR2(30)	NOT NULL	Name of the trigger
TABLE_OWNER	VARCHAR2(30)	NOT NULL	Owner of the table on which the trigger is defined
TABLE_NAME	VARCHAR2(30)	NOT NULL	Table on which the trigger is defined
COLUMN_NAME	VARCHAR2(4000)		Name of the column used in the trigger
COLUMN_LIST	VARCHAR2(3)		Column specified in UPDATE clause: Y/N
COLUMN_USAGE	VARCHAR2(17)		How the column is used in the trigger. All applicable combinations of NEW, OLD, IN, OUT, and IN OUT.

USER_TS_QUOTAS

This view contains information about tablespace quotas for the user.

Column	Datatype	NULL	Description
TABLESPACE_NAME	VARCHAR2(30)	NOT NULL	Tablespace name
BYTES	NUMBER		Number of bytes charged to the user
MAX_BYTES	NUMBER		User's quota in bytes, or -1 for UNLIMITED
BLOCKS	NUMBER	NOT NULL	Number of Oracle blocks charged to the user
MAX_BLOCKS	NUMBER		User's quota in Oracle blocks, or -1 or UNLIMITED

USER_TYPES

This view displays the user's types in a table.

Column	Datatype	NULL	Description
TYPE_NAME	VARCHAR2(30)	NOT NULL	Name of the type
TYPE_OID	RAW(16)	NOT NULL	Object identifier (OID) of the type
TYPECODE	VARCHAR2(30)		Typecode of the type
ATTRIBUTES	NUMBER		Number of attributes (if any) in the type
METHODS	NUMBER		Number of methods (if any) in the type
PREDEFINED	VARCHAR2(3)		Indicates whether the type is a predefined type
INCOMPLETE	VARCHAR2(3)		Indicates whether the type is an incomplete type

USER_TYPE_ATTRS

This view displays the attributes of the user's types.

Column	Datatype	NULL	Description
TYPE_NAME	VARCHAR2(30)	NOT NULL	Name of the type
ATTR_NAME	VARCHAR2(30)	NOT NULL	Name of the attribute
ATTR_TYPE_MOD	VARCHAR2(7)		Type modifier of the attribute
ATTR_TYPE_OWNER	VARCHAR2(30)		Owner of the type of the attribute
ATTR_TYPE_NAME	VARCHAR2(30)		Name of the type of the attribute
LENGTH	NUMBER		Length of the CHAR attribute or maximum length of the VARCHAR or VARCHAR2 attribute
PRECISION	NUMBER		Decimal precision of the NUMBER or DECIMAL attribute or binary precision of the FLOAT attribute
SCALE	NUMBER		Scale of the NUMBER or DECIMAL attribute

Column	Datatype	NULL	Description
CHARACTER_SET_NAME	VARCHAR2(44)		The name of the character set: CHAR_CS, NCHAR_CS

USER_TYPE_METHODS

This view is a description of the user's methods types.

Column	Datatype	NULL	Description
TYPE_NAME	VARCHAR2(30)	NOT NULL	Name of the type
METHOD_NAME	VARCHAR2(30)	NOT NULL	Name of the method
METHOD_NO	NUMBER		Method number for distinguishing overloaded method (not to be used as ID number)
METHOD_TYPE	VARCHAR2(6)		Type of the method
PARAMETERS	NUMBER	NOT NULL	Number of parameters to the method
RESULTS	NUMBER	NOT NULL	Number of results returned by the method

USER_UPDATABLE_COLUMNS

This view contains a description of columns that are updatable to the user in a join view.

Column	Datatype	NULL	Description
OWNER	VARCHAR2(30)	NOT NULL	Table owner
TABLE_NAME	VARCHAR2(30)	NOT NULL	Table name
COLUMN_NAME	VARCHAR2(30)	NOT NULL	Column name
UPDATABLE	VARCHAR2(3)		Indicates whether the column is updatable
INSERTABLE	VARCHAR2(3)		Indicates whether the column is insertable
DELETABLE	VARCHAR2(3)		Indicates whether the column is deletable

USER_USERS

This view contains information about the current user.

Column	Datatype	NULL	Description
USERNAME	VARCHAR2(30)	NOT NULL	Name of the user
USER_ID	NUMBER	NOT NULL	ID number of the user
ACCOUNT_STATUS	VARCHAR2(32)	NOT NULL	Indicates if the account is locked, expired, or unlocked

Column	Datatype	NULL	Description
LOCK_DATE	DATE		Date the account was locked if account status is locked
EXPIRY_DATE	DATE		Date of expiration of the account if account status is expired
DEFAULT_TABLESPACE	VARCHAR2(30)	NOT NULL	Default tablespace for data
TEMPORARY_TABLESPACE	VARCHAR2(30)	NOT NULL	Default tablespace for temporary tables
CREATED	DATE	NOT NULL	User creation date
EXTERNAL_NAME	VARCHAR2(4000)		User external name

USER_VIEWS

This view contains the text of views owned by the user.

Column	Datatype	NULL	Description
VIEW_NAME	VARCHAR2(30)	NOT NULL	Name of the view
TEXT_LENGTH	NUMBER		Length of the view text
TEXT	LONG		View text
TYPE_TEXT_LENGTH	NUMBER		Length of the type clause of the typed view
TYPE_TEXT	VARCHAR2(4000)		Type clause of the typed view
OID_TEXT_LENGTH	NUMBER		Length of the WITH OID clause of the typed view
OID_TEXT	VARCHAR2(4000)		WITH OID clause of the typed view
VIEW_TYPE_OWNER	VARCHAR2(30)		Owner of the type of the view if the view is a typed view
VIEW_TYPE	VARCHAR2(30)		Type of the view if the view is a typed view

3

Dynamic Performance (V$) Views

This chapter describes the dynamic performance views, which are also known as V$ views.

The following topics are included in this chapter:

- Dynamic Performance Views
- View Descriptions

Dynamic Performance Views

The Oracle Server contains a set of underlying views that are maintained by the server and accessible to the database administrator user SYS. These views are called *dynamic performance views* because they are continuously updated while a database is open and in use, and their contents relate primarily to performance.

Although these views appear to be regular database tables, they are not. These views provide data on internal disk structures and memory structures. These views can be selected from, but never updated or altered by the user.

The file CATALOG.SQL contains definitions of the views and public synonyms for the dynamic performance views. You must run CATALOG.SQL to create these views and synonyms.

V$ Views

Dynamic performance views are identified by the prefix V_$. Public synonyms for these views have the prefix V$. Database administrators or users should only access the V$ objects, not the V_$ objects.

The dynamic performance views are used by Enterprise Manager and Oracle Trace, which is the primary interface for accessing information about system performance.

Suggestion: Once the instance is started, the V$ views that read from memory are accessible. Views that read data from disk require that the database be mounted.

Warning: Information about the dynamic performance views is presented for completeness only; this information does not imply a commitment to support these views in the future.

GV$ Views

In Oracle, there is an additional class of fixed views, the GV$ (Global V$) fixed views. For each of the V$ views described in this chapter (with the exception of V$CACHE_LOCK, V$LOCK_ACTIVITY, V$LOCKS_WITH_COLLISIONS, and V$ROLLNAME), there is a GV$ view. In a parallel server environment, querying a GV$ view retrieves the V$ view information from all qualified instances. In addition to the V$ information, each GV$ view possesses an additional column named INST_ID with type integer. The INST_ID column displays the instance number from which the associated V$ view information was obtained. The INST_ID column can be used as a filter to retrieve V$ information from a subset of available instances. For example, the query:

```
SELECT * FROM GV$LOCK WHERE INST_ID = 2 OR INST_ID = 5
```

retrieves the information from the V$ views on instances 2 and 5.

The GV$ views can be used to return information on groups of instances defined with the OPS_ADMIN_GROUP parameter. For more information see "OPS_ADMIN_GROUP" on page 1-83 and *Oracle8 Parallel Server Concepts & Administration*.

Restrictions on GV$ Views

GV$ views have the following restrictions:

- The value of the PARALLEL_MAX_SERVERS parameter must be greater than zero on all instances mounting the database.

- The OPS_ADMIN_GROUP parameter must be defined with at least one member for a query to successfully complete.

Access to the Dynamic Performance Tables

After installation, only username SYS or anyone with SYSDBA ROLE has access to the dynamic performance tables.

For more information, see *Oracle Enterprise Manager: Performance Monitoring User's Guide*.

View Descriptions

This section lists the columns and public synonyms for the dynamic performance views.

FILEXT$

FILEXT$ is created the first time you turn on the AUTOEXTEND characteristic for a datafile.

Column	Datatype	Description
FILE#	NUMBER	File identifier
MAXEXTEND	NUMBER	Value from the MAXSIZE parameter
INC	NUMBER	Value from the NEXT parameter

For more information, see the *Oracle8 Server Administrator's Guide*.

V$ACCESS

This view displays objects in the database that are currently locked and the sessions that are accessing them.

Column	Datatype	Description
SID	NUMBER	Session number that is accessing an object
OWNER	VARCHAR2(64)	Owner of the object
OBJECT	VARCHAR2(1000)	Name of the object
TYPE	VARCHAR2(12)	Type identifier for the object

V$ACTIVE_INSTANCES

This view maps instance names to instance numbers for all instances that have the database currently mounted.

Column	Datatype	Description
INST_NUMBER	NUMBER	The instance number
INST_NAME	VARCHAR2(60)	The instance name

V$ARCHIVE

This view contains information on archive logs for each thread in the database system. Each row provides information for one thread. This information is also available in V$LOG. Oracle recommends that you use V$LOG. For more information, see "V$LOG" on page 3-57.

Column	Datatype	Description
GROUP#	NUMBER	Log file group number
THREAD#	NUMBER	Log file thread number
SEQUENCE#	NUMBER	Log file sequence number
CURRENT	VARCHAR2(3)	Archive log currently in use
FIRST_CHANGE#	NUMBER	First SCN stored in the current log

V$ARCHIVE_DEST

This view describes, for the current instance, all the archive log destinations, their current value, mode, and status.

Column	Datatype	Description
ARCMODE	VARCHAR2(12)	Archiving mode: • MUST SUCCEED: This is a must-succeed destination • BEST-EFFORT: This is a best-effort destination
STATUS	VARCHAR2(8)	Status: • NORMAL: This destination is normal • DISABLED: This destination has been disabled
DESTINATION	VARCHAR2(256)	Destination text string

For more information on archived log destinations, see "LOG_ARCHIVE_DEST" on page 1-58, "LOG_ARCHIVE_DUPLEX_DEST" on page 1-58, and "LOG_ARCHIVE_MIN_SUCCEED_DEST" on page 1-60

V$ARCHIVED_LOG

This view displays archived log information from the controlfile including archive log names. An archive log record is inserted after the online redo log is successfully archived or cleared (name column is NULL if the log was cleared). If the log is archived twice, there will be two archived log records with the same THREAD#, SEQUENCE#, and FIRST_CHANGE#, but with a different name. An archive log record is also inserted when an archive log is restored from a backup set or a copy.

Column	Datatype	Description
RECID	NUMBER	Archived log record ID
STAMP	NUMBER	Archived log record stamp
NAME	VARCHAR2(512)	Archived log file name. If set to NULL, the log file was cleared before it was archived
THREAD#	NUMBER	Redo thread number

Column	Datatype	Description
SEQUENCE#	NUMBER	Redo log sequence number
RESETLOGS_CHANGE#	NUMBER	Resetlogs change# of the database when this log was written
RESETLOGS_TIME	DATE	Resetlogs time of the database when this log was written
FIRST_CHANGE#	NUMBER	First change# in the archived log
FIRST_TIME	DATE	Timestamp of the first change
NEXT_CHANGE#	NUMBER	First change in the next log
NEXT_TIME	DATE	Timestamp of the next change
BLOCKS	NUMBER	Size of the archived log in blocks
BLOCK_SIZE	NUMBER	Redo log block size
COMPLETION_TIME	DATE	Time when the archiving completed
DELETED	VARCHAR2(3)	YES/NO

V$BACKUP

This view displays the backup status of all online datafiles.

Column	Datatype	Description
FILE#	NUMBER	File identifier
STATUS	VARCHAR2(18)	File status: NOT ACTIVE, ACTIVE (backup in progress), OFFLINE NORMAL, or description of an error
CHANGE#	NUMBER	System change number when backup started
TIME	DATE	Time the backup started

V$BACKUP_CORRUPTION

This view displays information about corruptions in datafile backups from the controlfile. Note that corruptions are not tolerated in the controlfile and archived log backups.

Column	Datatype	Description
RECID	NUMBER	Backup corruption record ID
STAMP	NUMBER	Backup corruption record stamp
SET_STAMP	NUMBER	Backup set stamp
SET_COUNT	NUMBER	Backup set count
PIECE#	NUMBER	Backup piece number
FILE#	NUMBER	Datafile number
BLOCK#	NUMBER	First block of the corrupted range
BLOCKS	NUMBER	Number of contiguous blocks in the corrupted range
CORRUPTION _CHANGE#	NUMBER	Change# at which the logical corruption was detected. Set to 0 to indicate media corruption
MARKED_CORRUPT	VARCHAR2(3)	YES/NO. If set to YES the blocks were not marked corrupted in the datafile, but were detected and marked as corrupted while making the datafile backup

V$BACKUP_DATAFILE

This view displays backup datafile and backup controlfile information from the controlfile.

Column	Datatype	Description
RECID	NUMBER	Backup datafile record ID
STAMP	NUMBER	Backup datafile record stamp
SET_STAMP	NUMBER	Backup set stamp
SET_COUNT	NUMBER	Backup set count
FILE#	NUMBER	Datafile number. Set to 0 for controlfile

Column	Datatype	Description
CREATION_CHANGE#	NUMBER	Creation change of the datafile
CREATION_TIME	DATE	Creation timestamp of the datafile
RESETLOGS_CHANGE#	NUMBER	Resetlogs change# of the datafile when it was backed up
RESETLOGS_TIME	DATE	Resetlogs timestamp of the datafile when it was backed up
INCREMENTAL_LEVEL	NUMBER	(0-4) incremental backup level
INCREMENTAL_CHANGE#	NUMBER	All blocks changed after incremental change# is included in this backup. Set to 0 for a full backup
CHECKPOINT_CHANGE#	NUMBER	All changes up to checkpoint change# are included in this backup
CHECKPOINT_TIME	DATE	Timestamp of the checkpoint
ABSOLUTE_FUZZY _CHANGE#	NUMBER	Highest change# in this backup
MARKED_CORRUPT	NUMBER	Number of blocks marked corrupt
MEDIA_CORRUPT	NUMBER	Number of blocks media corrupt
LOGICALLY_CORRUPT	NUMBER	Number of blocks logically corrupt
DATAFILE_BLOCKS	NUMBER	Size of the datafile in blocks at backup time. This value is also the number of blocks taken by the datafile restarted from this backup
BLOCKS	NUMBER	Size of the backup datafile in blocks. Unused blocks are not copied to the backup
BLOCK_SIZE	NUMBER	Block size
OLDEST_OFFLINE _RANGE	NUMBER	The RECID of the oldest offline range record in this backup controlfile. 0 for datafile backups
COMPLETION_TIME	DATE	The time completed.

V$BACKUP_DEVICE

This view displays information about supported backup devices. If a device type does not support named devices, then one row with the device type and a null device name is returned for that device type. If a device type supports named devices then one row is returned for each available device of that type. The special device type DISK is not returned by this view because it is always available.

Column	Datatype	Description
DEVICE_TYPE	VARCHAR2(17)	Type of the backup device
DEVICE_NAME	VARCHAR2(512)	Name of the backup device

V$BACKUP_PIECE

This view displays information about backup pieces from the controlfile. Each backup set consist of one or more backup pieces.

Column	Datatype	Description
RECID	NUMBER	Backup piece record ID
STAMP	NUMBER	Backup piece record stamp
SET_STAMP	NUMBER	Backup set stamp
SET_COUNT	NUMBER	Backup set count
PIECE#	NUMBER	Backup piece number (1-N)
DEVICE_TYPE	VARCHAR2(17)	Type of the device on which the backup piece resides. Set to DISK for backup sets on disk. See V$BACKUP_DEVICE
HANDLE	VARCHAR2(513)	Backup piece handle identifies the backup piece on restore
COMMENTS	VARCHAR2(81)	Comment returned by the operating system or storage subsystem. Set to NULL for backup pieces on disk. This value is informational only; not needed for restore.
MEDIA	VARCHAR2(65)	Name of the media on which the backup piece resides. This value is informational only; not needed for restore.
CONCUR	VARCHAR2(3)	YES/NO, Indicates whether the piece on a media that can be accessed concurrently
TAG	VARCHAR2(32)	Backup piece tag. The tag is specified at backup set level, but stored at piece level

Column	Datatype	Description
DELETED	VARCHAR2(3)	If set to YES indicates the piece is deleted, otherwise set to NO
START_TIME	DATE	The starting time.
COMPLETION_TIME	DATE	The completion time.
ELAPSED_SECONDS	NUMBER	The number of elapsed seconds.

V$BACKUP_REDOLOG

This view displays information about archived logs in backup sets from the controlfile. Note that online redo logs cannot be backed up directly; they must be archived first to disk and then backed up. An archive log backup set can contain one or more archived logs.

Column	Datatype	Description
RECID	NUMBER	Record ID for this row. It is an integer that identifies this row.
STAMP	NUMBER	Timestamp used with RECID to uniquely identify this row
SET_STAMP	NUMBER	One of the foreign keys for the row of the V$BACKUP_SET table that identifies this backup set
SET_COUNT	NUMBER	One of the foreign keys for the row of the V$BACKUP_SET table that identifies this backup set
THREAD#	NUMBER	Thread number for the log
SEQUENCE#	NUMBER	Log sequence number
RESETLOGS_CHANGE#	NUMBER	Change number of the last resetlogs before the log was written
RESETLOGS_TIME	DATE	Change time of the last resetlogs before the log was written. These will be the same for all logs in a backup set
FIRST_CHANGE#	NUMBER	SCN when the log was switched into. The redo in the log is at this SCN and greater
FIRST_TIME	DATE	Time allocated when the log was switched into

Column	Datatype	Description
NEXT_CHANGE#	NUMBER	SCN when the log was switched out of. The redo in the log is below this SCN
NEXT_TIME	DATE	Time allocated when the log was switched out of
BLOCKS	NUMBER	Size of the log in logical blocks including the header block
BLOCK_SIZE	NUMBER	Size of the log blocks in bytes

V$BACKUP_SET

This view displays backup set information from the controlfile. A backup set record is inserted after the backup set is successfully completed.

Column	Datatype	Description
RECID	NUMBER	Backup set record ID
STAMP	NUMBER	Backup set record timestamp
SET_STAMP	NUMBER	Backup set stamp. The backup set stamp and count uniquely identify the backup set. Primary key for the V$BACKUP_SET table, and the foreign key for the following tables: V$BACKUP_PIECE V$BACKUP_DATAFILE V$BACKUP_REDOLOG V$BACKUP_CORRUPTION
SET_COUNT	NUMBER	Backup set count. The backup set count is incremented by one every time a new backup set is started (if the backup set is never completed the number is "lost"). If the controlfile is recreated then the count is reset to 1. Therefore the count must be used with the stamp to uniquely identify a backup set. Primary key for the V$BACKUP_SET table, and the foreign key for the following tables: V$BACKUP_PIECE V$BACKUP_DATAFILE V$BACKUP_REDOLOG V$BACKUP_CORRUPTION
BACKUP_TYPE	VARCHAR2(1)	Type of files that are in this backup. If the backup contains archived redo logs, the value is `L'. If this is a datafile full backup, the value is `D'. If this is an incremental backup, the value is `I'.

Column	Datatype	Description
CONTROLFILE _INCLUDED	VARCHAR2(3)	Set to YES if there is a controlfile included in this backup set, otherwise set to NO.
INCREMENTAL _LEVEL	NUMBER	Location where this backup set fits into the database's backup strategy. Set to zero for full datafile backups, non-zero for incremental datafile backups, and NULL for archivelog backups.
PIECES	NUMBER	Number of distinct backup pieces in the backup set
COMPLETION_TIME	DATE	When the backup completes successfully, this is set to the completion time. This is the same time that was returned by backupEnd. If the backup is still in progress or has failed, this is set to NULL.
ELAPSED_SECONDS	NUMBER	The number of elapsed seconds.
BLOCK_SIZE	NUMBER	Block size of the backup set

V$BGPROCESS

This view describes the background processes.

Column	Datatype	Description
PADDR	RAW(4)	Address of the process state object
NAME	VARCHAR2	Name of this background process
DESCRIPTION	VARCHAR2	Description of the background process
ERROR	NUMBER	Error encountered

V$BH

This is a Parallel Server view. This view gives the status and number of pings for every buffer in the SGA.

Column	Datatype	Description
FILE#	NUMBER	Datafile identifier number (to find filename, query DBA_DATA_FILES or V$DBFILES)
BLOCK#	NUMBER	Block number

Column	Datatype	Description
STATUS	VARCHAR2(1)	FREE= not currently in use XCUR= exclusive SCUR= shared current CR= consistent read READ= being read from disk MREC= in media recovery mode IREC= in instance recovery mode
XNC	NUMBER	Number of PCM x to null lock conversions due to contention with another instance. This column is obsolete but is retained for historical compatibility.
LOCK_ELEMENT _ADDR	RAW(4)	The address of the lock element that contains the PCM lock that is covering the buffer. If more than one buffer has the same address, then these buffers are covered by the same PCM lock.
LOCK_ELEMENT _NAME	NUMBER	The address of the lock element that contains the PCM lock that is covering the buffer. If more than one buffer has the same address, then these buffers are covered by the same PCM lock.
LOCK_ELEMENT _CLASS	NUMBER	The address of the lock element that contains the PCM lock that is covering the buffer. If more than one buffer has the same address, then these buffers are covered by the same PCM lock.
FORCED_READS	NUMBER	Number of times the block had to be made re-read from disk because another instance had forced it out of this instance's cache by requesting the PCM lock on this block in lock mode.
FORCED_WRITES	NUMBER	Number of times DBWR had to write this block to disk because this instance had dirtied the block and another instance had requested the PCM lock on the block in conflicting mode.
DIRTY	VARCHAR2(1)	Y = block modified.
TEMP	VARCHAR2(1)	Y = temporary block
PING	VARCHAR2(1)	Y = block pinged
STALE	VARCHAR2(1)	Y = block is stale
DIRECT	VARCHAR2(1)	Y = direct block
NEW	VARCHAR2(1)	Always set to N. This column is obsolete but is retained for historical compatibility

Column	Datatype	Description
OBJD	NUMBER	Database object number of the block that the buffer represents

For more information, see *Oracle8 Parallel Server Concepts & Administration*.

V$BUFFER_POOL

This view displays information about all buffer pools available for the instance. The "sets" pertain to the number of LRU latch sets. For more information, see "DB_BLOCK_LRU_LATCHES" on page 1-28.

Column	Datatype	Description
INST_ID	NUMBER	Instance ID
ID	NUMBER	Buffer pool ID number
NAME	VARCHAR2	Buffer pool name
LO_SETID	NUMBER	Low set ID number
HI_SETID	NUMBER	High set ID number
SET_COUNT	NUMBER	Number of sets in this buffer pool. This is HI_SETID - LO_SETID + 1
SIZE	NUMBER	Number of buffers allocated to the buffer pool
LO_BNUM	NUMBER	Low buffer number for this pool
HI_BNUM	NUMBER	High buffer number for this pool

V$CACHE

This is a Parallel Server view. This view contains information from the block header of each block in the SGA of the current instance as related to particular database objects.

Column	Datatype	Description
FILE#	NUMBER	Datafile identifier number (to find filename, query DBA_DATA_FILES or V$DBFILES)
BLOCK#	NUMBER	Block number

Column	Datatype	Description
STATUS	VARCHAR2(1)	Status of block: FREE = not currently in use XCUR = exclusive SCUR = shared current CR = consistent read READ = being read from disk MREC = in media recovery mode IREC = in instance recovery mode
XNC	NUMBER	Number of PCM x to null lock conversions due to contention with another instance. This column is obsolete but is retained for historical compatibility.
NAME	VARCHAR2(30)	Name of the database object containing the block
KIND	VARCHAR2(12)	Type of database object. See Table 3-1.
OWNER#	NUMBER	Owner number
LOCK_ELEMENT_ADDR	RAW(4)	The address of the lock element that contains the PCM lock that is covering the buffer. If more than one buffer has the same address, then these buffers are covered by the same PCM lock.
LOCK_ELEMENT_ NAME	NUMBER	The address of the lock element that contains the PCM lock that is covering the buffer. If more than one buffer has the same address, then these buffers are covered by the same PCM lock.
PARTITION_NAME	VARCHAR2(30)	NULL for non-partitioned objects

For more information, see *Oracle8 Parallel Server Concepts & Administration.*

Table 3-1: Values for the KIND column

Type Number	KIND Value	Type Number	KIND Value
1	INDEX	11	PACKAGE BODY
2	TABLE	12	TRIGGER
3	CLUSTER	13	TYPE
4	VIEW	14	TYPE BODY
5	SYNONYM	19	TABLE PARTITION
6	SEQUENCE	20	INDEX PARTITION
7	PROCEDURE	21	LOB

Table 3-1: Values for the KIND column

Type Number	KIND Value	Type Number	KIND Value
8	FUNCTION	22	LIBRARY
9	PACKAGE	NULL	UNKNOWN
10	NON-EXISTENT	------	-------

V$CACHE_LOCK

This is a Parallel Server view.

Column	Datatype	Description
FILE#	NUMBER	Datafile identifier number (to find filename, query DBA_DATA_FILES or V$DBFILES)
BLOCK#	NUMBER	Block number
STATUS	VARCHAR2(4)	Status of block: FREE = not currently in use XCUR = exclusive SCUR = shared current CR = consistent read READ = being read from disk MREC = in media recovery mode IREC = in instance recovery mode
XNC	NUMBER	Number of parallel cache management (PCM) lock conversions due to contention with another instance
NAME	VARCHAR2(30)	Name of the database object containing the block
KIND	VARCHAR2(12)	Type of database object. See Table 3-1 on page 3-15.
OWNER#	NUMBER	Owner number
LOCK_ELEMENT _ADDR	RAW(4)	The address of the lock element that contains the PCM lock that is covering the buffer. If more than one buffer has the same address, then these buffers are covered by the same PCM lock.
LOCK_ELEMENT _NAME	NUMBER	The address of the lock element that contains the PCM lock that is covering the buffer. If more than one buffer has the same address, then these buffers are covered by the same PCM lock.

Column	Datatype	Description
FORCED_READS	NUMBER	Number of times the block had to be made re-read from disk because another instance had forced it out of this instance's cache by requesting the PCM lock on this block in lock mode.
FORCED_WRITES	NUMBER	Number of times DBWR had to write this block to disk because this instance had dirtied the block and another instance had requested the PCM lock on the block in conflicting mode.
INDX	NUMBER	Platform specific lock manager identifier
CLASS	NUMBER	Platform specific lock manager identifier

V$CACHE_LOCK is similar to V$CACHE, except for the platform-specific lock manager identifiers. This information may be useful if the platform-specific lock manager provides tools for monitoring the PCM lock operations that are occurring. For example, first query to find the lock element address using INDX and CLASS, then query V$BH to find the buffers that are covered by the lock. See also "V$CACHE" on page 3-14

For more information, see *Oracle8 Parallel Server Concepts & Administration*.

V$CIRCUIT

This view contains information about virtual circuits, which are user connections to the database through dispatchers and servers.

Column	Datatype	Description
CIRCUIT	RAW(4)	Circuit address
DISPATCHER	RAW(4)	Current dispatcher process address
SERVER	RAW(4)	Current server process address
WAITER	RAW(4)	Address of server process that is waiting for the (currently busy) circuit to become available
SADDR	RAW(4)	Address of session bound to the circuit
STATUS	VARCHAR2	Status of the circuit: BREAK (currently interrupted), EOF (about to be removed), OUTBOUND (an outward link to a remote database), NORMAL (normal circuit into the local database)

Column	Datatype	Description
QUEUE	VARCHAR2	Queue the circuit is currently on: COMMON (on the common queue, waiting to be picked up by a server process), DISPATCHER (waiting for the dispatcher), SERVER (currently being serviced), OUTBOUND (waiting to establish an outbound connection), NONE (idle circuit)
MESSAGE0	NUMBER	Size in bytes of the messages in the first message buffer
MESSAGE1	NUMBER	Size in bytes of the messages in the second message buffer.
MESSAGES	NUMBER	Total number of messages that have gone through this circuit
BYTES	NUMBER	Total number of bytes that have gone through this circuit
BREAKS	NUMBER	Total number of breaks (interruptions) for this circuit

V$CLASS_PING

V$CLASS_PING displays the number of blocks pinged per block class. Use this view to compare contentions for blocks in different classes.

Column	Datatype	Description
CLASS	NUMBER	Number that represents the block class
X_2_NULL	NUMBER	Number of lock conversions from Exclusive-to-NULL for all blocks of the specified CLASS
X_2_NULL_FORCED_WRITE	NUMBER	Number of forced writes that occur for blocks of the specified CLASS due to Exclusive-to-NULL conversions
X_2_NULL_FORCED_STALE	NUMBER	Number of times a block in the CLASS was made STALE due to Exclusive-to-NULL conversions
X_2_S	NUMBER	Number of lock conversions from Exclusive-to-Shared for all blocks of the specified CLASS
X_2_S_FORCED_WRITE	NUMBER	Number of forced writes that occur for blocks of the specified CLASS due to Exclusive-to-Shared conversions

Column	Datatype	Description
X_2_SSX	NUMBER	Number of lock conversions from Exclusive-to-Sub Shared Exclusive for all blocks of the specified CLASS
X_2_SSX_FORCED_WRITE	NUMBER	Number of forced writes that occur for blocks of the specified CLASS due to Exclusive-to-Sub Shared Exclusive conversions
S_2_NULL	NUMBER	Number of lock conversions from Shared-to-NULL for all blocks of the specified CLASS
S_2_NULL_FORCED_STALE	NUMBER	Number of times a block in the CLASS was made STALE due to Shared-to-NULL conversions
SS_2_NULL	NUMBER	Number of lock conversions from Sub Shared-to-NULL for all blocks of the specified CLASS
NULL_2_X	NUMBER	Number of lock conversions from NULL-to-Exclusive for all blocks of the specified CLASS
S_2_X	NUMBER	Number of lock conversions from Shared-to-Exclusive for all blocks of the specified CLASS
SSX_2_X	NUMBER	Number of lock conversions from Sub Shared Exclusive-to-Exclusive for all blocks of the specified CLASS
NULL_2_S	NUMBER	Number of lock conversions from NULL-to-Shared for all blocks of the specified CLASS
NULL_2_SS	NUMBER	Number of lock conversions from NULL-to-Sub Shared for all blocks of the specified CLASS

V$COMPATIBILITY

This view displays features in use by the database instance that may prevent downgrading to a previous release. This is the dynamic (SGA) version of this information, and may not reflect features that other instances have used, and may include temporary incompatibilities (like UNDO segments) that will not exist after the database is shut down cleanly.

Column	Datatype	Description
TYPE_ID	VARCHAR2(8	Internal feature identifier
RELEASE	VARCHAR2(60)	Release in which that feature appeared
DESCRIPTION	VARCHAR2(64)	Description of the feature

V$COMPATSEG

This view lists the permanent features in use by the database that will prevent moving back to an earlier release.

Column	Datatype	Description
TYPE_ID	VARCHAR2(8)	Internal feature identifier
RELEASE	VARCHAR2(60)	Release in which that feature appeared. The software must be able to interpret data formats added in that release
UPDATED	VARCHAR2(60)	Release that first used the feature

V$CONTROLFILE

This view lists the names of the control files.

Column	Datatype	Description
STATUS	VARCHAR2(7)	INVALID if the name cannot be determined, which should not occur. NULL if the name can be determined.
NAME	VARCHAR2(257)	The name of the control file.

V$CONTROLFILE_RECORD_SECTION

This view displays information about the controlfile record sections.

Column	Datatype	Description
TYPE	VARCHAR2(17)	DATABASE/CKPT PROGRESS/REDO THREAD/REDO LOG/DATAFILE/ FILENAME/TABLESPACE/LOG HISTORY/OFFLINE RANGE/ ARCHIVED LOG/BACKUP SET/ BACKUP PIECE/BACKUP DATAFILE/ BACKUP REDOLOG/DATAFILE COPY/BACKUP CORRUPTION/COPY CORRUPTION/DELETED OBJECT
RECORD_SIZE	NUMBER	Record size in bytes
RECORDS_TOTAL	NUMBER	Number of records allocated for the section
RECORDS_USED	NUMBER	Number of records used in the section
FIRST_INDEX	NUMBER	Index (position) of the first record
LAST_INDEX	NUMBER	Index of the last record
LAST_RECID	NUMBER	Record ID of the last record

V$COPY_CORRUPTION

This view displays information about datafile copy corruptions from the controlfile.

Column	Datatype	Description
RECID	NUMBER	Copy corruption record ID
STAMP	NUMBER	Copy corruption record stamp
COPY_RECID	NUMBER	Datafile copy record ID
COPY_STAMP	NUMBER	Datafile copy record stamp
FILE#	NUMBER	Datafile number
BLOCK#	NUMBER	First block of the corrupted range
BLOCKS	NUMBER	Number of contiguous blocks in the corrupted range

Column	Datatype	Description
CORRUPTION_CHANGE#	NUMBER	Change# at which the logical corruption was detected. Set to 0 to indicate media corruption
MARKED_CORRUPT	VARCHAR2(3)	YES/NO. If set to YES the blocks were not marked corrupted in the datafile, but were detected and marked as corrupted while making the datafile copy

V$DATABASE

This view contains database information from the control file.

Column	Datatype	Description
NAME	VARCHAR2	Name of the database
CREATED	DATE	Creation date
LOG_MODE	VARCHAR2	Archive log mode: NOARCHIVELOG or ARCHIVELOG
CHECKPOINT_ CHANGE#	NUMBER	Last SCN checkpointed
ARCHIVE_CHANGE#	NUMBER	Last SCN archived
DBID	NUMBER	Database ID calculated when database is created and stored in all file headers
RESETLOGS_CHANGE#	NUMBER	Change# at open resetlogs
RESETLOGS_TIME	DATE	Timestamp of open resetlogs
CONTROLFILE_TYPE	VARCHAR2(7)	CURRENT/STANDBY/CLONE/ BACKUP/CREATED. STANDBY indicates database is in standby mode. CLONE indicates a clone database. BACKUP/CREATED indicates database is being recovered using a backup or created controlfile. A standby database activate or database open after recovery changes the type to CURRENT
CONTROLFILE_CREATED	DATE	Controlfile creation timestamp
CONTROLFILE_SEQUENCE#	NUMBER	Controlfile sequence number incremented by controlfile transactions

Column	Datatype	Description
CONTROLFILE_CHANGE#	NUMBER	Last change# in backup controlfile. Set to NULL if the controlfile is not a backup
CONTROLFILE_TIME	DATE	Last timestamp in backup controlfile. Set to NULL if the controlfile is not a backup
OPEN_RESETLOGS	VARCHAR2(11)	NOT ALLOWED/ALLOWED/ REQUIRED. Indicates whether next database open allows or requires the resetlogs option

V$DATAFILE

This view contains datafile information from the control file. See also the "V$DATAFILE_HEADER" on page 3-26 view which displays information from datafile headers.

Column	Datatype	Description
FILE#	NUMBER	File identification number
STATUS	VARCHAR2	Type of file (system or user) and its status. Values: OFFLINE, ONLINE, SYSTEM, RECOVER, SYSOFF (an offline file from the SYSTEM tablespace).
ENABLED	VARCHAR2(10)	Describes how accessible the file is from SQL. It is one of the values in Table 3-2 on page 3-24.
CHECKPOINT_ CHANGE#	NUMBER	SCN at last checkpoint
CHECKPOINT_TIME	DATE	Time stamp of the checkpoint#
UNRECOVERABLE_ CHANGE#	NUMBER	Last unrecoverable change# made to this datafile. This column is always updated when an unrecoverable operation completes.
UNRECOVERABLE_ TIME	DATE	Time stamp of the last unrecoverable change
BYTES	NUMBER	Current size in bytes; 0 if inaccessible
CREATE_BYTES	NUMBER	Size when created, in bytes
NAME	VARCHAR2	Name of the file

Column	Datatype	Description
CREATION_CHANGE#	NUMBER	Change number at which the datafile was created
CREATION_TIME	DATE	Timestamp of the datafile creation
TS#	NUMBER	Tablespace number
RFILE#	NUMBER	Tablespace relative datafile number
LAST_CHANGE#	NUMBER	Last change# made to this datafile. Set to NULL if the datafile is being changed
LAST_TIME	DATE	Timestamp of the last change
OFFLINE_CHANGE#	NUMBER	Offline change# of the last offline range. This column is updated only when the datafile is brought online.
ONLINE_CHANGE#	NUMBER	Online change# of the last offline range
ONLINE_TIME	DATE	Online timestamp of the last offline range
BLOCKS	NUMBER	Current datafile size in blocks; 0 if inaccessible
BLOCK_SIZE	NUMBER	Block size of the datafile
NAME	VARCHAR2(512)	Datafile name

Table 3-2 describes values that can be entered in the ENABLED column.

Table 3-2: Values for the ENABLED Column

ENABLED Column Value	Description
DISABLED	No SQL access allowed
READ ONLY	No SQL updates allowed
READ WRITE	Full access allowed
UNKNOWN	Should not occur unless the control file is corrupted

V$DATAFILE_COPY

This view displays datafile copy information from the controlfile.

Column	Datatype	Description
RECID	NUMBER	Datafile copy record ID
STAMP	NUMBER	Datafile copy record stamp
NAME	VARCHAR2(512)	Filename of the datafile copy. The maximum length of the name is OS dependent
TAG	VARCHAR2(32)	Datafile copy tag
FILE#	NUMBER	Absolute datafile number
RFILE#	NUMBER	Tablespace relative datafile number
CREATION_CHANGE#	NUMBER	Datafile creation change#
CREATION_TIME	DATE	Datafile creation timestamp
RESETLOGS_CHANGE#	NUMBER	Resetlogs change# of the datafile when the copy was made
RESETLOGS_TIME	DATE	Resetlogs timestamp of the datafile when the copy was made
CHECKPOINT_CHANGE#	NUMBER	Checkpoint change# of the datafile when the copy was made
CHECKPOINT_TIME	DATE	Checkpoint timestamp of the datafile when the copy was made
ABSOLUTE_FUZZY _CHANGE#	NUMBER	Highest change seen when the datafile was copied
RECOVERY_FUZZY _CHANGE#	NUMBER	Highest change written to the file by media recovery
RECOVERY_FUZZY _TIME	DATE	Timestamp of the highest change written to the file by media recovery
ONLINE_FUZZY	VARCHAR2(3)	YES/NO. If set to YES, this is a copy taken using an operating system utility after a crash or offline immediate (or an invalid copy taken while datafile was online and the database open). Recovery will need to apply all redo up to the next crash recovery marker to make the file consistent.

Column	Datatype	Description
BACKUP_FUZZY	VARCHAR2(3)	YES/NO. If set to YES, this is a copy taken using the BEGIN BACKUP/END BACKUP technique. Recovery will need to apply all redo up to the end backup marker to make this copy consistent
MARKED_CORRUPT	NUMBER	Number of blocks marked corrupt by this copy operation. That is, blocks that were not marked corrupted in the source datafile, but were detected and marked as corrupted during the copy operation.
MEDIA_CORRUPT	NUMBER	Total number of media corrupt blocks. For example, blocks with checksum errors are marked media corrupt
LOGICALLY_CORRUPT	NUMBER	Total number of logically corrupt blocks. For example, applying redo for unrecoverable operations will mark affected blocks logically corrupt.
BLOCKS	NUMBER	Size of the datafile copy in blocks (also the size of the datafile when the copy was made)
BLOCK_SIZE	NUMBER	Block size of the datafile
OLDEST_OFFLINE _RANGE	NUMBER	The RECID of the oldest offline range record in this controlfile copy. 0 for datafile copies
COMPLETION_TIME	DATE	Time when the copy was completed
DELETED	VARCHAR2(3)	YES/NO. If set to YES the datafile copy has been deleted or overwritten

V$DATAFILE_HEADER

This view displays datafile information from the datafile headers.

Column	Datatype	Description
FILE#	NUMBER	Datafile number (from controlfile)
STATUS	VARCHAR2(7)	ONLINE/OFFLINE (from controlfile)

Column	Datatype	Description
ERROR	VARCHAR2(18)	NULL if the datafile header read and validation were successful. If the read failed then the rest of the columns are NULL. If the validation failed then the rest of columns may display invalid data. If there is an error then usually the datafile must be restored from a backup before it can be recovered or used.
FORMAT	NUMBER	Indicates the format for the header block. The possible values are 6, 7, 8, or 0. 6 - indicates Oracle Version 6 7 - indicates Oracle Version 7 8 - indicates Oracle Version 8 0 - indicates the format could not be determined (for example, the header could not be read)
RECOVER	VARCHAR2(3)	File needs media recovery YES/NO
FUZZY	VARCHAR2(3)	File is fuzzy YES/NO
CREATION_CHANGE#	NUMBER	Datafile creation change#
CREATION_TIME	DATE	Datafile creation timestamp
TABLESPACE_NAME	VARCHAR2(30)	Tablespace name
TS#	NUMBER	Tablespace number
RFILE#	NUMBER	Tablespace relative datafile number
RESETLOGS_CHANGE#	NUMBER	Resetlogs change#
RESETLOGS_TIME	DATE	Resetlogs timestamp
CHECKPOINT_CHANGE#	NUMBER	Datafile checkpoint change#
CHECKPOINT_TIME	DATE	Datafile checkpoint timestamp
CHECKPOINT_COUNT	NUMBER	Datafile checkpoint count
BYTES	NUMBER	Current datafile size in bytes
BLOCKS	NUMBER	Current datafile size in blocks
NAME	VARCHAR2(512)	Datafile name

V$DBFILE

This view lists all datafiles making up the database. This view is retained for historical compatibility. Use of V$DATAFILE is recommended instead. For more information, see "V$DATAFILE" on page 3-23.

Column	Datatype	Description
FILE#	NUMBER	File identifier
NAME	VARCHAR2	Name of file

V$DBLINK

This view describes all open database links (links with IN_TRANSACTION = YES). These database links must be committed or rolled back before being closed.

Column	Datatype	Description
DB_LINK	VARCHAR2(128)	Name of the database link
OWNER_ID	NUMBER	Owner of the database link UID
LOGGED_ON	VARCHAR2(3)	Whether the database link is currently logged on
HETEROGENEOUS	VARCHAR2(3)	Whether the database link is heterogeneous
PROTOCOL	VARCHAR2(6)	Communication protocol for the database link
OPEN_CURSORS	NUMBER	Whether there are open cursors for the database link
IN_TRANSACTION	VARCHAR2(3)	Whether the database link is currently in a transaction
UPDATE_SENT	VARCHAR2(3)	Whether there has been an update on the database link
COMMIT_POINT _STRENGTH	NUMBER	Commit point strength of the transactions on the database link

V$DB_OBJECT_CACHE

This view displays database objects that are cached in the library cache. Objects include tables, indexes, clusters, synonym definitions, PL/SQL procedures and packages, and triggers.

Column	Datatype	Description
OWNER	VARCHAR2	Owner of the object
NAME	VARCHAR2	Name of the object
DB_LINK	VARCHAR2	Database link name, if any
NAMESPACE	VARCHAR2	Library cache namespace of the object: TABLE/ PROCEDURE, BODY, TRIGGER, INDEX, CLUSTER, OBJECT
TYPE	VARCHAR2	Type of the object: INDEX, TABLE, CLUSTER, VIEW, SET, SYNONYM, SEQUENCE, PROCEDURE, FUNCTION, PACKAGE, PACKAGE BODY, TRIGGER, CLASS, OBJECT, USER, DBLINK
SHARABLE_MEM	NUMBER	Amount of sharable memory in the shared pool consumed by the object
LOADS	NUMBER	Number of times the object has been loaded. This count also increases when an object has been invalidated
EXECUTIONS	NUMBER	Not used. To see actual execution counts, see "V$SQLAREA" on page 3-102.
LOCKS	NUMBER	Number of users currently locking this object
PINS	NUMBER	Number of users currently pinning this object
KEPT	VARCHAR2(3)	YES or NO, depending on whether this object has been "kept" (permanently pinned in memory) with the PL/SQL procedure DBMS_SHARED_POOL.KEEP

V$DB_PIPES

This view displays the pipes that are currently in this database.

Column	Datatype	Description
OWNERID	NUMBER	The owner ID of the owner if this is a private pipe; NULL otherwise.
NAME	VARCHAR2	The name of the pipe; for example, scott.pipe
TYPE	VARCHAR2	PUBLIC or PRIVATE
PIPE_SIZE	NUMBER	The amount of memory the pipe uses

V$DELETED_OBJECT

This view displays information about deleted archived logs, datafile copies and backup pieces from the controlfile. The only purpose of this view is to optimize the recovery catalog resync operation. When an archived log, datafile copy, or backup piece is deleted, the corresponding record is marked deleted.

Column	Datatype	Description
RECID	NUMBER	Deleted object record ID
STAMP	NUMBER	Deleted object record stamp
TYPE	VARCHAR2(13)	ARCHIVED LOG/DATAFILE COPY/ BACKUP PIECE. Type of the deleted object
OBJECT_RECID	NUMBER	Record ID of the deleted object
OBJECT_STAMP	NUMBER	Record timestamp of the deleted object

V$DISPATCHER

This view provides information on the dispatcher processes.

Column	Datatype	Description
NAME	VARCHAR2	Name of the dispatcher process
NETWORK	VARCHAR2	Network protocol supported by this dispatcher. For example, TCP or DECNET.
PADDR	RAW(4)	Process address
STATUS	VARCHAR2	Dispatcher status: WAIT (idle), SEND (sending a message connection), RECEIVE (receiving a message), CONNECT (establishing a connection), DISCONNECT (handling a disconnect request), BREAK (handling a break), OUTBOUND (establishing an outbound connection)
ACCEPT	VARCHAR2	Whether this dispatcher is accepting new connections: YES, NO
MESSAGES	NUMBER	Number of messages processed by this dispatcher
BYTES	NUMBER	Size in bytes of messages processed by this dispatcher
BREAKS	NUMBER	Number of breaks occurring in this connection
OWNED	NUMBER	Number of circuits owned by this dispatcher
CREATED	NUMBER	Number of circuits created by this dispatcher
IDLE	NUMBER	Total idle time for this dispatcher in hundredths of a second
BUSY	NUMBER	Total busy time for this dispatcher in hundredths of a second
LISTENER	NUMBER	The most recent Oracle error number the dispatcher received from the listener

V$DISPATCHER_RATE

This view provides rate statistics for the dispatcher processes.

Column	Datatype	Description
NAME	CHAR	Process name

Column	Datatype	Description
PADDR	RAW	Process address
CUR_LOOP_RATE	NUMBER	Current rate of loop events
CUR_EVENT_RATE	NUMBER	Current rate of events
CUR_EVENTS_PER_LOOP	NUMBER	Current events per loop
CUR_MSG_RATE	NUMBER	Current rate of messages
CUR_SVR_BUF_RATE	NUMBER	Current rate of buffers for the server
CUR_SVR_BYTE_RATE	NUMBER	Current rate of bytes for the server
CUR_SVR_BYTE_PER_BUF	NUMBER	Current bytes per buffer for the server
CUR_CLT_BUF_RATE	NUMBER	Current rate of buffers for the client
CUR_CLT_BYTE_RATE	NUMBER	Current rate of bytes for the client
CUR_CLT_BYTE_PER_BUF	NUMBER	Current bytes per buffer for the client
CUR_BUF_RATE	NUMBER	Current rate of buffers
CUR_BYTE_RATE	NUMBER	Current rate of bytes
CUR_BYTE_PER_BUF	NUMBER	Current bytes per buffer
CUR_IN_CONNECT_RATE	NUMBER	Current inbound connects
CUR_OUT_CONNECT_RATE	NUMBER	Current outbound connects
CUR_RECONNECT_RATE	NUMBER	Current reconnects for connection pool and multiplexing
MAX_LOOP_RATE	NUMBER	Maximum rate of loop events
MAX_EVENT_RATE	NUMBER	Maximum rate of events
MAX_EVENTS_PER_LOOP	NUMBER	Maximum events per loop
MAX_MSG_RATE	NUMBER	Maximum rate of messages
MAX_SVR_BUF_RATE	NUMBER	Maximum rate of buffers for the server
MAX_SVR_BYTE_RATE	NUMBER	Maximum rate of bytes for the server
MAX_SVR_BYTE_PER_BUF	NUMBER	Maximum number of bytes per buffer for the server
MAX_CLT_BUF_RATE	NUMBER	Maximum rate of buffers for the client

Column	Datatype	Description
MAX_CLT_BYTE_RATE	NUMBER	Maximum rate of bytes for the client
MAX_CLT_BYTE_PER_BUF	NUMBER	Maximum number of bytes per buffer for the client
MAX_BUF_RATE	NUMBER	Maximum rate of buffers
MAX_BYTE_RATE	NUMBER	Maximum rate of bytes
MAX_BYTE_PER_BUF	NUMBER	Maximum number of bytes per buffer
MAX_IN_CONNECT_RATE	NUMBER	Maximum number of inbound connects
MAX_OUT_CONNECT_RATE	NUMBER	Maximum number of outbound connects
MAX_RECONNECT_RATE	NUMBER	Maximum number of reconnects for connection pool and multiplexing
AVG_LOOP_RATE	NUMBER	Average rate of loop events
AVG_EVENT_RATE	NUMBER	Average rate of events
AVG_EVENTS_PER_LOOP	NUMBER	Average events per loop
AVG_MSG_RATE	NUMBER	Average rate of messages
AVG_SVR_BUF_RATE	NUMBER	Average rate of buffers for the server
AVG_SVR_BYTE_RATE	NUMBER	Average rate of bytes for the server
AVG_SVR_BYTE_PER_BUF	NUMBER	Average bytes per buffer for the server
AVG_CLT_BUF_RATE	NUMBER	Average rate of buffers for the client
AVG_CLT_BYTE_RATE	NUMBER	Average rate of bytes for the client
AVG_CLT_BYTE_PER_BUF	NUMBER	Average bytes per buffer for the client
AVG_BUF_RATE	NUMBER	Average rate of buffers
AVG_BYTE_RATE	NUMBER	Average rate of bytes
AVG_BYTE_PER_BUF	NUMBER	Average bytes per buffer
AVG_IN_CONNECT_RATE	NUMBER	Average inbound connects
AVG_OUT_CONNECT_RATE	NUMBER	Average outbound connects
AVG_RECONNECT_RATE	NUMBER	Average reconnects for connection pool and multiplexing

Column	Datatype	Description
NUM_LOOPS_TRACKED	NUMBER	Number of loop tracked
NUM_MSG_TRACKED	NUMBER	Number of messages tracked
NUM_SVR_BUF_TRACKED	NUMBER	Number of buffers for the server tracked
NUM_CLT_BUF_TRACKED	NUMBER	Number of buffers for the client tracked
NUM_BUF_TRACKED	NUMBER	Number of buffers tracked
NUM_IN_CONNECT _TRACKED	NUMBER	Number inbound connects tracked
NUM_OUT_CONNECT _TRACKED	NUMBER	Number outbound connects tracked
NUM_RECONNECT _TRACKED	NUMBER	Number of reconnects tracked
SCALE_LOOPS	NUMBER	Scale of loop
SCALE_MSG	NUMBER	Scale of messages
SCALE_SVR_BUF	NUMBER	Scale of buffers for the server
SCALE_CLT_BUF	NUMBER	Scale of buffers for the client
SCALE_BUF	NUMBER	Scale of buffers
SCALE_IN_CONNECT	NUMBER	Scale of inbound connects
SCALE_OUT_CONNECT	NUMBER	Scale of outbound connects
SCALE_RECONNECT	NUMBER	Scale of reconnects

V$DLM_CONVERT_LOCAL

V$DLM_CONVERT_LOCAL displays the elapsed time for the local lock conversion operation.

Column	Datatype	Description
INST_ID	NUMBER	ID of the instance
CONVERT_TYPE	VARCHAR2(64)	Conversion types are listed in Table 3-3
AVERAGE _CONVERT_TIME	NUMBER	Average conversion time for each type of lock operation (in 100th of a second).

Column	Datatype	Description
CONVERT_COUNT	NUMBER	The number of operations.

V$DLM_CONVERT_REMOTE

V$DLM_CONVERT_REMOTE displays the elapsed time for the remote lock conversion operation.

Column	Datatype	Description
INST_ID	NUMBER	ID of the instance
CONVERT_TYPE	VARCHAR2(64)	Conversion types are listed in Table 3-3
AVERAGE_CONVERT _TIME	NUMBER	Average conversion time for each type of lock operation (in 100th of a second).
CONVERT_COUNT	NUMBER	The number of operations.

Table 3-3: Values for the CONVERT_TYPE column

Conversion Type	Description
NULL -> SS	NULL mode to sub shared mode
NULL -> SX	NULL mode to shared exclusive mode
NULL -> S	NULL mode to shared mode
NULL -> SSX	NULL mode to sub-shared exclusive mode
NULL -> X	NULL mode to exclusive mode
SS -> SX	sub shared mode to shared exclusive mode
SS -> S	sub shared mode to shared mode
SS -> SSX	sub shared mode to sub-shared exclusive mode
SS -> X	sub shared mode to exclusive mode
SX -> S	shared exclusive mode to shared mode
SX -> SSX	shared exclusive mode to sub-shared exclusive mode
SX -> X	shared exclusive mode to exclusive mode
S -> SX	shared mode to shared exclusive mode
S -> SSX	shared mode to sub-shared exclusive mode
S -> X	shared mode to exclusive mode
SSX -> X	sub-shared exclusive mode to exclusive mode

V$DLM_LATCH

V$DLM_LATCH displays statistics about DLM latch performance. The view includes totals for each type of latch rather than statistics for each individual latch. Ideally, the value IMM_GETS/TTL_GETS should be as close to 1 as possible.

Column	Datatype	Description
LATCH_TYPE	VARCHAR2(64)	The name of the latch type. See Table 3-4.
IMM_GETS	NUMBER	Immediate gets. The number of times that an attempt to acquire a latch of the specified type was satisfied immediately (that is, the process did not have to wait for another process to release the latch).
TTL_GETS	NUMBER	Total gets. The total number of times the latch was acquired.

Table 3-4: Values for the LATCH_TYPE column

deadlock list	domain lock latch
domain lock table latch	domain table latch
group lock latch	group lock table latch
group table freelist	lock table freelist
log/trace file latch	proc hash list
proc lock list	proc table freelist
rdomain record latch	rdomain table latch
resource hash list	resource scan list
resource structure	resource table freelist
shared comm. latch	stat table latch
sync data latch	timeout list

V$DLM_MISC

V$DLM_MISC displays miscellaneous DLM statistics.

Column	Datatype	Description
STATISTIC#	NUMBER	Statistic number
NAME	VARCHAR2(64)	Name of the statistic
VALUE	NUMBER	Value associated with the statistic

V$ENABLEDPRIVS

This view displays which privileges are enabled. These privileges can be found in the table SYS.SYSTEM_PRIVILEGES_MAP.

Column	Datatype	Description
PRIV_NUMBER	NUMBER	Numeric identifier of enabled privileges

V$ENQUEUE_LOCK

This view displays all locks owned by enqueue state objects. The columns in this view are identical to the columns in V$LOCK. For more information, see "V$LOCK" on page 3-51.

Column	Datatype	Description
ADDR	RAW(4)	Address of lock state object
KADDR	RAW(4)	Address of lock
SID	NUMBER	Identifier for session holding or acquiring the lock
TYPE	VARCHAR2(2)	Type of lock. For a list of user and system types that can have locks, see Table 3-5: "Values for the TYPE column: User Types" and Table 3-6: "Values for the TYPE column: System Types".
ID1	NUMBER	Lock identifier #1 (depends on type)
ID2	NUMBER	Lock identifier #2 (depends on type)

Column	Datatype	Description
LMODE	NUMBER	Lock mode in which the session holds the lock: 0, None 1, Null (NULL) 2, Row-S (SS) 3, Row-X (SX) 4, Share (S) 5, S/Row-X (SSX) 6, Exclusive (X)
REQUEST	NUMBER	Lock mode in which the process requests the lock: 0, None 1, Null (NULL) 2, Row-S (SS) 3, Row-X (SX) 4, Share (S) 5, S/Row-X (SSX) 6, Exclusive (X)
CTIME	NUMBER	Time since current mode was granted
BLOCK	NUMBER	The lock is blocking another lock

V$EVENT_NAME

This view contains information about wait events.

Column	Datatype	Description
EVENT#	NUMBER	The number of the wait event
NAME	VARCHAR2(64)	The name of the wait event
PARAMETER1	VARCHAR2(64)	The description of the first parameter for the wait event
PARAMETER2	VARCHAR2(64)	The description of the second parameter for the wait event
PARAMETER3	VARCHAR2(64)	The description of the third parameter for the wait event

V$EXECUTION

This view displays information on parallel query execution.

Column	Datatype	Description
PID	NUMBER	Session ID

Column	Datatype	Description
DEPTH	NUMBER	The depth
FUNCTION	VARCHAR2(10)	Session serial number
TYPE	VARCHAR2(7)	Name of the OBJECT_NODE in plan table
NVALS	NUMBER	Elapsed time for OBJECT_NODE
VAL1	NUMBER	The value for number 1
VAL2	NUMBER	The value for number 2
SEQH	NUMBER	A sequence
SEQL	NUMBER	A sequence

V$EXECUTION_LOCATION

This view displays detailed information on the parallel query execution tree location.

Column	Datatype	Description
SID	NUMBER	Session ID
SERIAL#	NUMBER	Session serial number
OBJECT_NODE	VARCHAR2(20)	Name of the OBJECT_NODE in plan table
ELAPSED_TIME	NUMBER	Elapsed time for OBJECT_NODE

V$FALSE_PING

V$FALSE_PING is a Parallel Server view. This view displays buffers that may be getting false pings. That is, buffers pinged more than 10 times that are protected by the same lock as another buffer that pinged more than 10 times. Buffers identified as getting false pings can be remapped in "GC_FILES_TO_LOCK" on page 1-44 to reduce lock collisions.

Column	Datatype	Description
FILE#	NUMBER	Datafile identifier number (to find filename, query DBA_DATA_FILES or V$DBFILES)

Column	Datatype	Description
BLOCK#	NUMBER	Block number
STATUS	VARCHAR2(1)	Status of block: FREE = not currently in use XCUR = exclusive SCUR = shared current CR = consistent read READ = being read from disk MREC = in media recovery mode IREC = in instance recovery mode
XNC	NUMBER	Number of PCM lock conversions from Exclusive mode due to contention with another instance. This column is obsolete but is retained for historical compatibility.
FORCED_READS	NUMBER	Number of times the block had to be reread from disk because another instance had forced it out of this instance's cache by requesting the PCM lock on the block in exclusive mode
FORCED_WRITES	NUMBER	Number of times DBWR had to write this block to disk because this instance had used the block and another instance had requested the lock on the block in a conflicting mode.
NAME	VARCHAR2(30)	Name of the database object containing the block
PARTITION_NAME	VARCHAR2	NULL for non-partitioned objects
KIND	VARCHAR2(12)	Type of database object. See Table 3-1 on page 3-15.
OWNER#	NUMBER	Owner number
LOCK_ELEMENT_ADDR	RAW(4)	The address of the lock element that contains the PCM lock that is covering the buffer. If more than one buffer has the same address, then these buffers are covered by the same PCM lock.
LOCK_ELEMENT_NAME	NUMBER	The name of the lock that contains the PCM lock that is covering the buffer.
LOCK_ELEMENT_CLASS	NUMBER	The lock element class

For more information, see "GC_FILES_TO_LOCK" on page 1-44 and also *Oracle8 Parallel Server Concepts & Administration*.

V$FILE_PING

The view V$FILE_PING displays the number of blocks pinged per datafile. This information in turn can be used to determine access patterns to existing datafiles and deciding new mappings from datafile blocks to PCM locks.

Column	Datatype	Description
FILE_NUMBER	NUMBER	Number of the datafile
FREQUENCY	NUMBER	The frequency
X_2_NULL	NUMBER	Number of lock conversions from Exclusive-to-NULL for all blocks in the file
X_2_NULL_FORCED _WRITE	NUMBER	Number of forced writes that occur for blocks of the specified file due to Exclusive-to-NULL conversions
X_2_NULL_FORCED _STALE	NUMBER	Number of times a block in the file was made STALE due to Exclusive-to-NULL conversions
X_2_S	NUMBER	Number of lock conversions from Exclusive-to-Shared for all blocks in the file
X_2_S_FORCED_WRITE	NUMBER	Number of forced writes that occur for blocks of the specified file due to Exclusive-to-Shared conversions
X_2_SSX	NUMBER	Number of lock conversions from Exclusive-to-Sub Shared Exclusive for all blocks in the file
X_2_SSX_FORCED _WRITE	NUMBER	Number of forced writes that occur for blocks of the specified file due to Exclusive-to-Sub Shared Exclusive conversions
S_2_NULL	NUMBER	Number of lock conversions from Shared-to-NULL for all blocks in the file
S_2_NULL_FORCED _STALE	NUMBER	Number of times a block in the file was made STALE due to Shared-to-NULL conversions
SS_2_NULL	NUMBER	Number of lock conversions from Sub Shared-to-NULL for all blocks in the file
WRB	NUMBER	Number of times the instance received a write single buffer cross instance call for this file
WRB_FORCED_WRITE	NUMBER	Number of blocks written due to write single buffer cross instance calls for this file

Column	Datatype	Description
RBR	NUMBER	Number of times the instance received a resuse block range cross instance call for this file
RBR_FORCED_WRITE	NUMBER	Number of blocks written due to resuse block range cross instance calls for this file
RBR_FORCED_STALE	NUMBER	Number of times a block in this file was made STALE due to resuse block range cross instance calls
CBR	NUMBER	Number of times the instance received a checkpoint block range cross instance call for this file
CBR_FORCED_WRITE	NUMBER	Number of blocks in this file which were written due to checkpoint cross range cross instance calls
NULL_2_X	NUMBER	Number of lock conversions from NULL-to-Exclusive for all blocks of the specified file
S_2_X	NUMBER	Number of lock conversions from Shared-to-Exclusive for all blocks of the specified file
SSX_2_X	NUMBER	Number of lock conversions from Sub Shared Exclusive-to-Exclusive for all blocks of the specified file
NULL_2_S	NUMBER	Number of lock conversions from NULL-to-Shared for all blocks of the specified file
NULL_2_SS	NUMBER	Number of lock conversions from NULL-to-Sub Shared for all blocks of the specified file

V$FILESTAT

This view contains information about file read/write statistics.

Column	Datatype	Description
FILE#	NUMBER	Number of the file
PHYRDS	NUMBER	Number of physical reads done
PHYWRTS	NUMBER	Number of times DBWR is required to write
PHYBLKRD	NUMBER	Number of physical blocks read

Column	Datatype	Description
PHYBLKWRT	NUMBER	Number of blocks written to disk; which may be the same as PHYWRTS if all writes are single blocks
READTIM	NUMBER	Time (in milliseconds) spent doing reads if the TIMED_STATISTICS parameter is TRUE; 0 if FALSE
WRITETIM	NUMBER	Time (in milliseconds) spent doing writes if the TIMED_STATISTICS parameter is TRUE; 0 if FALSE

V$FIXED_TABLE

This view displays all dynamic performance tables, views, and derived tables in the database.

Column	Datatype	Description
NAME	VARCHAR2(30)	Name of the object
OBJECT_ID	NUMBER	Identifier of the fixed object
TYPE	VARCHAR2(5)	Object type: TABLE, VIEW
TABLE_NUM	NUMBER	Number that identifies the dynamic performance table if it is of type TABLE

V$FIXED_VIEW_DEFINITION

This view contains the definitions of all the fixed views (views beginning with V$). Use this table with caution. Oracle tries to keep the behavior of fixed views the same from release to release, but the definitions of the fixed views can change without notice. Use these definitions to optimize your queries by using indexed columns of the dynamic performance tables.

Column	Datatype	Description
VIEW_NAME	VARCHAR2(30)	The name of the fixed view
VIEW_DEFINITION	VARCHAR2(2000)	The definition of the fixed view

V$GLOBAL_TRANSACTION

This view displays information on the currently active global transactions.

Column	Datatype	Description
FORMATID	NUMBER	Format identifier of the global transaction
GLOBALID	RAW(64)	Global transaction identifier of the global transaction
BRANCHID	RAW(64)	Branch qualifier of the global transaction
BRANCHES	NUMBER	Total number of branches in the global transaction
REFCOUNT	NUMBER	Number of siblings for this global transaction, must be the same as branches.
PREPARECOUNT	NUMBER	Number of branches of the global transaction that have prepared
STATE	VARCHAR2(18)	State of the branch of the global transaction
FLAGS	NUMBER	The numerical representation of the state
COUPLING	VARCHAR2(15)	Whether the branches are loosely coupled or tightly coupled

V$INDEXED_FIXED_COLUMN

This view displays the columns in dynamic performance tables that are indexed (X$ tables). The X$ tables can change without notice. Use this view only to write queries against fixed views (V$ views) more efficiently.

Column	Datatype	Description
TABLE_NAME	VARCHAR2(30)	The name of the dynamic performance table that is indexed
INDEX_NUMBER	NUMBER	Number that distinguishes to which index a column belongs
COLUMN_NAME	VARCHAR2(30)	Name of the column that is being indexed
COLUMN_POSITION	NUMBER	Position of the column in the index key (this is mostly relevant for multicolumn indexes)

V$INSTANCE

This view displays the state of the current instance. This version of V$INSTANCE is not compatible with earlier versions of V$INSTANCE.

Column	Datatype	Description
INSTANCE_NUMBER	NUMBER	Instance number used for instance registration . Corresponds to INSTANCE_NUMBER initialization parameter. See "INSTANCE_NUMBER" on page 1-49.
INSTANCE_NAME	VARCHAR2(16)	Instance name.
HOST_NAME	VARCHAR2(64)	Name of the host machine
VERSION	VARCHAR2(17)	RDBMS version
STARTUP_TIME	DATE	Time when instance was started up
STATUS	VARCHAR2(7)	STARTED/MOUNTED/OPEN STARTED after startup nomount MOUNTED after startup mount or alter database close OPEN after startup or after database open
PARALLEL	VARCHAR2(3)	YES/NO in parallel server mode
THREAD#	NUMBER	Redo thread opened by the instance
ARCHIVER	VARCHAR2(7)	STOPPED/STARTED/FAILED FAILED means that the archiver failed to archive a log last time, but will try again within 5 minutes
LOG_SWITCH_WAIT	VARCHAR2(11)	ARCHIVE LOG/CLEAR LOG/ CHECKPOINT event log switching is waiting for. Note that if ALTER SYSTEM SWITCH LOGFILE is hung, but there is room in the current online redo log, then value is NULL
LOGINS	VARCHAR2(10)	ALLOWED/RESTRICTED
SHUTDOWN_PENDING	VARCHAR2(3)	YES/NO

V$LATCH

This view lists statistics for non-parent latches and summary statistics for parent latches. That is, the statistics for a parent latch include counts from each of its children.

Note: Columns SLEEP5, SLEEP6,... SLEEP11 are present for compatibility with previous versions of Oracle. No data are accumulated for these columns.

Column	Datatype	Description
ADDR	RAW(4)	Address of latch object
LATCH#	NUMBER	Latch number
LEVEL#	NUMBER	Latch level
NAME	VARCHAR2(64)	Latch name
GETS	NUMBER	Number of times obtained a wait
MISSES	NUMBER	Number of times obtained a wait but failed on the first try
SLEEPS	NUMBER	Number of times slept when wanted a wait
IMMEDIATE_GETS	NUMBER	Number of times obtained without a wait
IMMEDIATE_MISSES	NUMBER	Number of times failed to get without a wait
WAITERS_WOKEN	NUMBER	How many times a wait was awakened
WAITS_HOLDING _LATCH	NUMBER	Number of waits while holding a different latch
SPIN_GETS	NUMBER	Gets that missed first try but succeeded on spin
SLEEP1	NUMBER	Waits that slept 1 time
SLEEP2	NUMBER	Waits that slept 2 times
SLEEP3	NUMBER	Waits that slept 3 times
SLEEP4	NUMBER	Waits that slept 4 times
SLEEP5	NUMBER	Waits that slept 5 times
SLEEP6	NUMBER	Waits that slept 6 times
SLEEP7	NUMBER	Waits that slept 7 times

Column	Datatype	Description
SLEEP8	NUMBER	Waits that slept 8 times
SLEEP9	NUMBER	Waits that slept 9 times
SLEEP10	NUMBER	Waits that slept 10 times
SLEEP11	NUMBER	Waits that slept 11 times

V$LATCHHOLDER

This view contains information about the current latch holders.

Column	Datatype	Description
PID	NUMBER	Identifier of process holding the latch
SID	NUMBER	Identifier of the session that owns the latch
LADDR	RAW(4)	Latch address
NAME	VARCHAR2	Name of latch being held

V$LATCHNAME

This view contains information about decoded latch names for the latches shown in V$LATCH. The rows of V$LATCHNAME have a one-to-one correspondence to the rows of V$LATCH. For more information, see "V$LATCH" on page 3-46.

Column	Datatype	Description
LATCH#	NUMBER	Latch number
NAME	VARCHAR2(64)	Latch name

V$LATCH_CHILDREN

This view contains statistics about child latches. This view includes all columns of V$LATCH plus the CHILD# column. Note that child latches have the same parent if their LATCH# columns match each other. For more information, see "V$LATCH" on page 3-46.

Column	Datatype	Description
ADDR	RAW(4)	Address of latch object
LATCH#	NUMBER	Latch number for a parent latch
CHILD#	NUMBER	Child number of a parent latch shown in LATCH#
LEVEL#	NUMBER	Latch level
NAME	VARCHAR2(64)	Latch name
GETS	NUMBER	Number of times obtained a wait
MISSES	NUMBER	Number of times obtained a wait but failed on the first try
SLEEPS	NUMBER	Number of times slept when wanted a wait
IMMEDIATE_GETS	NUMBER	Number of times obtained without a wait
IMMEDIATE_MISSES	NUMBER	Number of time failed to get without a wait
WAITERS_WOKEN	NUMBER	How many times a wait was awakened
WAITS_HOLDING_LATCH	NUMBER	Number of waits while holding a different latch
SPIN_GETS	NUMBER	Gets that missed first try but succeeded on spin
SLEEPn	NUMBER	Waits that slept n times

V$LATCH_MISSES

This view contains statistics about missed attempts to acquire a latch.

Column	Datatype	Description
PARENT_NAME	VARCHAR2	Latch name of a parent latch
WHERE	VARCHAR2	Location that attempted to acquire the latch
NWFAIL_COUNT	NUMBER	Number of times that no-wait acquisition of the latch failed
SLEEP_COUNT	NUMBER	Number of times that acquisition attempts caused sleeps

V$LATCH_PARENT

This view contains statistics about the parent latch. The columns of V$LATCH_PARENT are identical to those in V$LATCH. For more information, see "V$LATCH" on page 3-46.

V$LIBRARYCACHE

This view contains statistics about library cache performance and activity.

Column	Datatype	Description
NAMESPACE	VARCHAR2(15)	The library cache namespace
GETS	NUMBER	The number of times a lock was requested for objects of this namespace
GETHITS	NUMBER	The number of times an object's handle was found in memory
GETHITRATIO	NUMBER	The ratio of GETHITS to GETS
PINS	NUMBER	The number of times a PIN was requested for objects of this namespace
PINHITS	NUMBER	The number of times all of the meta data pieces of the library object were found in memory
PINHITRATIO	NUMBER	The ratio of PINHITS to PINS

Column	Datatype	Description
RELOADS	NUMBER	Any PIN of an object that is not the first PIN performed since the object handle was created, and which requires loading the object from disk
INVALIDATIONS	NUMBER	The total number of times objects in this namespace were marked invalid because a dependent object was modified
DLM_LOCK_REQUESTS	NUMBER	The number of GET requests lock instance locks
DLM_PIN_REQUESTS	NUMBER	The number of PIN requests lock instance locks
DLM_PIN_RELEASES	NUMBER	The number of release requests PIN instance locks
DLM_INVALIDATION _REQUESTS	NUMBER	The number of GET requests for invalidation instance locks
DLM_INVALIDATIONS	NUMBER	The number of invalidation pings received from other instances

V$LICENSE

This view contains information about license limits.

Column	Datatype	Description
SESSIONS_MAX	NUMBER	Maximum number of concurrent user sessions allowed for the instance
SESSIONS_WARNING	NUMBER	Warning limit for concurrent user sessions for the instance
SESSIONS_CURRENT	NUMBER	Current number of concurrent user sessions
SESSIONS _HIGHWATER	NUMBER	Highest number of concurrent user sessions since the instance started
USERS_MAX	NUMBER	Maximum number of named users allowed for the database

V$LOADCSTAT

This view contains SQL*Loader statistics compiled during the execution of a direct load. These statistics apply to the whole load. Any SELECT against this table results in "no rows returned" since you cannot load data and do a query at the same time.

Column	Datatype	Description
READ	NUMBER	Number of records read
REJECTED	NUMBER	Number of records rejected
TDISCARD	NUMBER	Total number of discards during the load
NDISCARD	NUMBER	Number of discards from the current file
SAVEDATA	NUMBER	Whether save data points are used

V$LOADTSTAT

SQL*Loader statistics compiled during the execution of a direct load. These statistics apply to the current table. Any SELECT against this table results in "no rows returned" since you cannot load data and do a query at the same time.

Column	Datatype	Description
LOADED	NUMBER	Number of records loaded
REJECTED	NUMBER	Number of records rejected
FAILWHEN	NUMBER	Number of records that failed to meet any WHEN clause
ALLNULL	NUMBER	Number of records that were completely null and were therefore not loaded
LEFT2SKIP	NUMBER	Number of records yet to skip during a continued load

V$LOCK

This view lists the locks currently held by the Oracle Server and outstanding requests for a lock or latch.

Column	Datatype	Description
ADDR	RAW(4)	Address of lock state object

Column	Datatype	Description
KADDR	RAW(4)	Address of lock
SID	NUMBER	Identifier for session holding or acquiring the lock
TYPE	VARCHAR2(2)	Type of lock. For a list of user and system types that can have locks, see Table 3-5: "Values for the TYPE column: User Types" and Table 3-6: "Values for the TYPE column: System Types".
ID1	NUMBER	Lock identifier #1 (depends on type)
ID2	NUMBER	Lock identifier #2 (depends on type)
LMODE	NUMBER	Lock mode in which the session holds the lock: 0, None 1, Null (NULL) 2, Row-S (SS) 3, Row-X (SX) 4, Share (S) 5, S/Row-X (SSX) 6, Exclusive (X)
REQUEST	NUMBER	Lock mode in which the process requests the lock: 0, None 1, Null (NULL) 2, Row-S (SS) 3, Row-X (SX) 4, Share (S) 5, S/Row-X (SSX) 6, Exclusive (X)
CTIME	NUMBER	Time since current mode was granted
BLOCK	NUMBER	The lock is blocking another lock

The locks on the user types in Table 3-5 are obtained by user applications. Any process that is blocking others is likely to be holding one of these locks.

Table 3-5: Values for the TYPE column: User Types

User Type	Description
TM	DML enqueue
TX	Transaction enqueue
UL	User supplied

The locks on the system types in Table 3-6 are held for extremely short periods of time.

Table 3-6: Values for the TYPE column: System Types

System Type	Description
BL	Buffer hash table instance
CF	Control file schema global enqueue
CI	Cross-instance function invocation instance
CU	Cursor bind
DF	Data file instance
DL	Direct loader parallel index create
DM	Mount/startup db primary/secondary instance
DR	Distributed recovery process
DX	Distributed transaction entry
FS	File set
HW	Space management operations on a specific segment
IN	Instance number
IR	Instance recovery serialization global enqueue
IS	Instance state
IV	Library cache invalidation instance
JQ	Job queue
KK	Thread kick
LA .. LP	Library cache lock instance lock (A..P = namespace)
MM	Mount definition global enqueue
MR	Media recovery
NA..NZ	Library cache pin instance (A..Z = namespace)
PF	Password File
PI, PS	Parallel operation

Table 3-6: Values for the TYPE column: System Types

System Type	Description
PR	Process startup
QA..QZ	Row cache instance (A..Z = cache)
RT	Redo thread global enqueue
SC	System commit number instance
SM	SMON
SN	Sequence number instance
SQ	Sequence number enqueue
SS	Sort segment
ST	Space transaction enqueue
SV	Sequence number value
TA	Generic enqueue
TS	Temporary segment enqueue (ID2=0)
TS	New block allocation enqueue (ID2=1)
TT	Temporary table enqueue
UN	User name
US	Undo segment DDL
WL	Being-written redo log instance

V$LOCK_ACTIVITY

This is a Parallel Server view. V$LOCK_ACTIVITY displays the DLM lock operation activity of the current instance. Each row corresponds to a type of lock operation.

Column	Datatype	Description
FROM_VAL	VARCHAR2(4)	PCM lock initial state: NULL S X SSX

Column	Datatype	Description
TO_VAL	VARCHAR2(4)	PCM lock initial state: NULL S X SSX
ACTION_VAL	VARCHAR2(51)	Description of lock conversions Lock buffers for read Lock buffers for write Make buffers CR (no write) Upgrade read lock to write Make buffers CR (write dirty buffers) Downgrade write lock to read (write dirty buffers) Write transaction table/undo blocks Transaction table/undo blocks (write dirty buffers) Make transaction table/undo blocks available share Rearm transaction table write mechanism
COUNTER	NUMBER	Number of times the lock operation executed

For more information, see *Oracle8 Parallel Server Concepts & Administration*.

V$LOCK_ELEMENT

This is a Parallel Server view. There is one entry in v$LOCK_ELEMENT for each PCM lock that is used by the buffer cache. The name of the PCM lock that corresponds to a lock element is {'BL', indx, class}.

Column	Datatype	Description
LOCK_ELEMENT_ ADDR	RAW(4)	The address of the lock element that contains the PCM lock that is covering the buffer. If more than one buffer has the same address, then these buffers are covered by the same PCM lock.

Column	Datatype	Description
LOCK_ELEMENT_NAME	NUMBER	The name of the lock that contains the PCM lock that is covering the buffer.
INDX	NUMBER	Platform specific lock manager identifier
CLASS	NUMBER	Platform specific lock manager identifier
MODE_HELD	NUMBER	Platform dependent value for lock mode held; often: 3 = share 5 = exclusive
BLOCK_COUNT	NUMBER	Number of blocks covered by PCM lock
RELEASING	NUMBER	Non-zero if PCM lock is being downgraded
ACQUIRING	NUMBER	Non-zero if PCM lock is being upgraded
INVALID	NUMBER	Non-zero if PCM lock is invalid. (A lock may become invalid after a system failure.)
FLAGS	NUMBER	Process level flags for the LE

For more information, see *Oracle8 Parallel Server Concepts & Administration*.

V$LOCKED_OBJECT

This view lists all locks acquired by every transaction on the system.

Column	Datatype	Description
XIDUSN	NUMBER	Undo segment number
XIDSLOT	NUMBER	Slot number
XIDSQN	NUMBER	Sequence number
OBJECT_ID	NUMBER	Object ID being locked
SESSION_ID	NUMBER	Session ID
ORACLE_USERNAME	VARCHAR2(30)	Oracle user name
OS_USER_NAME	VARCHAR2(15)	OS user name
PROCESS	VARCHAR2(9)	OS process ID
LOCKED_MODE	NUMBER	Lock mode

V$LOCKS_WITH_COLLISIONS

This is a Parallel Server view. Use this view to find the locks that protect multiple buffers, each of which has been either force-written or force-read at least 10 times. It is very likely that those buffers are experiencing false pings due to being mapped to the same lock.

Column	Datatype	Description
LOCK_ELEMENT_ ADDR	RAW(4)	The address of the lock element that contains the PCM lock covering the buffer. If more than one buffer has the same address, then these buffers are covered by the same PCM lock.

For more information, see *Oracle8 Parallel Server Concepts & Administration.*

V$LOG

This view contains log file information from the control files.

Column	Datatype	Description
GROUP#	NUMBER	Log group number
THREAD#	NUMBER	Log thread number
SEQUENCE#	NUMBER	Log sequence number
BYTES	NUMBER	Size of the log in bytes
MEMBERS	NUMBER	Number of members in the log group
ARCHIVED	VARCHAR2	Archive status: YES, NO
STATUS	VARCHAR2(16)	Log status. The STATUS column can have the values in Table 3-7.
FIRST_CHANGE#	NUMBER	Lowest SCN in the log
FIRST_TIME	DATE	Time of first SCN in the log

Table 3-7 describes values in the log STATUS column.

Table 3-7: Values for the STATUS column

STATUS	Meaning
UNUSED	Indicates the online redo log has never been written to. This is the state of a redo log that was just added, or just after a RESETLOGS, when it is not the current redo log.
CURRENT	Indicates this is the current redo log. This implies that the redo log is active. The redo log could be open or closed.
ACTIVE	Indicates the log is active but is not the current log. It is needed for crash recovery. It may be in use for block recovery. It might or might not be archived.
CLEARING	Indicates the log is being recreated as an empty log after an ALTER DATABASE CLEAR LOGFILE command. After the log is cleared, the status changes to UNUSED.
CLEARING _CURRENT	Indicates that the current log is being cleared of a closed thread. The log can stay in this status if there is some failure in the switch such as an I/O error writing the new log header.
INACTIVE	Indicates the log is no longer needed for instance recovery. It may be in use for media recovery. It might or might not be archived.

V$LOGFILE

This view contains information about redo log files.

Column	Datatype	Description
GROUP#	NUMBER	Redo log group identifier number
STATUS	VARCHAR2	Status of this log member: INVALID (file is inaccessible), STALE (file's contents are incomplete), DELETED (file is no longer used), or blank (file is in use)
MEMBER	VARCHAR2	Redo log member name

V$LOGHIST

This view contains log history information from the control file. This view is retained for historical compatibility. Use of V$LOG_HISTORY is recommended instead. For more information, see "V$LOG_HISTORY" on page 3-59.

Column	Datatype	Description
THREAD#	NUMBER	Log thread number
SEQUENCE#	NUMBER	Log sequence number
FIRST_CHANGE#	NUMBER	Lowest SCN in the log
FIRST_TIME	DATE	Time of first SCN in the log
SWITCH_CHANGE#	NUMBER	SCN at which the log switch occurred; one more than highest SCN in the log

V$LOG_HISTORY

This view contains log history information from the control file.

Column	Datatype	Description
THREAD#	NUMBER	Thread number of the archived log
SEQUENCE#	NUMBER	Sequence number of the archived log
FIRST_TIME	DATE	Time of first entry (lowest SCN) in the log. This column was previously named TIME.
FIRST_CHANGE#	NUMBER	Lowest SCN in the log. This column was previously named LOW_CHANGE#.
NEXT_CHANGE#	NUMBER	Highest SCN in the log. This column was previously named HIGH_CHANGE#.
RECID	NUMBER	Controlfile record ID
STAMP	NUMBER	Controlfile record stamp

V$MLS_PARAMETERS

This is a Trusted Oracle Server view that lists Trusted Oracle Server-specific initialization parameters. For more information, see the *Trusted Oracle Server Administrator's Guide*.

V$MTS

This view contains information for tuning the multi-threaded server.

Column	Datatype	Description
MAXIMUM _CONNECTIONS	NUMBER	The maximum number of connections each dispatcher can support. This value is determined at startup time using Net8 constants and other port-specific information, or can be lowered using the mls_dispatchers parameter.
SERVERS _STARTED	NUMBER	The total number of multi-threaded servers started since the instance started (but not including those started during startup)
SERVERS _TERMINATED	NUMBER	The total number of multi-threaded servers stopped by Oracle since the instance started
SERVERS _HIGHWATER	NUMBER	The highest number of servers running at one time since the instance started. If this value reaches the value set for the MTS_MAX_SERVERS initialization parameter, consider raising the value of MTS_SERVERS. For more information, see "MTS_SERVERS" on page 1-75.

V$MYSTAT

This view contains statistics on the current session.

Column	Datatype	Description
SID	NUMBER	The ID of the current session
STATISTIC#	NUMBER	The number of the statistic
VALUE	NUMBER	The value of the statistic

V$NLS_PARAMETERS

This view contains current values of NLS parameters.

Column	Datatype	Description
PARAMETER	VARCHAR2	Parameter name: NLS_CALENDAR NLS_CHARACTERSET NLS_CURRENCY NLS_DATE_FORMAT NLS_DATE_LANGUAGE NLS_ISO_CURRENCY NLS_LANGUAGE NLS_NUMERIC_CHARACTERS NLS_SORT NLS_TERRITORY
VALUE	VARCHAR2	NLS parameter value

V$NLS_VALID_VALUES

This view lists all valid values for NLS parameters.

Column	Datatype	Description
PARAMETER	VARCHAR2(64)	Parameter name: NLS_LANGUAGE NLS_SORT NLS_TERRITORY NLS_CHARACTERSET
VALUE	VARCHAR2(64)	NLS parameter value

V$OBJECT_DEPENDENCY

This view can be used to determine what objects are depended on by a package, procedure, or cursor that is currently loaded in the shared pool. For example, together with V$SESSION and V$SQL, it can be used to determine which tables are used in the SQL statement that a user is currently executing. For more information, see "V$SESSION" on page 3-78 and "V$SQL" on page 3-96.

Column	Datatype	Description
FROM_ADDRESS	RAW(4)	The address of a procedure, package, or cursor that is currently loaded in the shared pool

Column	Datatype	Description
FROM_HASH	NUMBER	The hash value of a procedure, package, or cursor that is currently loaded in the shared pool
TO_OWNER	VARCHAR2(64)	The owner of the object that is depended on
TO_NAME	VARCHAR2(1000)	The name of the object that is depended on
TO_ADDRESS	RAW(4)	The address of the object that is depended on. These can be used to look up more information on the object in V$DB_OBJECT_CACHE.
TO_HASH	NUMBER	The hash value of the object that is depended on. These can be used to look up more information on the object in V$DB_OBJECT_CACHE.
TO_TYPE	NUMBER	The type of the object that is depended on

V$OFFLINE_RANGE

This view displays datafile offline information from the controlfile. Note that the last offline range of each datafile is kept in the DATAFILE record. For more information, see "V$DATAFILE" on page 3-23.

An offline range is created for a datafile when its tablespace is first ALTERed to be OFFLINE NORMAL or READ ONLY, and then subsequently ALTERed to be ONLINE or read-write. Note that no offline range is created if the datafile itself is ALTERed to be OFFLINE or if the tablespace is ALTERed to be OFFLINE IMMEDIATE.

Column	Datatype	Description
RECID	NUMBER	Record ID
STAMP	NUMBER	Record stamp
FILE#	NUMBER	Datafile number
OFFLINE_CHANGE#	NUMBER	SCN at which offlined
ONLINE_CHANGE#	NUMBER	SCN at which onlined
ONLINE_TIME	DATE	Time of offline SCN

V$OPEN_CURSOR

This view lists cursors that each user session currently has opened and parsed.

Column	Datatype	Description
SADDR	RAW	Session address .
SID	NUMBER	Session identifier
USER_NAME	VARCHAR2(30)	User that is logged in to the session
ADDRESS	RAW	Used with HASH_VALUE to identify uniquely the SQL statement being executed in the session
HASH_VALUE	NUMBER	Used with ADDRESS to identify uniquely the SQL statement being executed in the session
SQL_TEXT	VARCHAR2(60)	First 60 characters of the SQL statement that is parsed into the open cursor

V$OPTION

This view lists options that are installed with the Oracle Server.

Column	Datatype	Description
PARAMETER	VARCHAR2(64)	The name of the option
VALUE	VARCHAR2(64)	TRUE if the option is installed

V$PARAMETER

This view lists information about initialization parameters.

Column	Datatype	Description
NUM	NUMBER	Parameter number
NAME	VARCHAR2(64)	Parameter name
TYPE	NUMBER	Parameter type; 1 = Boolean, 2 = string, 3 = integer
VALUE	VARCHAR2(512)	Parameter value
ISDEFAULT	VARCHAR2(9)	Whether the parameter value is the default

Column	Datatype	Description
ISSES_MODIFIABLE	VARCHAR2(5)	TRUE = the parameter can be changed with ALTER SESSION FALSE= the parameter cannot be changed with ALTER SESSION
ISSYS_MODIFIABLE	VARCHAR2(9)	IMMEDIATE = the parameter can be changed with ALTER SYSTEM DEFERRED=the parameter cannot be changed until the next session FALSE= the parameter cannot be changed with ALTER SYSTEM
ISMODIFIED	VARCHAR2(10)	Indicates how the parameter was modified. If an ALTER SESSION was performed, the value will be MODIFIED. If an ALTER SYSTEM (which will cause all the currently logged in sessions' values to be modified) was performed the value will be SYS_MODIFIED.
ISADJUSTED	VARCHAR2(5)	Indicates that the rdbms adjusted the input value to a more suitable value (e.g., the parameter value should be prime, but the user input a non-prime number, so the rdbms adjusted the value to the next prime number)
DESCRIPTION	VARCHAR2(64)	A descriptive comment about the parameter

V$PING

This is a Parallel Server view. The V$PING view is identical to the V$CACHE view but only displays blocks that have been pinged at least once. This view contains information from the block header of each block in the SGA of the current instance as related to particular database objects. For more information, see "V$CACHE" on page 3-14.

Column	Datatype	Description
FILE#	NUMBER	Datafile identifier number (to find filename, query "DBA_DATA_FILES" on page 2-55 or "V$DBFILE" on page 3-28)
BLOCK#	NUMBER	Block number
CLASS#	NUMBER	Class number

Column	Datatype	Description
STATUS	VARCHAR2(4)	Status of block: FREE= not currently in use XCUR= exclusive SCUR= shared current CR= consistent read READ= being read from disk MREC= in media recovery mode IREC= in instance recovery mode
XNC	NUMBER	Number of PCM lock conversions due to contention with another instance. This column is obsolete but is retained for historical compatibility
FORCED_READS	NUMBER	Number of times the block had to be reread from disk because another instance had forced it out of this instance's cache by requesting the PCM lock on the block in exclusive mode
FORCED_WRITES	NUMBER	Number of times DBWR had to write this block to disk because this instance had used the block and another instance had requested the lock on the block in a conflicting mode.
NAME	VARCHAR2(30)	Name of the database object containing the block
PARTITION_NAME	VARCHAR2(30)	NULL for non-partitioned objects
KIND	VARCHAR2(15)	Type of database object. See Table 3-1 on page 3-15.
OWNER#	NUMBER	Owner number
LOCK_ELEMENT _ADDR	RAW(4)	The address of the lock element that contains the PCM lock that is covering the buffer. If more than one buffer has the same address, then these buffers are covered by the same PCM lock.
LOCK_ELEMENT _NAME	NUMBER	The name of the lock that contains the PCM lock that is covering the buffer.

For more information, see *Oracle8 Parallel Server Concepts & Administration*.

V$PQ_SESSTAT

This view lists session statistics for parallel queries.

Column	Datatype	Description
STATISTIC	VARCHAR2(30)	Name of the statistic. See Table 3-8 on page 3-66
LAST_QUERY	NUMBER	The value of the statistic for the last operation
SESSION_TOTAL	NUMBER	The value of the statistic for the entire session to this point in time

The statistics (fixed rows) in Table 3-8 have been defined for this view. After you have run a query or DML operation, you can use the information derived from V$PQ_SESSTAT to view the number of slave processes used, and other information for the session and system.

Table 3-8: Names of Statistics in the STATISTIC Column

Statistic (Fixed Row)	Description
Queries Parallelized	Number of queries that were run in parallel
DML Parallelized	Number of DML operations that were run in parallel.
DFO Trees	Number of executed DFO trees
Server Threads	Total number of parallel servers used
Allocation Height	Requested number of servers per instance
Allocation Width	Requested number of instances
Local Msgs Sent	Number of local (intra-instance) messages sent
Distr Msgs Sent	Number of remote (inter-instance) messages sent
Local Msgs Recv'd	Number of local (intra-instance) messages received
Distr Msgs Recv'd	Number of remote (inter-instance) messages received

V$PQ_SLAVE

This view lists statistics for each of the active parallel query servers on an instance.

Column	Datatype	Description
SLAVE_NAME	VARCHAR2(4)	Name of the parallel query server
STATUS	VARCHAR2(4)	The current status of the parallel query server (BUSY or IDLE)
SESSIONS	NUMBER	The number of sessions that have used this parallel query server
IDLE_TIME_CUR	NUMBER	The amount of time spent idle while processing statements in the current session
BUSY_TIME_CUR	NUMBER	The amount of time spent busy while processing statements in the current session
CPU_SECS_CUR	NUMBER	The amount of CPU time spent on the current session
MSGS_SENT_CUR	NUMBER	The number of messages sent while processing statements for the current session
MSGS_RCVD_CUR	NUMBER	The number of messages received while processing statements for the current session
IDLE_TIME_TOTAL	NUMBER	The total amount of time this query server has been idle
BUSY_TIME_TOTAL	NUMBER	The total amount of time this query server has been active
CPU_SECS_TOTAL	NUMBER	The total amount of CPU time this query server has used to process statements
MSGS_SENT_TOTAL	NUMBER	The total number of messages this query server has sent
MSGS_RCVD_TOTAL	NUMBER	The total number of messages this query server has received

V$PQ_SYSSTAT

This view lists system statistics for parallel queries.

Column	Datatype	Description
STATISTIC	VARCHAR2(30)	Name of the statistic See Table 3-9 on page 3-68
VALUE	NUMBER	The value of the statistic

The statistics (fixed rows) in Table 3-9 have been defined for this view. After you have run a query or DML operation, you can use the information derived from V$PQ_SYSSTAT to view the number of slave processes used, and other information for the system.

Table 3-9: Names of Statistics in the STATISTIC Column

Statistic (Fixed Row)	Description
Servers Busy	Number of currently busy servers on this instance
Servers Idle	Number of currently idle servers on this instance
Servers Highwater	Number of active servers on this instance that have partaken in >= 1 operation so far
Server Sessions	Total number of operations executed in all servers on this instance
Servers Started	Total number of servers started on this instance
Servers Shutdown	Total number of servers shutdown on this instance
Servers Cleaned Up	Total number of servers on this instance cleaned up due to process death
Queries Initiated	Total number of parallel queries initiated on this instance
DML Initiated	Total number of parallel DML operations that were initiated
DFO Trees	Total number of DFO trees executed on this instance
Local Msgs Sent	Total number of local (intra-instance) messages sent on this instance
Distr Msgs Sent	Total number of remote (inter-instance) messages sent on this instance

Table 3-9: Names of Statistics in the STATISTIC Column

Statistic (Fixed Row)	Description
Local Msgs Recv'd	Total number of remote (inter-instance) messages received on this instance
Distr Msgs Recv'd	Total number of remote (inter-instance) messages received on this instance

V$PQ_TQSTAT

This view contains statistics on parallel query operations. The statistics are compiled after the query completes and only remain for the duration of the session. It displays the number of rows processed through each parallel query server at each stage of the execution tree. This view can help determine skew problems in a query's execution.

Column	Datatype	Description
DFO_NUMBER	NUMBER	The data flow operator (DFO) tree number to differentiate queries
TQ_ID	NUMBER	The table queue ID within the query, which represents the connection between two DFO nodes in the query execution tree
SERVER_TYPE	VARCHAR2(10)	The role in table queue - producer/consumer/ranger
NUM_ROWS	NUMBER	The number of rows produced/consumed
BYTES	NUMBER	The number of bytes produced/consumed
OPEN_TIME	NUMBER	Time (secs) the table queue remained open
AVG_LATENCY	NUMBER	Time (ms) for a message to be dequeued after it enters the queue
WAITS	NUMBER	The number of waits encountered during dequeue
TIMEOUTS	NUMBER	The number of timeouts when waiting for a message
PROCESS	VARCHAR2(10)	Process ID
INSTANCE	NUMBER	Instance ID

V$PROCESS

This view contains information about the currently active processes. While the LATCHWAIT column indicates what latch a process is waiting for, the LATCHSPIN column indicates what latch a process is spinning on. On multi-processor machines, Oracle processes will spin on a latch before waiting on it.

Column	Datatype	Description
ADDR	RAW(4)	Address of process state object
PID	NUMBER	Oracle process identifier
SPID	VARCHAR2	Operating system process identifier
USERNAME	VARCHAR2	Operating system process username. Any Two-Task user coming across the network has "-T" appended to the username.
SERIAL#	NUMBER	Process serial number
TERMINAL	VARCHAR2	Operating system terminal identifier
PROGRAM	VARCHAR2	Program in progress
BACKGROUND	VARCHAR2	1 for a background process; NULL for a normal process
LATCHWAIT	VARCHAR2	Address of latch the process is waiting for; NULL if none
LATCHSPIN	VARCHAR2	Address of latch the process is being spun on; NULL if none

V$PWFILE_USERS

This view lists users who have been granted SYSDBA and SYSOPER privileges as derived from the password file.

Column	Datatype	Description
USERNAME	VARCHAR2(30)	The name of the user that is contained in the password file.
SYSDBA	VARCHAR2(5)	If the value of this column is TRUE, the user can connect with SYSDBA privileges.
SYSOPER	VARCHAR2(5)	If the value of this column is TRUE, the user can connect with SYSOPER privileges

V$QUEUE

This view contains information on the multi-thread message queues.

Column	Datatype	Description
PADDR	RAW(4)	Address of the process that owns the queue
TYPE	VARCHAR2	Type of queue: COMMON (processed by servers), OUTBOUND (used by remote servers), DISPATCHER.
QUEUED	NUMBER	Number of items in the queue
WAIT	NUMBER	Total time that all items in this queue have waited. Divide by TOTALQ for average wait per item.
TOTALQ	NUMBER	Total number of items that have ever been in the queue

V$RECOVER_FILE

This view displays the status of files needing media recovery.

Column	Datatype	Description
FILE#	NUMBER	File identifier number
ONLINE	VARCHAR2	Online status: ONLINE, OFFLINE
ERROR	VARCHAR2	Why the file needs to be recovered: NULL if reason unknown, or OFFLINE NORMAL if recovery not needed
CHANGE#	NUMBER	SCN where recovery must start
TIME	DATE	Time of SCN when recovery must start

V$RECOVERY_FILE_STATUS

V$RECOVERY_FILE_STATUS contains one row for each datafile for each RECOVER command. This view contains useful information only for the Oracle process doing the recovery. When Recovery Manager directs a server process to perform recovery, only Recovery Manager is able to view the relevant information in this view. V$RECOVERY_FILE_STATUS will be empty to all other Oracle users.

Column	Datatype	Description
FILENUM	NUMBER	The number of the file being recovered
FILENAME	VARCHAR2(257)	The filename of the datafile being recovered
STATUS	VARCHAR2(13)	The status of the recovery. Contains one of the following values: IN RECOVERY CURRENT NOT RECOVERED

For further information, see The *Oracle8 Server Backup and Recovery Guide.*

V$RECOVERY_LOG

This view lists information about archived logs that are needed to complete media recovery. This information is derived from the log history view, V$LOG_HISTORY. For more information, see "V$LOG_HISTORY" on page 3-59.

V$RECOVERY_LOG contains useful information only for the Oracle process doing the recovery. When Recovery Manager directs a server process to perform recovery, only Recovery Manager is able to view the relevant information in this view. V$RECOVERY_LOG will be empty to all other Oracle users.

Column	Datatype	Description
THREAD#	NUMBER	Thread number of the archived log
SEQUENCE#	NUMBER	Sequence number of the archived log
TIME	VARCHAR2	Time of first entry (lowest SCN) in the log
ARCHIVE_NAME	VARCHAR2	Name of the file when archived, using the naming convention specified by "LOG_ARCHIVE_FORMAT" on page 1-59.

For further information, see The *Oracle8 Server Backup and Recovery Guide.*

V$RECOVERY_STATUS

V$RECOVERY_STATUS contains statistics of the current recovery process. This view contains useful information only for the Oracle process doing the recovery. When Recovery Manager directs a server process to perform recovery, only Recovery Manager is able to view the relevant information in this view. V$RECOVERY_STATUS will be empty to all other Oracle users.

Column	Datatype	Description
RECOVERY_CHECKPOINT	DATE	The point in time to which the recovery has occurred. If no logs have been applied, this is the point in time the recovery starts.
THREAD	NUMBER	The number of the redo thread currently being processed.
SEQUENCE_NEEDED	NUMBER	Log sequence number of the log needed by the recovery process. The value is 0 if no log is needed.
SCN_NEEDED	VARCHAR2(16)	The low SCN of the log needed by recovery. The value is 0 if unknown or no log is needed.
TIME_NEEDED	DATE	Time when the log was created. The value is midnight on 1/1/88 if the time is unknown or if no log is needed.
PREVIOUS_LOG_NAME	VARCHAR2(257)	The filename of the log.
PREVIOUS_LOG_STATUS	VARCHAR2(13)	The status of the previous log. Contains one of the following values: RELEASE WRONG NAME MISSING NAME UNNEEDED NAME NONE
REASON	VARCHAR2(13)	The reason recovery is returning control to the user. Contains one of the following values: NEED LOG LOG REUSED THREAD DISABLED

For further information, see The *Oracle8 Server Backup and Recovery Guide*.

V$REQDIST

This view lists statistics for the histogram of MTS dispatcher request times, divided into 12 buckets, or ranges of time. The time ranges grow exponentially as a function of the bucket number.

Column	Datatype	Description
BUCKET	NUMBER	Bucket number: 0 - 11; the maximum time for each bucket is (4 * 2^N)/100 seconds
COUNT	NUMBER	Count of requests whose total time to complete (excluding wait time) falls in this range

V$RESOURCE

This view contains resource name and address information.

Column	Datatype	Description
ADDR	RAW(4)	Address of resource object
TYPE	VARCHAR2	Resource type. The resource types are listed in Table 3-5: "Values for the TYPE column: User Types" and Table 3-6: "Values for the TYPE column: System Types"
ID1	NUMBER	Resource identifier #1
ID2	NUMBER	Resource identifier #2

V$RESOURCE_LIMIT

This view displays information about global resource use for some of the system resources. Use this view to monitor the consumption of resources so that you can take corrective action, if necessary. Many of the resources correspond to initialization parameters listed in Table 3-10.

Some resources, those used by DLM for example, have an initial allocation (soft limit), and the hard limit, which is theoretically infinite (although in practice it is limited by SGA size). During SGA reservation/initialization, a place is reserved in SGA for the INITIAL_ALLOCATION of resources, but if this allocation is exceeded, additional resources are allocated up to the value indicated by LIMIT_VALUE. The CURRENT_UTILIZATION column indicates whether the initial allocation has been exceeded. When the initial allocation value is exceeded, the additional required resources are allocated from the shared pool, where they must compete for space with other resources.

A good choice for the value of INITIAL_ALLOCATION will avoid the contention for space. For most resources, the value for INITIAL_ALLOCATION is the same as the LIMIT_VALUE. Exceeding LIMIT_VALUE results in an error.

Column	Datatype	Description
RESOURCE_NAME	VARCHAR2(30)	Name of the resource (see Table 3-10)
CURRENT _UTILIZATION	NUMBER	Number of (resources, locks, or processes) currently being used
MAX_UTILIZATION	NUMBER	Maximum consumption of this resource since the last instance start-up
INITIAL_ALLOCATION	VARCHAR2(10)	Initial allocation. This will be equal to the value specified for the resource in the initialization parameter file. (UNLIMITED for infinite allocation)
LIMIT_VALUE	VARCHAR2(10)	Unlimited for resources and locks. This can be greater than the initial allocation value. (UNLIMITED for infinite limit)

Table 3-10: Values for RESOURCE_NAME column

Resource Name	Corresponds to this Initialization Parameter
DISTRIBUTED_TRANSACTIONS	DISTRIBUTED_TRANSACTIONS For more information on this parameter, see "DISTRIBUTED_TRANSACTIONS" on page 1-39.
DML_LOCKS	DML_LOCKS For more information on this parameter see "DML_LOCKS" on page 1-39.
ENQUEUE_LOCKS	This value is computed by Oracle. Use the V$ENQUEUE_LOCK view (described on page 3-37) to obtain more information about the enqueue locks.
ENQUEUE_RESOURCES	ENQUEUE_RESOURCES For more information on this parameter see "ENQUEUE_RESOURCES" on page 1-41.
LM_PROCESSES	LM_PROCS For more information on this parameter see "LM_PROCS" on page 1-55.
LM_RESOURCES	LM_RESS For more information on this parameter see "LM_RESS" on page 1-55.

Table 3-10: Values for RESOURCE_NAME column

Resource Name	Corresponds to this Initialization Parameter
LM_LOCKS	LM_LOCKS For more information on this parameter see "LM_LOCKS" on page 1-54.
MTS_MAX_SERVERS	MTS_MAX_SERVERS For more information on this parameter see "MTS_MAX_SERVERS" on page 1-72.
PARALLEL_SLAVES	PARALLEL_MAX_SERVERS For more information on this parameter, see "PARALLEL_MAX_SERVERS" on page 1-89.
PROCESSES	PROCESSES For more information on this parameter, see "PROCESSES" on page 1-95.
ROLLBACK_SEGMENTS	MAX_ROLLBACK_SEGMENTS For more information on this parameter, see "MAX_ROLLBACK_SEGMENTS" on page 1-67.
SESSIONS	SESSIONS For more information on this parameter, see "SESSIONS" on page 1-103.
SORT_SEGMENT_LOCKS	This value is computed by Oracle
TEMPORARY_LOCKS	This value is computed by Oracle
TRANSACTIONS	TRANSACTIONS For more information on this parameter, see "TRANSACTIONS" on page 1-114.

V$ROLLNAME

This view lists the names of all online rollback segments. This view can only be accessed when the database is open.

Column	Datatype	Description
USN	NUMBER	Rollback (undo) segment number
NAME	VARCHAR2	Rollback segment name

V$ROLLSTAT

This view contains rollback segment statistics.

Column	Datatype	Description
USN	NUMBER	Rollback segment number
EXTENTS	NUMBER	Number of extents in rollback segment
RSSIZE	NUMBER	Size in bytes of rollback segment

Column	Datatype	Description
WRITES	NUMBER	Number of bytes written to rollback segment
XACTS	NUMBER	Number of active transactions
GETS	NUMBER	Number of header gets
WAITS	NUMBER	Number of header waits
OPTSIZE	NUMBER	Optimal size of rollback segment
HWMSIZE	NUMBER	High water mark of rollback segment size
SHRINKS	NUMBER	Number of times the size of a rollback segment decreases
WRAPS	NUMBER	Number of times rollback segment is wrapped
EXTENDS	NUMBER	Number of times rollback segment size is extended
AVESHRINK	NUMBER	Average shrink size
AVEACTIVE	NUMBER	Current size of active extents, averaged over time.
STATUS	VARCHAR2(15)	Rollback segment status
CUREXT	NUMBER	Current extent
CURBLK	NUMBER	Current block

V$ROWCACHE

This view displays statistics for data dictionary activity. Each row contains statistics for one data dictionary cache.

Column	Datatype	Description
CACHE#	NUMBER	Row cache ID number
TYPE	VARCHAR2	Parent or subordinate row cache type
SUBORDINATE#	NUMBER	Subordinate set number
PARAMETER	VARCHAR2	Name of the initialization parameter that determines the number of entries in the data dictionary cache
COUNT	NUMBER	Total number of entries in the cache

Column	Datatype	Description
USAGE	NUMBER	Number of cache entries that contain valid data
FIXED	NUMBER	Number of fixed entries in the cache
GETS	NUMBER	Total number of requests for information on the data object
GETMISSES	NUMBER	Number of data requests resulting in cache misses
SCANS	NUMBER	Number of scan requests
SCANMISSES	NUMBER	Number of times a scan failed to find the data in the cache
SCANCOMPLETES	NUMBER	For a list of subordinate entries, the number of times the list was scanned completely
MODIFICATIONS	NUMBER	Number of inserts, updates, and deletions
FLUSHES	NUMBER	Number of times flushed to disk

V$SESSION

This view lists session information for each current session.

Column	Datatype	Description
SADDR	RAW(4)	Session address
SID	NUMBER	Session identifier
SERIAL#	NUMBER	Session serial number. Used to identify uniquely a session's objects. Guarantees that session-level commands are applied to the correct session objects if the session ends and another session begins with the same session ID.
AUDSID	NUMBER	Auditing session ID
PADDR	RAW(4)	Address of the process that owns this session
USER#	NUMBER	Oracle user identifier
USERNAME	VARCHAR2(30)	Oracle username
COMMAND	NUMBER	Command in progress (last statement parsed); for a list of values, see Table 3-11 on page 3-81

Column	Datatype	Description
OWNERID	NUMBER	The column contents are invalid if the value is 2147483644. Otherwise, this column contains the identifier of the user who owns the migratable session.
TADDR	VARCHAR2(8)	Address of transaction state object
LOCKWAIT	VARCHAR2(8)	Address of lock waiting for; NULL if none
STATUS	VARCHAR2(8)	Status of the session: ACTIVE (currently executing SQL), INACTIVE, KILLED (marked to be killed), CACHED (temporarily cached for use by Oracle*XA), SNIPED (session inactive, waiting on the client)
SERVER	VARCHAR2(9)	Server type: DEDICATED, SHARED, PSEUDO, NONE
SCHEMA#	NUMBER	Schema user identifier
SCHEMANAME	VARCHAR2(30)	Schema user name
OSUSER	VARCHAR2(15)	Operating system client user name
PROCESS	VARCHAR2(9)	Operating system client process ID
MACHINE	VARCHAR2(64)	Operating system machine name
TERMINAL	VARCHAR2(10)	Operating system terminal name
PROGRAM	VARCHAR2(48)	Operating system program name
TYPE	VARCHAR2(10)	Session type
SQL_ADDRESS	RAW(4)	Used with SQL_HASH_VALUE to identify the SQL statement that is currently being executed
SQL_HASH_VALUE	NUMBER	Used with SQL_ADDRESS to identify the SQL statement that is currently being executed
MODULE	VARCHAR2(48)	Contains the name of the currently executing module as set by calling the DBMS_APPLICATION_INFO.SET_MODULE procedure.
MODULE_HASH	NUMBER	The hash value of the above MODULE
ACTION	VARCHAR2(32)	Contains the name of the currently executing action as set by calling the DBMS_APPLICATION_INFO.SET_ACTION procedure.
ACTION_HASH	NUMBER	The hash value of the above action name

Column	Datatype	Description
CLIENT_INFO	VARCHAR2(64)	Information set by the DBMS_APPLICATION_INFO.SET_CLIENT_INFO procedure.
FIXED_TABLE _SEQUENCE	NUMBER	This contains a number that increases every time the session completes a call to the database and there has been an intervening select from a dynamic performance table. This column can be used by performance monitors to monitor statistics in the database. Each time the performance monitor looks at the database, it only needs to look at sessions that are currently active or have a higher value in this column than the highest value that the performance monitor saw the last time. All the other sessions have been idle since the last time the performance monitor looked at the database.
ROW_WAIT_OBJ#	NUMBER	Object ID for the table containing the ROWID specified in ROW_WAIT_ROW#
ROW_WAIT_FILE#	NUMBER	Identifier for the datafile containing the ROWID specified in ROW_WAIT_ROW#. This column is valid only if the session is currently waiting for another transaction to commit and the value of ROW_WAIT_OBJ# is non-zero.
ROW_WAIT _BLOCK#	NUMBER	Identifier for the block containing the ROWID specified in ROW_WAIT_ROW#. This column is valid only if the session is currently waiting for another transaction to commit and the value of ROW_WAIT_OBJ# is non-zero.
ROW_WAIT_ROW#	NUMBER	The current ROWID being locked. This column is valid only if the session is currently waiting for another transaction to commit and the value of ROW_WAIT_OBJ# is non-zero.
PDML_ENABLED	VARCHAR2(3)	If set to YES, the session is in a PARALLEL DML enabled mode, otherwise set to NO
FAILOVER_TYPE	VARCHAR2(10)	NONE if failover is disabled for this session, SESSION if client is able to failover its session following a disconnect, and SELECT if client is able to fail over selects in progress as well
FAILOVER _METHOD	VARCHAR2(3)	NONE if failover is disabled for this session, BASIC if client reconnects following a disconnect, PRECONNECT if the backup instance is able to support all connections from every instance that it is backup for
FAILED_OVER	VARCHAR2(13)	TRUE if running in failover mode and have failed over, otherwise FALSE

Table 3-11 lists numeric values corresponding to commands that may be in progress during a session. These values can appear in the V$SESSION COMMAND column. They also appear in the data dictionary view SYS.AUDIT_ACTIONS.

Table 3-11: Command Numbers for the COMMAND Column

Command Number	Command
0	No command in progress. Occurs when process is in a transitory state, usually when terminating.
1	CREATE TABLE
2	INSERT
3	SELECT
4	CREATE CLUSTER
5	ALTER CLUSTER
6	UPDATE
7	DELETE
8	DROP CLUSTER
9	CREATE INDEX
10	DROP INDEX
11	ALTER INDEX
12	DROP TABLE
13	CREATE SEQUENCE
14	ALTER SEQUENCE
15	ALTER TABLE
16	DROP SEQUENCE
17	GRANT
18	REVOKE

Table 3-11: Command Numbers for the COMMAND Column

Command Number	Command
19	CREATE SYNONYM
20	DROP SYNONYM
21	CREATE VIEW
22	DROP VIEW
23	VALIDATE INDEX
24	CREATE PROCEDURE
25	ALTER PROCEDURE
26	LOCK TABLE
27	NO OPERATION
28	RENAME
29	COMMENT
30	AUDIT
31	NOAUDIT
32	CREATE DATABASE LINK
33	DROP DATABASE LINK
34	CREATE DATABASE
35	ALTER DATABASE
36	CREATE ROLLBACK SEGMENT
37	ALTER ROLLBACK SEGMENT
38	DROP ROLLBACK SEGMENT
39	CREATE TABLESPACE
40	ALTER TABLESPACE

Table 3-11: Command Numbers for the COMMAND Column

Command Number	Command
41	DROP TABLESPACE
42	ALTER SESSION
43	ALTER USER
44	COMMIT
45	ROLLBACK
46	SAVEPOINT
47	PL/SQL EXECUTE
48	SET TRANSACTION
49	ALTER SYSTEM SWITCH LOG
50	EXPLAIN
51	CREATE USER
52	CREATE ROLE
53	DROP USER
54	DROP ROLE
55	SET ROLE
56	CREATE SCHEMA
57	CREATE CONTROL FILE
58	ALTER TRACING
59	CREATE TRIGGER
60	ALTER TRIGGER
61	DROP TRIGGER
62	ANALYZE TABLE

Table 3-11: Command Numbers for the COMMAND Column

Command Number	Command
63	ANALYZE INDEX
64	ANALYZE CLUSTER
65	CREATE PROFILE
66	DROP PROFILE
67	ALTER PROFILE
68	DROP PROCEDURE
69	DROP PROCEDURE
70	ALTER RESOURCE COST
71	CREATE SNAPSHOT LOG
72	ALTER SNAPSHOT LOG
73	DROP SNAPSHOT LOG
74	CREATE SNAPSHOT
75	ALTER SNAPSHOT
76	DROP SNAPSHOT
79	ALTER ROLE
85	TRUNCATE TABLE
86	TRUNCATE CLUSTER
88	ALTER VIEW
91	CREATE FUNCTION
92	ALTER FUNCTION
93	DROP FUNCTION
94	CREATE PACKAGE

Table 3-11: Command Numbers for the COMMAND Column

Command Number	Command
95	ALTER PACKAGE
96	DROP PACKAGE
97	CREATE PACKAGE BODY
98	ALTER PACKAGE BODY
99	DROP PACKAGE BODY

V$SESSION_CONNECT_INFO

This view displays information about network connections for the current session.

Column	Datatype	Description
SID	NUMBER	Session identifier (can be used to join this view with V$SESSION)
AUTHENTICATION _TYPE	VARCHAR2(15)	How the user was authenticated: OS, PROTOCOL, or NETWORK.
OSUSER	VARCHAR2(30)	The external username for this database user
NETWORK _SERVICE_BANNER	VARCHAR2(2000)	Product banners for each Net8 service used for this connection (one row per banner)

V$SESSION_CURSOR_CACHE

This view displays information on cursor usage for the current session. Note: the V$SESSION_CURSOR_CACHE view is not a measure of the effectiveness of the SESSION_CACHED_CURSORS initialization parameter.

Column	Datatype	Description
MAXIMUM	NUMBER	Maximum number of cursors to cache. Once you hit this number, some cursors will need to be closed in order to open more. The value in this column is derived from the initialization parameter OPEN_CURSORS.
COUNT	NUMBER	The current number of cursors (whether they are in use or not)
OPENED_ONCE	NUMBER	Number of cursors opened at least once
OPEN	NUMBER	Current number of open cursors
OPENS	NUMBER	Cumulative total of cursor opens minus one. This is because the cursor that is currently open and being used for this query is not counted in the OPENS statistic.
HITS	NUMBER	Cumulative total of cursor open hits
HIT_RATIO	NUMBER	Ratio of the number of times an open cursor was found divided by the number of times a cursor was sought

V$SESSION_EVENT

This view lists information on waits for an event by a session. Note that the TIME_WAITED and AVERAGE_WAIT columns will contain a value of zero on those platforms that do not support a fast timing mechanism. If you are running on one of these platforms and you want this column to reflect true wait times, you must set TIMED_STATISTICS to TRUE in the parameter file. Please remember that doing this will have a small negative effect on system performance. For more information, see "TIMED_STATISTICS" on page 1-113.

Column	Datatype	Description
SID	NUMBER	The ID of the session
EVENT	VARCHAR2(64)	The name of the wait event. For more information, see Appendix A, "Oracle Wait Events"
TOTAL_WAITS	NUMBER	The total number of waits for this event by this session
TOTAL_TIMEOUTS	NUMBER	The total number of timeouts for this event by this session
TIME_WAITED	NUMBER	The total amount of time waited for this event by this session, in hundredths of a second
AVERAGE_WAIT	NUMBER	The average amount of time waited for this event by this session, in hundredths of a second

V$SESSION_LONGOPS

This view displays the status of certain long-running operations. It provides progression reports on operations using the columns SOFAR and TOTALWORK. For example, the operational status for the following components can be monitored:

- hash cluster creations
- backup operations
- recovery operations

Column	Datatype	Description
SID	NUMBER	Session identifier
SERIAL#	NUMBER	Session serial number
UPDATE_COUNT	NUMBER	The updated count
COMPNAM	VARCHAR2(30)	The component name
OBJID	NUMBER	If present, displays the dictionary object ID on which the operation is being done

Column	Datatype	Description
CONTEXT	NUMBER	A context specific to the component
STEPID	NUMBER	A number assigned by the component for the execution step
MSG	VARCHAR2(512)	Text describing work done so far and total anticipated work on an object
STEPSOFAR	NUMBER	Units of work done so far in the step
STEPTOTAL	NUMBER	Total amount of work to be done in the step
SOFAR	NUMBER	Total units of work done so far
TOTALWORK	NUMBER	Total amount of work to be done. Zero if unknown
APPLICATION _DATA_1	NUMBER	This column may contain additional data relating to the long-running operation described by this row. The contents of this row vary depending on the type of long-running operation.
APPLICATION _DATA_2	NUMBER	This column may contain additional data relating to the long-running operation described by this row. The contents of this row vary depending on the type of long-running operation.
APPLICATION _DATA_3	NUMBER	This column may contain additional data relating to the long-running operation described by this row. The contents of this row vary depending on the type of long-running operation.
START_TIME	DATE	The starting time
CURRENT_TIME	DATE	The current time
ELAPSED _SECONDS	NUMBER	The number of elapsed seconds

V$SESSION_OBJECT_CACHE

This view displays object cache statistics for the current user session on the local server (instance).

Column	Datatype	Description
PINS	NUMBER	Number of object pins or look-ups in the cache
HITS	NUMBER	Number of object pins that found the object already in the cache
TRUE_HITS	NUMBER	Number of object pins that found the object already in the cache and in the desired state (thus, not requiring refresh from the database)
HIT_RATIO	NUMBER	The ratio of HITS/PINS
TRUE_HIT_RATIO	NUMBER	The ratio of TRUE_HITS/PINS
OBJECT_REFRESHES	NUMBER	Number of objects in the cache that were refreshed with a new value from the database
CACHE_REFRESHES	NUMBER	Number of times the whole cache (all objects) were refreshed
OBJECT_FLUSHES	NUMBER	Number of objects in the cache that were flushed to the database
CACHE_FLUSHES	NUMBER	Number of times the whole cache (all objects) were flushed to the database
CACHE_SHRINKS	NUMBER	Number of times the cache was shrunk to the optimal size
CACHED_OBJECTS	NUMBER	Number of objects currently cached
PINNED_OBJECTS	NUMBER	Number of objects currently pinned
CACHE_SIZE	NUMBER	Current size of the cache in bytes
OPTIMAL_SIZE	NUMBER	Optimal size of the cache in bytes
MAXIMUM_SIZE	NUMBER	Maximum size of the cache in bytes

V$SESSION_WAIT

This view lists the resources or events for which active sessions are waiting.

The following are tuning considerations:

- P1RAW, P2RAW, and P3RAW display the same values as the P1, P2, and P3 columns, except that the numbers are displayed in hexadecimal.

- The WAIT_TIME column contains a value of -2 on platforms that do not support a fast timing mechanism. If you are running on one of these platforms and you want this column to reflect true wait times, you must set the TIMED_STATISTICS parameter to TRUE. Remember that doing this has a small negative effect on system performance. For more information, see "TIMED_STATISTICS" on page 1-113.

  In previous releases the WAIT_TIME column contained an arbitrarily large value instead of a negative value to indicate the platform did not have a fast timing mechanism.

- The STATE column interprets the value of WAIT_TIME and describes the state of the current or most recent wait.

For more information on session waits, see Appendix A, "Oracle Wait Events".

Column	Datatype	Description
SID	NUMBER	Session identifier
SEQ#	NUMBER	Sequence number that uniquely identifies this wait. Incremented for each wait.
EVENT	VARCHAR2(64)	Resource or event for which the session is waiting. For more information, see Appendix A, "Oracle Wait Events"
P1TEXT	VARCHAR2	Description of first additional parameter
P1	NUMBER	First additional parameter
P1RAW	RAW(4)	First additional parameter
P2TEXT	VARCHAR2	Description of second parameter
P2	NUMBER	Second additional parameter
P2RAW	RAW(4)	Second additional parameter
P3TEXT	VARCHAR2	Description of third parameter
P3	NUMBER	Third additional parameter
P3RAW	RAW(4)	Third additional parameter
WAIT_TIME	NUMBER	A non-zero value is the session's last wait time. A zero value means the session is currently waiting.

Column	Datatype	Description
STATE	VARCHAR2	Wait state (see Table 3-12)

Table 3-12 defines values in the V$SESSION_WAIT STATE column.

Table 3-12: Wait State listed in the STATE Column

STATE	Value	Meaning
WAITING	0	The session is currently waiting
WAITED UNKNOWN TIME	-2	Duration of last wait is unknown
WAITED SHORT TIME	-1	Last wait < 1/100th of a second
WAITED KNOWN TIME	>0	WAIT_TIME = duration of last wait

V$SESSTAT

This view lists user session statistics. To find the name of the statistic associated with each statistic number (STATISTIC#), see "V$STATNAME" on page 3-105.

Column	Datatype	Description
SID	NUMBER	Session identifier
STATISTIC#	NUMBER	Statistic number (identifier)
VALUE	NUMBER	Statistic value

V$SESS_IO

This view lists I/O statistics for each user session.

Column	Datatype	Description
SID	NUMBER	Session identifier
BLOCK_GETS	NUMBER	Block gets for this session
CONSISTENT_GETS	NUMBER	Consistent gets for this session
PHYSICAL_READS	NUMBER	Physical reads for this session
BLOCK_CHANGES	NUMBER	Block changes for this session
CONSISTENT _CHANGES	NUMBER	Consistent changes for this session

V$SGA

This view contains summary information on the System Global Area.

Column	Datatype	Description
NAME	VARCHAR2	SGA component group
VALUE	NUMBER	Memory size in bytes

V$SGASTAT

This view contains detailed information on the System Global Area.

Column	Datatype	Description
NAME	VARCHAR2	SGA component name
BYTES	NUMBER	Memory size in bytes
POOL	VARCHAR2	Designates the pool in which the memory in NAME resides. Value can be LARGE POOL - Memory is allocated from the large pool or SHARED POOL - Memory is allocated from the shared pool

V$SHARED_POOL_RESERVED

This fixed view lists statistics that help you tune the reserved pool and space within the shared pool.

The following columns of V$SHARED_POOL_RESERVED are valid only if the initialization parameter SHARED_POOL_RESERVED_SIZE is set to a valid value. For more information, see "SHARED_POOL_RESERVED_SIZE" on page 1-104.

Column	Datatype	Description
FREE_SPACE	NUMBER	Total amount of free space on the reserved list
AVG_FREE_SIZE	NUMBER	Average size of the free memory on the reserved list
FREE_COUNT	NUMBER	Number of free pieces of memory on the reserved list
MAX_FREE_SIZE	NUMBER	Size of the largest free piece of memory on the reserved list
USED_SPACE	NUMBER	Total amount of used memory on the reserved list
AVG_USED_SIZE	NUMBER	Average size of the used memory on the reserved list
USED_COUNT	NUMBER	Number of used pieces of memory on the reserved list
MAX_USED_SIZE	NUMBER	Size of the largest used piece of memory on the reserved list
REQUESTS	NUMBER	Number of times that the reserved list was searched for a free piece of memory
REQUEST_MISSES	NUMBER	Number of times the reserved list did not have a free piece of memory to satisfy the request, and started flushing objects from the LRU list
LAST_MISS_SIZE	NUMBER	Request size of the last request miss, when the reserved list did not have a free piece of memory to satisfy the request and started flushing objects from the LRU list
MAX_MISS_SIZE	NUMBER	Request size of the largest request miss, when the reserved list did not have a free piece of memory to satisfy the request and started flushing objects from the LRU list

The following columns of V$SHARED_POOL_RESERVED contain values which are valid even if SHARED_POOL_RESERVED_SIZE is not set.

Column	Datatype	Description
REQUEST_FAILURES	NUMBER	Number of times that no memory was found to satisfy a request (that is, the number of times the error ORA-4031 occurred)
LAST_FAILURE_SIZE	NUMBER	Request size of the last failed request (that is, the request size for the last ORA-4031 error)
ABORTED_REQUEST _THRESHOLD	NUMBER	Minimum size of a request which signals an ORA-4031 error without flushing objects
ABORTED_REQUESTS	NUMBER	Number of requests that signalled an ORA-4031 error without flushing objects
LAST_ABORTED_SIZE	NUMBER	Last size of the request that returned an ORA-4031 error without flushing objects from the LRU list

V$SHARED_SERVER

This view contains information on the shared server processes.

Column	Datatype	Description
NAME	VARCHAR2	Name of the server
PADDR	RAW(4)	Server's process address
STATUS	VARCHAR2	Server status: EXEC (executing SQL) WAIT (ENQ) (waiting for a lock), WAIT (SEND) (waiting to send data to user) WAIT (COMMON) (idle; waiting for a user request) WAIT (RESET) (waiting for a circuit to reset after a break) QUIT (terminating)
MESSAGES	NUMBER	Number of messages processed
BYTES	NUMBER	Total number of bytes in all messages
BREAKS	NUMBER	Number of breaks
CIRCUIT	RAW(4)	Address of circuit currently being serviced
IDLE	NUMBER	Total idle time in hundredths of a second
BUSY	NUMBER	Total busy time in hundredths of a second
REQUESTS	NUMBER	Total number of requests taken from the common queue in this server's lifetime

V$SORT_SEGMENT

This view contains information about every sort segment in a given instance.

Column	Datatype	Description
TABLESPACE_NAME	VARCHAR2(31)	Name of tablespace
SEGMENT_FILE	NUMBER	File number of the first extent
SEGMENT_BLOCK	NUMBER	Block number of the first extent
EXTENT_SIZE	NUMBER	Extent size
CURRENT_USERS	NUMBER	Number of active users of the segment
TOTAL_EXTENTS	NUMBER	Total number of extents in the segment
TOTAL_BLOCKS	NUMBER	Total number of blocks in the segment
RELATIVE_FNO	NUMBER	Relative file number of the sort segment header
USED_EXTENTS	NUMBER	Extents allocated to active sorts
USED_BLOCKS	NUMBER	Blocks allocated to active sorts
FREE_EXTENTS	NUMBER	Extents not allocated to any sort
FREE_BLOCKS	NUMBER	Blocks not allocated to any sort
ADDED_EXTENTS	NUMBER	Number of extent allocations
EXTENT_HITS	NUMBER	Number of times an unused extent was found in the pool
FREED_EXTENTS	NUMBER	Number of deallocated extents
FREE_REQUESTS	NUMBER	Number of requests to deallocate
MAX_SIZE	NUMBER	Maximum number of extents ever used
MAX_BLOCKS	NUMBER	Maximum number of blocks ever used
MAX_USED_SIZE	NUMBER	Maximum number of extents used by all sorts
MAX_USED_BLOCKS	NUMBER	Maximum number of blocks used by all sorts

Column	Datatype	Description
MAX_SORT_SIZE	NUMBER	Maximum number of extents used by an individual sort
MAX_SORT_BLOCKS	NUMBER	Maximum number of blocks used by an individual sort

V$SORT_USAGE

This view describes sort usage.

Column	Datatype	Description
USER	VARCHAR2(30)	User who requested temporary space
SESSION_ADDR	RAW(4)	Address of shared SQL cursor
SESSION_NUM	NUMBER	Serial number of session
SQLADDR	RAW(4)	Address of SQL statement
SQLHASH	NUMBER	Hash value of SQL statement
TABLESPACE	VARCHAR2(31)	Tablespace in which space is allocated
CONTENTS	VARCHAR2(9)	Indicates whether tablespace is TEMPORARY/PERMANENT
SEGFILE#	NUMBER	File number of initial extent
SEGBLK#	NUMBER	Block number of the initial extent
EXTENTS	NUMBER	Extents allocated to the sort
BLOCKS	NUMBER	Extents in blocks allocated to the sort
SEGRFNO#	NUMBER	Relative file number of initial extent

V$SQL

This view lists statistics on shared SQL area without the GROUP BY clause and contains one row for each child of the original SQL text entered.

Column	Datatype	Description
SQL_TEXT	VARCHAR2(1000)	The first eighty characters of the SQL text for the current cursor

Column	Datatype	Description
SHARABLE_MEM	NUMBER	The amount of sharable memory, in bytes used by this child cursor
PERSISTENT_MEM	NUMBER	The amount of persistent memory, in bytes used by this child cursor
RUNTIME_MEM	NUMBER	The size of the ephemeral frame used by this child cursor
SORTS	NUMBER	The number of sorts that was done for this child cursor
LOADED_VERSIONS	NUMBER	1 if context heap is loaded, 0 otherwise
OPEN_VERSIONS	NUMBER	1 if the child cursor is locked, 0 otherwise
USERS_OPENING	NUMBER	The number of users executing the statement
EXECUTIONS	NUMBER	The number of executions that took place on this object since it was brought into the library cache
USERS_EXECUTING	NUMBER	The number of users executing the statement
LOADS	NUMBER	The number of times the object was loaded or reloaded
FIRST_LOAD_TIME	VARCHAR2(19)	The time stamp of the parent creation time
INVALIDATIONS	NUMBER	The number of times this child cursor has been invalidated
PARSE_CALLS	NUMBER	The number of parse calls for this child cursor
DISK_READS	NUMBER	The number of disk reads for this child cursor
BUFFER_GETS	NUMBER	The number of buffer gets for this child cursor
ROWS_PROCESSED	NUMBER	The total number of rows the parsed SQL statement returns
COMMAND_TYPE	NUMBER	The Oracle command type definition
OPTIMIZER_MODE	VARCHAR2(10)	Mode under which the SQL statement is executed

Column	Datatype	Description
OPTIMIZER_COST	NUMBER	The cost of this query given by the optimizer
PARSING_USER_ID	NUMBER	The user ID of the user who originally built this child cursor
PARSING_SCHEMA_ID	NUMBER	The schema ID that was used to originally build this child cursor
KEPT_VERSIONS	NUMBER	Indicates whether this child cursor has been marked to be kept pinned in cache using the DBMS_SHARED_POOL package
ADDRESS	RAW(4)	The address of the handle to the parent for this cursor
TYPE_CHK_HEAP	RAW(4)	The descriptor of the type check heap for this child cursor
HASH_VALUE	NUMBER	The hash value of the parent statement in the library cache
CHILD_NUMBER	NUMBER	The number of this child cursor
MODULE	VARCHAR2(64)	Contains the name of the module that was executing at the time that the SQL statement was first parsed as set by calling DBMS_APPLICATION _INFO.SET_MODULE
MODULE_HASH	NUMBER	The hash value of the module that is named in the MODULE column
ACTION	VARCHAR2(64)	Contains the name of the action that was executing at the time that the SQL statement was first parsed as set by calling DBMS_APPLICATION _INFO.SET_ACTION
ACTION_HASH	NUMBER	The hash value of the action that is named in the ACTION column
SERIALIZABLE_ABORTS	NUMBER	The number of times the transaction fails to serialize, producing ORA-8177 errors, per cursor

V$SQL_BIND_DATA

This view displays the actual bind data sent by the client for each distinct bind variable in each cursor owned by the session querying this view if the data is available in the server.

Column	Datatype	Description
CURSOR_NUM	NUMBER	Cursor number for this bind
POSITION	NUMBER	Bind position
DATATYPE	NUMBER	Bind datatype
SHARED_MAX_LEN	NUMBER	Shared maximum length for this bind from the shared cursor object associated with this bind
PRIVATE_MAX_LEN	NUMBER	Private maximum length for this bind sent from the client
ARRAY_SIZE	NUMBER	Maximum number of array elements (for array binds only)
PRECISION	NUMBER	Precision (for numeric binds)
SCALE	NUMBER	Scale (for numeric binds)
SHARED_FLAG	NUMBER	Shared bind data flags
SHARED_FLAG2	NUMBER	Shared bind data flags (continued)
BUF_ADDRESS	RAW(4)	Bind buffer memory address
BUF_LENGTH	NUMBER	Bind buffer length
VAL_LENGTH	NUMBER	Actual bind value length
BUF_FLAG	NUMBER	Bind buffer flags
INDICATOR	NUMBER	Bind indicator
VALUE	VARCHAR2(4000)	Contents of the bind buffer

V$SQL_BIND_METADATA

This view displays bind metadata provided by the client for each distinct bind variable in each cursor owned by the session querying this view.

Column	Datatype	Description
ADDRESS	RAW(4)	Memory address of the child cursor that owns this bind variable
POSITION	NUMBER	Bind position
DATATYPE	NUMBER	Bind datatype
MAX_LENGTH	NUMBER	Maximum length of the bind value
ARRAY_LEN	NUMBER	Maximum number of array elements (for array binds only)
BIND_NAME	VARCHAR2(30)	Bind variable name (if used)

V$SQL_CURSOR

This view displays debugging information for each cursor associated with the session querying this view.

Column	Datatype	Description
CURNO	NUMBER	Cursor number
FLAG	NUMBER	Flags set in the cursor
STATUS	VARCHAR2(9)	Status of the cursor; that is, what state the cursor is in
PARENT_HANDLE	RAW(4)	Pointer to the parent cursor handle
PARENT_LOCK	RAW(4)	Pointer to the parent cursor lock
CHILD_LOCK	RAW(4)	Pointer to the child cursor lock
CHILD_PIN	RAW(4)	Pointer to the child cursor pin
PERS_HEAP_MEM	NUMBER	Total amount of memory allocated from persistent heap for this cursor
WORK_HEAP_MEM	NUMBER	Total amount of memory allocated from the work heap for this cursor

Column	Datatype	Description
BIND_VARS	NUMBER	Total number of bind positions in the query currently parsed into this cursor
DEFINE_VARS	NUMBER	Total number of define variables in the query currently parsed into this cursor
BIND_MEM_LOC	VARCHAR2(64)	Which memory heap the bind variables are stored in: either the UGA or the CGA
INST_FLAG	VARCHAR2(64)	Instantiation object flags
INST_FLAG2	VARCHAR2(64)	Instantiation object flags (continued)

V$SQL_SHARED_MEMORY

This view displays information about the cursor shared memory snapshot. Each SQL statement stored in the shared pool has one or more child objects associated with it. Each child object has a number of parts, one of which is the context heap, which holds, among other things, the query plan.

Column	Datatype	Description
SQL_TEXT	VARCHAR2(1000)	The SQL text of the shared cursor child object that this row is displaying information for.
HASH_VALUE	NUMBER	The hash value of the above SQL text in the shared pool.
HEAP_DESC	RAW(4)	The address of the descriptor for the context heap of the child cursor described in this row.
STRUCTURE	VARCHAR2(16)	If the memory chunk described in this row was allocated using a comment of the form "X : Y", then this is the "X" part of the comment.
FUNCTION	VARCHAR2(16)	Similar to the STRUCTURE column, this is the "Y" field of the comment.
COMMENT	VARCHAR2(16)	This is the whole comment field that was supplied when this memory chunk was allocated.
CHUNK_PTR	RAW(4)	This is the starting address of the allocated memory chunk.
CHUNK_SIZE	NUMBER	The amount of memory allocated for this chunk.

Column	Datatype	Description
ALLOC_CLASS	VARCHAR2(8)	Class of memory that this chunk of memory belongs to. It will usually be either FREEABLE or PERMANENT.
CHUNK_TYPE	NUMBER	An index into a table of callback functions that tell the server how to recreate this chunk of memory should it need to be LRU'd out of the shared pool.
SUBHEAP_DESC	RAW(4)	If the parent heap of this context heap is itself a subheap, then this is the address of the descriptor of the parent heap.

V$SQLAREA

This view lists statistics on shared SQL area and contains one row per SQL string. It provides statistics on SQL statements that are in memory, parsed, and ready for execution.

Column	Datatype	Description
SQL_TEXT	VARCHAR2(1000)	The first eighty characters of the SQL text for the current cursor
SHARABLE_MEM	NUMBER	The sum of all sharable memory, in bytes, of all the child cursors under this parent
PERSISTENT_MEM	NUMBER	The sum of all persistent memory, in bytes, of all the child cursors under this parent
RUNTIME_MEM	NUMBER	The sum of all the ephemeral frame sizes of all the children
SORTS	NUMBER	The sum of the number of sorts that was done for all the children
VERSION_COUNT	NUMBER	The number of children that are present in the cache under this parent
LOADED_VERSIONS	NUMBER	The number of children that are present in the cache AND have their context heap (KGL heap 6) loaded
OPEN_VERSIONS	NUMBER	The number of child cursors that are currently open under this current parent
USERS_OPENING	NUMBER	The number of users that have any of the child cursors open

Column	Datatype	Description
EXECUTIONS	NUMBER	The total number of executions, totalled over all the children
USERS_EXECUTING	NUMBER	The total number of users executing the statement over all children
LOADS	NUMBER	The number of times the object was loaded or reloaded
FIRST_LOAD_TIME	VARCHAR2(19)	The time stamp of the parent creation time
INVALIDATIONS	NUMBER	The total number of invalidations over all the children
PARSE_CALLS	NUMBER	The sum of all parse calls to all the child cursors under this parent
DISK_READS	NUMBER	The sum of the number of disk reads over all child cursors
BUFFER_GETS	NUMBER	The sum of buffer gets over all child cursors
ROWS_PROCESSED	NUMBER	The total number of rows processed on behalf of this SQL statement
COMMAND_TYPE	NUMBER	The Oracle command type definition
OPTIMIZER_MODE	VARCHAR2(10)	Mode under which the SQL statement is executed
PARSING_USER_ID	NUMBER	The user ID of the user that has parsed the very first cursor under this parent
PARSING_SCHEMA_ID	NUMBER	The schema ID that was used to parse this child cursor
KEPT_VERSIONS	NUMBER	The number of child cursors that have been marked to be kept using the DBMS_SHARED_POOL package
ADDRESS	RAW(4)	The address of the handle to the parent for this cursor
HASH_VALUE	NUMBER	The hash value of the parent statement in the library cache
MODULE	VARCHAR2(64)	Contains the name of the module that was executing at the time that the SQL statement was first parsed as set by calling DBMS_APPLICATION _INFO.SET_MODULE

Column	Datatype	Description
MODULE_HASH	NUMBER	The hash value of the module that is named in the MODULE column
ACTION	VARCHAR2(64)	Contains the name of the action that was executing at the time that the SQL statement was first parsed as set by calling DBMS_APPLICATION _INFO.SET_ACTION
ACTION_HASH	NUMBER	The hash value of the action that is named in the ACTION column
SERIALIZABLE_ABORTS	NUMBER	The number of times the transaction fails to serialize, producing ORA-8177 errors, totalled over all the children

V$SQLTEXT

This view contains the text of SQL statements belonging to shared SQL cursors in the SGA.

Column	Datatype	Description
ADDRESS	RAW	Used with HASH_VALUE to identify uniquely a cached cursor
HASH_VALUE	NUMBER	Used with ADDRESS to identify uniquely a cached cursor
PIECE	NUMBER	Number used to order the pieces of SQL text
SQL_TEXT	VARCHAR2	A column containing one piece of the SQL text
COMMAND_TYPE	NUMBER	Code for the type of SQL statement (SELECT, INSERT, etc.)

V$SQLTEXT_WITH_NEWLINES

This view is identical to the V$SQLTEXT view except that, to improve legibility, V$SQLTEXT_WITH_NEWLINES does not replace newlines and tabs in the SQL statement with spaces. For more information, see "V$SQLTEXT" on page 3-104.

Column	Datatype	Description
ADDRESS	RAW	Used with HASH_VALUE to identify uniquely a cached cursor
HASH_VALUE	NUMBER	Used with ADDRESS to identify uniquely a cached cursor
PIECE	NUMBER	Number used to order the pieces of SQL text
SQL_TEXT	VARCHAR2	A column containing one piece of the SQL text
COMMAND_TYPE	NUMBER	Code for the type of SQL statement (SELECT, INSERT, etc.)

V$STATNAME

This view displays decoded statistic names for the statistics shown in the V$SESSTAT and V$SYSSTAT tables. For more information, see "V$SESSTAT" on page 3-91 and "V$SYSSTAT" on page 3-108.

Column	Datatype	Description
STATISTIC#	NUMBER	Statistic number
NAME	VARCHAR2	Statistic name. See also Table 3-13
CLASS	NUMBER	Statistic class: 1 (User), 2 (Redo), 4 (Enqueue), 8 (Cache), 16 (OS), 32 (Parallel Server), 64 (SQL), 128 (Debug)

Table 3-13 lists the generic Oracle Server statistics returned by V$STATNAME. For a complete description of each statistic, see Appendix C, "Statistics Descriptions".

Additional Information: On some platforms, the NAME and CLASS columns will contain additional operating system-specific statistics. See your operating system-specific Oracle documentation for more information about these statistics.

Table 3-13: V$SESSTAT and V$SYSSTAT Statistics Names

CPU used by this session	CR blocks created
Current blocks converted for CR	DBWR Flush object call found no dirty buffers
DBWR Flush object cross instance calls	DBWR buffers scanned
DBWR checkpoints	DBWR cross instance writes
DBWR free buffers found	DBWR lru scans
DBWR make free requests	DBWR summed scan depth
DBWR timeouts	DDL statements parallelized
DML statements parallelized	PX local messages received
PX local messages sent	PX remote messages received
PX remote messages sent	SQL*Net roundtrips to/from client
SQL*Net roundtrips to/from dblink	Unnecessary process cleanup for SCN batching
background checkpoints completed	background checkpoints started
bytes received via SQL*Net from client	bytes received via SQL*Net from client
bytes sent via SQL*Net to client	bytes sent via SQL*Net to dblink
calls to get snapshot scn: kcmgss	change write time
cluster key scan block gets	cluster key scans
commit cleanout failures: block lost	commit cleanout failures: buffer being written
commit cleanout failures: callback failure	commit cleanout failures: cannot pin
commit cleanout failures: hot backup in progress	commit cleanout failures: write disabled
commit cleanouts	commit cleanouts successfully completed
consistent changes	consistent gets
cross instance CR read	db block changes
db block gets	dirty buffers inspected
enqueue conversions	enqueue deadlocks
enqueue releases	enqueue requests
enqueue timeouts	enqueue waits
exchange deadlocks	execute count
free buffer inspected	free buffer requested
global cache defers	global cache freelist waits

Table 3-13: V$SESSTAT and V$SYSSTAT Statistics Names

global cache hash latch waits	global lock convert time
global lock converts (async)	global lock converts (non async)
global lock get time	global lock gets (async)
global lock gets (non async)	global lock release time
global lock releases	kcmccs called get current scn
kcmccs read scn without going to DLM	kcmccs waited for batching
lock element waits	logons cumulative
logons current	next scns gotten without going to DLM
opened cursors cumulative	opened cursors current
opens of replaced files	pens requiring cache replacement
parse count (hard)	parse count (soft)
parse count (total)	parse time cpu
parse time elapsed	physical reads
physical writes	queries parallelized
recovery array read time	recovery array reads
recovery blocks read	recursive calls
recursive cpu usage	redo entries
redo entries linearized	redo log space requests
redo log space wait time	redo log switch interrupts
redo ordering marks	redo size
redo synch time	redo sync writes
redo wastage	redo write time
redo writer latching time	redo writes
remote instance undo block writes	remote instance undo header writes
remote instance undo requests	serializable aborts
session connect time	session cursor cache count
session cursor cache hits	session logical reads
session pga memory	session pga memory max
session stored procedure space	session uga memory
session uga memory max	sorts (disk)
sorts (memory)	sorts (rows)
summed dirty queue length	table fetch by rowid
table fetch continued row	table scan blocks gotten
table scan rows gotten	table scans (cache partitions)
table scans (direct read)	table scans (long tables)

Table 3-13: V$SESSTAT and V$SYSSTAT Statistics Names

table scans (rowid ranges)	table scans (short tables)
total file opens	user calls
user commits	user rollbacks
write requests	

V$SUBCACHE

This view displays information about the subordinate caches currently loaded into library cache memory. The view walks through the library cache, printing out a row for each loaded subordinate cache per library cache object.

Column	Datatype	Description
OWNER_NAME	VARCHAR2(64)	Owner of object containing these cache entries
NAME	VARCHAR2(1000)	Object Name
TYPE	NUMBER	Object Type
HEAP_NUM	NUMBER	Heap number containing this subordinate cache
CACHE_ID	NUMBER	Subordinate cache ID
CACHE_CNT	NUMBER	Number of entries for this cache in this object
HEAP_SZ	NUMBER	Amount of extent space allocated to this heap
HEAP_ALOC	NUMBER	Amount of extent space allocated from this heap
HEAP_USED	NUMBER	Amount of space utilized in this heap

V$SYSSTAT

This view lists system statistics. To find the name of the statistic associated with each statistic number (STATISTIC#), see "V$STATNAME" on page 3-105.

Column	Datatype	Description
STATISTIC#	NUMBER	Statistic number
NAME	VARCHAR2(64)	Statistic name. See Table 3-13 on page 107.
CLASS	NUMBER	Statistic class: 1 (User), 2 (Redo), 4 (Enqueue), 8 (Cache), 16 (OS), 32 (Parallel Server), 64 (SQL), 128 (Debug)
VALUE	NUMBER	Statistic value

V$SYSTEM_CURSOR_CACHE

This view displays similar information to the V$SESSION_CURSOR_CACHE view except that this information is system wide. For more information, see "V$SESSION_CURSOR_CACHE" on page 3-86.

Column	Datatype	Description
OPENS	NUMBER	Cumulative total of cursor opens
HITS	NUMBER	Cumulative total of cursor open hits
HIT_RATIO	NUMBER	Ratio of the number of times you found an open cursor divided by the number of times you looked for a cursor

V$SYSTEM_EVENT

This view contains information on total waits for an event. Note that the TIME_WAITED and AVERAGE_WAIT columns will contain a value of zero on those platforms that do not support a fast timing mechanism. If you are running on one of these platforms and you want this column to reflect true wait times, you must set TIMED_STATISTICS to TRUE in the parameter file.

Please remember that doing this will have a small negative effect on system performance. For more information, see "TIMED_STATISTICS" on page 1-113.

Column	Datatype	Description
EVENT	VARCHAR2(64)	The name of the wait event
TOTAL_WAITS	NUMBER	The total number of waits for this event
TOTAL_TIMEOUTS	NUMBER	The total number of timeouts for this event
TIME_WAITED	NUMBER	The total amount of time waited for this event, in hundredths of a second
AVERAGE_WAIT	NUMBER	The average amount of time waited for this event, in hundredths of a second

V$SYSTEM_PARAMETER

This view contains information on system parameters.

Column	Datatype	Description
NUM	NUMBER	Parameter number
NAME	VARCHAR2(64)	Parameter name
TYPE	NUMBER	Parameter type; 1 = Boolean, 2 = string, 3 = integer
VALUE	VARCHAR2(512)	Value assigned to the parameter
ISDEFAULT	VARCHAR2(9)	Is the value assigned to the parameter the default
ISSES_MODIFIABLE	VARCHAR2(5)	Whether the parameter can be modified by ALTER SESSION
ISSYS_MODIFIABLE	VARCHAR2(9)	Whether the parameter can be modified by ALTER SYSTEM
ISMODIFIED	VARCHAR2(8)	Indicates how the parameter was modified. If an ALTER SESSION was performed, the value will be MODIFIED. If an ALTER SYSTEM (which will cause all the currently logged in sessions' values to be modified) was performed the value will be SYS_MODIFIED.

Column	Datatype	Description
ISADJUSTED	VARCHAR2(5)	Indicates that the rdbms adjusted the input value to a more suitable value (e.g., the parameter value should be prime, but the user input a non-prime number, so the rdbms adjusted the value to the next prime number)
DESCRIPTION	VARCHAR2(64)	Descriptive text about the parameter

V$TABLESPACE

This view displays tablespace information from the controlfile.

Column	Datatype	Description
TS#	NUMBER	Tablespace number
NAME	VARCHAR2 (30)	Tablespace name

V$THREAD

This view contains thread information from the control file.

Column	Datatype	Description
THREAD#	NUMBER	Thread number
STATUS	VARCHAR2	Thread status: OPEN, CLOSED
ENABLED	VARCHAR2	Enabled status: DISABLED, (enabled) PRIVATE, or (enabled) PUBLIC
ENABLE_CHANGE#	NUMBER	SCN at which thread was enabled
ENABLE_TIME	DATE	Time of enable SCN
DISABLE_CHANGE#	NUMBER	SCN at which thread was disabled
DISABLE_TIME	DATE	Time of disable SCN
GROUPS	NUMBER	Number of log groups assigned to this thread
INSTANCE	VARCHAR2	Instance name, if available
OPEN_TIME	DATE	Last time the thread was opened.

Column	Datatype	Description
CURRENT_GROUP#	NUMBER	Current log group
SEQUENCE#	NUMBER	Sequence number of current log
CHECKPOINT _CHANGE#	NUMBER	SCN at last checkpoint
CHECKPOINT_TIME	DATE	Time of last checkpoint

V$TIMER

This view lists the elapsed time in hundredths of seconds. Time is measured since the beginning of the epoch, which is operating system specific, and wraps around to 0 again whenever the value overflows four bytes (roughly 497 days).

Column	Datatype	Description
HSECS	NUMBER	Elapsed time in hundredths of a second

V$TRANSACTION

This view lists the active transactions in the system.

Column	Datatype	Description
ADDR	RAW(4)	Address of transaction state object
XIDUSN	NUMBER	Undo segment number
XIDSLOT	NUMBER	Slot number
XIDSQN	NUMBER	Sequence number
UBAFIL	NUMBER	Undo block address (UBA) filenum
UBABLK	NUMBER	UBA block number
UBASQN	NUMBER	UBA sequence number
UBAREC	NUMBER	UBA record number
STATUS	VARCHAR2(16)	Status
START_TIME	VARCHAR2(20)	Start time (wall clock)

Column	Datatype	Description
START_SCNB	NUMBER	Start system change number (SCN) base
START_SCNW	NUMBER	Start SCN wrap
START_UEXT	NUMBER	Start extent number
START_UBAFIL	NUMBER	Start UBA file number
START_UBABLK	NUMBER	Start UBA block number
START_UBASQN	NUMBER	Start UBA sequence number
START_UBAREC	NUMBER	Start UBA record number
SES_ADDR	RAW(4)	User session object address
FLAG	NUMBER	Flag
SPACE	VARCHAR2(3)	"Yes", if a space transaction
RECURSIVE	VARCHAR2(3)	"Yes", if a recursive transaction
NOUNDO	VARCHAR2(3)	"Yes" if a no undo transaction
PTX	VARCHAR 2(3)	YES if parallel transaction, otherwise set to NO
PRV_XIDUSN	NUMBER	Previous transaction undo segment number
PRV_XIDSLT	NUMBER	Previous transaction slot number
PRV_XIDSQN	NUMBER	Previous transaction sequence number
PTX_XIDUSN	NUMBER	Rollback segment number of the parent XID
PTX_XIDSLT	NUMBER	Slot number of the parent XID
PTX_XIDSQN	NUMBER	Sequence number of the parent XID
DSCN_B	NUMBER	Dependent SCN base
DSCN_W	NUMBER	Dependent SCN wrap
USED_UBLK	NUMBER	Number of undo blocks used
USED_UREC	NUMBER	Number of undo records used
LOG_IO	NUMBER	Logical I/O
PHY_IO	NUMBER	Physical I/O

Column	Datatype	Description
CR_GET	NUMBER	Consistent gets
CR_CHANGE	NUMBER	Consistent changes

V$TRANSACTION_ENQUEUE

V$TRANSACTION_ENQUEUE displays locks owned by transaction state objects.

Column	Datatype	Description
ADDR	RAW(4)	Address of lock state object
KADDR	RAW(4)	Address of lock
SID	NUMBER	Identifier for session holding or acquiring the lock
TYPE	VARCHAR2(2)	Type of lock. TX = transaction enqueue.
ID1	NUMBER	Lock identifier #1 (depends on type)
ID2	NUMBER	Lock identifier #2 (depends on type)
LMODE	NUMBER	Lock mode in which the session holds the lock: 0, None 1, Null (NULL) 2, Row-S (SS) 3, Row-X (SX) 4, Share (S) 5, S/Row-X (SSX) 6, Exclusive (X)
REQUEST	NUMBER	Lock mode in which the process requests the lock: 0, None 1, Null (NULL) 2, Row-S (SS) 3, Row-X (SX) 4, Share (S) 5, S/Row-X (SSX) 6, Exclusive (X)
CTIME	NUMBER	Time since current mode was granted
BLOCK	NUMBER	The lock is blocking another lock

V$TYPE_SIZE

This view lists the sizes of various database components for use in estimating data block capacity.

Column	Datatype	Description
COMPONENT	VARCHAR2	Component name, such as segment or buffer header
TYPE	VARCHAR2	Component type
DESCRIPTION	VARCHAR2	Description of component
TYPE_SIZE	NUMBER	Size of component

V$VERSION

Version numbers of core library components in the Oracle Server. There is one row for each component.

Column	Datatype	Description
BANNER	VARCHAR2	Component name and version number

V$WAITSTAT

This view lists block contention statistics. This table is only updated when timed statistics are enabled.

Column	Datatype	Description
CLASS	VARCHAR2	Class of block
COUNT	NUMBER	Number of waits by this OPERATION for this CLASS of block
TIME	NUMBER	Sum of all wait times for all the waits by this OPERATION for this CLASS of block

4

National Language Support

This chapter describes features that enable Oracle Server applications to operate with multiple languages using conventions specified by the application user. The following topics are included:

- What Does National Language Support Provide?
- Oracle Server NLS Architecture
- Background Information
- Choosing Character Sets for Database Character Set and National Character Set
- Specifying Language-Dependent Behavior
- Specifying Language-Dependent Behavior for a Session
- Specifying Language-Dependent Application Behavior
- Specifying Default Language-Dependent Behavior
- Runtime Loadable NLS Data
- NLS Parameters
- Specifying Character Sets
- Date and Number Formats
- Additional NLS Environment Variables

- Using NLS Parameters in SQL Functions
- Obsolete NLS Data
- Unicode (UTF-8) Support
- NLS Data
- Calendar Systems

What Does National Language Support Provide?

Oracle Server National Language Support allows users to interact with the database in their native language. It also allows applications to run in different language environments.

To achieve these goals, NLS provides

- support for processing data in the various character encoding schemes used by computer hardware
  - both single-byte and multi-byte character encoding schemes
  - client and server can use different character encoding schemes in client/server environments, with transparent conversion of data between them
- language-dependent operation of end-user applications
  - Oracle Server messages displayed in multiple languages
  - dates and numbers formatted using language and territory conventions
  - character data sorted according to cultural conventions
  - language-dependent operation specifiable for each session

The remainder of this chapter provides background on these issues and describes the mechanisms NLS provides to handle them.

Oracle Server NLS Architecture

The NLS architecture has two components: language-independent functions and language-dependent data. The former provides generic language-oriented features; the latter provides data required to operate these features for a specific language.

Because the language-dependent data is separate from the code, the operation of NLS functions is governed by data supplied at runtime. New languages can be added and language-specific application characteristics can be altered without requiring any code changes. This architecture also enables language-dependent features to be specified for each session.

Background Information

This section provides background information on the issues involved in multi-lingual applications, and shows how they are resolved by the National Language Support (NLS) features of the Oracle Server. The remaining sections of this chapter discuss the specific parameters that control NLS operation.

Character Encoding Schemes

To understand how Oracle Server deals with character data, it is important to understand the general features of character representation on computers. The appearance of a character on a terminal depends on the convention for character representation used by that terminal. When you press a character key on the keyboard, the terminal generates a numeric code specified by the character encoding scheme in use on that device. When the terminal receives a number representing a character, it displays the character shape specified by that encoding scheme.

Encoding schemes define the representation of alphabetic characters, numerals, and punctuation characters, together with codes that control terminal display and communication. A *character encoding scheme* (also known as a character set or code page) specifies numbers corresponding to each character that the terminal can display. Examples are 7-bit ASCII, EBCDIC Code Page 500, and Japanese Extended UNIX Code.

Many encoding schemes are used by hardware manufacturers to support different languages. All support the 26 letters of the Latin alphabet, A to Z. In general, single-byte encoding schemes are used for European and Middle Eastern languages and multi-byte encoding schemes for Asian languages.

Restrictions on Character Sets Used to Express Names and Text

Table 4-1 lists the restrictions on the character sets that can be used to express names and other text in Oracle.

Table 4-1: Restrictions on Character Sets Used to Express Names and Text

Name	1-Byte Fixed	Varying Width	Multi-byte fixed width character sets
comments	Yes	Yes	Yes
database link names	Yes	No	No
database names	Yes	No	No
filenames (datafile, logfile, controlfile, initialization file)	Yes	No	No
instance names	Yes	No	No
directory names	Yes	No	No
keywords (see **Note** below)	Yes	No	No
recovery manager filenames	Yes	No	No
rollback segment names (see **Note** below)	Yes	No	No
stored script names	Yes	Yes	No
tablespace names (see **Note** below)	Yes	Yes*	No

Note: Keywords can be expressed only in English (single byte).

Note: The ROLLBACK_SEGMENTS parameter does not support NLS.

Note: Recovery Manager doesn't support varying width character set tablespace names.

For a list of supported string formats and character sets, including LOB data (LOB, BLOB, CLOB, NCLOB), see Table 4-3: "Supported Character String Functionality and Character Sets" on page 4-27.

Single-Byte 7-Bit Encoding Schemes

Single-byte 7-bit encoding schemes can define up to 128 characters, and normally support just one language. The only characters defined in 7-bit ASCII are the 26 Latin alphabetic characters. Various other 7-bit schemes are used where certain characters (normally punctuation) in 7-bit ASCII are replaced with additional alphanumeric characters required for a specific language.

Single-Byte 8-Bit Encoding Schemes

Single-byte 8-bit encoding schemes can define up to 256 characters, and normally support a group of languages. For example, ISO 8859/1 supports many Western European languages.

Varying-Width Multi-Byte Encoding Schemes

Multi-byte encoding schemes are needed for Asian languages because these languages use thousands of characters. Some multi-byte encoding schemes use the value of the most significant bit to indicate if a byte represents a single-byte character or is the first or second byte of a double-byte character. In other schemes, control codes differentiate single-byte from double-byte characters. A *shift-out* code indicates that the following bytes are double-byte characters until a *shift-in* code is encountered.

There are two general groups of encoding schemes, those based on 7-bit ASCII and those based on IBM EBCDIC. Within each group, all schemes normally use the same encoding for the 26 Latin characters (A to Z), but use different encoding for other characters used in languages other than English. ASCII and EBCDIC use different encodings, even for the Latin characters.

Fixed-Width Multi-Byte Encoding Schemes

A fixed-width multi-byte character set is a subset of a corresponding varying-width multi-byte character set. A fixed-width multi-byte character set contains all of the characters of a certain width which belong to a corresponding varying-width multi-byte character set. In fixed-width multi-byte character sets, no *shift-out* or *shift-in* codes are used even if they are needed in their corresponding varying-width multi-byte character set.

A fixed-width multi-byte character set can be used as the national character set, but cannot be used as a database character set. This is because database character sets must have either EBCDIC or 7-bit ASCII as a subset in order to represent identifiers and to hold SQL and PL/SQL source code.

Pattern Matching Characters for Fixed-width Multi-byte Character Sets

The LIKE operator is used in character string comparisons with pattern matching. Its syntax requires the use of two special pattern matching characters: the underscore (_) and the percent sign(%).

Table 4-2: Encoding for the Underscore, Percent Sign, and Pad Character

For this Character Set	Use these Code Point Values		
	underscore	percent sign	pad character (space)
JA16SJISFIXED	0x8151	0x8193	0x8140
JA16EUCFIXED	0xa162	0xa1f3	0xa1a1
JA16DBCSFIXED	0x426d	0x426c	0x4040
ZHT32TRISFIXED	0x8eb1a1df	0x8eb1a1a5	0x8ebla1a10

UTF8 Encoding

The UNICODE encoding scheme, UTF-8 (character set name AL24UTFFSS for UNICODE Version 1.1 and character set name UTF8 for UNICODE Version 2.0), a variable-width, multi-byte format, is supported with Oracle8.

Arabic/Hebrew Display Character Set Support

Semitic languages consist of ligatures and typically two sets of digits (that is, Arabic and Hindi numbers), in addition to their alphabetical characters. Using a display character set allows front-end input and output of ligatures and Arabic/Hindi numbers. Some of the display character sets even contain different shapes of a character whose form is context sensitive to its position in a word. However, a display character set should not be used for data storage purposes. A storage character set is defined for the use of data storage. Oracle Server supports conversion between display and storage character sets. The environment variable NLS_LANG defines the storage character set while NLS_DISPLAY sets the display character set. It is the client's responsibility to ensure that no display character set is defined as a storage character set and vice versa.

Choosing Character Sets for Database Character Set and National Character Set

This section describes the uses for the database character set and the national character set. It also presents some general guidelines for choosing character sets to represent the database character set and the national character set.

Uses for the Database Character Set

Oracle uses the database character set for these items:

- identifiers such as table names, column names, and PL/SQL variables
- data stored in CHAR, VARCHAR2, CLOB, and LONG columns
- entering and storing SQL and PL/SQL program source

Since SQL and PL/SQL keywords are expected to appear in either 7-bit ASCII or in EBCDIC, whichever is native to the host, the database character set must be a superset of one of these encodings. If the platform operating system supports an encoding with a larger set of glyphs (or *repertoire*), the corresponding Oracle character set might be a natural choice for use as the database character set.

Uses for the National Character Set

Oracle uses the national character set for these items:

- data stored in NCHAR, NVARCHAR2, and NCLOB columns

As described in "Varying-Width Multi-Byte Encoding Schemes" and "Fixed-Width Multi-Byte Encoding Schemes" on page 4-5, a varying-width multi-byte character set can be used as a national character set or a database character set. A fixed-width multi-byte character set, on the other hand, can be used for a national character set but not a database character set.

Guidelines for Choosing Character Sets

There does not have to be a close relationship between the character sets which you choose for your database character set and your national character set. However, these guidelines are suggested:

Consider your need to use national character literals

Consider your need for character literals to represent national character set values when choosing the database character set and national character set to use together on a platform. Only characters in the repertoire of both the database character set and the national character set can be meaningfully used in a national character literal. Thus, you might want to choose a national character set and a database character set which are closely-related. For example, many Japanese customers will probably choose JA16EUC as their database character set and JA16EUCFIXED as their national character set.

You might find that there are characters in your chosen national character set which do not occur in your chosen database character set. You create the needed characters with the CHR(n USING NCHAR_CS) function where n represents the codepoint value of the character.

Consider performance

Some string operations will be faster if you choose a fixed-width character set for the national character set. A separate performance issue is space efficiency (and thus speed) when using smaller-width character sets. These issues potentially trade-off against each other when the choice is between a varying-width and a fixed-width character set.

Be careful when mixing fixed-width and varying-width character sets

Because fixed-width multi-byte character sets are measured in characters but varying-width character sets are measured in bytes, be careful if you use a fixed-width multi-byte character set as your national character set on one platform and a varying-width character set on another platform.

For example, if you use %TYPE or a named type to declare an item on one platform using the declaration information of an item from the other platform, you might receive a constraint limit too small to support the data. For example, "NCHAR (10)" on the platform using the fixed-width multi-byte set will allocate enough space for 10 characters, but if %TYPE or use of a named type creates a correspondingly typed item on the other platform, it will allocate only 10 bytes. Usually, this is not enough for 10 characters. To be safe, do one of the following:

- do not mix fixed-width multi-byte and varying-width character sets as the national character set on different platforms
- if you do mix fixed-width multi-byte and varying-width character sets as the national character set on different platforms, use varying-length type declarations with relatively large constraint values

Consider the shortcomings of converting between character sets

Character set conversions can be silently lossy. Characters not in the destination character set will convert to "?" or some other designated codepoint. If you have distributed environments, consider using character sets with similar repertoires as your database character sets on your various platforms. Also consider using character sets with similar repertoires as your national character sets, to avoid either undesirable loss of data or results which vary depending on which platform evaluates a particular expression.

Specifying Language-Dependent Behavior

This section discusses the parameters that specify language-dependent operation. You can set language-dependent behavior defaults for the server and set language dependent behavior for the client that overrides these defaults.

Most NLS parameters can be used in three ways:

- As initialization parameters to specify language-dependent behavior defaults for the server.

  For example, in your initialization parameter file, include

  ```
  NLS_TERRITORY = FRANCE
  ```

- As environment variables on client machines to specify language-dependent behavior defaults for a session. These defaults override the defaults set for the server.

  For example, on a UNIX system

  ```
  setenv NLS_SORT FRANCE
  ```

- As ALTER SESSION parameters to change the language-dependent behavior of a session. These parameters override the defaults set for the session or for the server.

  For example:

  ```
  ALTER SESSION SET NLS_SORT = FRANCE
  ```

The following NLS parameters can be initialization parameters, environment variables, and ALTER SESSION parameters:

- NLS_CURRENCY
- NLS_DATE_FORMAT
- NLS_DATE_ LANGUAGE
- NLS_ISO_CURRENCY
- NLS_NUMERIC_CHARACTERS

- NLS_SORT

The following parameters can be specified as initialization parameters and ALTER SESSION parameters, but not as environment variables:

- NLS_LANGUAGE
- NLS_TERRITORY

For more information on these parameters, see "NLS Parameters" on page 4-19.

The following NLS parameters can be set only as environment variables:

- NLS_CREDIT
- NLS_DEBIT
- NLS_DISPLAY
- NLS_LANG
- NLS_LIST_SEPARATOR
- NLS_MONETARY_CHARACTERS
- NLS_NCHAR

For more information on these parameters, see "NLS Parameters" on page 4-19. For additional information on NLS_DISPLAY, see "NLS_DISPLAY" on page 4-32. For additional information on NLS_LANG, see "Specifying Language-Dependent Behavior for a Session" below.

Specifying Language-Dependent Behavior for a Session

This section discusses the NLS parameters that specify language-dependent operation of applications.

NLS_LANG

Note: If the NLS_LANG parameter is *not* set, then the values assigned to other NLS parameters are ignored.

The NLS_LANG environment variable has three components (*language*, *territory*, and *charset*) in the form:

```
NLS_LANG = language_territory.charset
```

Each component controls the operation of a subset of NLS features.

language	Specifies conventions such as the language used for Oracle messages, day names, and month names. Each supported language has a unique name; for example, American, French, or German. The language argument specifies default values for the territory and character set arguments, so either (or both) territory or charset can be omitted. If language is not specified, the value defaults to american. For a complete list of languages, see "Supported Languages" on page 4-41.
territory	Specifies conventions such as the default date format and decimal character used for numbers. Each supported territory has a unique name; for example, America, France, or Canada. If territory is not specified, the value defaults to america. For a complete list of territories, see "Supported Territories" on page 4-42.
charset	Specifies the character set used by the client application (normally that of the user's terminal). Each supported character set has a unique acronym, for example, US7ASCII, WE8ISO8859P1, WE8DEC, WE8EBCDIC500, or JA16EUC. Each language has a default character set associated with it. Default values for the languages available on your system are listed in your installation or user's guide. For a complete list of character sets, see "Storage Character Sets" on page 4-45 and "Arabic/Hebrew Display Character Sets" on page 4-50.

Note: All components of the NLS_LANG definition are optional; any item left out will default. If you specify *territory* or *charset*, you *must* include the preceding delimiter [underscore (_) for *territory*, period (.) for *charset*], otherwise the value will be parsed as a language name.

The three arguments of NLS_LANG can be specified in any combination, as in the following examples:

```
NLS_LANG = AMERICAN_AMERICA.US7ASCII
```

or

```
NLS_LANG = FRENCH_FRANCE.WE8ISO8859P1
```

or

```
NLS_LANG = FRENCH_CANADA.WE8DEC
```

or

```
NLS_LANG = JAPANESE_JAPAN.JA16EUC
```

Specifying NLS_LANG

NLS_LANG is defined for each session by means of an environment variable or equivalent platform-specific mechanism. Different sessions connected to the same database can specify different values for NLS_LANG.

For example, on VMS you could specify the value of NLS_LANG by entering the following line at the VMS prompt:

```
$ DEFINE NLS_LANG FRENCH_FRANCE.WE8DEC
```

If you do not specify a value for NLS_LANG, the language-dependent behavior defaults to the language specified by the NLS_LANGUAGE database initialization parameter and the territory specified by the NLS_TERRITORY database initialization parameter. Additionally, if you do not specify a value for NLS_LANG, other NLS environment variables you may have set are ignored.

If you *do* specify a value for NLS_LANG, the values set in initialization parameters are ignored.

For more information on how to set NLS_LANG on your system, see your operating system-specific Oracle documentation.

Client/Server Architecture

NLS_LANG sets the NLS language and territory environment used by the database for both the server session and for the client application. Using the one parameter ensures that the language environments of both database and client application are automatically the same.

Because NLS_LANG is an environment variable, it is read by the client application at startup time. The client communicates the information defined in NLS_LANG to the server when it connects.

Overriding Language and Territory Specifications

The default values for language and territory can be overridden for a session by using the ALTER SESSION statement. For example:

```
ALTER SESSION SET NLS_LANGUAGE = FRENCH NLS_TERRITORY = FRANCE
```

This feature implicitly determines the language environment of the database for each session. An ALTER SESSION statement is automatically executed when a session connects to a database to set the values of the database parameters NLS_LANGUAGE and NLS_TERRITORY to those specified by the *language* and *territory* arguments of NLS_LANG. If NLS_LANG is not defined, no ALTER SESSION statement is executed.

When NLS_LANG is defined, the implicit ALTER SESSION is executed for all instances to which the session connects, for both direct and indirect connections. If the values of NLS parameters are changed explicitly with

ALTER SESSION during a session, the changes are propagated to all instances to which that user session is connected.

The NLS_NCHAR parameter specifies the character set used by the client application for national character set data. For more information on this parameter, see "NLS_NCHAR" on page 4-33.

Specifying Language-Dependent Application Behavior

Language-Dependent Functions

Setting the values of various NLS parameters allows applications to function in a language-dependent manner. The language-dependent functions controlled by NLS include

- Messages and Text
- Number Format
- Date Format, Currency Symbols, and First Day of the Week

Messages and Text

All messages and text should be in the same language. For example, when running a Developer 2000 application, messages and boilerplate text seen by the user originate from three sources:

- messages from the server
- messages and boilerplate text generated by SQL*Forms
- messages and boilerplate text defined as part of the application

The application is responsible for meeting the last requirement. NLS takes care of the other two.

Number Format

The database must know the number-formatting convention used in each session to interpret numeric strings correctly. For example, the database needs to know whether numbers are entered with a period or a comma as the decimal character (234.00 or 234,00). In the same vein, the application needs to be able to display numeric information in the format expected at the client site.

Date Format, Currency Symbols, and First Day of the Week

Similarly, date and currency information need to be interpreted properly when they are input to the server, and formatted in the expected manner when output to the user's terminal. These functions are all controlled by the NLS parameters. For more information, see "NLS Parameters" on page 4-19.

Sorting Character Data

Conventionally, when character data is sorted, the sort sequence is based on the numeric values of the characters defined by the character encoding scheme. Such a sort is called a *binary* sort. Such a sort produces reasonable results for the English alphabet because the ASCII and EBCDIC standards define the letters A to Z in ascending numeric value.

Note however, that in the ASCII standard all uppercase letters appear before any lowercase letters. In the EBCDIC standard, the opposite is true: all lowercase letters appear before any uppercase letters.

Binary Sorts

When characters used in other languages are present, a *binary* sort generally does not produce reasonable results. For example, an ascending ORDER BY query would return the character strings ABC, ABZ, BCD, ÄBC, in that sequence, when the Ä has a higher numeric value than B in the character encoding scheme.

Linguistic Sorts

To produce a sort sequence that matches the alphabetic sequence of characters for a particular language, another sort technique must be used that sorts characters independently of their numeric values in the character encoding scheme. This technique is called a *linguistic* sort. A linguistic sort operates by replacing characters with other binary values that reflect the character's proper linguistic order so that a binary sort returns the desired result.

Oracle Server provides both sort mechanisms. Linguistic sort sequences are defined as part of language-dependent data. Each linguistic sort sequence has a unique name. NLS parameters define the sort mechanism for ORDER BY queries. A default value can be specified, and this value can be overridden for each session with the NLS_SORT parameter. A complete list of linguistic definitions is provided in "Linguistic Definitions" on page 4-51.

Warning: Linguistic sorting is not supported on multi-byte character sets. If the database character set is multi-byte, you get binary sorting, which makes the sort sequence dependent on the character set specification.

Linguistic Special Cases

Linguistic special cases are character sequences that need to be treated as a single character when sorting. Such special cases are handled automatically when using a linguistic sort. For example, one of the linguistic sort sequences for Spanish specifies that the double characters *ch* and *ll* are sorted as single characters appearing between *c* and *d* and between *l* and *m* respectively.

Another example is the German language sharp s (ß). The linguistic sort sequence *German* can sort this sequence as the two characters *SS*, while the linguistic sort sequence *Austrian* sorts it as *SZ*.

Special cases like these are also handled when converting uppercase characters to lowercase, and vice versa. For example, in German the uppercase of the sharp s is the two characters *SS*. Such case-conversion issues are handled by the NLS_UPPER, NLS_LOWER, and NLS_INITCAP functions, according to the conventions established by the linguistic sort sequence. (The standard functions UPPER, LOWER, and INITCAP do not handle these special cases.)

Specifying Default Language-Dependent Behavior

This section describes NLS_LANGUAGE and NLS_TERRITORY, the database initialization parameters that specify the default language-dependent behavior for a session.

NLS_LANGUAGE

NLS_LANGUAGE specifies the default conventions for the following session characteristics:

- language for server messages
- language for day and month names and their abbreviations (specified in the SQL functions TO_CHAR and TO_DATE)
- symbols for equivalents of AM, PM, AD, and BC
- default sorting sequence for character data when ORDER BY is specified (GROUP BY uses a binary sort, unless ORDER BY is specified)
- writing direction

- affirmative/negative response strings

The value specified for NLS_LANGUAGE in the initialization file is the default for all sessions in that instance.

For more information on which language conventions supported, see your operating system-specific Oracle documentation.

For example, to specify the default session language as French, the parameter should be set as follows:

```
NLS_LANGUAGE = FRENCH
```

In this case, the server message

```
ORA-00942: table or view does not exist
```

will appear as

```
ORA-00942: table ou vue inexistante
```

Messages used by the server are stored in binary-format files that are placed in the ORA_RDBMS directory, or the equivalent.

Multiple versions of these files can exist, one for each supported language, using the filename convention

<product_id><language_id>.MSB

For example, the file containing the server messages in French is called ORAF.MSB, "F" being the language abbreviation for French.

Messages are stored in these files in one specific character set, depending on the particular machine and operating system. If this is different from the database character set, message text is automatically converted to the database character set. If necessary, it will be further converted to the client character set if it is different from the database character set. Hence, messages will be displayed correctly at the user's terminal, subject to the limitations of character set conversion.

The default value of NLS_LANGUAGE may be operating system specific. You can alter the NLS_LANGUAGE parameter by changing the value in the initialization file and then restarting the instance. For more information on NLS_LANGUAGE as an initialization parameter, see "NLS_LANGUAGE" on page 1-78.

For more information on the default value, see your operating system-specific Oracle documentation.

NLS_TERRITORY

NLS_TERRITORY specifies the conventions for the following default date and numeric formatting characteristics:

- date format
- decimal character and group separator
- local currency symbol
- ISO currency symbol
- week start day
- credit and debit symbol
- ISO week flag
- list separator

The value specified for NLS_TERRITORY in the initialization file is the default for the instance. For example, to specify the default as France, the parameter should be set as follows:

```
NLS_TERRITORY = FRANCE
```

In this case, numbers would be formatted using a comma as the decimal character.

The default value of NLS_TERRITORY can be operating system specific.

You can alter the NLS_TERRITORY parameter by changing the value in the initialization file and then restarting the instance. For more information on NLS_TERRITORY as an initialization parameter, see "NLS_TERRITORY" on page 1-80.

For more information on the default value and to see which territory conventions are supported on your system, see your operating system-specific Oracle documentation.

Runtime Loadable NLS Data

Data Loading

Language-independent data (NLSDATA) is loaded into memory at runtime; this determines the behavior of an application in a given language environment that is defined by the NLSDATA. In conjunction with NLSDATA, a boot file is used to determine the availability of NLS objects which can be loaded.

On initialization, the boot file is loaded into memory, where it serves as the master list of available NLS objects, prior to loading NLSDATA files. Oracle supports both system and user boot files. A user boot file may only contain a subset of the system boot file. When loading, the user boot file takes precedence over the system boot file. If the user boot file is not present, the system boot file will be used; this way, all NLS data defined in the system boot file will be available for loading. If neither user nor system boot file is found, then a default linked-in boot file and some default linked-in data objects (language American, territory America, character set US7ASCII) will be loaded. NLS functionality, however, will be limited to what is provided by the linked-in data objects. After a boot file (either user or system) is loaded, the NLSDATA files are read into memory based on the availability of the NLS objects defined in the boot file.

The idea behind a user boot file is to give an application further flexibility to tailor exactly which NLS objects it needs for its language environment, thus controlling the application's memory consumption.

Utilities

Oracle Server includes the following two utilities to assist you in maintaining NLS data:

NLS Data Installation Utility	Generate binary-format data objects from their text-format versions. Use this when you receive NLS data updates or if you create your own data objects.
NLS Configuration Utility (LXBCNF)	Create and edit user boot files.

For more information, see *Oracle8 Server Utilities*.

NLS Parameters

The NLS_LANGUAGE and NLS_TERRITORY parameters implicitly specify several aspects of language-dependent operation. Additional NLS parameters provide explicit control over these operations. Most of the parameters listed below can be specified in the initialization file; they can also be specified for each session with the ALTER SESSION command.

Parameter	Description
NLS_CALENDAR	Calendar system
NLS_CURRENCY	Local currency symbol
NLS_DATE_FORMAT	Default date format
NLS_DATE_ LANGUAGE	Default language for dates
NLS_ISO_CURRENCY	ISO international currency symbol
NLS_LANGUAGE	Default language
NLS_NUMERIC_CHARACTERS	Decimal character and group separator
NLS_SORT	Character sort sequence
NLS_TERRITORY	Default territory

For a complete description of ALTER SESSION, see *Oracle8 Server SQL Reference*.

NLS_CALENDAR

Parameter type:	string
Parameter class:	dynamic, scope = ALTER SESSION
Default value:	Gregorian
Range of values:	any valid calendar format name

Many different calendar systems are in use throughout the world. NLS_CALENDAR specifies which calendar system Oracle uses.

NLS_CALENDAR can have one of the following values:

- Arabic Hijrah
- English Hijrah
- Gregorian
- Japanese Imperial
- Persian
- ROC Official (Republic of China)
- Thai Buddha

For example, if NLS_CALENDAR is set to "Japanese Imperial", the date format is "E YY-MM-DD", and the date is May 17, 1997, then the SYSDATE is displayed as follows:

```
SELECT SYSDATE FROM DUAL;

SYSDATE

--------

H 09-05-15
```

NLS_CURRENCY

This parameter specifies the character string returned by the number format mask L, the local currency symbol, overriding that defined implicitly by NLS_TERRITORY. For example, to set the local currency symbol to "Dfl" (including a space), the parameter should be set as follows:

```
NLS_CURRENCY = "Dfl "
```

In this case, the query

```
SELECT TO_CHAR(TOTAL, 'L099G999D99') "TOTAL"
     FROM ORDERS WHERE CUSTNO = 586
```

would return

```
TOTAL

-------------

Dfl 12.673,49
```

You can alter the default value of NLS_CURRENCY by changing its value in the initialization file and then restarting the instance, and you can alter its value during a session using an ALTER SESSION SET NLS_CURRENCY command.

For more information on NLS_CURRENCY as an initialization parameter, see "NLS_CURRENCY" on page 1-76.

NLS_DATE_FORMAT

Defines the default date format to use with the TO_CHAR and TO_DATE functions. The default value of this parameter is determined by NLS_TERRITORY. The value of this parameter can be any valid date format mask, and the value must be surrounded by double quotes. For example:

```
NLS_DATE_FORMAT = "MM/DD/YYYY"
```

To add string literals to the date format, enclose the string literal with double quotes. Note that every special character (such as the double quote) must be preceded with an escape character. The entire expression must be surrounded with single quotes. For example:

```
NLS_DATE_FORMAT = '\"Today\'s date\" MM/DD/YYYY'
```

As another example, to set the default date format to display Roman numerals for months, you would include the following line in your initialization file:

```
NLS_DATE_FORMAT = "DD RM YYYY"
```

With such a default date format, the following SELECT statement would return the month using Roman numerals (assuming today's date is February 12, 1997):

```
SELECT TO_CHAR(SYSDATE) CURRDATE
    FROM DUAL;

CURRDATE

---------

12 II 1997
```

The value of this parameter is stored in the tokenized internal date format. Each format element occupies two bytes, and each string occupies the number of bytes in the string plus a terminator byte. Also, the entire format mask has a two-byte terminator. For example, "MM/DD/YY" occupies 12 bytes internally because there are three format elements, two one-byte strings (the two slashes), and the two-byte terminator for the format mask. The tokenized format for the value of this parameter cannot exceed 24 bytes.

Note: The applications you design may need to allow for a variable-length default date format. Also, the parameter value must be surrounded by double quotes: single quotes are interpreted as part of the format mask.

You can alter the default value of NLS_DATE_FORMAT by changing its value in the initialization file and then restarting the instance, and you can alter the value during a session using an ALTER SESSION SET NLS_DATE_FORMAT command.

For more information on NLS_DATE_FORMAT as an initialization parameter, see "NLS_DATE_FORMAT" on page 1-76.

Date Formats and Partition Bound Expressions

Partition bound expressions for a date column must specify a date using a format which requires that the month, day, and 4-digit year are fully specified. For example, the date format MM-DD-YYYY requires that the month, day, and 4-digit year are fully specified. In contrast, the date format DD-MON-YY (11-jan-97, for example) is invalid because it relies on the current date for the century.

Use TO_DATE() to specify a date format which requires the full specification of month, day, and 4-digit year. For example:

```
TO_DATE('11-jan-1997', 'dd-mon-yyyy')
```

If the default date format, specified by NLS_DATE_FORMAT, of your session does not support specification of a date independent of current century (that is, if your default date format is MM-DD-YY), you must take one of the following actions:

- Use TO_DATE() to express the date in a format which requires you to fully specify the day, month, and 4-digit year.

- Change the value of NLS_DATE_FORMAT for the session to support the specification of dates in a format which requires you to fully specify the day, month, and 4-digit year.

For a more information on using TO_DATE(), see *Oracle8 Server SQL Reference*.

NLS_DATE_ LANGUAGE

This parameter specifies the language for the spelling of day and month names by the functions TO_CHAR and TO_DATE, overriding that specified implicitly by NLS_LANGUAGE. NLS_DATE_LANGUAGE has the same syntax as the NLS_LANGUAGE parameter, and all supported languages are valid values. For example, to specify the date language as French, the parameter should be set as follows:

```
NLS_DATE_LANGUAGE = FRENCH
```

In this case, the query

```
SELECT TO_CHAR(SYSDATE, 'Day:Dd Month yyyy')
    FROM DUAL;
```

would return

```
Mercredi:12 Février 1997
```

Month and day name abbreviations are also in the language specified, for example:

```
Me:12 Fév 1997
```

The default date format also uses the language-specific month name abbreviations. For example, if the default date format is DD-MON-YYYY, the above date would be inserted using:

```
INSERT INTO tablename VALUES ('12-Fév-1997');
```

The abbreviations for AM, PM, AD, and BC are also returned in the language specified by NLS_DATE_LANGUAGE. Note that numbers spelled using the TO_CHAR function always use English spellings; for example:

```
SELECT TO_CHAR(TO_DATE('12-Fév'),'Day: ddspth Month')
    FROM DUAL;
```

would return:

```
Mercredi: twenty-seventh Février
```

You can alter the default value of NLS_DATE_LANGUAGE by changing its value in the initialization file and then restarting the instance, and you can alter the value during a session using an ALTER SESSION SET NLS_DATE_LANGUAGE command.

For more information on NLS_DATE_LANGUAGE as an initialization parameter, see "NLS_DATE_LANGUAGE" on page 1-77.

NLS_ISO_CURRENCY

This parameter specifies the character string returned by the number format mask C, the ISO currency symbol, overriding that defined implicitly by NLS_TERRITORY.

Local currency symbols can be ambiguous; for example, a dollar sign ($) can refer to US dollars or Australian dollars. ISO Specification 4217 1987-07-15 defines unique "international" currency symbols for the currencies of specific territories (or countries).

For example, the ISO currency symbol for the US Dollar is USD, for the Australian Dollar AUD. To specify the ISO currency symbol, the corresponding territory name is used.

NLS_ISO_CURRENCY has the same syntax as the NLS_TERRITORY parameter, and all supported territories are valid values. For example, to specify the ISO currency symbol for France, the parameter should be set as follows:

```
NLS_ISO_CURRENCY = FRANCE
```

In this case, the query

```
SELECT TO_CHAR(TOTAL, 'C099G999D99') "TOTAL"
    FROM ORDERS WHERE CUSTNO = 586
```

would return

```
TOTAL

------------

FRF12.673,49
```

You can alter the default value of NLS_ISO_CURRENCY by changing its value in the initialization file and then restarting the instance, and you can alter its value during a session using an ALTER SESSION SET NLS_ISO_CURRENCY command.

For more information on NLS_ISO_CURRENCY as an initialization parameter, see "NLS_ISO_CURRENCY" on page 1-77.

NLS_NUMERIC_CHARACTERS

This parameter specifies the decimal character and grouping separator, overriding those defined implicitly by NLS_TERRITORY. The group separator is the character that separates integer groups (that is, the thousands, millions, billions, and so on). The decimal character separates the integer and decimal parts of a number.

Any character can be the decimal or group separator. The two characters specified must be single-byte, and both characters must be different from each other. The characters cannot be any numeric character or any of the following characters: plus (+), hyphen (-), less than sign (<), greater than sign (>).

The characters are specified in the following format:

```
NLS_NUMERIC_CHARACTERS = "<decimal_character><group_separator>"
```

The grouping separator is the character returned by the number format mask G. For example, to set the decimal character to a comma and the grouping separator to a period, the parameter should be set as follows:

```
NLS_NUMERIC_CHARACTERS = ",."
```

Both characters are single byte and must be different. Either can be a space.

Note: When the decimal character is not a period (.) or when a group separator is used, numbers appearing in SQL statements must be enclosed in quotes. For example, with the value of NLS_NUMERIC_CHARACTERS above, the following SQL statement requires quotation marks around the numeric literals:

```
INSERT INTO SIZES (ITEMID, WIDTH, QUANTITY)
    VALUES (618, '45,5', TO_NUMBER('1.234','9G999'));
```

You can alter the default value of NLS_NUMERIC_CHARACTERS in either of these ways:

- Change the value of NLS_NUMERIC_CHARACTERS in the initialization file and then restart the instance.
- Use the ALTER SESSION SET NLS_DATE_LANGUAGE command to change the parameter's value during a session.

For more information on NLS_NUMERIC_CHARACTERS as an initialization parameter, see "NLS_NUMERIC_CHARACTERS" on page 1-78.

NLS_SORT

This parameter specifies the type of sort for character data, overriding that defined implicitly by NLS_LANGUAGE.

The syntax of NLS_SORT is:

```
NLS_SORT = { BINARY | name }
```

BINARY specifies a binary sort and *name* specifies a particular linguistic sort sequence. For example, to specify the linguistic sort sequence called German, the parameter should be set as follows:

```
NLS_SORT = German
```

The name given to a linguistic sort sequence has no direct connection to language names. Usually, however, each supported language will have an appropriate linguistic sort sequence defined that uses the same name.

Note: When the NLS_SORT parameter is set to BINARY, the optimizer can in some cases satisfy the ORDER BY clause without doing a sort (by choosing an index scan). But when NLS_SORT is set to a linguistic sort, a sort is always needed to satisfy the ORDER BY clause.

You can alter the default value of NLS_SORT by changing its value in the initialization file and then restarting the instance, and you can alter its value during a session using an ALTER SESSION SET NLS_SORT command.

For more information on NLS_SORT as an initialization parameter, see "NLS_SORT" on page 1-79.

A complete list of linguistic definitions is provided in Table 4-9: "Linguistic Definitions" on page 4-51.

Specifying Character Sets

The character encoding scheme used by the database is defined at database creation as part of the CREATE DATABASE statement. All data columns of type CHAR, CLOB, VARCHAR2, and LONG, including columns in the data dictionary, have their data stored in the database character set. In addition, the choice of database character set determines which characters can name objects in the database. Data columns of type NCHAR, NCLOB, NVARCHAR2 use the national character set.

Once the database is created, the character set choices cannot be changed without re-creating the database. Hence, it is important to consider carefully which character set(s) to use. The database character set should always be a superset or equivalent of the operating system's native character set. The character sets used by client applications that access the database will usually determine which superset is the best choice.

If all client applications use the same character set, then this is the normal choice for the database character set. When client applications use different character sets, the database character set should be a superset (or equivalent) of all the client character sets. This will ensure that every character is represented when converting from a client character set to the database character set.

When a client application operates with a terminal that uses a different character set, then the client application's characters must be converted to the database character set, and vice versa. This conversion is performed automatically, and is transparent to the client application. The character set used by the client application is defined by the NLS_LANG parameter. Similarly, the character set used for national character set data is defined by the NLS_NCHAR parameter. For more information on these parameters, see "NLS_LANG" on page 4-10 and "NLS_NCHAR" on page 4-33.

Supported Character Sets

Oracle Server National Language Support features solve the problems that result from the fact that different encoding schemes use different binary values to represent the same character. With NLS, data created with one encoding scheme can be correctly processed and displayed on a system that uses a different encoding scheme. Table 4-3 lists the supported string format and character sets.

Table 4-3: Supported Character String Functionality and Character Sets

Type	1-Byte Fixed	Varying Width	Multi-byte fixed width character sets	Object Type and Collection Type Support
CHAR	Yes	Yes	No	Yes
NCHAR	Yes	Yes	Yes	No
BLOB	Yes	Yes	Yes	Yes
CLOB	Yes	No	No	Yes
NCLOB	Yes	No	Yes	No

Note: CLOBs only support 1-byte fixed width database character sets. NCLOBs only support fixed-width NCHAR database character sets. BLOBs process characters as a series of byte sequences. The data is not subject to any NLS-sensitive operations.

Character Set Conversion

Where a character exists in both source and destination character sets, conversion presents no problem. However, data conversion has to accommodate characters that do not exist in the destination character set. In such cases, replacement characters are used. The source character is replaced by a character that does exist in the destination character set.

Replacement characters may be defined for specific characters as part of a character set definition. Where a specific replacement character is not defined, a default replacement character is used. To avoid the use of replacement characters when converting from client to database character set, the latter should be a superset (or equivalent) of all the client character sets.

The Concatenation Operator

If the database character set replaces the vertical bar ("|") with a national character, then all SQL statements that use the concatenation operator (ASCII 124) will fail. For example, creating a procedure will fail because it generates a recursive SQL statement that uses concatenation. When you use a 7-bit replacement character set such as D7DEC, F7DEC, or SF7ASCII for the database character set, then the national character which replaces the vertical bar is not allowed in object names because the vertical bar is interpreted as the concatenation operator.

On the user side, a 7-bit replacement character set can be used if the database character set is the same or compatible, that is, if both character sets replace the vertical bar with the same national character.

Storing Data in Multi-Byte Character Sets

Width specifications of the character datatypes CHAR and VARCHAR2 refer to bytes, not characters. Hence, the specification CHAR(20) in a table definition allows 20 bytes for storing character data.

If the database character set is single byte, the number of characters and number of bytes will be the same. If the database character set is multi-byte, there will in general be no such correspondence. A character can consist of one or more bytes, depending on the specific multi-byte encoding scheme and whether *shift-in/shift-out* control codes are present. Hence, column widths must be chosen with care to allow for the maximum possible number of bytes for a given number of characters.

When using the NCHAR and NVARCHAR2 data types, the width specification refers to characters if the national character set is fixed-width multi-byte. Otherwise, the width specification refers to bytes.

Loadable Character Sets

Oracle Server loads character sets upon first reference. Instead of linking all character sets as static data, each character set is read into dynamic memory upon first reference. The size of the executable is thus reduced by eliminating character set data not in use during execution.

Date and Number Formats

Several format masks are provided with the TO_CHAR, TO_DATE, and TO_NUMBER functions to format dates and numbers according to the relevant conventions.

Note: The TO_NUMBER function also accepts a format mask.

Date Formats

A format element RM (Roman Month) returns a month as a Roman numeral. Both uppercase and lowercase can be specified, using RM and rm respectively. For example, for the date 7 Sep 1998, "DD-rm-YYYY" will return "07-ix-1998" and "DD-RM-YYYY" will return "07-IX-1998".

Note that the MON and DY format masks explicitly support month and day abbreviations that may not be three characters in length. For example, the abbreviations "Lu" and "Ma" can be specified for the French "Lundi" and "Mardi", respectively.

Week and Day Number Conventions

The week numbers returned by the WW format mask are calculated according to the algorithm *int((day-ijan1)/7)*. This week number algorithm does not follow the ISO standard (2015, 1992-06-15).

To support the ISO standard, a format element IW is provided that returns the ISO week number. In addition, format elements I IY IYY and IYYY, equivalent in behavior to the format elements Y, YY, YYY, and YYYY, return the year relating to the ISO week number.

In the ISO standard, the year relating to an ISO week number can be different from the calendar year. For example 1st Jan 1988 is in ISO week number 53 of 1987. A week always starts on a Monday and ends on a Sunday.

- If January 1 falls on a Friday, Saturday, or Sunday, then the week including January 1 is the last week of the previous year, because most of the days in the week belong to the previous year.

- If January 1 falls on a Monday, Tuesday, Wednesday, or Thursday, then the week is the first week of the new year, because most of the days in the week belong to the new year.

For example, January 1, 1991, is a Tuesday, so Monday, December 31, 1990, to Sunday, January 6, 1991, is week 1. Thus the ISO week number and year for December 31, 1990, is 1, 1991. To get the ISO week number, use the format mask "IW" for the week number and one of the "IY" formats for the year.

Number Formats

Several additional format elements are provided for formatting numbers:

- D (Decimal) returns the decimal character
- G (Group) returns the group separator
- L (Local currency) returns the local currency symbol
- C (international Currency) returns the international currency symbol
- RN (Roman Numeral) returns the number as its Roman numeral equivalent

For Roman numerals, both uppercase and lowercase can be specified, using RN and rn, respectively. The number to be converted must be an integer in the range 1 to 3999.

For a more information on using date masks, see *Oracle8 Server SQL Reference*.

Additional NLS Environment Variables

SQL commands such as ALTER SESSION SET NLS_*parameter* = *value* can be issued to alter the NLS settings for the current session. In addition, Oracle Server supports the following NLS parameters as environment variables to provide greater flexibility for multi-lingual applications:

- NLS_DATE_FORMAT
- NLS_DATE_ LANGUAGE
- NLS_SORT
- NLS_NUMERIC_CHARACTERS
- NLS_CURRENCY
- NLS_ISO_CURRENCY

- NLS_CALENDAR

These variables work in a similar fashion to NLS_LANG. The syntax for the environments listed above is the same as that for the ALTER SESSION command.

Note: If NLS_LANG is *not* set, the other NLS environment variables are ignored.

The following is an example for a UNIX environment:

```
setenv NLS_DATE_FORMAT "dd/mon/yyyy"
```

For more information, see the *Oracle8 Server Administrator's Guide*.

Client-Only Environment Variables

The following environment variables can be set in the client environment:

- NLS_CREDIT
- NLS_DEBIT
- NLS_DISPLAY
- NLS_LANG
- NLS_LIST_SEPARATOR
- NLS_MONETARY_CHARACTERS
- NLS_NCHAR

NLS_CREDIT

Default value:	derived from NLS_TERRITORY
Range of values:	any string, maximum of 9 bytes (not including null)

NLS_CREDIT sets the symbol that displays a credit in financial reports. The default value of this parameter is determined by NLS_TERRITORY.

NLS_DEBIT

Default value:	derived from NLS_TERRITORY
Range of values:	any string, maximum of 9 bytes (not including null)

NLS_DEBIT sets the symbol that displays a debit in financial reports. The default value of this parameter is determined by NLS_TERRITORY.

NLS_DISPLAY

Default value:	none
Range of values:	any valid string

NLS_DISPLAY sets the client-side display environment. It is only applicable to Hebrew and Arabic languages. For a list of valid character sets, see Table 4-8: "Arabic/Hebrew Display Character Sets" on page 4-50.

The value of the parameter is a string of the form *locale_direction.characterset*, where *locale* is any string up to 20 bytes (not including NULL) containing only the characters [A-Z, a-z, 0-9 -], *direction* is either RTL or LTR (case-insensitive), and *characterset* specifies a valid display character set.

Specification of *locale* and *direction* is optional. If omitted, *locale* will default to an empty string, and *direction* will default to LTR. The *characterset* option must be specified. If you specify *direction* or *characterset*, you must include the preceding delimiter [underscore (_) for *direction*, period (.) for *characterset*], otherwise the value will be parsed as a language name.

NLS_LIST_SEPARATOR

Default value:	derived from NLS_TERRITORY
Range of values:	any valid character

NLS_LIST_SEPARATOR specifies the character to use to separate values in a list of values.

The character specified must be single-byte and cannot be the same as either the numeric or monetary decimal character, any numeric character, or any of the following characters: plus (+), hyphen (-), less than sign (<), greater than sign (>), period (.).

NLS_MONETARY_CHARACTERS

Default value:	derived from NLS_TERRITORY

NLS_MONETARY_CHARACTERS specifies the characters that indicate monetary units, such as the dollar sign ($) for U.S. Dollars, and the cent symbol (¢) for cents.

The two characters specified must be single-byte and cannot be the same as each other. They also cannot be any numeric character or any of the following characters: plus (+), hyphen (-), less than sign (<), greater than sign (>).

NLS_NCHAR

Default value:	derived from NLS_LANG
Range of values:	any valid character set name

NLS_NCHAR specifies the character set used by the client application for national character set data. If it is not specified, the client application uses the same character set which it uses for the database character set data.

Using NLS Parameters in SQL Functions

All character functions support both single-byte and multi-byte characters. Except where explicitly stated, character functions operate character-by-character, rather than byte-by-byte.

All SQL functions whose behavior depends on NLS conventions allow NLS parameters to be specified. These functions are

- TO_CHAR
- TO_DATE
- TO_NUMBER
- NLS_UPPER
- NLS_LOWER
- NLS_INITCAP

- NLS_SORT

Explicitly specifying the optional NLS parameters for these functions allows the function evaluations to be independent of the NLS parameters in force for the session. This feature may be important for SQL statements that contain numbers and dates as string literals.

For example, the following query is evaluated correctly only if the language specified for dates is American:

```
SELECT ENAME FROM EMP
WHERE HIREDATE > '1-JAN-91'
```

Such a query can be made independent of the current date language by using these statements:

```
SELECT ENAME FROM EMP
WHERE HIREDATE > TO_DATE('1-JAN-91','DD-MON-YY',
   'NLS_DATE_LANGUAGE = AMERICAN')
```

In this way, language-independent SQL statements can be defined where necessary. For example, such statements might be necessary when string literals appear in SQL statements in views, CHECK constraints, or triggers.

Default Specifications

When evaluating views and triggers, default values for NLS function parameters are taken from the values currently in force for the session. When evaluating CHECK constraints, default values are set by the NLS parameters that were specified at database creation.

Specifying Parameters

The syntax that specifies NLS parameters in SQL functions is:

```
'parameter = value'
```

The following NLS parameters can be specified:

- NLS_DATE_ LANGUAGE
- NLS_NUMERIC_CHARACTERS
- NLS_CURRENCY
- NLS_ISO_CURRENCY
- NLS_SORT

Only certain NLS parameters are valid for particular SQL functions, as follows:

SQL Function	NLS Parameter
TO_DATE:	NLS_DATE_LANGUAGE NLS_CALENDAR
TO_NUMBER:	NLS_NUMERIC_CHARACTERS NLS_CURRENCY NLS_ISO_CURRENCY
TO_CHAR	NLS_DATE_LANGUAGE NLS_NUMERIC_CHARACTERS NLS_CURRENCY NLS_ISO_CURRENCY NLS_CALENDAR
NLS_UPPER	NLS_SORT
NLS_LOWER	NLS_SORT
NLS_INITCAP	NLS_SORT
NLSSORT	NLS_SORT

Examples of the use of NLS parameters are

```
TO_DATE ('1-JAN-89', 'DD-MON-YY',
   'nls_date_language = American')

TO_CHAR (hiredate, 'DD/MON/YYYY',
   'nls_date_language = French')


TO_NUMBER ('13.000,00', '99G999D99',
   'nls_numeric_characters = ''.,''')

TO_CHAR (sal, '9G999D99L', 'nls_numeric_characters = ''.,''
   nls_currency = ''Dfl ''')

TO_CHAR (sal, '9G999D99C', 'nls_numeric_characters = '',.''
   nls_iso_currency = Japan')
NLS_UPPER (ename, 'nls_sort = Austrian')

NLSSORT (ename, 'nls_sort = German')
```

Note: For some languages, various lowercase characters correspond to a sequence of uppercase characters, or vice versa. As a result, the output from NLS_UPPER, NLS_LOWER, and NLS_INITCAP can differ from the length of the input.

Unacceptable Parameters

Note that NLS_LANGUAGE and NLS_TERRITORY are not accepted as parameters in SQL functions. Only NLS parameters that explicitly define the specific data items required for unambiguous interpretation of a format are accepted. NLS_DATE_FORMAT is also not accepted as a parameter for the reason described below.

If an NLS parameter is specified in TO_CHAR, TO_NUMBER, or TO_DATE, a format mask must also be specified as the second parameter. For example, the following specification is legal:

```
TO_CHAR (hiredate, 'DD/MON/YYYY', 'nls_date_language = French')
```

These are illegal:

```
TO_CHAR (hiredate, 'nls_date_language = French')
TO_CHAR (hiredate, 'nls_date_language = French',
   'DD/MON/YY')
```

This restriction means that a date format must always be specified if an NLS parameter is in a TO_CHAR or TO_DATE function. As a result, NLS_DATE_FORMAT is not a valid NLS parameter for these functions.

CONVERT Function

The SQL function CONVERT allows for conversion of character data between character sets.

For more information on CONVERT, see *Oracle8 Server SQL Reference*.

The CONVERT function converts the binary representation of a character string in one character set to another. It uses exactly the same technique as described previously for the conversion between database and client character sets. Hence, it uses replacement characters and has the same limitations.

If the CONVERT function is used in a stored procedure, the stored procedure will run independently of the client character set (that is, it will use the server's character set), which sometimes results in the last converted character being truncated. The syntax for CONVERT is:

convert

where *src_char_set* is the source and *dest_char_set* is the destination character set.

In client/server environments using different character sets, use the TRANSLATE (...USING...) statement to perform conversions instead of CONVERT. The conversion to client character sets will then properly know the server character set of the result of the TRANSLATE statement.

NLSSORT Function

The NLSSORT function replaces a character string with the equivalent sort string used by the linguistic sort mechanism. For a binary sort, the sort string is the same as the input string. The linguistic sort technique operates by replacing each character string with some other binary values, chosen so that sorting the resulting string produces the desired sorting sequence. When a linguistic sort is being used, NLSSORT returns the binary values that replace the original string.

String Comparisons in a WHERE Clause

NLSSORT allows applications to perform string matching that follows alphabetic conventions. Normally, character strings in a WHERE clause are compared using the characters' binary values. A character is "greater than" another if it has a higher binary value in the database character set. Because the sequence of characters based on their binary values might not match the alphabetic sequence for a language, such comparisons often do not follow alphabetic conventions. For example, if a column (COL1) contains the values ABC, ABZ, BCD and ÄBC in the ISO 8859/1 8-bit character set, the following query:

```
SELECT COL1 FROM TAB1 WHERE COL1 > 'B'
```

returns both BCD and ÄBC because Ä has a higher numeric value than B. However, in German, an Ä is sorted alphabetically before B. Such conventions are language dependent even when the same character is used. In Swedish, an Ä is sorted after Z. Linguistic comparisons can be made using NLSSORT in the WHERE clause, as follows:

```
WHERE NLSSORT(col) comparison_operator NLSSORT(comparison_string)
```

Note that NLSSORT has to be on both sides of the comparison operator. For example:

```
SELECT COL1 FROM TAB1 WHERE NLSSORT(COL1) > NLSSORT('B')
```

If a German linguistic sort is being used, this does not return strings beginning with Ä because in the German alphabet Ä comes before B. If a Swedish linguistic sort is being used, such names are returned because in the Swedish alphabet Ä comes after Z.

Other SQL Functions

Two SQL functions, NLS_CHARSET_NAME and NLS_CHARSET_ID, are provided to convert between character set ID numbers and character set names. They are used by programs which need to determine character set ID numbers for binding variables through OCI.

The NLS_CHARSET_DECL_LEN function returns the declaration length (in number of characters) for an NCHAR column.

For more information on these functions, see *Oracle8 Server SQL Reference*.

Converting from Character Set Number to Character Set Name

The NLS_CHARSET_NAME(n) function returns the name of the character set corresponding to ID number n. The function returns NULL if n is not a recognized character set ID value.

Converting from Character Set Name to Character Set Number

NLS_CHARSET_ID(*TEXT*) returns the character set ID corresponding to the name specified by *TEXT*. *TEXT* is defined as a run-time VARCHAR2 quantity, a character set name. Values for *TEXT* can be NLSRTL names that resolve to sets other than the database character set or the national character set.

If the value CHAR_CS is entered for *TEXT*, the function returns the ID of the server's database character set. If the value NCHAR_CS is entered for *TEXT*, the function returns the ID of the server's national character set. The function returns NULL if *TEXT* is not a recognized name. The value for *TEXT* must be entered in all uppercase.

Returning the Length of an NCHAR Column

NLS_CHARSET_DECL_LEN(*BYTECNT, CSID*) returns the declaration length (in number of characters) for an NCHAR column. The *BYTECNT* argument is the byte length of the column. The *CSID* argument is the character set ID of the column.

Partitioned Tables and Indexes

String comparison for partition VALUES LESS THAN collation for DDL and DML always follows BINARY order.

Controlling an ORDER BY Clause

If a linguistic sorting sequence is in use, then NLSSORT is used implicitly on each character item in the ORDER BY clause. As a result, the sort mechanism (linguistic or binary) for an ORDER BY is transparent to the application. However, if the NLSSORT function is explicitly specified for a character item in an ORDER BY item, then the implicit NLSSORT is not done.

In other words, the NLSSORT linguistic replacement is only applied once, not twice. The NLSSORT function is generally not needed in an ORDER BY clause when the default sort mechanism is a linguistic sort. However, when the default sort mechanism is BINARY, then a query such as:

```
SELECT ENAME FROM EMP
ORDER BY ENAME
```

will use a binary sort. A German linguistic sort can be obtained using:

```
SELECT ENAME FROM EMP
ORDER BY NLSSORT(ENAME, 'NLS_SORT = GERMAN')
```

Obsolete NLS Data

Prior to Oracle Server release 7.2, when a character set was renamed the old name was usually supported along with the new name for several releases after the change. Beginning with release 7.2, the old names are no longer supported. Table 4-4 lists the affected character sets. If you reference any of these character sets in your code, please replace them with their new name:

Table 4-4: New Names for Obsolete NLS Data Character Sets

Old Name	New Name
AR8MSAWIN	AR8MSWIN1256
JVMS	JA16VMS
JEUC	JA16EUC
SJIS	JA16SJIS
JDBCS	JA16DBCS
KSC5601	KO16KSC5601
KDBCS	KO16DBCS
CGB2312-80	ZHS16CGB231280

Table 4-4: New Names for Obsolete NLS Data Character Sets

Old Name	New Name
CNS 11643-86	ZHT32EUC
ZHT32CNS1164386	ZHT32EUC
TSTSET2	JA16TSTSET2
TSTSET	JA16TSTSET

Character set CL8MSWINDOW31 has been de-supported. The newer character set CL8MSWIN1251 is actually a duplicate of CL8MSWINDOW31 and includes some characters omitted from the earlier version. Change any usage of CL8MSWINDOW31 to CL8MSWIN1251 instead.

Unicode (UTF-8) Support

Unicode has two major encoding schemes: UCS-2 and UTF-8. UCS-2 is a two-byte fixed-width format; UTF-8 is a multi-byte format with variable width. Oracle8 provides support for the UTF-8 format because this enhancement is transparent to clients who already provide support for multi-byte character sets.

The character set name for UTF-8 is AL24UTFFSS for UNICODE Version 1.1 and UTF8 for UNICODE Version 2.0. Conversion between UTF-8 and other existing character sets is provided in this release of Oracle Server. Conversion between UTF-8 and single-byte character sets is performed through an internal number matching mechanism; conversion between UTF-8 and multi-byte character sets is performed with conversion functions and tables.

Clients should be aware that UTF8 is now officially supported as a new character set. Since UTF8 is the UTF-8 encoding for UNICODE Version 2.0, it is recommended for use in UNICODE support. The encoding scheme of UTF8 is very similar to some existing character sets, thus no major impact on existing products is expected.

Note: UNICODE no longer supports the encoding scheme UTF-2. UTF-8 replaces UTF-2.

NLS Data

This section lists supported languages, territories, storage character sets, Arabic/Hebrew display character sets, linguistic definitions, and calendars.

You can also obtain information about supported character sets, languages, territories, and sorting orders by querying the dynamic data view V$NLS_VALID_VAUES. For more information on the data which can be returned by this view, see "V$NLS_VALID_VALUES" on page 3-61.

Supported Languages

Table 4-5 lists the 46 languages supported by the Oracle Server.

Table 4-5: Oracle Supported Languages

Abbreviation	Name
us	AMERICAN
ar	ARABIC
bn	BENGALI
ptb	BRAZILIAN PORTUGUESE
bg	BULGARIAN
frc	CANADIAN FRENCH
ca	CATALAN
hr	CROATIAN
cs	CZECH
dk	DANISH
nl	DUTCH
eg	EGYPTIAN
gb	ENGLISH
et	ESTONIAN
sf	FINNISH
f	FRENCH
din	GERMAN DIN
d	GERMAN
el	GREEK
iw	HEBREW
hu	HUNGARIAN

Table 4-5: Oracle Supported Languages

Abbreviation	Name
is	ICELANDIC
in	INDONESIAN
i	ITALIAN
ja	JAPANESE
ko	KOREAN
esa	LATIN AMERICAN SPANISH
lv	LATVIAN
lt	LITHUANIAN
ms	MALAY
esm	MEXICAN SPANISH
n	NORWEGIAN
pl	POLISH
pt	PORTUGUESE
ro	ROMANIAN
ru	RUSSIAN
zhs	SIMPLIFIED CHINESE
sk	SLOVAK
sl	SLOVENIAN
e	SPANISH
s	SWEDISH
th	THAI
zht	TRADITIONAL CHINESE
tr	TURKISH
uk	UKRAINIAN
vn	VIETNAMESE

Supported Territories

Table 4-6 lists the 67 territories supported by the Oracle Server.

Table 4-6: Oracle Supported Territories

Abbreviation	Name
dz	ALGERIA
us	AMERICA

Table 4-6: Oracle Supported Territories

Abbreviation	Name
at	AUSTRIA
bh	BAHRAIN
bd	BANGLADESH
br	BRAZIL
bg	BULGARIA
ca	CANADA
cat	CATALONIA
cn	CHINA
cis	CIS
hr	CROATIA
cz	CZECH REPUBLIC
cs	CZECHOSLOVAKIA
dk	DENMARK
dj	DJIBOUTI
eg	EGYPT
ee	ESTONIA
fi	FINLAND
fr	FRANCE
de	GERMANY
gr	GREECE
hk	HONG KONG
hu	HUNGARY
is	ICELAND
id	INDONESIA
iq	IRAQ
il	ISRAEL
it	ITALY
jp	JAPAN
jo	JORDAN
kr	KOREA
kw	KUWAIT
lv	LATVIA
lb	LEBANON
ly	LIBYA

Table 4-6: Oracle Supported Territories

Abbreviation	Name
lit	LITHUANIA
my	MALAYSIA
mr	MAURITANIA
mx	MEXICO
ma	MOROCCO
no	NORWAY
om	OMAN
pl	POLAND
pt	PORTUGAL
qa	QATAR
ro	ROMANIA
sa	SAUDI ARABIA
sk	SLOVAKIA
si	SLOVENIA
so	SOMALIA
es	SPAIN
sd	SUDAN
se	SWEDEN
ch	SWITZERLAND
sy	SYRIA
tw	TAIWAN
th	THAILAND
nl	THE NETHERLANDS
tn	TUNISIA
tr	TURKEY
ua	UKRAINE
ae	UNITED ARAB EMIRATES
gb	UNITED KINGDOM
vn	VIETNAM
ye	YEMEN
cy	CYPRUS

Storage Character Sets

Table 4-7 lists the 180 storage character sets supported by the Oracle Server.

Table 4-7: Storage Character Sets

Name	Description
US7ASCII	ASCII 7-bit American
WE8DEC	DEC 8-bit West European
WE8HP	HP LaserJet 8-bit West European
US8PC437	IBM-PC Code Page 437 8-bit American
WE8EBCDIC37	EBCDIC Code Page 37 8-bit West European
WE8EBCDIC500	EBCDIC Code Page 500 8-bit West European
WE8EBCDIC285	EBCDIC Code Page 285 8-bit West European
WE8PC850	IBM-PC Code Page 850 8-bit West European
D7DEC	DEC VT100 7-bit German
F7DEC	DEC VT100 7-bit French
S7DEC	DEC VT100 7-bit Swedish
E7DEC	DEC VT100 7-bit Spanish
SF7ASCII	ASCII 7-bit Finnish
NDK7DEC	DEC VT100 7-bit Norwegian/Danish
I7DEC	DEC VT100 7-bit Italian
NL7DEC	DEC VT100 7-bit Dutch
CH7DEC	DEC VT100 7-bit Swiss (German/French)
YUG7ASCII	ASCII 7-bit Yugoslavian
SF7DEC	DEC VT100 7-bit Finnish
TR7DEC	DEC VT100 7-bit Turkish
IW7IS960	Israeli Standard 960 7-bit Latin/Hebrew
IN8ISCII	Multiple-Script Indian Standard 8-bit Latin/Indian Languages
WE8ISO8859P1	ISO 8859-1 West European
EE8ISO8859P2	ISO 8859-2 East European
SE8ISO8859P3	ISO 8859-3 South European
NEE8ISO8859P4	ISO 8859-4 North and North-East European
CL8ISO8859P5	ISO 8859-5 Latin/Cyrillic
AR8ISO8859P6	ISO 8859-6 Latin/Arabic
EL8ISO8859P7	ISO 8859-7 Latin/Greek
IW8ISO8859P8	ISO 8859-8 Latin/Hebrew

Table 4-7: Storage Character Sets

Name	Description
WE8ISO8859P9	ISO 8859-9 West European & Turkish
NE8ISO8859P10	ISO 8859-10 North European
TH8TISASCII	Thai Industrial Standard 620-2533 - ASCII 8-bit
TH8TISEBCDIC	Thai Industrial Standard 620-2533 - EBCDIC 8-bit
BN8BSCII	Bangladesh National Code 8-bit BSCII
VN8VN3	VN3 8-bit Vietnamese
WE8NEXTSTEP	NeXTSTEP PostScript 8-bit West European
AR8EBCDICX	EBCDIC XBASIC Server 8-bit Latin/Arabic
EL8DEC	DEC 8-bit Latin/Greek
TR8DEC	DEC 8-bit Turkish
WE8EBCDIC37C	EBCDIC Code Page 37 8-bit Oracle/c
WE8EBCDIC500C	EBCDIC Code Page 500 8-bit Oracle/c
IW8EBCDIC424	EBCDIC Code Page 424 8-bit Latin/Hebrew
TR8EBCDIC1026	EBCDIC Code Page 1026 8-bit Turkish
WE8EBCDIC871	EBCDIC Code Page 871 8-bit Icelandic
WE8EBCDIC284	EBCDIC Code Page 284 8-bit Latin American/Spanish
EEC8EUROASCI	EEC Targon 35 ASCI West European / Greek
EEC8EUROPA3	EEC EUROPA3 8-bit West European/Greek
LA8PASSPORT	German Government Printer 8-bit All-European Latin
BG8PC437S	IBM-PC Code Page 437 8-bit (Bulgarian Modification)
EE8PC852	IBM-PC Code Page 852 8-bit East European
RU8PC866	IBM-PC Code Page 866 8-bit Latin/Cyrillic
RU8BESTA	BESTA 8-bit Latin/Cyrillic
IW8PC1507	IBM-PC Code Page 1507/862 8-bit Latin/Hebrew
RU8PC855	IBM-PC Code Page 855 8-bit Latin/Cyrillic
TR8PC857	IBM-PC Code Page 857 8-bit Turkish
CL8MACCYRILLIC	Mac Client 8-bit Latin/Cyrillic
CL8MACCYRILLICS	Mac Server 8-bit Latin/Cyrillic
WE8PC860	IBM-PC Code Page 860 8-bit West European
IS8PC861	IBM-PC Code Page 861 8-bit Icelandic
EE8MACCES	Mac Server 8-bit Central European
EE8MACCROATIANS	Mac Server 8-bit Croatian
TR8MACTURKISHS	Mac Server 8-bit Turkish
IS8MACICELANDICS	Mac Server 8-bit Icelandic

Table 4-7: Storage Character Sets

Name	Description
EL8MACGREEKS	Mac Server 8-bit Greek
IW8MACHEBREWS	Mac Server 8-bit Hebrew
EE8MSWIN1250	MS Windows Code Page 1250 8-bit East European
CL8MSWIN1251	MS Windows Code Page 1251 8-bit Latin/Cyrillic
ET8MSWIN923	MS Windows Code Page 923 8-bit Estonian
BG8MSWIN	MS Windows 8-bit Bulgarian Cyrillic
EL8MSWIN1253	MS Windows Code Page 1253 8-bit Latin/Greek
IW8MSWIN1255	MS Windows Code Page 1255 8-bit Latin/Hebrew
LT8MSWIN921	MS Windows Code Page 921 8-bit Lithuanian
TR8MSWIN1254	MS Windows Code Page 1254 8-bit Turkish
WE8MSWIN1252	MS Windows Code Page 1252 8-bit West European
BLT8MSWIN1257	MS Windows Code Page 1257 8-bit Baltic
D8EBCDIC273	EBCDIC Code Page 273/1 8-bit Austrian German
I8EBCDIC280	EBCDIC Code Page 280/1 8-bit Italian
DK8EBCDIC277	EBCDIC Code Page 277/1 8-bit Danish
S8EBCDIC278	EBCDIC Code Page 278/1 8-bit Swedish
EE8EBCDIC870	EBCDIC Code Page 870 8-bit East European
CL8EBCDIC1025	EBCDIC Code Page 1025 8-bit Cyrillic
F8EBCDIC297	EBCDIC Code Page 297 8-bit French
IW8EBCDIC1086	EBCDIC Code Page 1086 8-bit Hebrew
CL8EBCDIC1025X	EBCDIC Code Page 1025 (Modified) 8-bit Cyrillic
N8PC865	IBM-PC Code Page 865 8-bit Norwegian
BLT8CP921	Latvian Standard LVS8-92(1) Windows/Unix 8-bit Baltic
LV8PC1117	IBM-PC Code Page 1117 8-bit Latvian
LV8PC8LR	Latvian Version IBM-PC Code Page 866 8-bit Latin/Cyrillic
BLT8EBCDIC1112	EBCDIC Code Page 1112 8-bit Baltic Multilingual
LV8RST104090	IBM-PC Alternative Code Page 8-bit Latvian (Latin/Cyrillic)
CL8KOI8R	RELCOM Internet Standard 8-bit Latin/Cyrillic
BLT8PC775	IBM-PC Code Page 775 8-bit Baltic
F7SIEMENS9780X	Siemens 97801/97808 7-bit French
E7SIEMENS9780X	Siemens 97801/97808 7-bit Spanish
S7SIEMENS9780X	Siemens 97801/97808 7-bit Swedish
DK7SIEMENS9780X	Siemens 97801/97808 7-bit Danish
N7SIEMENS9780X	Siemens 97801/97808 7-bit Norwegian

Table 4-7: Storage Character Sets

Name	Description
I7SIEMENS9780X	Siemens 97801/97808 7-bit Italian
D7SIEMENS9780X	Siemens 97801/97808 7-bit German
WE8GCOS7	Bull EBCDIC GCOS7 8-bit West European
EL8GCOS7	Bull EBCDIC GCOS7 8-bit Greek
US8BS2000	Siemens 9750-62 EBCDIC 8-bit American
D8BS2000	Siemens 9750-62 EBCDIC 8-bit German
F8BS2000	Siemens 9750-62 EBCDIC 8-bit French
E8BS2000	Siemens 9750-62 EBCDIC 8-bit Spanish
DK8BS2000	Siemens 9750-62 EBCDIC 8-bit Danish
S8BS2000	Siemens 9750-62 EBCDIC 8-bit Swedish
WE8BS2000	Siemens EBCDIC.DF.04 8-bit West European
CL8BS2000	Siemens EBCDIC.EHC.LC 8-bit Cyrillic
WE8BS2000L5	Siemens EBCDIC.DF.04.L5 8-bit West European/Turkish
WE8DG	DG 8-bit West European
WE8NCR4970	NCR 4970 8-bit West European
WE8ROMAN8	HP Roman8 8-bit West European
EE8MACCE	Mac Client 8-bit Central European
EE8MACCROATIAN	Mac Client 8-bit Croatian
TR8MACTURKISH	Mac Client 8-bit Turkish
IS8MACICELANDIC	Mac Client 8-bit Icelandic
EL8MACGREEK	Mac Client 8-bit Greek
IW8MACHEBREW	Mac Client 8-bit Hebrew
US8ICL	ICL EBCDIC 8-bit American
WE8ICL	ICL EBCDIC 8-bit West European
WE8ISOICLUK	ICL special version ISO8859-1
WE8MACROMAN8	Mac Client 8-bit Extended Roman8 West European
WE8MACROMAN8S	Mac Server 8-bit Extended Roman8 West European
TH8MACTHAI	Mac Client 8-bit Latin/Thai
TH8MACTHAIS	Mac Server 8-bit Latin/Thai
HU8CWI2	Hungarian 8-bit CWI-2
EL8PC437S	IBM-PC Code Page 437 8-bit (Greek modification)
EL8EBCDIC875	EBCDIC Code Page 875 8-bit Greek
EL8PC737	IBM-PC Code Page 737 8-bit Greek/Latin
LT8PC772	IBM-PC Code Page 772 8-bit Lithuanian (Latin/Cyrillic)

Table 4-7: Storage Character Sets

Name	Description
LT8PC774	IBM-PC Code Page 774 8-bit Lithuanian (Latin)
EL8PC869	IBM-PC Code Page 869 8-bit Greek/Latin
EL8PC851	IBM-PC Code Page 851 8-bit Greek/Latin
CDN8PC863	IBM-PC Code Page 863 8-bit Canadian French
HU8ABMOD	Hungarian 8-bit Special AB Mod
AR8ASMO8X	ASMO Extended 708 8-bit Latin/Arabic
AR8NAFITHA711	Nafitha Enhanced 711 Server 8-bit Latin/Arabic
AR8SAKHR707	SAKHR 707 Server 8-bit Latin/Arabic
AR8MUSSAD768	Mussa'd Alarabi/2 768 Server 8-bit Latin/Arabic
AR8ADOS710	Arabic MS-DOS 710 Server 8-bit Latin/Arabic
AR8ADOS720	Arabic MS-DOS 720 Server 8-bit Latin/Arabic
AR8APTEC715	APTEC 715 Server 8-bit Latin/Arabic
AR8MSAWIN	MS Windows Code Page 1256 8-Bit Latin/Arabic
AR8MSWIN1256	MS Windows Code Page 1256 8-Bit Latin/Arabic
AR8NAFITHA721	Nafitha International 721 Server 8-bit Latin/Arabic
AR8SAKHR706	SAKHR 706 Server 8-bit Latin/Arabic
AR8ARABICMAC	Mac Client 8-bit Latin/Arabic
AR8ARABICMACS	Mac Server 8-bit Latin/Arabic
LA8ISO6937	ISO 6937 8-bit Coded Character Set for Text Communication
US8NOOP	No-op character set prohibiting conversions
JA16VMS	JVMS 16-bit Japanese
JA16EUC	EUC 16-bit Japanese
JA16EUCYEN	EUC 16-bit Japanese with '\' mapped to the Japanese yen character
JA16SJIS	Shift-JIS 16-bit Japanese
JA16DBCS	IBM DBCS 16-bit Japanese
JA16SJISYEN	Shift-JIS 16-bit Japanese with '\' mapped to the Japanese yen character
JA16EBCDIC930	IBM DBCS Code Page 290 16-bit Japanese
JA16MACSJIS	Mac client Shift-JIS 16-bit Japanese
KO16KSC5601	KSC5601 16-bit Korean
KO16DBCS	IBM DBCS 16-bit Korean
KO16KSCCS	KSCCS 16-bit Korean
ZHS16CGB231280	CGB2312-80 16-bit Simplified Chinese
ZHS16MACCGB231280	Mac client CGB2312-80 16-bit Simplified Chinese
ZHS16GBK	Windows95 16-bit PRC version Chinese character set

Table 4-7: Storage Character Sets

Name	Description
ZHS16DBCS	EBCDIC 16-bit Simplified Chinese character set
ZHT32EUC	EUC 32-bit Traditional Chinese
ZHT32SOPS	SOPS 32-bit Traditional Chinese
ZHT16DBT	Taiwan Taxation 16-bit Traditional Chinese
ZHT32TRIS	TRIS 32-bit Traditional Chinese
ZHT16DBCS	IBM DBCS 16-bit Traditional Chinese
ZHT16BIG5	BIG5 16-bit Traditional Chinese
ZHT16CCDC	HP CCDC 16-bit Traditional Chinese
AL24UTFFSS	Unicode 1.1 UTF-8 character set
UTF8	Unicode 2.0 UTF-8 character set
JA16EUCFIXED	16-bit Japanese. A fixed-width subset of JA16EUC (contains only the 2-byte characters of JA16EUC). Contains no 7- or 8-bit ASCII characters
JA16SJISFIXED	SJIS 16-bit Japanese. A fixed-width subset of JA16SJIS (contains only the 2-byte characters of JA16JIS). Contains no 7- or 8-bit ASCII characters
JA16DBCSFIXED	16-bit only JA16DBCS. A fixed-width subset of JA16DBCS which has only 16-bit (double byte character set-DBCS) characters. Contains no 7- or 8-bit ASCII characters
ZHT32TRISFIXED	TRIS 32-bit Fixed-width Traditional Chinese

Arabic/Hebrew Display Character Sets

Table 4-8 lists the 10 Arabic/Hebrew display character sets supported by the Oracle Server.

Table 4-8: Arabic/Hebrew Display Character Sets

Name	Description
AR8ASMO708PLUS	ASMO 708 Plus 8-bit Latin/Arabic
AR8XBASIC	XBASIC Right-to-Left Arabic Character Set
AR8NAFITHA711T	Nafitha Enhanced 711 Client 8-bit Latin/Arabic
AR8SAKHR707T	SAKHR 707 Client 8-bit Latin/Arabic
AR8MUSSAD768T	Mussa'd Alarabi/2 768 Client 8-bit Latin/Arabic
AR8ADOS710T	Arabic MS-DOS 710 Client 8-bit Latin/Arabic
AR8ADOS720T	Arabic MS-DOS 720 Client 8-bit Latin/Arabic
AR8APTEC715T	APTEC 7 15 Client 8-bit Latin/Arabic
AR8NAFITHA721T	Nafitha International 721 Client 8-bit Latin/Arabic
AR8HPARABIC8T	HP ARABIC8 8-bit Latin/Arabic

Linguistic Definitions

Linguistic definitions define linguistic cases for particular languages. Extended linguistic definitions include some special linguistic cases for the language. Table 4-9 lists the 63 linguistic definitions supported by the Oracle Server.

Table 4-9: Linguistic Definitions

Basic Name	Extended Name
ARABIC	--
ASCII7	--
BENGALI	--
BULGARIAN	--
CANADIAN FRENCH	--
CATALAN	XCATALAN
CROATIAN	XCROATIAN
CZECH	XCZECH
DANISH	XDANISH
DUTCH	XDUTCH
EEC_EURO	--
ESTONIAN	--
FINNISH	--
FRENCH	XFRENCH
GERMAN	XGERMAN
GERMAN_DIN	XGERMAN_DIN
GREEK	--
HEBREW	--
HUNGARIAN	XHUNGARIAN
ICELANDIC	--
ITALIAN	--
JAPANESE	--
LATIN	--
LATVIAN	--
LITHUANIAN	--
MALAY	--
NORWEGIAN	--

Table 4-9: Linguistic Definitions

Basic Name	Extended Name
POLISH	--
PUNCTUATION	XPUNCTUATION
ROMANIAN	--
RUSSIAN	--
SLOVAK	XSLOVAK
SLOVENIAN	XSLOVENIAN
SPANISH	XSPANISH
SWEDISH	--
SWISS	XSWISS
THAI_DICTIONARY	--
THAI_TELEPHONE	--
TURKISH	XTURKISH
UKRAINIAN	--
VIETNAMESE	--
WEST_EUROPEAN	XWEST_EUROPEAN
INDONESIAN	
ARABIC_MATCH	
ARABIC_ABJ_SORT	
ARABIC_ABJ_MATCH	
EEC_EUROPA3	

Calendar Systems

Table 4-10 lists the calendar systems supported by the Oracle Server.

Table 4-10: NLS Supported Calendars

Name	Abbreviation	Character Set Texts	Default Format
Japanese Imperial	ji	JA16EUC	EEYY"\307\257"MM"\267\356"DD"\306\374"
ROC Official	co	ZHT32EUC	EEyy"\310\241 "mm"\305\314"dd"\305\312"
Thai Buddha	tb	TH8TISASCII	"\307\321\27 1\267\325\350" dd month EE yyyy
Persian	pg	AR8ASMO8X	DD Month YYYY
Arabic Hijrah	hl	AR8ISO8859P6	DD Month YYYY

Note: By default, the Gregorian system is used.

CHAPTER

5

Database Limits

This chapter lists the limits of values associated with database functions and objects. The following topic is included in this chapter:

- Database Limits

Database Limits

Limits exist on several levels in the database. There is usually a hard-coded limit in the database that cannot be exceeded. This value may be further restricted for any given operating system. For more information on the maximum value of such limits, see your operating system-specific Oracle documentation.

Table 5-1 lists datatype limits.

Table 5-2 lists physical database limits

Table 5-3 lists logical database limits.

Table 5-4 lists process/runtime limits.

Table 5-1: Datatype Limits

Datatypes	Limit	Comments
BFILE	maximum size: 4 GB maximum size of file name: 255 characters maximum size of directory name: 255 characters maximum number of open BFILEs: see comments	The maximum number of BFILEs is limited by the value of SESSION_MAX_OPEN_FILES, which is itself limited by the maximum number of open files the operating system will allow.
CHAR	2000 bytes maximum	
CHAR VARYING	4000 bytes	
CLOB	4 GB maximum	The number of LOB columns per table is limited only by the maximum number of columns per table (i.e., 1000)
Literals (characters or numbers in SQL or PL/SQL)	4000 characters maximum	
LOB	maximum size of 4 GB -1 byte	
LONG	2^{31}-1 bytes (2 GB) maximum	Only one LONG column allowed per table
NCHAR	2000 bytes	
NCHAR VARYING	4000 bytes	
NUMBER	999...(38 9's) x10^{125}maximum value	Can be represented to full 38-digit precision (the mantissa).
	-999...(38 9's) x10^{125}minimum value	Can be represented to full 38-digit precision (the mantissa).
Precision	38 significant digits	
RAW	2000 bytes maximum	
VARCHAR	4000 bytes maximum	
VARCHAR2	4000 bytes maximum	

Table 5-2: Physical Database Limits

Item	Type of Limit	Limit Value
Database Block Size	minimum	2048 bytes; must be a multiple of O/S physical block size
	maximum	O/S-dependent ; never more than 32 KB
Database Blocks	minimum in initial extent of a segment	2 blocks
	maximum per datafile	platform dependent; typically 2^{22} blocks
Controlfiles	number of controlfiles	1 minimum: 2 or more (on separate devices) strongly recommended
	size of a controlfile	dependent on O/S and database creation options; maximum of 20,000 x (database block size)
Database files	maximum per tablespace	O/S dependent, usually 1022
	maximum per database	65533; may be less on some operating systems; limited also by size of database blocks, and by the DB_FILES init parameter for a particular instance
Database file size	maximum	O/S dependent, limited by maximum O/S file size; typically 2^{22} or 4M blocks
MAXEXTENTS	default value	derived from tablespace default storage or DB_BLOCK_SIZE
	maximum	unlimited
Redo Log Files	maximum number of logfiles	LOG_FILES initialization parameter, or MAXLOGFILES in CREATE DATABASE; controlfile can be resized to allow more entries; ultimately an O/S limit
	maximum number of logfiles per group	unlimited
Redo Log File Size	minimum size	50K bytes
	maximum size	O/S limit, typically 2GB
Tablespaces	maximum number per database	64K Number of tablespaces cannot exceed the number of database files, as each tablespace must include at least one file.

Table 5-3: Logical Database Limits

Item	Type	Limit
GROUP BY clause	maximum length	The group-by expression and all of the non-distinct aggregates (e.g., sum, avg) need to fit within a single database block.
Indexes	maximum per table	unlimited
	total size of indexed column	40% of the database block size minus some overhead.
Columns	table	1000 columns maximum
	indexed (or clustered index)	32 columns maximum
	bitmapped index	30 columns maximum
Constraints	maximum per column	unlimited
Nested Queries	maximum number	255
Partitions	maximum length of linear partitioning key	4KB - overhead
	maximum number of columns in partition key	16 columns
	maximum number of partitions allowed per table or index	64K-1 partitions
Rollback Segments	maximum number per database	no limit; limited within a session by MAX_ROLLBACK_SEGMENTS init parameter
Rows	maximum number per table	no limit
SQL Statement Length	maximum length of statements	64K maximum; particular tools may impose lower limits
Stored Packages	maximum size	PL/SQL and Developer/2000 may have limits on the size of stored procedures they can call. Consult your PL/SQL or Developer/2000 documentation for details. The limits typically range from 2000-3000 lines of code.
Trigger Cascade Limit	maximum value	O/S dependent, typically 32
Users and Roles	maximum	65525 (combined)
Tables	maximum per clustered table	32 tables
	maximum per database	unlimited

Table 5-4: Process / Runtime Limits

Item	Type	Limit
Instances per database	maximum number of OPS instances per database	O/S dependent
Locks	row-level	unlimited
	Distributed Lock Manager	O/S dependent
SGA size	maximum value	O/S dependent, typically 2-4 GB for 32-bit O/S, > 4 GB for 64 bit O/S
Job Queue Processes	maximum per instance	36
I/O Slave Processes	maximum per background process (DBWR, LGWR, etc.)	15
	maximum per Backup session	15
Sessions	maximum per instance	32K, limited by PROCESSES and SESSIONS init parameters
LCK Processes	maximum per instance	10
MTS Servers	maximum per instance	Unlimited within constraints set by PROCESSES and SESSIONS init parameters, for instance.
Dispatchers	maximum per instance	Unlimited within constraints set by PROCESSES and SESSIONS init parameters, for instance.
Parallel Query Slaves	maximum per instance	Unlimited within constraints set by PROCESSES and SESSIONS init parameters, for instance.
Backup Sessions	maximum per instance	Unlimited within constraints set by PROCESSES and SESSIONS init parameters, for instance.

6

SQL Scripts

This chapter describes the SQL scripts that are required for optimal operation of the Oracle Server. The SQL scripts are described in the following sections:

- Creating the Data Dictionary
- Creating Additional Data Dictionary Structures
- The "NO" Scripts
- Migration Scripts

Note: Check the header of each SQL script for more detailed information and examples.

Creating the Data Dictionary

The data dictionary is automatically created when a database is created. Thereafter, whenever the database is in operation, Oracle updates the data dictionary in response to every DDL statement.

The data dictionary base tables are the first objects created in any Oracle database. They are created and must remain in the SYSTEM tablespace. The data dictionary base tables are present to store information about all user-defined objects in the database.

Table 6-1 lists the scripts that are required for the Oracle Server with the indicated options. The appropriate scripts for your Oracle Server options are run automatically when you create a database. They are described here because you might need to run them again, when upgrading to a new release of Oracle8. Your release notes and *Oracle8 Server Migration* indicate when this is necessary. Run these scripts connected to the Oracle Server as the user SYS.

The exact names and locations of these scripts are operating system dependent. See your operating system specific Oracle documentation for the names and locations on your system.

For more information about scripts with names starting with DBMS, see the *Oracle8 Server Administrator's Guide*.

Table 6-1: Required SQL Scripts

Script Name	Needed For	Description
CATALOG.SQL	All databases	Creates the data dictionary and public synonyms for many of its views, and grants PUBLIC access to the synonyms
CATPROC.SQL	All databases	Runs all scripts required for or used with PL/SQL. It is required for all Oracle8 databases.

Creating Additional Data Dictionary Structures

Oracle supplies other scripts with the Oracle Server that create additional structures you can use in managing your database and creating database applications. These scripts are listed in Table 6-2.

The exact names and locations of these scripts are operating system dependent. See your operating system-specific Oracle documentation for the names and locations on your system.

Table 6-2: Additional SQL Scripts

Script Name	Needed For	Run By	Description
CATBLOCK.SQL	Performance Management	Must be run when connected to SYS	Creates views that can dynamically display lock dependency graphs
CATEXP7.SQL	Exporting data to Oracle7	Must be run when connected to SYS	Creates the dictionary views needed for the Oracle7 Export utility to export data from Oracle8 in Oracle7 Export file format
CATHS.SQL	Heterogeneous Services	Must be run when connected to SYS	Installs packages for administering heterogeneous services.

Table 6-2: Additional SQL Scripts

Script Name	Needed For	Run By	Description
CATIO.SQL	Performance Management	Must be run when connected to SYS	Allows I/O to be traced on a table-by-table basis
CATOCTK.SQL	Security	Must be run when connected to SYS	Creates the Oracle Cryptographic Toolkit package
CATPARR.SQL	Parallel Server	SYS or SYSDBA	Creates parallel server data dictionary views.
CATREP.SQL	Advanced Replication	Must be run when connected to SYS	Runs all SQL scripts for enabling database replication.
CATRMAN.SQL	Recovery Manager	RMAN or any user with grant_recovery_ catalog_owner role	Creates recovery manager tables and views (schema) to establish an external recovery catalog for the backup, restore and recovery functionality provided by the Recovery Manager (RMAN) utility
DBMSIOTC.SQL	Storage Management	any user	Analyzes chained rows in index-organized tables
DBMSOTRC.SQL	Performance Management	SYS or SYSDBA	Used to enable and disable Oracle Trace trace generation
DBMSPOOL.SQL	Performance Management	SYS or SYSDBA	Enables DBA to lock PL/SQL packages, SQL statements, and triggers into the shared pool
USERLOCK.SQL	Concurrency Control	SYS or SYSDBA	Provides a facility for user-named locks that can be used in a local or clustered environment to aid in sequencing application actions.
UTLBSTAT.SQL and UTLESTAT.SQL	Performance Monitoring	SYS	Respectively start and stop collecting performance tuning statistics
UTLCHAIN.SQL	Storage Management	any user	Creates tables for storing the output of the ANALYZE command with CHAINED ROWS option
UTLCONST.SQL	Year 2000 Compliance	any user	Provides functions to validate CHECK constraints on date columns are year 2000 compliant
UTLDTREE.SQL	Metadata Management	any user	Creates tables and views that show dependencies between objects
UTLEXCPT.SQL	Constraints	any user	Creates the default table (EXCEPTIONS) for storing exceptions from enabling constraints
UTLHTTP.SQL	Web Access	SYS or SYSDBA	PL/SQL package retrieve data from Internet or intranet web servers via HTTP protocol
UTLLOCKT.SQL	Performance Monitoring	SYS or SYSDBA	Displays a lock wait-for graph, in tree structure format
UTLPG.SQL	Data Conversion	SYS or SYSDBA	Provides a package that converts IBM/370 VS COBOL II
UTLPWDMG.SQL	Security	SYS or SYSDBA	Creates PL/SQL function for default password complexity verification. Sets the default password profile parameters and enables password management features

Table 6-2: Additional SQL Scripts

Script Name	Needed For	Run By	Description
UTLSAMPL.SQL	Examples	SYS or any user with DBA role	Creates sample tables, such as EMP and DEPT, and users, such as SCOTT
UTLSCLN.SQL	Advanced Replication	any user	Copies a snapshot schema from another snapshot site
UTLTKPROF.SQL	Performance Management	SYS	Creates the TKPROFER role to allow the TKPROF profiling utility to be runs by non-DBA users
UTLVALID.SQL	Partitioned Tables	any user	Creates table required for storing output of ANALYZE TABLE ...VALIDATE STRUCTURE of a partitioned table.
UTLXPLAN.SQL	Performance Management	any user	Creates the table PLAN_TABLE, which holds output from the EXPLAIN PLAN command

The "NO" Scripts

The scripts in Table 6-3 are used to remove dictionary information for certain optional services or components.

Table 6-3: The "NO" Scripts

Script Name	Needed For	Run By	Description
CATNOADT.SQL	Objects	Must be run when connected to SYS	Drops views and synonyms on dictionary metadata that relate to Object types
CATNOAUD.SQL	Security	Must be run when connected to SYS	Drops views and synonyms on auditing metadata
CATNOHS.SQL	Heterogeneous Services	Must be run when connected to SYS	Removes Heterogeneous Services dictionary metadata
CATNOPRT.SQL	Partitioning	Must be run when connected to SYS	Drops views and synonyms on dictionary metadata that relate to partitioned tables and indexes
CATNOQUEUE.SQL	Advanced Queuing	Must be run when connected to SYS	Removes Advanced Queuing dictionary metadata
CATNORMN.SQL	Recovery Manager	Owner of recovery catalog	Removes recovery catalog schema
CATNOSVM.SQL	Server Manager	Must be run when connected to SYS	Removes Oracle7 Server Manager views and synonyms
CATNOSNMP.SQL	Distributed Management	SYS	Drops the DBSNMP user and SNMPAGENT role

For more information, see *Oracle8 Server Migration*.

Migration Scripts

The scripts in Table 6-4 are useful when migrating to another version or release.

For more information, see *Oracle8 Server Migration*.

Table 6-4: Migration SQL Scripts

Script Name	Needed For	Run By	Description
CAT8000.SQL	Migration from Oracle7	SYS or SYSDBA	Creates new Oracle8 dictionary metadata
CATREP8M.SQL	Advanced Replication	SYS	Loads replication packages/views and adjusts 7.3 replication-specific packages/views
DROPCAT6.SQL	Removing legacy metadata	SYS	Loads replication packages/views and adjusts 7.3 replication-specific packages/views
DROPCAT5.SQL	Removing legacy metadata	SYS	Loads replication packages/views and adjusts 7.3 replication-specific packages/views

Oracle Wait Events

Introduction

The V$SESSION_WAIT view displays the events for which sessions have just completed waiting or are currently waiting. The V$SYSTEM_EVENT displays the total number of times all the sessions have waited for the events in that view. The V$SESSION_EVENT is similar to V$SYSTEM_EVENT, but displays all waits for each session. For more information on these views, see "V$SESSION_EVENT" on page 3-86, "V$SESSION_WAIT" on page 3-89, and "V$SYSTEM_EVENT" on page 3-109.

This appendix describes the event name, wait time, and parameters for each event. The following SQL statement displays all Oracle events:

```
select *
    from v$event_name;
```

Oracle Wait Events

The following wait events are present in the Oracle Server. The columns P1, P2, and P3 represent parameters for the wait event.

Table A-1: Wait Events for Oracle Parallel Server

Event Name	P1	P2	P3
DFS db file lock	file#	not used	not used
DFS lock handle	typelmode	id1	id2
KOLF: Register LFI close	lfictx	fileop	0
KOLF: Register LFI exists	lfictx	nameop	0
KOLF: Register LFI isopen	lifctx	nameop	0
KOLF: Register LFI length	lfictx	nameop	0
KOLF: Register LFI lfimkm	lfictx	path	0
KOLF: Register LFI lfimkpth	lfictx	pathobj	0
KOLF: Register LFI open	lfictx	fileop	nameop
KOLF: Register LFI read	lfictx	fileop	0
KOLF: Register LFI seek	lfictx	fileop	0
PL/SQL lock timer	duration	not used	not used
SQL*Net break/reset to client	driver id	break?	not used
SQL*Net break/reset to dblink	driver id	break?	not used
SQL*Net message from client	driver id	#bytes	not used
SQL*Net message from dblink	driver id	#bytes	not used
SQL*Net message to client	driver id	#bytes	not used
SQL*Net message to dblink	driver id	#bytes	not used
SQL*Net more data from client	driver id	#bytes	not used
SQL*Net more data from dblink	driver id	#bytes	not used
SQL*Net more data to client	driver id	#bytes	not used
SQL*Net more data to dblink	driver id	#bytes	not used
WMON goes to sleep	not used	not used	not used
alter system set mts_dispatcher	waited	not used	not used
batched allocate scn lock request	not used	not used	not used
buffer busy due to global cache	file#	block#	id
buffer busy waits	file#	block#	id
buffer deadlock	dba	class*10+mode	flag
buffer for checkpoint	buffer#	dba	state*10+mode
buffer latch	latch addr	chain#	not used
buffer read retry	file#	block#	not used
checkpoint completed	not used	not used	not used
checkpoint range buffer not saved	not used	not used	not used

Table A-1: Wait Events for Oracle Parallel Server

Event Name	P1	P2	P3
control file parallel write	files	blocks	requests
control file sequential read	file#	block#	blocks
control file single write	file#	block#	blocks
conversion file read	file#	block#	blocks
db file parallel read	files	blocks	requests
db file parallel write	files	blocks	requests
db file scattered read	file#	block#	blocks
db file sequential read	file#	block#	blocks
db file single write	file#	block#	blocks
debugger command	not used	not used	not used
direct path read	file number	first dba	block cnt
direct path write	file number	first dba	block cnt
dispatcher shutdown	waited	not used	not used
dispatcher timer	sleep time	not used	not used
dupl. cluster key	dba	not used	not used
enqueue	name|mode	id1	id2
file identify	fib	file name	opcode
file open	fib	iov	0
free buffer waits	file#	block#	set-id#
free global transaction table entry	tries	not used	not used
free process state object	not used	not used	not used
global cache freelist wait	lenum	not used	not used
global cache lock busy	file#	block#	lenum
global cache lock cleanup	file#	block#	lenum
global cache lock null to s	file#	block#	lenum
global cache lock null to x	file#	block#	lenum
global cache lock open null	file#	block#	class
global cache lock open s	file#	block#	lenum
global cache lock open ss	file#	block#	class
global cache lock open x	file#	block#	lenum
global cache locks s to x	file#	block#	lenum
imm op	msg ptr	not used	not used
inactive session	session#	waited	not used
inactive transaction branch	branch#	waited	not used

Table A-1: Wait Events for Oracle Parallel Server

Event Name	P1	P2	P3
index block split	rootdba	level	childdba
instance recovery	undo segment#	not used	not used
instance state change	layer	value	waited
io done	msg ptr	not used	not used
kcl bg acks	count	loops	not used
latch activity	address	number	process#
latch free	address	number	tries
library cache load lock	object address	lock address	10*mask+namespace
library cache lock	handle address	lock address	10*mode+namespace
library cache pin	handle address	pin address	10*mode+namespace
lock manager wait for remote message	waittime	not used	not used
log buffer space	not used	not used	not used
log file parallel write	files	blocks	requests
log file sequential read	log#	block#	blocks
log file single write	log#	block#	blocks
log file switch (archiving needed)	not used	not used	not used
log file switch (checkpoint incomplete	not used	not used	not used
log file switch (clearing log file)	not used	not used	not used
log file switch completion	not used	not used	not used
log file sync	buffer#	not used	not used
log switch/archive	thread#	not used	not used
on-going SCN fetch to complete	not used	not used	not used
parallel query create server	nservers	sleeptime	enqueue
parallel query dequeue wait	reason	sleeptime/senderid	passes
parallel query qref latch	function	sleeptime	qref
parallel query server shutdown	nalive	sleeptime	loop
parallel query signal server	serial	error	nbusy
pending ast	lenum	not used	not used
pending global transaction(s)	scans	not used	not used
pipe get	handle address	buffer length	timeout
pipe put	handle address	record length	timeout
pmon timer	duration	not used	not used
process startup	type	process#	waited
queue messages	queue id	process#	wait time

Table A-1: Wait Events for Oracle Parallel Server

Event Name	P1	P2	P3
queue wait	not used	not used	not used
rdbms ipc message	timeout	not used	not used
rdbms ipc message block	not used	not used	not used
rdbms ipc reply	from_process	timeout	not used
redo wait	not used	not used	not used
row cache lock	cache id	mode	request
scginq AST call	not used	not used	not used
single-task message	not used	not used	not used
slave exit	nalive	sleeptime	loop
smon timer	sleep time	failed	not used
switch logfile command	not used	not used	not used
timer in sksawat	not used	not used	not used
transaction	undo seg#l slot#	wrap#	count
unbound tx	not used	not used	not used
undo segment extension	segment#	not used	not used
undo segment recovery	segment#	tx flags	not used
undo segment tx slot	segment#	not used	not used
virtual circuit status	circuit#	status	not used
wait for DLM latch	latchtype	gets	immediate
wait for influx DLM latch	latchtype	latchaddr	not used
wakeup time manager	not used	not used	not used
write complete waits	file#	block#	id
writes stopped by instance recovery	by thread #	our thread#	not used

Parameter Descriptions

This section describes a number of common event parameters.

- block#
- blocks
- break?
- class
- dba
- driver id
- file#
- id1
- id2
- lenum
- mode
- name and type
- namespace
- requests
- session#
- waited

block#

This is the block number of the block for which Oracle needs to wait. The block number is relative to the start of the file. To find the object to which this block belongs, enter these SQL statements:

```
select name, kind
  from ext_to_obj_view
 where file#  = file#
   and lowb  <= block#
   and highb >= block#;
```

blocks

The number of blocks that is being either read from or written to the file. The block size is dependent on the file type:

- database files have a block size of DB_BLOCK_SIZE
- logfiles and controlfiles have a block size that is equivalent to the physical block size of the platform

break?

If the value for this parameter equals 0, a reset was sent to the client. A non-zero value indicates that a break was sent to the client.

class

The class of the block describes how the contents of the block are used. For example, class 1 represents data block, class 4 represents segment header.

dba

The initials "dba" represents the data block address. A dba consists of a file number and a block number.

driver id

The address of the disconnect function of the driver that is currently being used.

file#

The following query returns the name of the database file:

```
select *
 from v$datafile
 where file# = file#;
```

id1

The first identifier (*id1*) of the enqueue or global lock takes its value from P2 or P2RAW. The meaning of the identifier depends on the name (P1).

id2

The second identifier (*id2*) of the enqueue or global lock takes its value from P3 or P3RAW. The meaning of the identifier depends on the name (P1).

lenum

The relative index number into V$LOCK_ELEMENT.

mode

The *mode* is usually stored in the low order bytes of P1 or P1RAW and indicates the mode of the enqueue or global lock request. This parameter has one of the following values:

Table A-2: Lock Mode Values

Mode Value	Description
1	Null mode
2	Sub-Share
3	Sub-Exclusive
4	Share
5	Share/Sub-Exclusive
6	Exclusive

Use the following SQL statement to retrieve the name of the lock and the mode of the lock request:

```
select chr(bitand(p1,-16777216)/16777215)||
       chr(bitand(p1, 16711680)/65535) "Lock",
       bitand(p1, 65536) "Mode"
  from v$session_wait
 where event = 'DFS enqueue lock acquisition';
```

name and type

The name or "type" of the enqueue or global lock can be determined by looking at the two high order bytes of P1 or P1RAW. The name is always two characters. Use the following SQL statement to retrieve the lock name.

```
select chr(bitand(p1,-16777216)/16777215)||
       chr(bitand(p1,16711680)/65535) "Lock"
  from v$session_wait
 where event = 'DFS enqueue lock acquisition';
```

namespace

The name of the object namespace as it is displayed in V$DB_OBJECT_CACHE view.

requests

The number of I/Os that are "requested". This differs from the number of blocks in that one request could potentially contain multiple blocks.

session#

The number of the inactive session. Use the following SQL statement to find more information about the session:

```
select *
  from v$session
 where sid = session#;
```

waited

This is the total amount of time the session has waited for this session to die.

Wait Events

This section describes the Oracle events.

DFS db file lock

This event occurs only for the DBWR in the Parallel Server. Each DBWR of every instance holds a global lock on each file in shared mode. The instance that is trying to offline the file will escalate the global lock from shared to exclusive. This signals the other instances to synchronize their SGAs with the controlfile before the file can be taken offline. The name of this lock is **DF** (see Appendix B, "Enqueue and Lock Names" for more information).

Wait Time: 1 second in loop. The DBWR is waiting in a loop (sleep, check) for the other instances to downgrade to NULL mode. During this time, the DBWR cannot perform other tasks such as writing buffers.

Parameters:

file   See "file#" on page A-7.

DFS lock handle

The session waits for the lock handle of a global lock request. The lock handle identifies a global lock. With this lock handle, other operations can be performed on this global lock (to identify the global lock in future operations such as conversions or release). The global lock is maintained by the DLM.

Wait Time: The session waits in a loop until it has obtained the lock handle from the DLM. Inside the loop there is a wait of 0.5 seconds.

Parameters:

name	See "name and type" on page A-8.
mode	See "mode" on page A-8.
id1	See "id1" on page A-7.
id2	See "id2" on page A-8.

The session needs to get the lock handle.

KOLF: Register LFI close

The session waits for an external large object (LOB) to close.

Wait Time: The total elapsed time for the **close** call.

Parameters:

session#	See "session#" on page A-9.
waited	See "waited" on page A-9.

KOLF: Register LFI exists

The session waits to check if an external large object (LOB) exists.

Wait Time: The total elapsed time for the **exists** call.

Parameters:

session#	See "session#" on page A-9.
waited	See "waited" on page A-9.

KOLF: Register LFI isopen

The session waits to check if an external large object (LOB) has already been opened.

Wait Time: The total elapsed time for the **isopen** call.

Parameters:

session#	See "session#" on page A-9.
waited	See "waited" on page A-9.

KOLF: Register LFI length

The session waits on a call to check the size of an external large object (LOB).

Wait Time: The total elapsed time for the call to check the LOB size.

Parameters:

session#	See "session#" on page A-9.
waited	See "waited" on page A-9.

KOLF: Register LFI lfimkm

The session waits on a call to find or generate the external name of a external large object.

Wait Time: The total elapse time for **make external file name** to complete.

Parameters:

session#	See "session#" on page A-9.
waited	See "waited" on page A-9.

KOLF: Register LFI lfimkpth

The session is waiting on a call to find or generate the external path name of an external large object (LOB).

Wait Time: The total elapsed time for **make external path** to complete.

Parameters:

session#	See "session#" on page A-9.
waited	See "waited" on page A-9.

KOLF: Register LFI open

The session waits on a call to open the external large object (LOB).

Wait Time: The total elapsed time for the **open** call to complete.

Parameters:

session#	See "session#" on page A-9.
waited	See "waited" on page A-9.

KOLF: Register LFI read

The session waits for a read from a external large object (LOB) to complete.

Wait Time: The total elapse time for the **read** to complete.

Parameters:

session#	See "session#" on page A-9.
waited	See "waited" on page A-9.

KOLF: Register LFI seek

The session waits for a positioning call within the external large object (LOB) to complete.

Wait Time: The total elapse time for the **seek** to complete.

Parameters:

session#	See "session#" on page A-9.
waited	See "waited" on page A-9.

PL/SQL lock timer

This event is called through the DBMSLOCK.SLEEP procedure or USERLOCK.SLEEP procedure. This event will most likely originate from procedures written by a user.

Wait Time: The wait time is in hundredths of seconds and is dependent on the user context.

Parameters:

duration	The duration that the user specified in the DBMS_LOCK.SLEEP or USER_LOCK.SLEEP procedures.

SQL*Net break/reset to client

The server sends a break or reset message to the client. The session running on the server waits for a reply from the client.

Wait Time: The actual time it takes for the break or reset message to return from the client.

Parameters:

driver id	See "driver id" on page A-7.
break?	See "break?" on page A-7.

SQL*Net break/reset to dblink

Same as **SQL*Net break/reset to client**, but in this case, the break/reset message is sent to another server process over a database link.

Wait Time: The actual time it takes for the break or reset message to return from the other server process.

Parameters:

driver id	See "driver id" on page A-7.
break?	See "break?" on page A-7.

SQL*Net message from client

The server process (foreground process) waits for a message from the client process to arrive.

Wait Time: The time it took for a message to arrive from the client since the last message was sent to the client.

Parameters:

driver id	See "driver id" on page A-7.
#bytes	The number of bytes received by the server (foreground process) from the client.

SQL*Net message from dblink

The session waits while the server process (foreground process) receives messages over a database link from another server process.

Wait Time: The time it took for a message to arrive from another server (foreground process) since a message was sent to the other foreground process.

Parameters:

driver id	See "driver id" on page A-7.
#bytes	The number of bytes received by the server (foreground process) from another foreground process over a database link.

SQL*Net message to client

The server (foreground process) is sending a message to the client.

Wait Time: The actual time the **send** takes.

Parameters:

driver id	See "driver id" on page A-7.
#bytes	The number of bytes sent by the server process to the client.

SQL*Net message to dblink

The server process (foreground process) is sending a message over a database link to another server process.

Wait Time: The actual time the **send** takes.

Parameters:

driver id	See "driver id" on page A-7.
#bytes	The number of bytes sent by the server process to another server process over a database link.

SQL*Net more data from client

The server is performing another send to the client. The previous operation was also a send to the client.

Wait Time: The time waited depends on the time it took to receive the data (including the waiting time).

Parameters:

driver id	See "driver id" on page A-7.
#bytes	The number of bytes received from the client.

SQL*Net more data from dblink

The foreground process is expecting more data from a data base link.

Wait Time: The total time it takes to read the data from the database link (including the waiting time for the data to arrive).

Parameters:

driver id	See "driver id" on page A-7.
#bytes	The number of bytes received.

SQL*Net more data to client

The server process is sending more data/messages to the client. The previous operation to the client was also a **send**.

Wait Time: The actual time it took for the **send** to complete.

Parameters:

driver id	See "driver id" on page A-7.
#bytes	The number of bytes that are being sent to the client.

SQL*Net more data to dblink

The event indicates that the server is sending data over a database link again. The previous operation over this database link was also a **send**.

Wait Time: The actual time it takes to send the data to the other server.

Parameters:

driver id	See "driver id" on page A-7.
#bytes	The number of bytes that are sent over the database link to the other server process.

WMON goes to sleep

WMON is the UNIX-specific Wait Monitor, that can be used to reduce the number of system calls related to setting timers for posting or waiting in Oracle. You need to set an initialization parameter that enables the WMON process.

Wait Time: Depends on the next timeout.

Parameters: none

alter system set mts_dispatchers

A session has issued an alter system set mts_dispatchers=<string> and it waiting for the dispatchers to get started.

Wait Time: The session will wait 1/100 of a secondand check to see if the new dispatchers have started else the session will wait again.

Parameters:

waited	The number of times that the session has waited 1/100 of second.

batched allocate scn lock request

A session is waiting on another process to allocate an System Change Number (SCN). If the foreground timed out waiting on a process to get the SCN, the foreground will get the SCN.

Wait Time: The wait time is 1 second on the assumption that an SCN allocation should normally need much less than that.

Parameters: none

buffer busy waits

Wait until a buffer becomes available. This event happens because a buffer is either being read into the buffer cache by another session (and the session is waiting for that read to complete) or the buffer is the buffer cache, but in a incompatible mode (that is, some other session is changing the buffer).

Wait Time: Normal wait time is 1 second. If the session was waiting for a buffer during the last wait, then the next wait will be 3 seconds.

Parameters:

file#	See "file#" on page A-7.
block#	See "block#" on page A-6.
id	The buffer busy wait event is called from different places in the session. Each place in the kernel points to different reason, as described in

buffer deadlock

Oracle does not really wait on this event; the foreground only yields the CPU. Thus, the chances of catching this event are very low. This is not an application induced deadlock, but an assumed deadlock by the cache layer. The cache layer cannot get a buffer in a certain mode within a certain amount of time.

Wait Time: 0 seconds. The foreground process only yields the CPU and will usually be placed at the end of the CPU run queue.

Parameters:

class	See "class" on page A-7.
mode	See "mode" on page A-8.
flag	The flag points to the internal flags used by the session to get this block.
dba	See "dba" on page A-7.

buffer for checkpoint

The buffer could not be checkpointed, because some process is modifying it. This means that after the wait, the DBWR will scan the whole buffer cache again. This could happen during a database close or after a user does a local checkpoint. During this situation the database cannot be closed.

Wait Time: 1 second

Parameters:

dba	See "dba" on page A-7.
state	State refers to the status of the buffer contents.
mode	See "mode" on page A-8.
buffer#	This is the index of the block in the buffer cache (V$BH).

buffer latch

The session waits on the buffer hash chain latch. Primarily used in the dump routines.

Wait Time: 1 second

Parameters:

latch addr   The virtual address in the SGA where this latch is
                           located. Use the following command to find the
                           name of this latch:

```
select *
 from v$latch a, v$latchname b
 where addr = latch addr
   and a.latch# = b.latch#;
```

chain#   The index into array of buffer hash chains. When
                           the chain is 0xffffffff, the foreground waits on the
                           LRU latch.

buffer read retry

This event occurs only if the instance is mounted in shared mode (Parallel
Server). During the read of the buffer, the contents changed. This means that
either:

- the version number, dba, or the incarnation and sequence number
  stored in the block no longer match

- the checksum on the block does not match the checksum in the block

The block will be re-read (this may fail up to 3 times), then corruption is
assumed and the corrupt block is dumped in the trace file.

Wait Time: The wait time is the elapsed time of the read.

Parameters:

file#   See "file#" on page A-7.
block#   See "block#" on page A-6.

checkpoint completed

A session waits for a checkpoint to complete. This could happen, for example,
during a close database or a local checkpoint.

Wait Time: 5 seconds

Parameters: none

checkpoint range buffer not saved

During a range checkpoint operation a buffer was found that was not saved or written. Either:

- the session will wait on this event if the write batch is empty and it is the first time that the session waited on this event in the range checkpoint operation

- the current range checkpoint operation will be aborted and a new one will be started to complete the operation

Wait Time: 10 milliseconds

Parameters: none

control file parallel write

This event occurs while the session is writing physical blocks to all controlfiles. This happens when:

- the session starts a controlfile transaction (to make sure that the controlfiles are up to date in case the session crashes before committing the controlfile transaction)

- the session commits a transaction to a controlfile

- changing a generic entry in the controlfile, the new value is being written to all controlfiles

Wait Time: The wait time is the time it takes to finish all writes to all controlfiles.

Parameters:

files	The number of controlfiles to which the session is writing.
blocks	The number of blocks that the session is writing to the controlfile.
requests	The number of I/O requests which the session wants to write.

control file sequential read

Reading from the controlfile. This happens in many cases. For example, while:

- making a backup of the controlfiles

- sharing information (between instances) from the controlfile
- reading other blocks from the controlfiles
- reading the header block

Wait Time: The wait time is the elapsed time of the read.

Parameters:

file#	The controlfile from which the session is reading.
block#	Block number in the controlfile from where the session starts to read. The block size is the physical block size of the port (usually 512 bytes, some UNIX ports have 1 or 2 Kilobytes).
blocks	The number of blocks that the session is trying to read.

control file single write

This wait is signaled while the controlfile's shared information is written to disk. This is an atomic operation protected by an enqueue (CF), so that only one session at a time can write to the entire database.

Wait Time: The wait time is the elapsed time of the write.

Parameters:

file#	This identifies the controlfile to which the session is currently writing.
block#	Block number in the controlfile where the write begins. The block size is the as the physical block size of the port (usually 512 bytes, some UNIX ports have 1 or 2 Kilobytes).
blocks	The number of blocks that the session is trying to read.

conversion file read

This event occurs during a the creation of a Version 7 controlfile as part of converting a database to Version 7 from Version 6.

Wait Time: The wait time is the elapsed time of the read.

Parameters:

file#	The controlfile to which the session is currently writing.
block#	Block number in the controlfile where the write begins. The block size is the as the physical block size of the port (usually 512 bytes, some UNIX ports have 1 or 2 Kilobytes).
blocks	The number of blocks that the session is trying to read.

db file parallel read

This happens during recovery. Database blocks that need to be changed as part of recovery are read in paralle from the database.

Wait Time: Wait until all of the I/Os are completed.

Parameters:

files	This indicates the number of files to which the session is reading.
blocks	This indicates the total number of blocks to be read.
requests	This indicates the total number of I/O requests, which will be the same as blocks.

db file parallel write

This event occurs in the DBWR. It indicates that the DBWR is performing a parallel write to files and blocks. The parameter *requests* indicates the real number of I/Os that are being performed. When the last I/O has gone to disk, the wait ends.

Wait Time: Wait until all of the I/Os are completed.

Parameters:

files	This indicates the number of files to which the session is writing.

Parameters:

blocks	This indicates the total number of blocks to be written.
requests	This indicates the total number of I/O requests, which will be the same as blocks.

db file scattered read

Similar to **db file sequential read**, except that the session is reading multiple data blocks.

Wait Time: The wait time is the actual time it takes to do all of the I/Os.

Parameters:

file#	See "file#" on page A-7.
block#	See "block#" on page A-6.
blocks	The number of blocks that the session is trying to read from the *file#* starting at *block#*.

db file sequential read

The session waits while a sequential read from the database is performed. This event is also used for rebuilding the controlfile, dumping datafile headers, and getting the database file headers.

Wait Time: The wait time is the actual time it takes to do the I/O.

Parameters:

file#	See "file#" on page A-7.
block#	See "block#" on page A-6.
blocks	This is the number of blocks that the session is trying to read (should be 1).

db file single write

This event is used to wait for the writing of the file headers.

Wait Time: The wait time is the actual time it takes to do the I/O.

Parameters:

file#	See "file#" on page A-7.
block#	See "block#" on page A-6.
blocks	This is the number of blocks that the session is trying to write in *file#* starting at *block#*.

direct path read

During Direct Path operations the data is asynchronously read from the database files. At some stage the session needs to make sure that all outstanding asynchronous I/O have been completed to disk. This can also happen if during a direct read no more slots are available to store outstanding load requests (a load request could consist of multiple I/Os).

Wait Time: 10 seconds. The session will be posted by the completing asynchronous I/O. It will never wait the entire 10 seconds. The session waits in a tight loop until all outstanding I/Os have completed.

Parameters:

descriptor address	This is a pointer to the I/O context of outstanding direct I/Os on which the session is currently waiting.
first dba	The dba of the oldest I/O in the context referenced by the descriptor address.
block cnt	Number of valid buffers in the context referenced by the descriptor address.

direct path write

During Direct Path operations the data is asynchronously written to the database files. At some stage the session needs to make sure that all outstanding asynchronous I/O have been completed to disk. This can also happen if during a direct write no more slots are available to store outstanding load requests (a load request could consist of multiple I/Os).

Wait Time: 10 seconds. The session will be posted by the completing asynchronous I/O. It will never wait the entire 10 seconds. The session waits in a tight loop until all outstanding I/Os have completed.

Parameters:

descriptor address	This is a pointer to the I/O context of outstanding direct I/Os on which the session is currently waiting.
first dba	The dba of the oldest I/O in the context referenced by the descriptor address.
block cnt	Number of valid buffers in the context referenced by the descriptor address.

dispatcher shutdown

During shutdown immediate or normal, the shutdown process must wait for all the dispatchers to shutdown. As each dispatcher is signaled, the session that causes the shutdown is waits on this event until the requested dispatcher is no longer alive.

Wait Time: 1 second

Parameters:

waited	Indicates the cumulative wait time. After 5 minutes, the session writes to the alert and trace files to indicate that there might be a problem.

dispatcher timer

This basically means that the dispatcher is idle and waiting for some work to arrive.

Wait Time: 60 seconds

Parameters:

sleep time	The intended sleep time. The dispatcher will return to work sooner if it is posted by either data arriving on the network or by a post from a shared server process to send data back to the client.

duplicate cluster key

It is possible for a race condition to occur when creating a new cluster key. If it is found that another process has put the cluster key into the data/index block, then the session waits and retries. The retry should then find a valid cluster key.

Wait Time: 0.01 seconds

Parameters:

dba	The dba of the block into which the session is trying to insert a cluster key.

enqueue

The session is waiting for a local enqueue. The wait is dependent on the name of the enqueue (see Appendix B, "Enqueue and Lock Names").

Wait Time: Depends on the enqueue name.

Parameters:

name	See "name and type" on page A-8.
mode	See "mode" on page A-8.

file identify

The time it takes to identify a file so that it can be opened later.

file open

The time it takes to open the file.

free buffer waits

This will happen if:

- All buffer gets have been suspended. This could happen when a file was read-only and is now read-write. All the existing buffers need to be invalidated since they are not linked to lock elements (needed when mounted parallel (shared)). So cache buffers are not assigned to data block addresses until the invalidation is finished.

- The session moved some dirty buffers to the dirty queue and now this dirty queue is full. The dirty queue needs to be written first. The session will wait on this event and try again to find a free buffer

- This also happens after inspecting **free buffer inspected** buffers. If no free buffer is found, Oracle waits for one second, and then tries to get the buffer again (depends on the context). For more information, see Appendix , "free buffer inspected".

Wait Time: 1 second

Parameters:

file#	See "file#" on page A-7.
block#	See "block#" on page A-6.

free global transaction table entry

The session is waiting for a free slot in the global transaction table (used by the Distributed Database Option). It will wait for 1 second and try again.

Wait Time: 1 second

Parameters:

tries	The number of times the session tried to find a free slot in the global transaction table.

free process state object

Used during the creation of a process. The session will scan the process table and look for a free process slot. If none can be found, PMON is posted to check if all the processes currently in the process table are still alive. If there are dead processes, PMON will clean them and make the process slot available to new processes. The waiting process will then rescan the process table to find the new slot.

Wait Time: 1 second

Parameters: none

global cache freelist wait

All releasable locks are used and a new one has been requested. To make a lock element available, a lock element is pinged.

Wait Time: The duration of the lock get operation to ping the lock element.

Parameters:

lenum   See "lenum" on page A-8.

global cache lock busy

The session waits to convert a buffer up from Shared Current to Exclusive Current status.

Wait Time: 1 second

Parameters:

file#	See "file#" on page A-7.
block#	See "block#" on page A-6.
lenum	See "lenum" on page A-8.

global cache lock cleanup

PMON is waiting for an LCK process to cleanup the lock context after a foreground process died while doing a global cache lock operation.

Wait Time: 1 second

Parameters:

file#	See "file#" on page A-7.
block#	See "block#" on page A-6.
lenum	See "lenum" on page A-8.

global cache lock null to s

The session waits for a lock convert from NULL to SHARED mode on the block identified by file# and block#.

Wait Time: 1 second

Parameters:

file#	See "file#" on page A-7.
block#	See "block#" on page A-6.
class	See "class" on page A-7.

global cache lock null to x

The session waits for a lock convert from NULL to EXCLUSIVE mode on the block identified by file# and block#.

Wait Time: 1 second

Parameters:

file#	See "file#" on page A-7.
block#	See "block#" on page A-6.
lenum	See "lenum" on page A-8.

global cache lock open null

The session waits for a lock get in NULL mode on the block identified by file# and block#.

Wait Time: 1 second

Parameters:

file#	See "file#" on page A-7.
block#	See "block#" on page A-6.
class	See "class: on page A-6.

global cache lock open s

The session waits for a lock get in SHARED mode on the block identified by file# and block#.

Wait Time: 1 second

Parameters:

file#	See "file#" on page A-7.
block#	See "block#" on page A-6.
class	See "class: on page A-7.

global cache lock open ss

The session waits for a lock get in SUB SHARED mode on the block identified by file# and block#.

Wait Time: 1 second

Parameters:

file#	See "file#" on page A-7.
block#	See "block#" on page A-6.
lenum	See "lenum" on page A-8.

global cache lock open x

The session waits for a lock get in EXCLUSIVE mode on the block identified by file# and block#.

Wait Time: 1 second

Parameters:

file#	See "file#" on page A-7.
block#	See "block#" on page A-6.
lenum	See "lenum" on page A-8.

global cache lock s to x

The session waits for a lock convert from SHARED to EXCLUSIVE mode on the block identified by file# and block#.

Wait Time: 1 second

Parameters:

file#	See "file#" on page A-7.
block#	See "block#" on page A-6.
lenum	See "lenum" on page A-8.

inactive session

This event is used for two purposes:

- Switching sessions

  If a time-out period has been specified, then wait that amount of time for the session to be detached.

- Killing sessions

  From either KILL SESSION or internal request. Having posted a session that it should kill itself, wait for up to 1 minute for the session to die.

Wait Time: 1 second

Parameters:

session#	See "session#" on page A-9.
waited	See "waited" on page A-9.

inactive transaction branch

The session waits for a transaction branch that is currently used by another session.

Wait Time: 1 second

Parameters:

branch#	The serial number of the transaction for which the session is waiting.
waited	See "waited" on page A-9.

index block split

While trying to find an index key in an index block, Oracle noticed that the index block was being split. Oracle will wait for the split to finish and try to find the key again.

Wait Time: The session will yield the CPU, so there is no actual waiting time.

Parameters:

rootdba	The root of the index.
level	This is the level of the block that the session is trying to split in the index. The leaf blocks are level 0. If the level is > 0, it is a branch block. (The root block can be considered a special branch block).
childdba	The block that the session is trying to split.

instance recovery

The session waits for SMON to finish the instance, transaction recovery, or sort segment cleanup.

Wait Time: The wait time can vary and depends on the amount of recovery needed.

Parameters:

undo segment#	If the value is 0, SMON is probably performing instance recovery. If P1 > 0, use this query to find the undo segment:

```
select *
  from v$rollstat
 where usn = undo segment#;
```

instance state change

The session waits for SMON to enable or disable cache or transaction recovery. This usually happens during ALTER DATABASE OPEN or CLOSE.

Wait Time: Wait time depends on the amount of time the action takes (that is, the amount of recovery needed).

Parameters:

layer	This value can be 1 or 2. If 1, it means that the transaction layer wants transaction recovery to be performed. If 2, it means that cache recovery will be performed.
value	This value can be 0 (disable) or 1 (enable).
waited	The number of seconds waited so far.

io done

The session waits for an I/O to complete or it waits for a slave process to become available to submit the I/O request. This event occurs on platforms that do not support asynchronous I/O.

Wait Time: 50 milliseconds

Parameters:

msg ptr	A pointer to the I/O request.

kcl bg acks

The session waits for the background LCK process(es) to finish what they are doing. For example:

- lock recovery
- initializing the locks (start up)
- finalizing the locks (shut down)

Wait Time: 10 seconds

Parameters:

count	The number of LCK processes that have finished.
loops	The number times the process had to wait for the LCK processes to finish what they were doing.

latch activity

This event is used as part of the process of determining whether a latch needs to be cleaned.

Wait Time: 0.05 to 0.1 seconds

Parameters:

address	The address of the latch that is being checked.
number	The latch number of the latch that has activity. To find more information on the latch, use this SQL command:

```
select *
  from v$latchname
 where latch# = number;
```

process#	If this is 0, it is the first phase of the in-flux tests.

latch free

The process waits for a latch that is currently busy (held by another process).

Wait Time: The wait time increases exponentially and does not include spinning on the latch (active waiting). The maximum wait time also depends on the number of latches that the process is holding. There is an incremental wait of up to 2 seconds.

Parameters:

address	The address of the latch for which the process is waiting.
number	The latch number that indexes in the V$LATCHNAME view. To find more information on the latch, use this SQL command:

```
select *
  from v$latchname
 where latch# = number;
```

tries	A count of the number of times the process tried to get the latch (slow with spinning) and the process has to sleep.

library cache load lock

The session tries to find the load lock for the database object so that it can load the object. The load lock is always obtained in Exclusive mode, so that no other process can load the same object. If the load lock is busy the session will wait on this event until the lock becomes available.

Wait Time: 3 seconds (1 second for PMON)

Parameters:

object address	Address of the object being loaded.
lock address	Address of load lock being used.
mask	Indicates which data pieces of the object that needs to be loaded.

library cache lock

This event controls the concurrency between clients of the library cache. It acquires a lock on the object handle so that either:

- one client can prevent other clients from accessing the same object
- the client can maintain a dependency for a long time (e.g., no other client can change the object)

This lock is also obtained to locate an object in the library cache.

Wait Time: 3 seconds (1 second for PMON)

Parameters:

handle address	Address of the object being loaded.
lock address	Address of the load lock being used. This is not the same thing as a latch or an enqueue, it is a State Object.
mode	Indicates the data pieces of the object which need to be loaded.
namespace	See "namespace" on page A-9.

library cache pin

This event manages library cache concurrency. Pinning an object causes the heaps to be loaded into memory. If a client wants to modify or examine the object, the client must acquire a pin after the lock.

Wait Time: 3 seconds (1 second for PMON)

Parameters:

handle address	Address of the object being loaded.

Parameters:

pin address	Address of the load lock being used. This is not the same thing as a latch or an enqueue, it is basically a State Object.
mode	Indicates which data pieces of the object that needs to be loaded.
namespace	See "namespace" on page A-9.

lock manager wait for remote message

The lock manager waits for a message from a remote lock manager in the same configuration.

Wait Time: The elapsed time of the wait

Parameters:

waittime	The elapsed time of the actual wait.

log buffer space

Waiting for space in the log buffer because the session is writing data into the log buffer faster than LGWR can write it out. Consider making the log buffer bigger if it is small, or moving the log files to faster disks such as striped disks.

Wait Time: Usually 1 second, but 5 seconds if it is waiting for a Switch Logfile to complete.

Parameters: none

log file parallel write

Writing redo records to the redo log files from the log buffer.

Wait Time: Time it takes for the I/Os to complete. Even though redo records are written in parallel, the parallel write is not complete until the last I/O is on disk.

Parameters:

files	Number of files to be written.
blocks	Number of blocks to be written.

Parameters:

requests Number of I/O requests.

log file sequential read

Waiting for the read from this logfile to return. This is used to read redo records from the log file.

Wait Time: Time it takes to complete the physical I/O (read).

Parameters:

log# The relative sequence number of the logfiles within a log group (used only when dumping the logfiles).

block# See "block#" on page A-6.

blocks The number of blocks to read.

log file single write

Waiting for the write to this logfile to complete. This event is used while updating the header of the logfile. It is signaled when adding a log file member and when incrementing sequence numbers.

Wait Time: Time it takes for the physical I/O (write) to complete.

Parameters:

log# This is the number of the group/log to which the session is currently writing.

block# See "block#" on page A-6.

blocks The number of blocks to write.

log file switch (archiving needed)

Waiting for a log switch because the log that the LGWR will be switching into has not been archived yet. Check the alert file to make sure that archiving has not stopped due to a failed archive write. To speed archiving, consider adding more archive processes or putting the archive files on striped disks.

Wait Time: 1 second

Parameters: none

log file switch (checkpoint incomplete)

Waiting for a log switch because the session cannot wrap into the next log. Wrapping cannot be performed because the checkpoint for that log has not completed.

Wait Time: 1 second

Parameters: none

log file switch (clearing log file)

Waiting for a log switch because the log is being cleared due to a CLEAR LOGFILE command or implicit clear logfile executed by recovery.

Wait Time: 1 second

Parameters: none

log file switch completion

Waiting for a log switch to complete.

Wait Time: 1 second

Parameters: none

log file sync

When a user session commits, the session's redo information needs to be flushed to the redo logfile. The user session will post the LGWR to write the log buffer to the redo log file. When the LGWR has finished writing, it will post the user session.

Wait Time: The wait time includes the writing of the log buffer and the post.

Parameters:

buffer#   The number of the physical buffer in the redo log buffer that needs to be sync'ed

log switch/archive

Used as part of the ALTER SYSTEM ARCHIVE LOG CHANGE *scn* command. The session waits for the current log from all open threads to be archived.

Wait Time: Wait for up to 10 seconds.

Parameters:

thread#	The thread number of the thread that is currently archiving its current log.

on-going SCN fetch to complete

Another session is fetching the SCN (System Change Number). This session waits for the other session finish fetching the SCN.

Wait Time: 1 second

Parameters: none

parallel query create server

Used when creating or starting a Parallel Query Slave.

Wait Time: The time it takes to start all of the requested Parallel Query Slaves.

Parameters:

nservers	The number of Parallel Query Slaves that are being started.
sleeptime	Time it takes to get the processes started. The process should be started within *sleeptime*.
enqueue	The number of blocks to read.

parallel query dequeue wait

The process is waiting for a message during a parallel execute.

Wait Time: The wait time depends on how quickly the message arrives. Wait times can vary, but it will normally be a short period of time.

Parameters:

reason	The reason for dequeueing.
sleeptime	The amount of time that the session slept.
loop	The total number of times that the session has slept.

parallel query qref latch

Each Parallel Query Process has a parallel query qref latch, which needs to be acquired before the queue buffers can be manipulated.

Wait Time: Wait up to 1 second.

Parameters:

function	Indicates the type of wait that the session is doing.
sleeptime	The amount of time that the session waits (in hundredths of a second).
qref	The address of the process queue for which the session is waits.

parallel query server shutdown

During normal or immediate shutdown the Parallel Query Slaves are posted to shutdown cleanly. If any Parallel Query Slaves are still alive after 10 seconds, they are killed.

Wait Time: Wait up to 0.5 seconds.

Parameters:

nalive	The number of Parallel Query Slaves that are still running.
sleeptime	The total sleeptime since the session started to wait on this event.
loop	The number of times the session waited for this event.

parallel query signal server

This event occurs only in Exclusive mode. The Query Coordinator is signalling the Query Slaves that an error has occurred.

Wait Time: 0.5 seconds

Parameters:

serial	The serial number of the slave process queue.

Parameters:

error	The error that has occurred.
nbusy	The number of slave processes that are still busy.

pending ast

The session is waiting for an outstanding AST to be delivered before the lock element can be used.

Wait Time: The session yields the CPU.

Parameters:

lenum	See "lenum" on page A-8.

pending global transaction(s)

This event should happen only during testing. The session waits for pending transactions to clear.

Wait Time: 30 seconds

Parameters:

scans	Number of times the session has scanned the PENDING_TRANS$ table.

pipe get

The session waits for a message to be received on the pipe or for the pipe timer to expire.

Wait Time: There is a 5 second wake up (check) and the pipe timer set by the user.

Parameters:

handle address	The library cache object handle for this pipe.
buffer length	The length of the buffer.
timeout	The pipe timer set by the user.

pipe put

The session waits for the pipe send timer to expire or for space to be made available in the pipe.

Wait Time: There is the 5 second wakeup (check) and the user-supplied timeout value.

Parameters:

handle address	The library cache object handle for this pipe.
record length	The length of the record or buffer that has been put into the pipe.
timeout	The pipe timer set by the user.

pmon timer

This is the main wait event for PMON. When PMON is idle, it is waiting on this event.

Wait Time: Up to 3 seconds, if not posted before.

Parameters:

duration	The actual amount of time that the PMON is trying to sleep.

process startup

Wait for a Multi-Threaded Server (Shared Server), Dispatcher, or other background process to start.

Wait Time: Wait up to 1 second for a background process to start. If timed out, then re-wait until 5 minutes have passed and signal an error. If the process has started, the event will acknowledge this.

Parameters:

type	The process type that was started.
process#	The process number of the process being started.
waited	Cumulative time waited for the process to start.

queue messages

The session is waiting on an empty OLTP queue (Advanced Queue) for a message to arrive so that the session can dequeue that message.

Wait Time: The amount of time that the session wants to wait is determined by the parameter *wait time*.

Parameters:

queue id	The ID of the OLTP queue for which this session is waiting.
process#	The process number of the process in which this session runs.
wait time	The intended wait time for this session.

queue wait

The direct loader uses a queue of slots for managing buffers. These slots are used for read/write operations. If a new slot is requested, but none are available, then this wait event is signaled. This wait will only occur if the underlying operating system is using asynchronous I/O.

Wait Time: Wait up to 1 second for slots to be freed in the circular direct loader I/O buffer queue.

Parameters: none

rdbms ipc message

The background processes (LGWR, DBWR, LCK0) use this event to indicate that they are idle and are waiting for the foreground processes to send them an IPC message to do some work.

Wait Time: Up to 3 seconds. The parameter *timeout* shows the true sleep time.

Parameters:

timeout	The amount of time that the session waits for an IPC message.

rdbms ipc message block

This event indicates that all message blocks are in use and that the session had to wait for a message block to become available.

Wait Time: Wait up to 60 seconds.

Parameters: none

rdbms ipc reply

This event is used to wait for a reply from one of the background processes.

Wait Time: The wait time is specified by the user and is indicated by the parameter *timeout*.

Parameters:

from_process	The background process for which the session is waiting. The wait is for a reply to an IPC message sent by the session.
timeout	The amount of time in seconds that this process will wait for a reply.

redo wait

Defined but not used by the code.

row cache lock

The session is trying to get a data dictionary lock.

Wait Time: Wait up to 60 seconds.

Parameters:

cache id	The CACHE# column value in the V$ROWCACHE view.
mode	See "mode" on page A-8.
request	The pipe timer set by the user.

scginq AST call

Called by the session to find the highest lock mode that is held on a resource.

Wait Time: Wait up to 0.2 seconds, but the wait will continue until the NULL mode Acquisition AST has fired.

Parameters: none

single-task message

When running single task, this event indicates that the session waits for the client side of the executable.

Wait Time: Total elapsed time that this session spent in the user application.

Parameters: none

smon timer

This is the main idle event for SMON. SMON will be waiting on this event most of the time until it times out or is posted by another process.

Wait Time: 5 minutes (300 seconds)

Parameters:

sleeptime	The amount of time that SMON tries to wait on this event in seconds.
failed	The number of times SMON was posted when there some kind of error.

switch logfile command

The session waits on the user command SWITCH LOGFILE to complete.

Wait Time: 5 seconds

Parameters: none

timer in sksawat

The session waits for the Archiver (ARCH) asynchronous I/O to complete.

Wait Time: 0.01 seconds

Parameters: none

transaction

Wait for a blocking transaction to be rolled back. Continue waiting until the transaction has been rolled back.

Wait Time: 1 second

Parameters:

undo seg#	The rollback segment ID.
slot#	The slot ID inside the rollback segment.
wrap#	The sequence number that is incremented for each transaction.
count	The number of times that the session has waited on this transaction.

unbound tx

The session waits to see if there are any transactions that have been started but do not have a Rollback Segment associated with them.

Wait Time: 1 second

Parameters: none

undo segment extension

The undo segment is being extended or shrunk. The session must wait until the operation on the undo segment has finished.

Wait Time: 0.01 seconds

Parameters:

segment#	The ID of the rollback segment that is being extended or shrunk.

undo segment recovery

PMON is rolling back a dead transaction. The wait continues until rollback finishes.

Wait Time: 3 seconds

Parameters:

segment#   The ID of the rollback segment that contains the transaction that is being rolled back.

tx flags   The transaction flags (options) set for the transaction that is being rolled back.

undo segment tx slot

Wait for a transaction slot to become available within the selected rollback segment. Continue waiting until the slot is available.

Wait Time: 1 second

Parameters:

segment#   The ID of the rollback segment that contains the transaction that is being rolled back.

virtual circuit status

The session waits for a virtual circuit to return a message type indicated by *status*.

Wait Time: 30 seconds

Parameters:

circuit#   Indicates the virtual circuit# being waited on.

status   Indicates what the session is waiting for.

write complete waits

The session waits for a buffer to be written. The write is caused by normal aging or by a cross-instance call.

Wait Time: 1 second

Parameters:

file#   The rollback segment id that contains the transaction that is being rolled back.

Parameters:

block#	The transaction flags (options) set for the transaction that is being rolled back.
id	Identifies the reason for waiting.

writes stopped by instance recovery

The session is blocked until the instance that started Instance Recovery is finished.

Wait Time: 5 seconds

Parameters:

bythread#	The rollback segment id that contains the transaction that is being rolled back.
ourthread#	The current instance thread number.

B

Enqueue and Lock Names

Introduction

Table B-1 contains a list of the enqueues and locks that are used by Oracle. Locks and Resources are different structures used by Oracle, but sometimes the names are not used correctly. A *resource* uniquely identifies a certain object that can be locked by different sessions within an instance (Local Resource) or between instances (Global Resource). Each session will have a lock structure on the resource if it tries to lock the resource.

Note: The names of enqueues and locks and their definitions may change from release to release.

Table B-1: Oracle Enqueue and Lock Names

BL, Buffer Cache Management	CF, Controlfile Transaction
CI, Cross-instance Call Invocation	CU, Bind Enqueue
DF, Datafile	DL, Direct Loader Index Creation
DM, Database Mount	DR, Distributed Recovery
DX, Distributed TX	FS, File Set
IN, Instance Number	IR, Instance Recovery
IS, Instance State	IV, Library Cache Invalidation
JQ, Job Queue	KK, Redo Log "Kick"
L[A-P], Library Cache Lock	MR, Media Recovery
N[A-Z], Library Cache Pin	PF, Password File
PI, Parallel Slaves	PR, Process Startup
PS, Parallel Slave Synchronization	Q[A-Z], Row Cache
RT, Redo Thread	SC, System Commit Number
SM, SMON	SQ, Sequence Number Enqueue
SR, Synchronized Replication	SS, Sort Segment
ST, Space Management Transaction	SV, Sequence Number Value
TA, Transaction Recovery	TM, DML Enqueue
TS, Temporary Segment (also TableSpace)	TT, Temporary Table
TX, Transaction	UL, User-defined Locks
UN, User Name	US, Undo Segment, Serialization
WL, Being Written Redo Log	XA, Instance Attribute Lock
XI, Instance Registration Lock	------

Statistics Descriptions

This appendix briefly describes some of the statistics stored in the V$SESSTAT and V$SYSSTAT dynamic performance tables. These statistics are useful in identifying and correcting performance problems.

The V$SESSTAT view contains statistics on a per-session basis and is only valid for the session currently connected. When a session disconnects all statistics for the session are updated in V$SYSSTAT. The values for the statistics are cleared until the next session uses them.

The V$STATNAME view contains all of the statistics for an Oracle release.

For more information on these views, see "V$SESSTAT" on page 3-91, "V$STATNAME" on page 3-105, and "V$SYSSTAT" on page 3-108.

Statistics Descriptions

This section describes the statistics stored in the V$SESSTAT and V$SYSSTAT views.

CPU used by this session

This is the amount of CPU time (in 10s of milliseconds) used by a session between when a user call started and ended. Some user calls can complete within 10 milliseconds and as a result, the start and end user-call time can be the same. In this case, 0 milliseconds are added to the statistic.

A similar problem can exist in the reporting by the Operating System, especially on systems that suffer from many context switches.

CR blocks created

A buffer in the buffer cache was cloned. The most common reason for cloning is that the buffer is held in a incompatible mode.

Current blocks converted for CR

A CURRENT buffer (shared or exclusive) is made CR before it can be used.

DBWR Flush object call found no dirty buffers

The DBWR didn't find any dirty buffers for an object that was flushed from the cache.

DBWR Flush object cross instance calls

The number of times DBWR received a flush by object number cross instance call (from a remote instance). This includes both checkpoint and invalidate object.

DBWR buffers scanned

The total number of buffers looked at when scanning each LRU set for dirty buffers to clean. This count includes both dirty and clean buffers. Divide by **DBWR lru scans** to find the average number of buffers scanned.

DBWR checkpoints

Number of times the DBWR was asked to scan the cache and write all blocks marked for a checkpoint.

DBWR cross instance writes

The total number of blocks written for other instances so that they can access the buffers.

DBWR free buffers found

The number of buffers that DBWR found to be clean when it was requested to make free buffers. Divide by **DBWR make free requests** to find the average number of reusable buffers at the end of each LRU.

DBWR lru scans

The number of times that DBWR does a scan of the LRU queue looking for buffers to write. This includes times when the scan is to fill a batch being written for another purpose such as a checkpoint. This statistic is always greater than or equal to **DBWR make free requests**.

DBWR make free requests

Number of messages received requesting DBWR to make some more free buffers for the LRU.

DBWR summed scan depth

The current scan depth (number of buffers examined by DBWR) is added to this statistic every time DBWR scans the LRU for dirty buffers. Divide by **DBWR lru scans** to find the average scan depth.

DBWR timeouts

The number of times that the DBWR has been idle since the last timeout. These are the times that the DBWR looked for buffers to idle write.

DDL statements parallelized

The number of DDL statements that were parallelized.

DML statements parallelized.

The number of DML statements that were parallelized.

PX local messages recv'd

The number of local messages received for Parallel Executions.

PX local messages sent

The number of local messages send for Parallel Executions.

PX remote messages recv'd

The number of remote messages received for Parallel Executions.

PX remote messages sent

The number of remote messages sent for Parallel Executions.

SQL*Net roundtrips to/from client

Total number of Net8 messages sent to and received from the client.

SQL*Net roundtrips to/from dblink

Total number of Net8 messages sent over and received from a database link.

Unnecessary process cleanup for SCN batching

The total number of times that the process cleanup was performed unnecessarily because the session/process did not get the next batched SCN. The next batched SCN went to another session instead.

background checkpoints completed

The number of checkpoints completed by the background. This statistic is incremented when the background successfully advances the thread checkpoint.

background checkpoints started

The number of checkpoints started by the background. It can be larger than the number completed if a new checkpoint overrides an incomplete checkpoint. This only includes checkpoints of the thread, not individual file checkpoints for operations such as offline or begin backup. This statistic does not include the checkpoints performed in the foreground, such as ALTER SYSTEM CHECKPOINT LOCAL.

bytes received via SQL*Net from client

The total number of bytes received from the client over Net8.

bytes received via SQL*Net from dblink

The total number of bytes received from a database link over Net8.

bytes sent via SQL*Net to client

The total number of bytes sent to the client from the foreground process(es).

bytes sent via SQL*Net to dblink

The total number of bytes sent over a database link.

calls to get snapshot scn: kcmgss

The number of times a snap System Change Number (SCN) was allocated. The SCN is allocated at the start of a transaction.

change write time

The elapsed time for redo write for changes made to CURRENT blocks in 10s of milliseconds.

cluster key scan block gets

The number of blocks obtained in a cluster scan.

cluster key scans

The number of cluster scans that were started.

commit cleanout failures: block lost

The number of times a cleanout at commit was attempted and could not find the correct block due to forced write, replacement, or switch CURRENT.

commit cleanout failures: buffer being written

The number of times a cleanout at commit was attempted but the buffer was currently being written.

commit cleanout failures: callback failure

The number of times the cleanout callback function returns FALSE.

commit cleanout failures: cannot pin

The total number of times a commit cleanout was performed but failed because the block could not be pinned.

commit cleanout failures: hot backup in progress

The number of times cleanout at commit was attempted during hot backup. The image of the block needs to be logged before the buffer can be made dirty.

commit cleanout failures: write disabled

The number of times that a cleanout at commit time was performed but the writes to the database had been temporarily disabled.

commit cleanouts

The total number of times the cleanout block at commit time function was performed.

commit cleanouts successfully completed

The number of times the cleanout block at commit time function successfully completed.

consistent changes

The number of times a database block has applied rollback entries to perform a consistent read on the block.

Work loads that produce a great deal of consistent changes can consume a great deal of resources.

consistent gets

The number of times a consistent read was requested for a block. See also "consistent changes" above.

cross instance CR read

The number of times this instance made a cross instance call to write a particular block due to timeout on an instance lock get. The call allowed the block to be read CR rather than CURRENT.

db block changes

Closely related to **consistent changes**, this statistics counts the total number of changes that were made to all blocks in the SGA that were part of an update or delete operation. These are changes that are generating redo log entries and hence will be permanent changes to the database if the transaction is committed.

This statistic is a rough indication of total database work. This statistic indicates (possibly on a per-transaction level) the rate at which buffers are being dirtied.

db block gets

This statistic tracks the number of blocks obtained in CURRENT mode.

dirty buffers inspected

The number of dirty buffers found by the foreground while the foreground is looking for a buffer to reuse.

enqueue conversions

The total number of enqueue converts.

enqueue deadlocks

The total number of enqueue deadlocks between different sessions.

enqueue releases

The total number of enqueue releases.

enqueue requests

The total number of enqueue gets.

enqueue timeouts

The total number of enqueue operations (get and convert) that timed out before they could complete.

enqueue waits

The total number of waits that happened during an enqueue convert or get because the enqueue could not be granted right away.

exchange deadlocks

The number of times that a process detected a potential deadlock when exchanging two buffers and raised an internal, restartable error. Index scans are currently the only operations which perform exchanges.

execute count

The total number of calls (user and recursive) that execute SQL statements.

free buffer inspected

The number of buffers skipped over from the end of an LRU queue in order to find a reusable buffer. The difference between this statistic and **dirty buffers inspected** is the number of buffers that could not be used because they were busy, needed to be written after rapid aging out, or they have a user, a waiter, or are being read/written. For more information, see "dirty buffers inspected" on page C-7.

free buffer requested

The count of the number of times a reusable buffer or a free buffer was requested to create or load a block.

global cache defers

The number of times a ping request was defered until later.

global cache freelist waits

The number of pings for free lock elements (when all releasable locks are inuse)

global cache hash latch waits

The number of times that the buffer cache hash chain latch couldn't be acquired immediately, when processing a lock element.

global lock convert time

The total elapsed time of all synchronous (non-asynchronous) global lock converts in 10s of milliseconds.

global lock converts (async)

The total number of asynchronous global lock converts.

global lock converts (non async)

The total number of synchronous global lock converts.

global lock get time

The total elapsed time of all synchronous (non-asynchronous) global lock gets in 10s of milliseconds.

global lock gets (async)

The total number of asynchronous global lock gets.

global lock gets (non async)

The total number of synchronous global lock gets.

global lock release time

The elapsed time of all synchronous global lock releases.

global lock releases

The total number of synchronous global lock releases.

kcmccs called get current scn

The number of times the kernel got the CURRENT SCN when there was a need to casually confirm the SCN.

kcmccs read scn without going to DLM

The number of times the kernel casually confirmed the SCN without going to the LM.

kcmgss waited for batching

The number of times the kernel waited on a snapshot SCN.

lock element waits

The number of times a lock element was busy.

logons cumulative

The total number of logons since the instance started. This statistic is useful only in V$SYSSTAT. It gives an instance overview of all processes that logged on.

logons current

The total number of current logons. This statistic is useful only in V$SYSSTAT.

next scns gotten without going to DLM

The number of SCNs (System Change Numbers) obtained without going to the DLM.

opened cursors cumulative

The total number of opened cursors since the instance has started (in V$SYSSTAT). In V$SESSTAT, this statistic shows the total number of cursors opened since the start of the session.

opened cursors current

> The total number of current open cursors.

opens of replaced files

> The total number of files that needed to be reopened because they were no longer in the process file cache.

opens requiring cache replacement

> The total number of file opens that caused a current file to be closed in the process file cache.

parse count (hard)

> The total number of parse calls (real parses). A hard parse means allocating a workheap and other memory structures, and then building a parse tree. A hard parse is a very expensive operation in terms of memory use.

parse count (soft)

> The total number of parse calls that didn't result in a hard parse.

parse count (total)

> Total number of parse calls (hard and soft). A soft parse is a check to make sure that the permissions on the underlying object have not changed.

parse time cpu

> The total CPU time used for parsing (hard and soft) in 10s of milliseconds.

parse time elapsed

> The total elapsed time for parsing in 10s of milliseconds. By subtracting **parse time cpu** from the this statistic, the total waiting time for parse resources is determined. For more information see "parse time cpu" above.

physical reads

> This statistic stores the number of I/O requests to the operating system to retrieve a database block from the disk subsystem. This is a buffer cache miss.

Logical reads is **consistent gets** + **database block gets**. Logical reads and physical reads are used to calculate the buffer cache hit ratio.

physical writes

This statistic stores the number of I/O requests to the operating system to write a database block to the disk subsystem. The bulk of the writes are performed either by DBWR or LGWR.

queries parallelized

The number of SELECT statements that got parallelized.

recovery array read time

The elapsed time of I/O while doing recovery.

recovery array reads

The number of reads performed during recovery.

recovery blocks read

The number of blocks read during recovery.

recursive calls

Oracle maintains tables used for internal processing. When Oracle needs to make a change to these tables, it internally generates a SQL statement. These internal SQL statements generate recursive calls.

recursive cpu usage

The total CPU time used by non-user calls (recursive calls). Subtract this value from **CPU used by this session** to determine how much CPU time was used by the user calls.

redo entries

This statistic increments each time redo entries are copied into the redo log buffer.

redo entries linearized

The total number of entries of size <= REDO_ENTRY_PREBUILD_THRESHOLD. Building these entries increase CPU time, but may increase concurrency on a multi-processor system.

redo log space requests

The active log file is full and Oracle is waiting for disk space to be allocated for the redo log entries. Space is created by performing a log switch.

Small Log files in relation to the size of the SGA or the commit rate of the work load can cause problems. When the log switch occurs, Oracle must ensure that all committed dirty buffers are written to disk before switching to a new log file. If you have a large SGA full of dirty buffers and small redo log files, a log switch must wait for DBWR to write dirty buffers to disk before continuing.

Also examine the **log file space** and **log file space switch** wait events in V$SESSION_WAIT.

redo log space wait time

The total elapsed time of waiting for **redo log space request** in 10s of milliseconds.

redo log switch interrupts

The number of times that another instance asked this instance to advance to the next log file.

redo ordering marks

The number of times that an SCN had to be allocated to force a redo record to have an higher SCN than a record generated in another thread using the same block.

redo size

The total amount of redo generated in bytes.

redo synch time

The elapsed time of all **redo sync writes** calls in 10s of milliseconds.

redo sync writes

Usually, redo that is generated and copied into the log buffer need not be flushed out to disk immediately. The log buffer is a circular buffer that LGWR periodically flushes. Redo sync writes increments when changes being applied must be written out to disk due to a commit.

redo wastage

Number of bytes wasted because redo blocks needed to be written before they are completely full. Early writing may be needed to commit transactions, to be able to write a database buffer or to switch logs.

redo write time

The total elapsed time of the write from the redo log buffer to the current redo log file in 10s of milliseconds.

redo writer latching time

The elapsed time need by LWGR to obtain and release each copy latch in 10s of milliseconds. This is only used if the initialization parameter LOG_SIMULTANEOUS_COPIES > 0. For more information, see "LOG_SIMULTANEOUS_COPIES" on page 1-65.

redo writes

Count of the total number of writes by LGWR to the redo log files.

remote instance undo block writes

The number of times this instance wrote a dirty undo block so that another instance could read it.

remote instance undo header writes

The number of times this instance wrote a dirty undo header block so that another instance could read it.

remote instance undo requests

The number of times this instance requested undo from another instance so it could be read CR.

serializable aborts

> The number of times a SQL statement in serializable isolation level had to abort.

session connect time

> The connect time for the session in 1/100 seconds. This value is useful only in V$SESSTAT. It is the wall clock time of when the logon to this session occurred.

session cursor cache count

> The total number of cursor cached. This is only incremented if SESSION_CACHED_CURSORS > 0. This statistic is the most useful in V$SESSTAT. If the value for this statistic in V$SESSTAT is close to the setting of the initialization parameter SESSION_CACHED_CURSORS, the value of the initialization parameter should be increased.

session cursor cache hits

> The count of the number of hits in the session cursor cache. A hit means that the SQL statement did not have to be reparsed. By subtracting this statistic from **parse count (total)** one can determine the real number of parses that happened. For more information, see "parse count (soft)" on page C-11.

session logical reads

> This statistic is basically **db block gets + consistent gets**. For more information, see "db block gets" on page C-7 and "consistent gets" on page C-7.

session pga memory

> This statistic shows the current PGA size for a session. This statistic is useful only in V$SESSTAT; it has no meaning in V$SYSSTAT.

session pga memory max

> This statistic shows the peak PGA size for a session. This statistic is useful only in V$SESSTAT; it has no meaning in V$SYSSTAT.

session stored procedure space

This statistic shows the amount of memory that this session is using for stored procedures.

session uga memory

This statistic shows the current UGA size for a session. This statistic is useful only in V$SESSTAT; it has no meaning in V$SYSSTAT.

session uga memory max

This statistic shows the peak UGA size for a session. This statistic is useful only in V$SESSTAT; it has no meaning in V$SYSSTAT.

sorts (disk)

If the number of disk writes is non-zero for a given sort operation, then this statistic is incremented.

Sorts that require I/O to disk are quite resource intensive. Try increasing the size of the initialization parameter SORT_AREA_SIZE. For more information, see "SORT_AREA_SIZE" on page 1-106.

sorts (memory)

If the number of disk writes is zero, then the sort was performed completely in memory and this statistic is incremented.

This is more an indication of sorting activity in the application work load. You cannot do much better than memory sorts, except maybe no sorts at all. Sorting is usually caused by selection criteria specifications within table join SQL operations.

sorts (rows)

The total number of rows sorted.

summed dirty queue length

The sum of the dirty LRU queue length after every write request. Divide by **write requests** to get the average queue length after write completion. For more information, see "write requests" on page C-19.

table fetch by rowid

When rows are fetched using a ROWID (usually recovered from an index), each row returned increments this counter.

This statistic is an indication of row fetch operations being performed with the aid of an index. Because doing table scans usually indicates either non-optimal queries or tables without indexes, this statistic should increase as the above issues have been addressed in the application.

table fetch continued row

When a row that spans more than one block is encountered during a fetch, this statistic is incremented.

Retrieving rows that span more than one block increases the logical I/O by a factor that corresponds to the number of blocks than need to be accessed. Exporting and re-importing may eliminate this problem. Taking a closer look at the STORAGE parameters PCT_FREE and PCT_USED. This problem cannot be fixed if rows are larger than database blocks (for example, if the LONG datatype is used and the rows are extremely large).

table scan blocks gotten

During scanning operations, each row is retrieved sequentially by Oracle. Each block encountered during the scan increments this statistic.

This statistic informs you of the number of database blocks that you had to get from the buffer cache for the purpose of scanning. Compare the value of this parameter to the value of **consistent gets** to get a feeling for how much of the consistent read activity can be attributed to scanning. For more information, see "consistent gets" on page C-7.

table scan rows gotten

This statistic is collected during a scan operation, but instead of counting the number of database blocks, it counts the rows being processed.

table scans (cache partitions)

Count of range scans on tables that have the CACHE option enabled.

table scans (direct read)

Count of table scans performed with direct read (bypassing the buffer cache).

table scans (long tables)

Long (or conversely short) tables can be defined as tables that do not meet the short table criteria as described in "table scans (short tables)" below.

table scans (rowid ranges)

Count of table scans with specified ROWID endpoints. This is performed for Parallel Query.

table scans (short tables)

Long (or conversely short) tables can be defined by optimizer hints coming down into the row source access layer of Oracle. The table must have the CACHE option set.

total file opens

The total number of file opens being performed by the instance. Each process needs a number of files (control file, log file, database file) in order to work against the database.

user calls

Oracle allocates resources (Call State Objects) to keep track of relevant user call data structures every time you log in, parse, or execute.

When determining activity, the ratio of user calls to RPI calls, give you an indication of how much internal work gets generated as a result of the type of requests the user is sending to Oracle.

user commits

When a user commits a transaction, the redo generated that reflects the changes made to database blocks must be written to disk. Commits often represent the closest thing to a user transaction rate.

user rollbacks

This statistic stores the number of times users manually issue the ROLLBACK statement or an error occurs during users' transactions.

write requests

This statistic stores the number of times DBWR takes a batch of dirty buffers and writes them to disk.

Index

V

W

X

Reader's Comment Form

Oracle8 Server Reference
A54645-01

Oracle Corporation welcomes your comments and suggestions on the quality and usefulness of this publication. Your input is an important part of the information used for revision.

- Did you find any errors?
- Is the information clearly presented?
- Do you need more information? If so, where?
- Are the examples correct? Do you need more examples?
- What features did you like most about this manual?

If you find any errors or have suggestions for improvement, please indicate the topic, chapter, and page number below:

_____

_____

_____

_____

_____

_____

_____

_____

_____

_____

Please send your comments to:

Server Technologies Documentation Manager
Oracle Corporation
500 Oracle Parkway
Redwood Shores, CA 94065

or e-mail comments to: infodev@us.oracle.com

If you would like a reply, please give your name, address, and telephone number below:

_____

_____

Thank you for helping us improve our documentation.